S0-BZD-135

Lighthouse Keeper, Cove Point - October 17, 1948   MSA SC 1890 - MI - 12, 673 - 9

"Cove Point was the first lighthouse I photographed in Maryland. We had only lived in Annapolis a year and we went on a 'club run' with our photography group down near Solomons to photograph the lighthouse. I set up on the beach and was very fortunate... the flag was blowing and there were wonderful clouds. You photograph something when you see it or you may not get another chance. The keeper came outside and talked to us for awhile. Then he asked me if I wanted to go inside. I sure did. I grew up in Missouri, so I thought a lighthouse was really something."

Marion E. Warren, Maryland Photographer, August 1996

OVERLEAF:
Cove Point Lighthouse - October 17, 1948 MSA SC 1890 - MI - 1154

Maryland
Lighthouses
of the Chesapeake Bay

F. Ross Holland

The Maryland Historical Trust Press
Department of Housing and Community Development,
Crownsville, Maryland

The Friends of St. Clement's Island Museum, Inc.
Colton's Point, Maryland

Published by
The Maryland Historical Trust Press and
The Friends of St. Clement's Island Museum, Inc.

©1997 Maryland Historical Trust

All rights reserved. Published 1997

Printed in the United States of America

Maryland Historical Trust
Department of Housing and
Community Development
100 Community Place
Crownsville, Maryland 21032-2032

The Friends of St. Clement's Island Museum, Inc.
38370 Point Breeze Road
Colton's Point, Maryland 20626

ISBN 1-878399 -70 - 5

This publication has been financed in part with
state funds from the Maryland Historical Trust,
an agency of the Department of Housing and
Community Development of the State of
Maryland. However, the contents and opinions
do not necessarily reflect the views or policies
of the Maryland Historical Trust or the
Department of Housing and Community
Development.

As an agency of the Maryland Department of
Housing and Community Development, we
pledge to foster the letter and spirit of the law
for achieving equal opportunity in Maryland.

Publication of this book has been made possible
in part by donations from NationsBank and BGE.

Library of Congress Cataloging-in-Publication Data

Holland, F. Ross (Francis Ross), 1927-
    Maryland lighthouses of the Chesapeake
Bay : an illustrated history / F. Ross Holland.
        p.   cm.
    Includes bibliographical references and
    index.
    ISBN 1-878399-70-5
    1. Lighthouses—Chesapeake Bay (Md. and
Va.) 2. Lighthouses-Maryland-. I. Title.
VK1024.M3H65   1996
387.1'55'097521—DC20
                        96-42187
                         CIP

Contents

Acknowledgements

DEDICATION

For

Stephen Ross Holland

Corey Douglas Holland

Samantha Desiree Holland

Who have brought

so much joy

to their grandparents.

I am most grateful to a number of people for their assistance. First of all, I thank David Policansky for the time we spent in his boat, getting close to Maryland's off-shore lighthouses. Dr. Policansky is a fine photographer and his pictures were useful in comparing the lighthouses of today with those of the past.

During the 35 years that I have been gathering information on lighthouses, I have found the U.S. Coast Guard always to be exceedingly helpful. This book project was no exception, and I was provided, among other things, access to several caisson lighthouses. These trips gave me a much better understanding of this type of lighthouse.

No study of lighthouses and other aids to navigation can be considered complete without an examination of the records on the subject in our National Archives. During my many visits,

Aloha Smith rendered great assistance as did William Sherman, who seemed to know intuitively which records I needed to examine. The National Archives Regional Office in Philadelphia was also helpful in locating the drawings of the Fifth District lighthouses.

I also want to thank Pamela Blumgart and Lillian Wray, both editors, who have worked diligently in guiding this work to its final form. I appreciate the good work each has done, and my deep thanks go to them.

My special thanks to Dr. Elaine Eff of the Maryland Historical Trust, who generously shared her oral history files and photos.

Finally, I wish to acknowledge Theresa Schaefer, who ably handled the indexing and Gerry Valerio, whose design talents have given us a beautiful book.

F. ROSS HOLLAND

Colesville, Maryland
August 1996

Editorial Notes

Behind every book lies another story - a tale of stewardship - often with a little-known cast of characters. The publication of "the lighthouse book," as it has been known for years at the Maryland Historical Trust, is the culmination of a long period of "stop-start" work, which reflected the presence or absence of funding and staff. But even in the leanest times, this massive project inched slowly along, as Ross Holland and Pamela Blumgart continued the tedious process of reading, questioning and refining the first version of the manuscript. By the time Pamela passed the baton - and the manuscript - to me, much had been done, but there was much more to do. The "doing of it" has been both a challenge and a collaborative adventure.

There were surprises... a cache of more than 100 photos wasn't enough, so a massive search for images began. We often became dependent upon the kindness of strangers - knowledgeable people who dug into personal collections, institutional archives and boxes of old negatives for the elusive photo, drawing or postcard. Special thanks go to: Jack Kelbaugh, who shared his extensive collection of Maryland postcards; Kenneth G. Lay of Havre de Grace and Mark Schatz of the Ann Arrundell County Historical Society, who both located and loaned rare photos. Invaluable assistance came from Mary Markey of the Peale Museum; Rob Hurry and Richard Dodds of the Calvert Marine Museum; Lydia Wood and Michael Humphries of the St. Clement's Island - Potomac River Museum; Emily Murphy and Nancy Bramucci of the Maryland State Archives; Peter Lesher of the Chesapeake Bay Maritime Museum; Reed Macmillan and Teresa Kaltenbacher of the Cultural Resources Program, Aberdeen Proving Ground; Theresa Hopkins of Environmental Public Affairs, Naval Air Station Patuxent River; Nancy Roberts of the Paw Paw Museum, and Dot Sappington of the U.S. Naval Institute Photo Library.

We are indebted to Elaine Eff of the Trust's Cultural Conservation Program, who loaned unpublished photos, historic news clippings and oral history transcripts from her "Keepers and Kin" project. She also urged us on – contributing insight and enthusiasm.

Many people generously furnished research information, and later became caught up in the excitement of the project. We thank Anne M. Saba, Archivist at the U.S. Customs Service, who furnished new information on the early Maryland collectors, and Fred Kelso, an expert on Port Deposit granite, the building material used for many of John Donahoo's early lighthouses.

A number of Trust staff members made the finished product possible. Becky Bartlett Hutchison deftly handled administrative problems, contributed proofreading services and volunteered sound advice. Mary Louise de Sarran cheerfully loaned library tables, books, supplies and photographs. Michael Bourne, Charity Davidson, Stephen Bilicki, Sue King and Elizabeth Hughes all deserve sincere thanks: they were never too busy to stop their work to demystify a technicality, identify an architectural element, explain a nautical puzzle, or simply to share the delight of a discovery. Ralph Eshelman, a Trust Board member and lighthouse scholar, also generously shared his knowledge, insight and time.

Others helped in more unusual ways: Ellsworth B. Shank and Jane S. Jacksteit furnished information on lighthouse builder John Donahoo that allowed us to locate his great-great-granddaughter Lauren. (Mr. Shank also fought his way through Fourth of July parade traffic in Havre de Grace to guide visitors through an old cemetery and to John Donahoo's gravesite.)

Lauren Donahoo also gave up a holiday, driving to Annapolis for a rainy day of photography and hours of research at the State Archives.

We were honored to welcome Gerry Valerio, one of the nation's most respected book designers, to the project. He was a natural, in many ways. A master of elegant graphic understatement, he provides constant visual excitement on a printed page as he weaves text and image into an impressive tapestry for the reader. He's also a veteran Chesapeake Bay sailor who knows his lighthouses.

We also thank our publishing partners, The Friends of St. Clement's Island Museum, Inc. for their interest and faithful support of the book. Scores of loyal volunteers have been, and will continue to be, involved.

Finally, spouses deserve recognition. June Holland, a very brave lady, and Bill Hathaway, a very patient man, have contributed greatly to this work.

LILLIAN B. WRAY, Editor

1821
1. Upper Cedar Point Lightboat [D]

1822
2. Bodkin Island [D]

1823
3. North Point Range Lights [D] (Eastern and Western)

1825
4. Lower Cedar Point Lightboat [D]
5. Pooles Island
6. Thomas Point [D]

1827
7. Fog Point [D]
8. Concord Point
9. Hooper Strait Lightboat [D]

1828
10. Cove Point

1830
11. Point Lookout

1831
12. Lazaretto Point [D]

1832
13. Clay Island [D]

1833
14. Turkey Point

1836
15. Piney Point

1837
16. Upper Cedar Point Lightboat II [D]

1838
17. Sharp's Island [D]

1839
18. Lower Cedar Point Lightboat II [D]

1840
19. Thomas Point II [D]

1848
20. Greenbury Point [D]

1851
21. Blackistone Island [D]

1853
22. Fishing Battery Island
23. Janes Island Lightboat [D]

1854
24. Fort Carroll [D]

1856
25. Seven Foot Knoll (Relocated to Baltimore Inner Harbor 1988)

1857
26. Fort Washington

1858
27. Sandy Point [D]

1864
28. Upper Cedar Point Lightboat III [D]
29. Lower Cedar Point Lightboat III [D]

1866
30. Sharp's Island II [D]

1867
31. Hooper Strait [D]
32. Janes Island [D]

1868
36. Hawkins Point and Leading Point [D] (Brewerton Channel Range Lights)

1871
37. Choptank River [D]

1872
33. Upper Cedar Point [D]
34. Lower Cedar Point [D]
38. Love Point [D]

1873
35. Somers Cove [D]
39. Craighill Channel Range Lights (Front and Rear)

1875
40. Solomons Lump [D]

1876
41. Thomas Point Shoal
42. Mathias Point Shoal [D]

1879
43. Janes Island II [D]
44. Hooper Strait II (Relocated to Chesapeake Bay Maritime Museum, 1966)

1882
45. Sharp's Island III
46. Bloody Point Bar

1883
47. Sandy Point Shoal
48. Drum Point (Relocated to Calvert Marine Museum, 1975)

1884
49. Great Shoals [D]

1886
50. Craighill Channel Upper Range Lights (Cut-Off Channel Front and Rear)

1889
51. Cobb Point Bar [D]
52. Holland Island Bar [D]

1891
53. Greenbury Point Shoal [D]

1892
54. Maryland Point [D]

1895
55. Sharkfin Shoal [D]

1896
56. Solomons Lump II
57. Lower Cedar Point II [D]

1898
58. Cedar Point [D]

1902
59. Fort Carroll II

1905
60. Hooper Island

1908
61. Point No Point

1910
62. Baltimore
63. Ragged Point [D]

1921
64. Choptank River II [D]

Maryland
Lighthouses
of the Chesapeake Bay

Although the Chesapeake Bay had lighthouses as early as 1792, the story of aids to navigation in Maryland's waters begins in the early decades of the 19th century. This volume of lighthouse history - summarized above pictorially - deals with the eight lightboats and 60 individual lighthouses that became active between 1821 and 1921. While most, marked [D], have been destroyed, the surviving structures - on land, in the rivers and on the bay - are tangible symbols of Maryland's proud maritime heritage.

Detail, The New Topographical Atlas of the State of Maryland and the District of Columbia, S.J. Martenet, H.F. Walling, and O.W. Gray, Baltimore, 1873. MHT Library.

Chapter 1

"And in the Beginning..."

1819 - 1830

Lighthouses have been around at least since 300 B.C., when a firelight first shone from a tower on the Island of Pharos at Alexandria in Egypt. Dedicated to the safety of mariners, travelers and others who plied the waters of the area, this tower, estimated to be 450 feet tall, guided vessels to the entrance to the harbor of the great city of Alexandria. Over the next millennium or so, other lighthouses, lighted by wood or coal fires, came into use as coastal lights or to mark entrances to harbors.[1]

In time, lighthouse operators experimented with using both tallow candles and oil lamps to provide the light mariners needed. Both of these methods required an enclosed room to keep the wind from disturbing the flames, thus a small room of glass and metal came into use atop the towers. This room became known as the lantern (spelled lanthorn until well into the nineteenth century).

Although both candles and lamps were used in early lighthouses, an invention by Ami Argand in 1781 confirmed the lamp's superiority. The Argand lamp had a hollow wick, which permitted the flame to burn more brightly (equivalent in brilliance to seven candles). To focus the light and make it brighter still, each lamp was fitted with a parabolic reflector.[2]

Later in the nineteenth century the principle of the circular hollow wick was adapted to lamps used with the Fresnel lens. Looking like a glass beehive and coming in various sizes, the Fresnel lens was the most important development in the history of lighthouse illumination. It gave off a bright and reliable light. In the lens's larger sizes, visibility was limited only by the curvature of the earth and fog. The lens, although costly, was durable and is still used in many coastal lighthouses.

The first lighthouse in what is now the United States came into use in 1716 and served as a guide to Boston harbor. It is not known what lighting was first used there, but by the end of the Revolution the tower was lighted with spider lamps. Each of these lamps had several wicks, and was hung from a metal framework or chandelier.

By the time of the Revolution, eleven lighthouses were operating along the Atlantic coast from Portsmouth, New Hampshire, to Tybee Island, Georgia, though at the latter the tower was probably not lighted. Most of these colonial lighthouses were damaged during the war. The most severely injured was the Boston lighthouse, maimed beyond repair by a British gunpowder charge. It was rebuilt after the war.

For a few years following the Revolution, the country was governed by the Articles of Confederation. Under this form of government, each state was responsible for its own lighthouses, including repair and construction. Massachusetts was the only state to build any lighthouses during this period, putting two into service and beginning another—at Portland Head in what is now Maine.

When the federal government was established in 1789, Congress, in one of its earliest acts, made lighthouses and other aids to navigation the responsibility of the central government. This legislation placed the administration of lighthouses in the Department of the Treasury. Until 1820 the secretary of the Treasury or the commissioner of revenue supervised aids to navigation. Generally, local supervision devolved onto collectors of customs, for which duty they received the title of superintendent of lighthouses and 2.5 percent of the lighthouse money that passed through their hands.

The same law that assigned responsibilty for

Fiat Lux. Maryland's inland sea, Chesapeake Bay, and its mighty rivers were devoid of lighthouses in 1794 when cartographer Samuel Lewis published "The State of Maryland from the best Authorities." By the time of the Revolution there were eleven Atlantic Coast lighthouses but Maryland, and her premier port of Baltimore would wait until 1819 for a Congressional authorization and until 1822 for a lighthouse.

(Huntingfield Corporation Map Collection, MSA SC 1399 – 1 – 195)

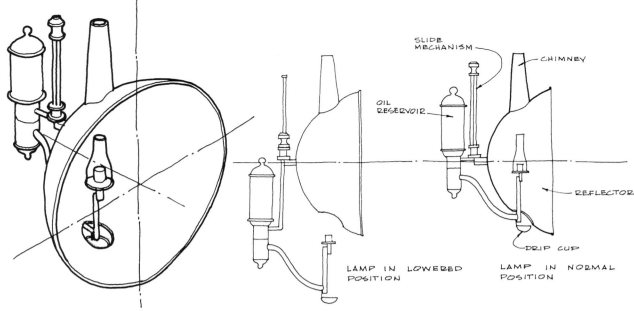

SLIDE
MECHANISM

CHIMNEY

OIL
RESERVOIR

REFLECTOR

DRIP CUP

LAMP IN LOWERED
POSITION

LAMP IN NORMAL
POSITION

The Argand lamp and parabolic reflector system had been used successfully in Europe for many years before it was introduced in American lighthouses by Winslow Lewis in 1812. Lewis's version of the system was never fully satisfactory and eventually received vitriolic criticism from much of the American maritime community. A British lighthouse historian said Lewis stole the lighting system from the South Stack lighthouse in England. In 1889 a Lighthouse Service official said Lewis's reflector approached the paraboloid about as closely as did a barber's basin. Despite the criticism, the system was used for forty years in America.

(Drawing by David Battle, F. Ross Holland Collection)

Developed by French physicist, Augustin Jean Fresnel in 1822, the Fresnel (frä–něl′) lens revolutionized lighthouse illumination throughout the world, but was not adopted for U.S. lighthouses until 1852. The fourth–order fixed lens pictured, right, was in use for decades at the Thomas Point Shoal lighthouse.

(MHT photo by Mark R. Edwards, 1985)

lighthouses also authorized a new lighthouse at the capes of the Chesapeake Bay. Completed in October 1792 on Cape Henry at the southern side of the entrance to the bay, this light was the first public works project of the new government and the first aid to navigation in Chesapeake Bay. In 1790 Congress appropriated funds for the partially finished lighthouse at Portland Head, and it went into service in 1791.

Soon after, other lighthouses were authorized and erected by the federal government, several in Virginia's portion of Chesapeake Bay. By 1820,

as Maryland's first lighthouses were being constructed, 55 lighthouses and 156 buoys guided ships along the seacoast and into harbors of the young republic, from northern Maine to the Georgia-Florida border.[3]

A light did not shine from a lighthouse in Maryland waters until 1822. Congress, in an act dated March 3, 1819, provided for the placing of buoys in the Patapsco River and construction of lighthouses on Bodkin Point (or Island as it was then known), on North Point, and on Sparrows Point.[4] All of these lights were primarily to serve traffic entering the Patapsco River, bound for the port of Baltimore. Bodkin is at the southern side of the river's entrance; North Point on the north; and Sparrows Point just inside the mouth of the river. Baltimore was Maryland's premier port, an appropriate place to begin to build lighthouses for Maryland shipping.

Just what the motivation was for getting these lighthouses authorized is not clear from the records, but Stephen Pleasonton, fifth auditor of the Treasury, shortly after he took over the administration of lighthouses in 1820, hinted there had been some opposition to these aids to navigation. He wrote to William B. Barney, naval officer of the Baltimore district, regarding the owner of the land at North Point, who was asking an astronomically high price for his land. If the state legislature could do nothing to get a fairer price, he instructed, Barney was to cease prosecution of the effort, "an object calculated not so much to benefit the trade of the United States as that of Maryland, particularly of Baltimore."[5] The statement reflected a strange attitude toward lighthouses in the United States since the only level of government in the lighthouse business after 1789 was the federal government.

Coincidentally, the building of these Patapsco River lighthouses straddled a change in the

administration of lighthouses—from the commissioner of revenue to the fifth auditor of the Treasury. Prior to Pleasonton's emergence on the scene, lighthouses were administered by the commissioner of the revenue, one Samuel H. Smith. In 1817 Congress passed an act abolishing the position, effective July 1, 1820. When Smith departed, the secretary of the Treasury assigned the commissioner's duties, including overseeing lighthouses, to Pleasonton, fifth auditor of the Treasury. Pleasonton was already responsible for all the accounts of the State Department and the Patent Office, as well as of the census and boundary commissioners. Although he carried a heavy workload and his new duties brought only a couple of additional clerks, he seemed to take them on without complaint.

For the next twenty years Pleasonton signed his letters "Fifth Auditor of the Treasury and Acting Commissioner of the Revenue." He administered lighthouses under delegation from the secretary of the Treasury until 1845, when Congress passed an act formally recognizing the fifth auditor's responsibility for lighthouses.[6]

Before Commissioner Smith departed, he had contracted with Lewis Brantz of Baltimore to implement the act authorizing the establishment of Maryland's first lighthouses. Brantz, a German immigrant, and his partner, Christian Mayer, conducted trade with Europe and the East Indies. Brantz persuaded the Marine Insurance Companies of Maryland to commission a survey of the Patapsco River. The insurers agreed, and Brantz undertook the work. The knowledge he gained from the survey work made him an excellent choice to place the buoys in the Patapsco and to select the lighthouse sites at the entrance to the river for which he was to be paid $300.[7]

Smith instructed Brantz to locate and purchase the sites for the three lighthouses and to develop designs and plans for them and attendant dwellings. He was also to send out proposals for their construction and obtain cessions of the land from the State of Maryland. At this time, the building of lighthouses was not an organized operation with proper staff. All work was done under contract.

Brantz first approached the owner of Bodkin

Boston Harbor lighthouse, the first in what is now the United States, was lighted in 1716. Three years later the colonial government provided a cannon to serve as a fog signal. In the 1750s the wooden portion of the tower burned and through the years lightning struck the tower; officials refused to provide a lightning rod. By the time of the Revolution the tower had been fitted with spider lamps. They were fueled by whale oil which produced an acrid odor, often driving the keepers out of the lantern. As the Revolution dawned, Americans, fearing the lighthouse was of greater use to the British, tried to put it out of business. Where they failed, the British succeeded, and in 1776 it was blown up. The Massachusetts legislature had it reconstructed in 1789 and in 1790 turned it over to the U.S. government.
(U.S. Naval Institute Photo Library)

Stephen Pleasonton, fifth auditor of the Treasury, was given responsibility for aids to navigation in 1820 when Congress abolished the office of commissioner of the revenue. A controversial bureaucrat, Pleasonton was known to have political influence, and luckily, a beautiful and intelligent wife who understood Washington society. He served for 32 years, but experienced widespread criticism of his management policies, especially in the area of lighthouse illumination. He felt the Fresnel lens was too expensive, and did not accept the argument that the savings in oil would, within a few years pay for the lens. During the Civil War his son, Alfred Pleasonton, served in the Union army as a major general.

(Library of Congress photo)

Island, Richard Caton, who wanted $1,000 for the site. A month later Caton said he would sell four acres and an access way for $600. The remaining two-thirds of the island was marsh, which Caton wanted to harvest for its sixteen tons of hay. Brantz encouraged Caton to keep the marsh, since he felt the government needed only the four acres. However, he thought the land worth no more than $25 per acre, as he found that land in that area usually sold for $10 an acre.[8]

Across the river at Sparrows Point, Brantz had been unsuccessful in getting Dr. James Stewart (or Steuart), owner of the site, even to name a price, although he had met with him twice.[9] The other aid to navigation was to be a range light, and in April 1819 Brantz, in the interest of economy, suggested putting both lights at North Point, about 500 yards apart, rather than one light at North Point and one at Sparrows Point. One keeper, he said, could look after both lights and "the range would be equally good." Two months later he reported establishing the ship channel range. "This line was established by Sending the Revenue Cutter out into the Bay . . . running up the range with a fine steady breeze, while the Vessel was in this line Piles were drove [sic] with great accuracy."[10]

Brantz wanted to get on with erecting the lighthouses, but he was frustrated by what he considered the unreasonable prices being asked for the sites. "The want of a lighthouse on the [Bodkin Island] Scite [sic] becomes very evident to one who is a few days in its vicinity. The Bar was never without one or more vessels aground while I was in that neighborhood." Apparently his idea for placing both the range lights on North Point was not approved, for by September he had staked out the sites for lighthouses on both North and Sparrows Points.[11]

Meanwhile Smith and Brantz were contacting others knowledgeable about lighthouse construction. Smith wrote Winslow Lewis, developer of the lamp and reflector system used to light lighthouses in the United States at that time. Lewis, who was himself the builder of several lighthouses, responded with information on wooden structures. Brantz wrote Benjamin Latrobe, the leading architect of the day and a friend of his, for advice. Latrobe answered openly and fully, urging that the lighthouses be built of stone rather than wood because of the fire hazard. He felt that the foundation at Bodkin Island, sandy loam, was adequate for the heaviest structure, but that the foundation of the North Point lighthouse should be built in a caisson so any sinking would be even. The "lanthorn," he suggested, should be anchored securely onto the tower.[12]

As of January 1821 the land had not been purchased nor had cession of the land from Maryland been obtained. Nonetheless, things were looking up, for on January 10, Naval Officer William Barney, who had been put in charge of building the Bodkin Island and North Point lighthouses the previous June, sent Pleasonton a copy of the bill ceding jurisdiction of the sites to the federal government. Two months later the commission created under this bill awarded $562 for the land at North Point. The owner, a Dr. Todd, agreed to accept the award, despite the fact that six months earlier he had felt he could take nothing less than $5,000 for the six acres. The government had purchased the Bodkin Island site from Richard Caton the previous August for $600.[13]

Advertisements for bids to build the Bodkin Point lighthouse had gone out and by mid-March Barney had received seven proposals, ranging from $4,300 to $9,000. He didn't trust the low bidders and felt the two highest were too high. He leaned towards the fifth highest bidder, Yernell and Macguire, who had built the buoy storage shed at Lazaretto Point.[14] Barney did think their price a little high and asked them if they could

An influential German immigrant engaged in international trade, Lewis Brantz of Baltimore, was contracted to identify locations for Maryland's first lighthouses. After surveying the Patapsco River, he selected strategic sites to serve vessels bound for the port of Baltimore: Bodkin Point on the southern side of the entrance to the river and North Point on the opposite side. Work on the Bodkin Island lighthouse began in June 1821 and was completed in January 1822. The lighthouse was abandoned in 1856 and the early

image above shows visitors at the ruins prior to 1914 when the tower blew down.
Far left: Detail, *The New Topographical Atlas of the State of Maryland and the District of Columbia*, S.J. Martenet, H.F. Walling, and O.W. Gray, Baltimore 1873. *MHT Library*
Left: Bodkin Island, with approximately 20 acres as shown in a 1844 U.S. Coast Survey map, has also vanished.

(Archives of The Ann Arrundell County Historical Society; Topographic Surveys 1803–1846, Register No. 175 BIS. MHT Library)

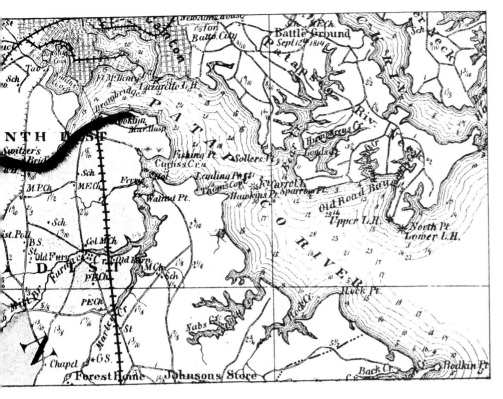

Lewis Brantz selected range lights for the northern entrance to the Patapsco River. He considered positioning one at Sparrows Point and one at North Point, but for reasons of economy, finally recommended placing both lighthouses at North Point, about 500 yards apart. "They are range lights," one early Light List explained, "to lead vessels, when up with Swan Point, into the Patapsco through the ship channel, also through the Swash."

(The American Pharos or Light-house Guide, Robert Mills, 1832, Detail, The New Topographical Atlas.....MHT Library)

reduce it. They took off $800, making their bid $6,500. Meanwhile, he had eliminated the lowest bidder, who he did not feel could obtain surety. The second lowest bidder, Thomas Evans and William Coppeck, shaved $600 off their bid, reducing it to $4,600, making their proposal more attractive to Barney. He decided to enter into contract with them.[15]

Evans and Coppeck had trouble getting surety, but by April 10, 1821, Barney had signed a contract with them. Barney didn't know he couldn't take such action without the approval of the fifth auditor, but he quickly found out and sent the contract to Washington. In June Barney received Pleasonton's approval, and Evans and Coppeck began work. By early August the tower was up 15 feet "and the dwelling and out House in proportion." By the middle of the month the builders had the soapstone deck laid on the top of the tower, and they expected to finish the lighthouse by the first of September. On that date Evans and Coppeck announced the lighthouse and other structures were finished and ready for inspection. Barney conducted the inspection and found a few things wrong, which he felt the builders could correct in a few days.[16]

Pleasonton had told Barney to hire a Captain Bunker as temporary keeper at Bodkin Island. The blunt-tongued Barney responded that he hoped the man would not be made permanent keeper, since "he is not qualified were he even sound in intellect, and surely much less so, deranged as he is in mind."[17]

Though the tower was completed, it was not

ready to go into service, for it needed a light. Near the end of September, Barney received a shipment from Winslow Lewis that contained thirteen lamps, each with a 16-inch reflector; glass chimneys; wicks; winter and summer oil; a stove to warm the oil; and tools and other equipment. In November the permanent keeper, Captain John Gray, was appointed. However, the light remained unlighted because, as Barney reported in the middle of December, the spindle on which the ventilator and weathercock rotated was defective and needed to be repaired by the contractor.[18] The light apparently went into service in early January 1822. Its mission was to serve Baltimore-bound vessels.

Pleasonton earlier had decided to follow Brantz's plan to have two lights at North Point, and in late January 1821 Barney visited the site, where he "laid off and surveyed" the land necessary for the light station. In March Pleasonton instructed him to prepare an advertisement soliciting bidders for the work at North Point based on Brantz's plan, with one important change. "Instead of having both Towers of the Light Houses of one height, say thirty one feet," he told Barney, "one of them ought to be twenty eight and the other thirty six feet, so that both lights when in range should be seen." Though often accused of having little understanding of aids to navigation, Pleasonton understood range lights better than Brantz did. Barney's draft was satisfactory to Pleasonton, but the money available to erect the lighthouses was inadequate, and Pleasonton instructed Barney to revise the advertisement to reflect a request for two bids, one for each lighthouse.[19]

Of the bids received, including one from Boston, Pleasonton thought that of Evans and Coppeck was the best. He directed Barney to enter into a contract with the two for the Eastern North Point light tower, if they could give satisfactory security. Though he apparently did not say anything at this time, Barney did make critical remarks about the contractors in September, reporting that he found Evans and Coppeck to be "tricky, slippery men [who] have completely forfeited my confidence." In working on the Bodkin lighthouse, he said, "they have made many attempts to deceive and impose upon me that I fortunately detected, but there is no knowing in how many they succeeded." For example, he continued, they built the first fifteen feet of the tower using an inadequate quantity of lime in the mortar and beach sand so "strongly impregnated with salt, as to preclude the possibility of its ever forming a cement." He said he had previously told them not to use the sand, so he had the

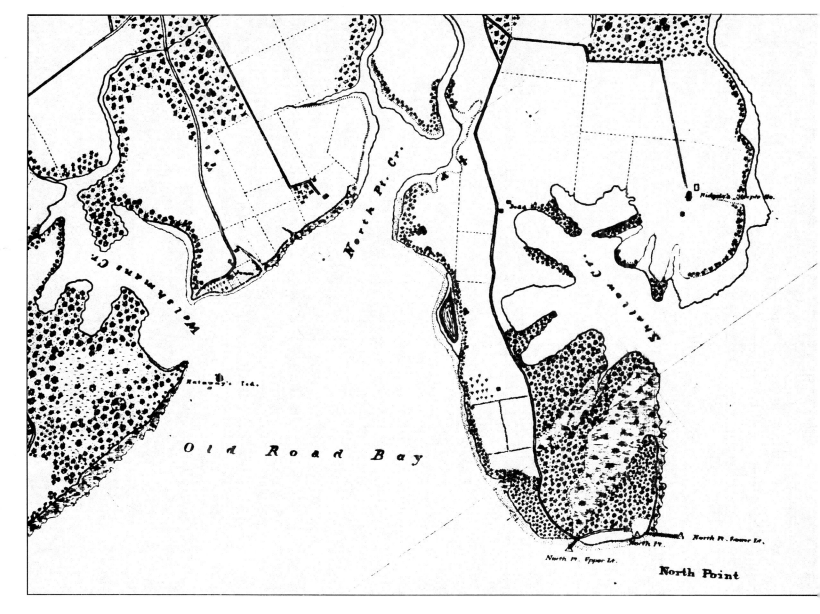

Map labels: Welchman Cr. · North Pt. Cr. · Old Road Bay · Bodkin's Island · North Point · North Pt. Upper Lt. · North Pt. Lower Lt. · North Pt.

tower pulled down. Barney said he was fearful the contractors would not do good work on either the foundation, which was to be built on piles, or the tower, wharf, and footbridge. He wanted to hire an overseer to make sure they performed the work competently.[20]

Evans and Coppeck did not execute the work on the Eastern North Point light tower with alacrity. By November 1, the deadline of the contract, they had nearly completed the dwelling, had dug the well, and built, "tho not fully completing, the foundation of the Light House." Dismayed at this performance, Barney asked Pleasonton what he should do. Pleasonton told him to notify the contractors that if they did not finish the work by the middle of December, penalties would be imposed. Evans and Coppeck wrote Pleasonton on December 8 that the sickly season had overtaken their workers, and they had not been able to keep men on the site except for more than two weeks without them coming

down with the illness. The contractors said if he would delay imposing penalties on their bond for four weeks they could get their work done. Pleasonton replied by telling Barney that if he felt they could complete the work in that time, then delay the suit. A few days before Christmas, one of the contractors' sureties visited Pleasonton in his office and handed him doctors' statements reporting that so many of their workers were sick they couldn't finish on time. Their case seemed so compelling to Pleasonton that he gave Evans and Coppeck until May 1 to finish the work at North Point.

Barney was probably able to work up some sympathy for Evans and Coppeck himself, because he too had been ill for much of the autumn of 1821. He said his sickness began September 25, and two months later he was only slowly recovering from it. Doctors, he wrote, say the illness is caused by too frequent exposure to sun and rain, visits to Bodkin Island and North

William B. Barney, son of the famous Commodore Joshua Barney, had been put in charge of building Maryland's lighthouses in 1820. As naval officer for the port of Baltimore he struggled with bidding and building problems, as well as "the Sickly season" for two years at the North Point site. For visibility, the two tall stone towers had to be placed offshore in five feet of water and the foundation of each was built in a coffer dam. A long footbridge connected each tower to the shore. The North Point range lights finally went into service on February 1, 1823.

(U.S. Coast Survey, 1845, T–218, MHT Library)

9

Point, and several hours standing in water selecting a site for the North Point lighthouse.[21]

In April 1822 the contractors had done enough additional work to receive a second payment, but Barney was less than sanguine about their finishing all the work by the deadline of May 1. He reported that the bondsmen were also concerned and had taken over management of the work. Visits to Bodkin Island had brought Barney's sickness back, giving him "rheumatism accompanied with highly bilious fever," for which he had been bled 100 ounces.

Work was permitted to continue, without penalties, and in the middle of May Barney asked that Evans and Coppeck be given the third payment. A month later he authorized the fourth payment. By July 5 the work had been finished and was ready for inspection by Barney, who found several serious defects. The tower was two feet taller than called for, in some places materials of lesser quality had been used, and the soapstone deck consisted of too many pieces and was flaking. By the first of August the eastern tower had been accepted and Barney authorized final payment. All told, the government had paid $6,637 for the light tower, dwelling, and outhouse.[22]

In May Pleasonton had instructed Barney to advertise in the *Baltimore Gazette* twice a week for a month for a proposal to build the Western North Point light tower. The tower was to be 35 feet high and situated 700 feet west of the eastern tower. By the first of August Barney had three proposals in hand. One, interestingly, was from Evans and a new partner, Robert Walcott, who submitted a bid of $6,500. Apparently the bid was handed to Barney when he last inspected Evans and Coppeck's work. Though it was the low bid, Barney looked upon it with considerable disfavor, writing Pleasonton that Evans should never get another government contract.[23]

The next lowest bidder was the partnership of James Boyd and James Hamilton, who proposed to do the work for $7,000. The third bidder was $2,800 higher and wanted to delay construction, not finishing until June of the following year.

Barney was not enthusiastic about Boyd and Hamilton, calling them journeymen masons who had never taken on a project on their own before. In addition, he believed the securities they offered were men who, combined, were not worth half the value of the project. Later Boyd and Hamilton submitted others as securities with whom Barney felt comfortable. In the meantime, however, Barney had readvertised for proposals and received one from Simon Frieze of Port Deposit, who said he would do the work for $7,800. Barney was pleased, saying he considered him "a man well worthy of confidence." Boyd and Hamilton were unable to deliver adequate securities, and Barney let the contract to build the western lighthouse on September 3 to Frieze and George Ring. Winslow Lewis received the contract to supply the lamps and reflectors and other pertinent equipment for the lighting apparatus.[24]

Work progressed steadily on the western tower, and on January 10, 1823, Barney wrote Pleasonton that the structure would be completed in a few days. He also reported less than salutary news about the status of the eastern tower, which, he said, "has been rather on the retrograde." The contractors, he reported, had early in the work "failed to make good their contracts to different mechanics and others under them and not being able to get along without advances, assigned over to their securities the several payments receivable from me, as they might respectively come due." The blacksmith heard that he might not get full payment for the ironwork, so, to ensure payment, he took a considerable portion of the completed work with him. Barney tried to get the contractors to have the work put back, but they had no money to pay the blacksmith, who stood firm in the position he had taken.[25] The record is not clear as to how this situation was resolved, but the work ultimately was completed.

On January 19 Barney heard that the eastern tower was finished, and five days later he reported to Pleasonton that the western tower was nearly completed, certainly, he said, far enough along for Lewis to install the lighting apparatus. Lewis had already put the lamps and reflectors in the eastern tower.[26]

On January 25 Barney inspected the lighting equipment in the two towers. He found that although the western or rear tower was fitted with nine Melville and Black patent lamps as called for in the contract, they were not arranged to produce the best light. The lamps were too few for a good light, but worse, "the apparatus was put up in a loose and crazy manner." Except for one or two, the reflectors were not fourteen inches across as called for in the contract, and the lamp chimneys were two inches too short, causing the reflectors to become smoked. They also were made of inferior material and were easily broken, often just through handling.

The eastern light tower's apparatus was, he thought, better hung and arranged. The reflectors did not measure fourteen inches, however, and some were not even thirteen inches wide. The chimneys were of better quality, but were as

"The blacksmith heard that he might not get full payment for the ironwork, so, to ensure payment, he took a considerable portion of the completed work with him. Barney tried to get the contractor to have the work put back, but they had no money to pay the blacksmith, who stood firm in the position he had taken."

much as four inches too short, causing the reflectors to become smoked. The oil butts at both towers were also inferior. Their metal was too thin, and though they were supposed to hold ninety gallons, testing revealed they held just eighty. Barney somewhat bitterly noted his impression that Lewis was charging the government "a high retail price for any article furnished."[27]

Despite Barney's misgivings about the lamps, the North Point range lights went into service for the first time on February 1, 1823, with Solomon Frazier as keeper.[28] Because he had two lights to attend, Frazier's salary was greater than that of the keeper at Bodkin Island. The usual keeper's pay at that time was $350 a year. Frazier received $600, the last $100 having been justified on the great distance he had to walk to tend the lights and the fact that the well supplied poor water, forcing him to haul water some distance.[29]

Lewis Brantz, though he liked the Bodkin light, criticized the quality of the North Point lights, particularly the eastern tower, adding that many captains and pilots had complained to him about them. He attributed the poor quality to the keeper, who he felt did not pay "proper attention to . . . trimming and filling the Lamps, and keeping the reflectors and the Lanthorn clear and bright."[30]

Complaints about the lamp and reflector system were not new, and over the years they increased in intensity. But at this period the maritime community had not yet focused on these problems, and some years were to pass before they did.

The Bodkin Island and North Point range lights, plus the buoys that had been placed in the Patapsco, made a good start at improving safety for mariners entering the accessway to Baltimore harbor. Now the time had come to build lighthouses in other parts of Maryland's portion of the Chesapeake Bay.

In 1824 Congress authorized two additional lighthouses for Maryland, one on Pooles Island in the upper part of the Chesapeake and one at Thomas Point just south of Annapolis at the entrance to the South River. The Pooles Island light would serve both traffic bound to and from the Gunpowder River and traffic coming from the north, through the shallow channel on the west side of Pooles Island. The eastern channel, more popular because it was deeper, would not be served by the lighthouse.

William Barney characterized the need for a light at Thomas Point in a letter to Pleasonton in 1823: "Many ship owners and seafaring men of respectability have frequently spoken to me on

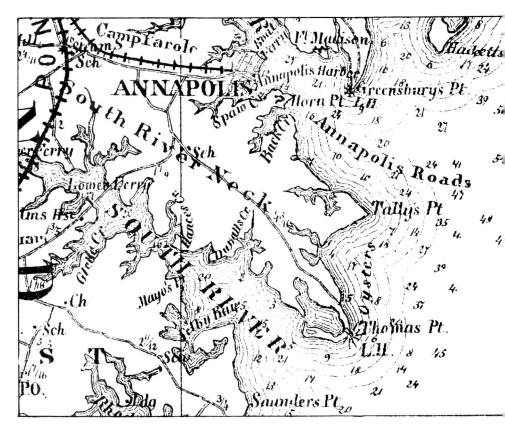

the subject of a light to be placed at the end of Thomas' Point bar, a few miles below Annapolis; which extends a considerable distance out into the Bay, cutting the direct track of vessels bound up or down; at the end of which from four feet, you instantly deepen to six and seven fathoms water. A light placed here, would be of as great utility as perhaps any one in the Chesapeak [sic] Bay."[31] For this light Congress appropriated $6,500 and $5,000 for the Pooles Island light.

In July Pleasonton instructed Barney to purchase the lighthouse sites. A month later he bought the seven-acre Thomas Point site for $75 per acre. But he did not have the same success on Pooles Island, where the owners wanted $250 for each of the four acres required. Barney thought this amount much too high and recommended going to the Maryland legislature to have the land condemned and valued.

With the Thomas Point site in hand, Barney advertised for bids to erect the light tower. It was to be a round structure made of brick or stone, 30 feet tall, 18 feet across at the base, and 9 feet at the top, with the wall 3 feet thick at the base and gradually decreasing to 20 inches at the top. Also to be built were a dwelling, similarly of stone or hard brick, 24 feet by 20 feet, with two rooms and a chimney supplying a fireplace for each room. The kitchen was to be attached, 14 feet by 12 feet, with a chimney containing a fireplace and an oven with an iron door. A well producing good water was to be lined with brick or

Authorized by Congress in 1824, the Thomas Point lighthouse was needed to mark a troublesome bar at the entrance to the South River, just south of the capital city, Annapolis.

(Detail, The New Topographical Atlas....MHT Library)

The 1824 specifications for the Thomas Point lighthouse are detailed and standard for the period. In addition to the tower, to be built of brick or stone, a two–room keeper's dwelling with attached kitchen, an outhouse or privy and a well were called for. Although such details as an iron bucket for the well were spelled out, many decisions were left to the builder. The privy was to be placed "a convenient distance from the dwelling," the interior wood-work of the buildings was to be painted with two coats of "good paint" and " the whole was to be completed in a faithful and workman like manner...." Later lighthouse specifications would consist of numerous detailed draw-ings of the structure, lists of materials to be used, and details of how parts were to be fitted together.

(Lighthouse Superintendent's Correspondence, Baltimore, 1825 –1852, R.G. 26, National Archives)

with the Dwelling-house a Chimney with a fire-place and sizable oven with an iron door, iron crane, trammel and hooks in the fire-place and on one side of the Chimney a sink with a spout leading through the wall.

Also an (out house) or privy at a convenient distance from the dwelling of Stone or brick five feet by four in the clear, with a wall at least eight feet deep, walled up with stone or brick, the roof to be well shingled.

Also a well to be sunk of such depth as to procure good water at a convenient distance from the house, to be stoned or bricked up and furnished with a pump or with a curb, windlass and an iron chain, and a strong iron hooped bucket.

All the wood-work of the dwelling-house, Kitchen and out-house to be painted with two coats of good paint exclusive of priming.

The inside walls and ceilings to be lathed and plas-tered and finished in a plain neat style. Gutters of double tin to lead round the dwelling house and kitchen with spouts of same materials to carry off the rain-water. Also the lumber used to be of well seasoned yellow heart pine, consequently en-tirely free from sap.

The sand used in making the mortar must be inland sand and the water must be spring or well-water, so that there shale be nothing of a saline nature in the cement or mortar.

Above and below each window frame of the right thickness must be lintels of sufficient dimension to reach from out to out of the frame and extend inwards the whole thickness of the wall. And in building up the walls, if of stone there must be an entire range of thorough stones every three feet besides that in the intermediate spaces the stones must tie.

The whole to be completed in a faithful and work-man-like manner by the first day of October next.

Separate proposals will be received for Fitting-up said Light-House within one month after it shall be built, with Patent-lamps and reflectors, tin-butts for keeping the oil and also the necessary apparatus in the same manner as the Light-houses of the United States have been fitted up by Mr Winslow Lewis.

The Whole to be approved by the Superintendent.

Payment to be made when the whole shall be completed and approved.

(Signed) William B. Barney
Naval Officer Dist. Baltimore

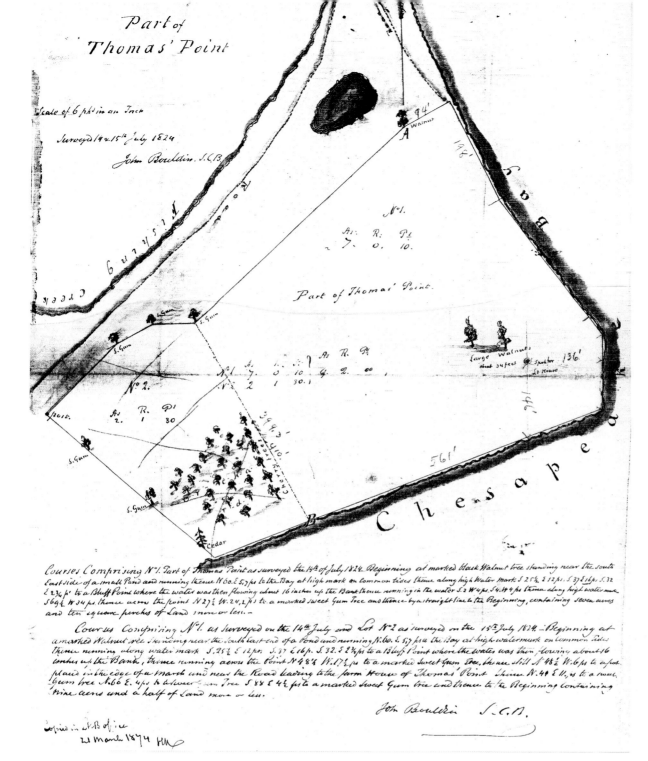

Part of
Thomas' Point

Scale of 6 phs in an Inch

Surveyed 14 & 15th July 1824

John Bouldin. S.C.B.

Part of Thomas' Point.

No. 1.

A: R: P¼
7. 0. 10.

Courses Comprising Nº 1. Part of Thomas Point as surveyed the 14th of July, 1824. Beginning at marked Black Walnut tree standing near the south East side of a small Pond and running thence N 60. E. 57 ps to the Bay at high mark on common tides thence along high Water Mark S 25½ E 12 ps. S 37 E 16 ps. S 32 E 23½ ps to a Bluff Point where the waters was then flowing about 16 inches up the Bank thence running in the water S 2 W 4 ps. S 4. 14 4 ps thence along high water mark S 69¼ W 34 ps thence across the point N 27½ W. 24, 2 ps to a marked sweet Gum Tree and thence by a straight line to the Beginning, containing seven acres and ten square perches of Land more or less.—

Courses Comprising Nº 1. as surveyed on the 14th July and Lot Nº 2 as surveyed on the 15th July 1824.— Beginning at a marked Walnut tree standing near the south East end of a Pond and running N 60. E 57 ps the Bay at high watermark on common tides thence running along water mark S 25½ E 12 ps. S 37 E 16 ps. S 32 E 23½ ps to a Bluff Point where the waters was then flowing about 16 inches up the Bank, thence running across the Point N 48¾ W 17½ ps to a marked Sweet Gum Tree, thence still N 48½ W 6 ps to a post place in the edge of a Marsh and near the Road leading to the farm House of Thomas' Point Thence N 44 E 11, ps to a sweet Gum tree N 60 E 4 ps to another Gum Tree S 88 E 4½ ps to a marked Sweet Gum tree and thence to the Beginning containing Nine acres and a half of Land more or less.

John Bouldin   S.C.B.

Copies in S.B. office
21 March 1874 H.M.

Left: The Thomas Point site was surveyed in July 1824 and the "space for Lt. House" is clearly marked near the two large walnut trees. William Barney acquired the seven–acre site a month later, paying $75 per acre, and by February 1825 had contracted with John Donahoo and Simon Frieze for construction. There are no known pictures of the lighthouse, but it may have been built of Port Deposit granite, a material Donahoo would use at other sites. (His building partner, Frieze, had quarried the Port Deposit granite used for the 1817 toll bridge across the Susquehanna River and then continued to work the opening until about 1829.)

The Thomas Point land mass, pictured above in an 1847 Coastal Survey map, bears little resemblance to the area today and helps to explain why the lighthouse was rebuilt in 1840 and eventually replaced by a screw-pile structure on the shoal. The thin land link has vanished and build– up has been extensive on the western side of the point.

(Thomas Point Site File, Folder A, National Archives)

(U.S. Coast Survey, 1847, Register No. 248, MHT Library)

stone and have a pump or windlass with an iron bucket. A privy was also to be constructed.[32]

The advertisement elicited several good proposals from reliable people with what Barney considered to be good bondsmen. The low bid was $5,626, proposed by John Donahoo and Simon Frieze. Donahoo had built a retaining wall at the Bodkin lighthouse, and Frieze, with George Ring, had erected the western tower at North Point. The second lowest bid, at $6,000, was from Jeremiah H. Boyd and George Ring, and the highest was submitted by Joseph Jamieson, who bid $6,500.[33] In his bid, Donahoo exhibited a technique that would serve him well over the years to come: He bid at least in the general vicinity of

the money available. He took into account that the money Congress appropriated for a lighthouse was to pay for everything—the land, the 2.5 percent due the collector of customs, the lighting apparatus and any incidental expenses associated with the project. His bid was just a few hundred dollars over the money on hand.

Barney negotiated with Donahoo and by February 23 had reached an agreement with the partners and begun to draw up a contract. A week before he had employed John Bovis of Baltimore to supply the lighting apparatus.[34]

During construction of the Thomas Point light, Donahoo exhibited another characteristic that would continue to bring him lighthouse con-

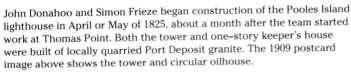

John Donahoo and Simon Frieze began construction of the Pooles Island lighthouse in April or May of 1825, about a month after the team started work at Thomas Point. Both the tower and one–story keeper's house were built of locally quarried Port Deposit granite. The 1909 postcard image above shows the tower and circular oilhouse.

(Jack Kelbaugh Collection)

Long-time keeper Captain Stephen Andrew Cohee welcomed visitors to the island, and his wife Agnes photographed this group on the gallery deck about 1910.

(Courtesy Mrs. Stephen William Cohee)

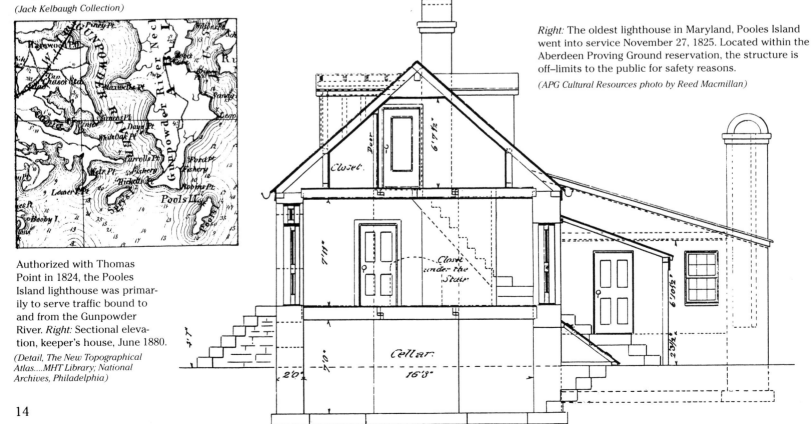

Authorized with Thomas Point in 1824, the Pooles Island lighthouse was primarily to serve traffic bound to and from the Gunpowder River. *Right:* Sectional elevation, keeper's house, June 1880.

(Detail, The New Topographical Atlas....MHT Library; National Archives, Philadelphia)

Right: The oldest lighthouse in Maryland, Pooles Island went into service November 27, 1825. Located within the Aberdeen Proving Ground reservation, the structure is off–limits to the public for safety reasons.

(APG Cultural Resources photo by Reed Macmillan)

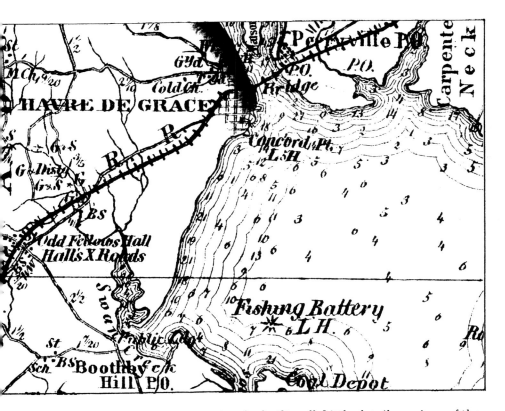

Authorized in 1825, the Concord Point lighthouse (also called the Susquehannah Light) at Havre de Grace marked the entrance to the Susquehanna River near the head of the bay. Native son John Donahoo built the tower and dwelling during the summer and fall of 1827, while simultaneously constructing the Fog Point lighthouse on Smith Island in the southernmost reaches of Maryland's part of Chesapeake Bay.

(Detail, The New Topographical Atlas....MHT Library)

tracts—he built well. Little detail survives of the progress of construction, but apparently the work went steadily. In early October Barney inspected it and found a few things unsuitable, especially the well water, which smelled foul, but he was pleased with much of the work. The record is skimpy, and it is not known whether this was an interim inspection or the final one. Barney and Donahoo disagreed over some of the work, but principally over the smelly well water. They agreed to call in a referee, and near the end of December 1825 the three visited the site. Barney later reported that the referee agreed the water had a potent odor, but found it clear and not unhealthful. The referee also said the construction work was the best he had seen.[35]

Whether the light was exhibited before the visit is not known for sure. The *Light Lists* issued by Pleasonton, starting in 1838, has the Thomas Point light going into service in 1825, as did Robert Mills' *The American Pharos,* which of course, indicates it was in use before Barney's last visit. The light guarded vessels against a shoal that made out from that point, but more important it served as a guide to Annapolis harbor, and later, into it, with the aid of five buoys that had been placed there in 1831. Its position also made it a good general light for navigating the bay.

There was no shortage of people interested in the keeper's position at Thomas Point. Barney said he had fifteen applicants and others had made their application directly to Washington. These men came from many professions—post-men, pilots, ship captains, masons, and boat-builders, among them.[36] Unfortunately, who ultimately won the post has not been revealed in the records.

While this work had been going on, the construction of the Pooles Island light station was also underway. Pleasonton had instructed Barney in late December 1824 not to pay more than $500 for the desired acreage on Pooles Island. Barney talked to the owner, Peregrine Wethered, who agreed to sell nearly seven acres for $500, which he did on March 10, 1825.[37]

Little is known about the construction of this lighthouse. Several people bid on the work, but the contract went to Donahoo and Frieze, and the illuminating apparatus was installed by Mr. Bovis. The lighthouse went into service on the evening of November 27, 1825.[38]

Three years later the Chesapeake Bay received its first fog signal. The idea had been talked about as early as February 1828. Pleasonton planned to put the bell on a tower, and he said the only other place with such a structure was at Passamaquoddy, in Maine. The Passamaquoddy tower, however, was not a good model for the one needed at Pooles Island since it was 12-feet-square at the base and 18 feet tall, with a small bell. The one at Pooles Island needed to be 25 to 30 feet tall and required a bell weighing at least 1,100 lbs. The tower proposed for Pooles Island would cost $2,500, more than twice the price of the Passamaquoddy tower.

On May 23, 1828, Congress appropriated $2,800 for a fog bell, tower, and striking machinery to be positioned near the light tower on Pooles Island. The bell was to be struck ten times every minute and the machinery would run at least sixteen hours without being wound. These fog bell towers looked like metronomes and came to be quite common, but today only a few survive at light stations in New England. The New England towers were made of wood, but Pleasonton thought the Pooles Island structure should be built of brick or stone. The machinery was operated by weights: the higher the tower, the further the weight had to fall, which allowed for a longer interval between times when the weight had to be rewound. The same mechanism, on a smaller and more delicate scale, was used to turn Fresnel lenses in order to achieve a flashing light.

In the fall of 1828, Barney advertised for proposals to erect the bell tower and install the bell. By the middle of November he had received only one response, which was for $1,600. When the bidders, Hugh Devalin and Jarvis Kile, heard theirs was the only bid, they visited Barney in his

office and said that they had made a mistake—the bid should have been $2,000. When he learned of this, Pleasonton told Barney to accept Devalin and Jarvis's bid, if they would do the work for their initial figure of $1,600. If they did not accept this offer, Barney was to readvertise the work.[39]

Apparently Devalin and Jarvis refused the offer, for Barney advertised again, adding that the work was to be completed by June 1, 1829. This time he received two proposals. The low bidder was William Simpson, who said he would put up the tower and place the bell for $1,900. Pleasonton directed Barney to accept Simpson's proposal. The fog signal was put in place, and the keeper's salary went up $50 per year to compensate him for taking care of the fog bell.

In two years time the tower was threatened by erosion. Pleasonton could not understand why it had not been placed far enough back to prevent this danger for fifty years. There was no answer, and with a choice of moving the bell tower or putting in a breakwater, Pleasonton took the latter course.[40] It apparently solved the problem for a fog bell continued to operate at the site for a number of years.

The year following the authorization for the Thomas Point and Pooles Island lighthouses, Congress appropriated $2,500 for a lighthouse on Concord Point in Havre de Grace and $4,000

for a light vessel at Hooper Strait. Neither sum was adequate for the project, and the next year Congress provided an additional $1,500 for the lighthouse and $1,826 for the light vessel.[41]

The initial appropriation, Pleasonton figured, was sufficient to begin advertising for bids to build the lighthouse at Concord Point. Barney first visited Havre de Grace to select a site and commented, "I found as is usual when Government want [sic] property, that it had increased in value in so prompt and extravagant a manner as to render the probability of a purchase quite impracticable, without the aid of the state Legislature." He figured the land had an estimated value of $100 per acre, but the asking price was $320 per acre. In looking for a site, Barney felt the best one would be on the river bank, but he discovered fisheries occupied these banks. With such crowding at the site, the keeper's dwelling would have to be erected 100 yards away. The town commissioners were willing to sell a small piece of land on the bank for the light tower, but "the solitary proprietor of the adjacent lots conceives himself [so] immensely aggrieved, that he will not give his consent . . . ." The other owners of fisheries would not sell even a minuscule piece of land for the tower, nor a larger piece for the tower and dwelling. Finally, the commissioners and the fishery owners agreed for the lighthouse to be built in the street and the dwelling

Purchasing the land for the Concord Point lighthouse and keeper's dwelling was more daunting than the tasks associated with construction. William Barney was able to locate a small plot of land near the river's bank for the tower, but the keeper's house had to be built further inland, mandating brisk walks for a century's worth of keepers.

(Postcard view c. 1898, Kenneth G. Lay Collection)

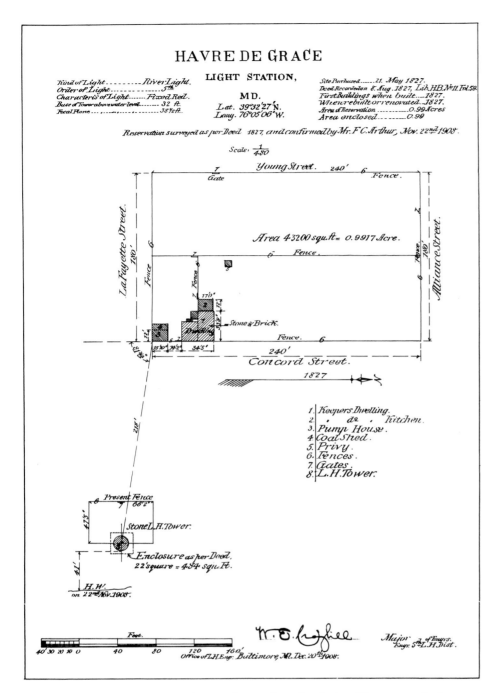

HAVRE DE GRACE

LIGHT STATION,

MD.

Kind of Light .... River Light.
Order of Light .... 5th.
Characteris of Light .... Fixed Red.
Base of Tower above water level ..... 32 ft.
Focal Plane .... 38½ ft.

Lat. 39°32´27˝ N.
Long. 76°05´06˝ W.

Site Purchased .... 21. May 1827.
Deed Recorded on 8. Aug. 1827, Lib. H.B. No. 11. Fol. 59.
First Buildings when built ... 1827.
When rebuilt or renovated ... 1827.
Area of Reservation .... 0.99 Acres
Area enclosed 0.99

Reservation surveyed as per Deed 1827, and confirmed by Mr. F.C. Arthur, Nov. 22nd 1908.

Scale ⅟₄₈₀

1. Keepers Dwelling.
2. do. Kitchen.
3. Pump House.
4. Coal Shed.
5. Privy.
6. Fences.
7. Gates.
8. L.H. Tower.

Major A. of Engrs.
Engr. 5th L.H. Dist.

Office of L.H. Eng: Baltimore, Md. Dec. 20th 1908.

The Concord Point complex, purchased in 1827 for $225, offered the keeper a spacious garden area along with outbuildings. John O'Neill, a local hero in the War of 1812, beat out seven other applicants, including John Donahoo, for the keeper's position. Many of O'Neill's descendants kept the light, including the last keeper, a great-grandson.

(Site plan, National Archives, Philadelphia)

located at a detached site. The commissioners asked Barney to have the legislature give them the authority to cede the street to the federal government. He did, and the legislature eventually authorized the town to transfer one acre of land for the light tower. So in the end Barney acquired a lot twenty-two-feet square for the tower and a separate site at the corner of Concord and Lafayette streets for a dwelling and garden. For both pieces he paid $225, $175 of it to Sarah Hall and her son William B. Stokes, who sold the dwelling site to the government on May 21, 1827. As these negotiations were drawing to a close, Pleasonton directed Barney to advertise for proposals to erect the tower, to be similar to those at Thomas Point and Pooles Island, and the dwelling.[42]

Barney advertised, and the low bidder at $3,500 was John Donahoo, a native of Havre de Grace. Pleasonton told Barney to enter into a contract with him and also with James Geddes and a Mr. Stewart, who were to fit up the lantern with patent lamps and reflectors for $493. Pleasonton added that if the tower was to be built of stone, Donahoo was to cover it with Roman cement, for which he would be paid an extra $50. It was later covered with this plaster.

Donahoo erected the conical stone light tower and the dwelling. In August 1827 Barney reported he expected the structures to be completed in September. Something must have delayed construction, however, for it wasn't until early November that Barney received notification the Concord Point lighthouse was ready for inspection. Possibly there was a delay in the arrival of the lamps and reflectors.

In the meantime, Pleasonton had received an application from John O'Neill, a hero of the War of 1812, and several others for the keeper's position. In late October Pleasonton sent the president O'Neill's name, along with seven others, including that of John Donahoo, who had applied for the job. O'Neill's name was at the top of the list. On November 3, 1827, Pleasonton notified Barney that President John Quincy Adams had appointed O'Neill keeper of the Concord Point lighthouse. The lighthouse went into service during that month, probably within a week of the appointment. By November 22 Barney had made the final payment on the light tower, and on December 3 he sent Pleasonton a final accounting of his disbursements for the lighthouse.[43]

As Barney was carrying through with this effort, he was also engaged in getting a light vessel for Hooper Strait, which was needed to keep other vessels clear of the bar off Hoopers Island. With specifications prepared by a naval architect in Washington, Barney advertised, apparently in July 1826, for proposals to build a 50-ton light vessel. None of the bids came close to the money available, which was $4,000. Pleasonton obtained an additional appropriation, and Barney readvertised. The second ad may have been for a larger vessel, perhaps of seventy tons. This time several bids were received, and the low bidder was William Harrison, who proposed to build the vessel for $7,500. In May 1827 Pleasonton instructed Barney to enter into a contract with Harrison, but when Barney approached him, Harrison declined to enter the contract. Barney was then authorized to go to the next lowest bidder, who was William Price, a Baltimore shipbuilder. His bid had been $1,000 higher than Harrison's.

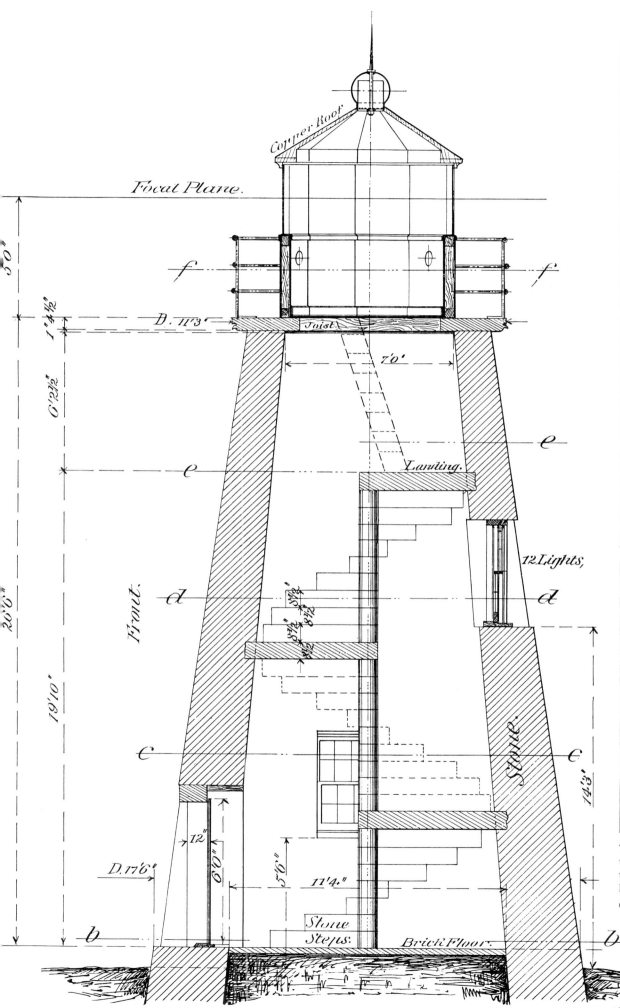

Focal Plane.

Copper Roof

Joist.

7'0'

Landing.

12 Lights,

Front.

Stone.

12"

6'0"

5'6"

11'4."

Stone
Steps.

Brick Floor.

D.11'3'

D.17'6'

5'0"

1"4½"

0'2½"

20'6"

19'10'

14'3'

John Donahoo built the Concord Point tower of Port Deposit granite, tapering the massive walls from an exterior diameter of 17' 6" at the base to 10' 0" below the lantern deck. Sectional elevation, 1891.

(MHT photo by Catherine Adams Masek, 1982; National Archives, Philadelphia)

The tower steps are stacked blocks of triangular granite which spiral up from the brick floor to the quarter–circle lantern landing.

(MHT photo by Catherine Adams Masek, 1981)

19

Donahoo's Dozen

Nov. 1825
POOLES ISLAND,
4th lighthouse in Maryland;
built with Simon Frieze,
white stone tower. *(Standing)*

Dec. 1825
THOMAS POINT,
5th lighthouse in Maryland;
built with Simon Frieze,
white stone or brick tower.
(Destroyed)

Sept. 1827
FOG POINT,
6th lighthouse, house with
tower on roof.
(Destroyed)

Nov. 1827
CONCORD POINT,
7th lighthouse, white stone
tower. *(Standing)*

Dec. 1828
COVE POINT,
8th lighthouse, white brick
tower. *(Standing)*

Sept. 1830
POINT LOOKOUT,
9th lighthouse, story-and-a-
half house with tower on
roof. *(Standing)*

Fall 1831
LAZARETTO POINT,
10th lighthouse, white brick
tower. *(Destroyed)*

Nov. 1832
CLAY ISLAND,
11th lighthouse, story-and-a-
half house with a square
tower on roof. *(Destroyed)*

Aug. 1833
TURKEY POINT,
12th lighthouse, white brick
tower. *(Standing)*

Sept. 1836
PINEY POINT,
13th lighthouse, white brick
tower. *(Standing)*

Dec. 1851
BLACKISTONE
ISLAND,
16th lighthouse, white brick
tower rising through a brick
keeper's house. *(Destroyed)*

Jan. 1853
FISHING BATTERY,
17th lighthouse, story-and-a-
half brick house with an
hexagonal wooden tower.
(Standing)

*John Donahoo built 12 of the
first 17 lighthouses in Maryland.*

The Man Who Lit the Maryland Coast

For years Lauren Donahoo thought her great-great-grandfather had been a light-house keeper somewhere near Havre de Grace. Reality turned out to be far more interesting than legend however, and her research, originally just a family project, has served to flesh out the fascinating and virtually unknown figure who built 12 of the first 17 lighthouses in Maryland.

Early federal census records indicate that John Donahoo was born in Harford County to Daniel and Sarah Donahoo in 1786. Little is known of his early life, but in February 1812 he married Eliza-beth Wood and in June enlisted in the Maryland Militia when Con-gress declared war on Britain. He rose from private to sergeant, served until December 1814, and returned to a Havre de Grace that had been burned and savaged by Admiral Sir George Cockburn's fleet in 1813. Early handwritten records of the Havre de Grace City Council indicate that John Dona-hoo was involved in efforts to rebuild the town, says long-time resident Jane S. Jacksteit, an active

Jane S. Jacksteit helped establish the Friends of the Concord Point Lighthouse shortly after the original fifth–order Fresnel lens was stolen in 1975. She once got very close to the replacement lens, loaned by the Chesapeake Bay Maritime Museum, as she perched in the back of a volun-teer's van hugging and steadying it on the long trip home.

(MHT Cultural Conservation Program photo by Dave Harp, 1993)

Lauren Donahoo's Maryland roots run deep – from 18th century Eastern Shore planters to a hero of the Great Baltimore Fire. But sandwiched between the centuries is her favorite ancestor, the lighthouse builder of Havre de Grace.

(MHT photo by Lillian Wray)

member of the Friends of the Con-cord Point Lighthouse, Inc.

Apparently attracted to politics, Donahoo served as the town's judge of elections for four terms and in 1819 was himself elected a town commissioner. According to a former mayor, David Craig, writ-ing in *Havre de Grace, An Informal History*, 96 men held the office of town commissioner from the first election in 1812 to the last in 1876. The longest term of service was that of J. Thompson Frieze who held office for 22 years; second was John Donahoo with 16 years of service. (Interestingly Frieze, who was first elected in 1852, was the grandson of Simon Frieze, John Donahoo's building partner on the 1825 Pooles Island and Thomas Point lighthouses).

According to Mrs. Jacksteit's records, Donahoo dabbled in real estate, buying and selling many parcels of land in and around Havre de Grace beginning about 1815. He and John O'Neill, an often elected commissioner and the Havre de Grace hero who stood his ground when the British

attacked the town, served on the school committee. Among other tasks, they oversaw the lottery which permitted "poor children" to attend the public school. A fish-erman for much of his life, Dona-hoo leased in-town fishing wharf space for his sloop, got the con-tract to repair the town wharf, and finally in 1839 constructed his own with 170 feet of water frontage.

John Donahoo's lighthouses were built over a period of 28 years, with the last two, Blacki-stone Island (1851) and Fishing Battery (1853), constructed when he was in his sixties. Yet Lauren Donahoo notes that her great-great-grandfather is listed in the 1850 census as a "farmer" and the head of an extended family of 15. He died in Havre de Grace on March 18, 1858 and the inventory of his possessions included farm equipment, beds and tables, a shaving stand, four mahogany chairs, an "old desk," an armchair, "old books" and "one old map." Ask Ms. Donahoo how she thinks her ancestor should be remem-bered and the response is quick and simple. "As a man who cared about his town and its people; a man who believed in hard work and teamwork; and as a man who created structures that have lasted."

Sources as noted, also correspondence Jacksteit to Donahoo 1991, Donahoo to L. Wray 1995 and conversations with Ms. Donahoo.

After work had begun on the vessel, Pleasonton noticed that the specifications called for only one anchor. He felt the second anchor had been overlooked, since all other such vessels had two anchors, and directed Barney to acquire a second anchor. Barney agreed with Pleasonton, feeling more than one mushroom anchor and sixty fathoms of chain would be required to hold the floating light on station. The purchase added $371 to the cost of the vessel.

By December the oak, schooner-rigged vessel was ready for inspection. Richard F. Fox had been appointed captain or keeper of the floating light the previous month. His crew was to consist of three seamen, who would be paid merchant service wages plus 25 cents subsistence per day, and a boy.[44] It is not clear exactly when the vessel went into service, but it was probably December 1827.

The Hooper Strait lightboat was not the first one in Maryland waters. Two light vessels had been placed in the "narrows of the Potomac," where the present bridge carries U.S. 301 across the river. In 1821 a light vessel was placed at Upper Cedar Point, where the river bends sharply nearly three miles upriver from the bridge. A second light vessel was established in 1825 at Lower Cedar Point, about a mile downriver from the bridge. Little is known about the early history of these vessels, but both were replaced by newly built lightboats in the late 1830s. James T. Hunter of Norfolk built the Lower Cedar Point vessel, completing it in late 1838, though it did not go on station until March 1, 1839. Captain William Easby of Washington, D.C., built the Upper Cedar Point lightboat in 1837, finishing it in early October. The old Lower Cedar Point light vessel was disposed of at auction.[45]

As the Hooper Strait lightboat was being built, Barney was also engaged in establishing lighthouses in southern Maryland, particularly at Cove Point, Point Lookout, and Fog Point.

Fog Point is located on the northwestern point of Smith Island, an island mostly in Maryland waters with a small portion of the southern end belonging to Virginia. The northern end of the island forms the southern side of Kedges Straits, which is the accessway from Chesapeake Bay to Tangier Sound. In 1826 Congress authorized a light there to guide vessels through the strait into Tangier Sound and provided $3,500 for its establishment.[46]

Pleasonton must have been exceedingly confident the lighthouse would be authorized, for in January 1826, a full four months before the bill passed, he instructed Barney to advertise for proposals to erect it. The specifications sent

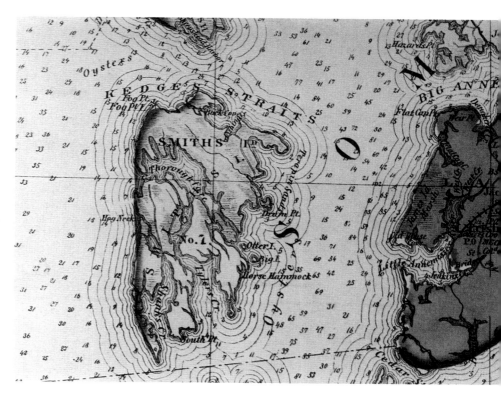

were the same as those for Warrick Neck lighthouse in Rhode Island. Pleasonton felt this structure could be erected at Fog Point for a sum less than the appropriation so money would be left to pay for the land and the lighting apparatus.

During the summer of 1826 Littleton Dennis Teackle, acting for the government, negotiated with Richard Evans to buy a three-acre site at Fog Point. In August Barney forwarded to Pleasonton the fruits of Teackle's effort—an agreement whereby Evans would sell the land for $200. Teackle urged immediate approval of this agreement, for he felt the Maryland commissioners would award a much higher sum. Barney asked the commissioners to cease their effort, but they did not desist and after adding an acre of marsh to the site, they placed a valuation of $400 on the property. Pleasonton was not happy and urged Barney to settle quickly with Evans before he heard about the value the commissioners had set on the land. In November 1826 Evans sold the property to the government.[47]

Barney received only one bid in response to his advertisement, and that was from John Donahoo, who said he would do the work for $3,500, which was the total appropriation. Low bidder on fitting up the lantern with lamps and reflectors was Winslow Lewis, who bid $500.

When Pleasonton received Donahoo's bid, he said he could not accept it and asked Barney to write Lewis and inquire what sum he would require to build the structure. Lewis had, Pleasonton said, built a similar lighthouse at Provincetown Harbor, Massachusetts, for $2,395.

Fog Point, the sixth lighthouse built in Maryland, was located on the northwest side of Smith Island on Kedges Strait, the accessway to Tangier Sound. John Donahoo followed specifications that had been used for a Rhode Island lighthouse, erecting a saltbox–type structure with a tower over the center. Ten years later the lighthouse was threatened by erosion and a series of breakwaters were built.

(Detail :The New Topographical Atlas.... MHT Library)

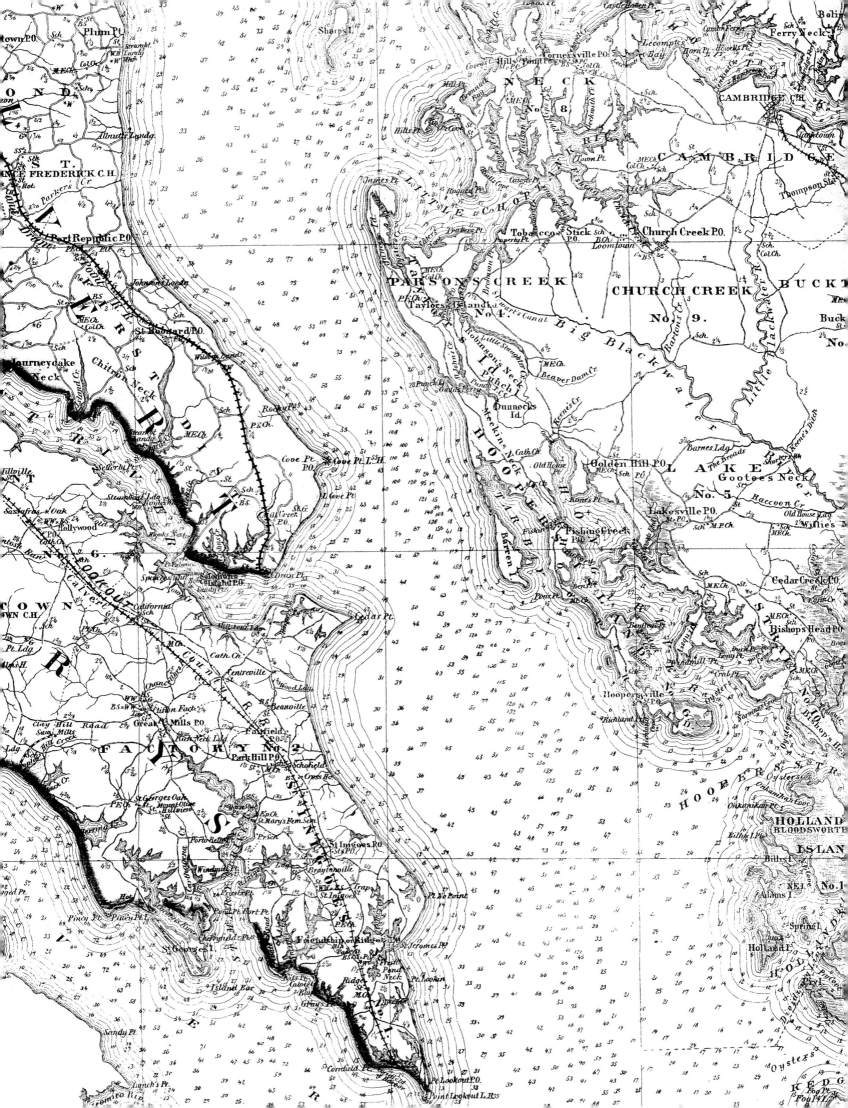

Barney wrote Lewis, who responded he would erect a lighthouse similar to the one he had built at Sandy Neck at Barnstable, Massachusetts, and fit the lantern with lamps and reflectors for $3,450. In transmitting the reply to Pleasonton, Barney expressed his lack of confidence in Lewis, reflecting, perhaps, his unhappiness in the past with lighting equipment and materials Lewis had supplied to Chesapeake Bay lighthouses. Barney felt Lewis's response was vague and that the plan he proposed did not conform to the advertisement and was patently inferior to the structure proposed therein. He pointed out that Donahoo's bid conformed to the advertisement and was just $50 more than Lewis's. He would be inclined, he wrote, to give the preference to Donahoo. Apparently Pleasonton accepted Barney's contention since on April 25, 1827, Barney entered into a contract with the veteran builder to erect the lighthouse for $3,500.

By late August Donahoo had completed the lighthouse and notified Barney it was ready for inspection. In mid-September Barney visited the the island, saw the lighthouse and reported it "completed to the letter of the contract." The house with a tower over the center had cost $3,500. A sketch in the Fog Point site file in the National Archives shows such a structure, but the dwelling appears somewhat strange, with the rear roof line extending to the ground. It looks as if the artist was attempting to draw a saltbox structure. In 1857 the Lighthouse Board had a plan done of the lighthouse on Clay Island. This structure was a story-and-a-half dwelling with an attached kitchen that continued the slope of the house roof, making that end of the dwelling look like a saltbox. The Fog Point lighthouse was probably a similar structure.

During this period Barney forwarded Richard Evans's application to be keeper of the Fog Point lighthouse to Pleasonton. Barney's regard for this applicant was not high; he found Evans very old and "not . . . adequate to the duties." Evans and his son, who would succeed him, Barney wrote, had a marked appearance of "indolence and ignorance." After he returned from inspecting the lighthouse, Barney asked Pleasonton not to appoint a keeper until he wrote again because he was expecting to receive the application of a good person. The delay would be no problem, he explained, since Lewis wouldn't be able to get the lighting supplies there until October. This time Pleasonton did not heed Barney's advice, for he recommended to the president that Richard Evans be appointed keeper of the Fog Point lighthouse.

Evans did not serve long, for he died in late

June 1828. In notifying Pleasonton, Barney wrote that several people had applied, including Solomon Evans. Barney said he did not know him but presumed "him equally ignorant of the duties and detail of a lightkeeper as was the deceased, for innumerable have been the complaints made to me of the manner the light was kept, frequently no light at all." Barney recommended a Mr. Wilson. Pleasonton once again did not take his advice, recommending to the president that John M. White be appointed in Evans's place. White was appointed.[48]

The lighthouse erected during this period at Cove Point was initially scheduled to be built at Cedar Point on the southern side of the mouth of

Left: A lighthouse had been approved for Cedar Point on the southern side of the mouth of the Patuxent, but after a site visit William Barney suggested an alternative, Cove Point, five miles to the north.

(The New Topographical Atlas.....MHT Library)

John Donahoo built the brick Cove Point tower and standard keeper's house for $5,685, finishing the work in about three months. The lighthouse went into service in 1828.

(MHT photo, c.1967)

"Barney later said he had selected an acre of land on 'a bleak sand point without the least particle of vegetation and utterly useless for any other purpose' and two acres about 200 yards away for a garden. The land, he said was 'hardly tillable'."

the Patuxent River. Because of the change, a lighthouse was not established there until 1896.

In the early spring of 1825 Congress appropriated $6,000 to build a lighthouse at Cedar Point at the mouth of the Patuxent River, but it was nine months before William Barney visited southern Maryland to select a site. On the way he stopped by Cove Point, at the suggestion of Pleasonton, who felt it might be a better location for a lighthouse. After viewing both sites, Barney reported "a light at Cove Point would be of ten fold the utility than one at Cedar Point would be, but . . . a Light Boat immediately abreast of the mouth of Patuxent would be of still greater benefit." Properly placed, he added, such a vessel could guide mariners in their approach to Cove and Cedar Points and guide them out of the Patuxent River or to a harbor in the river. He said his view was supported by many ship captains and pilots in Chesapeake Bay.

Probably thinking of the cost of a light vessel and its future operational expense, Pleasonton apparently accepted the suggestion to move the light to Cove Point, five miles south of Cedar Point. On February 12, 1826, Congress authorized the placement of a lighthouse at Cove Point in place of the one it had approved for Cedar Point.[49]

In June Pleasonton wrote to Barney telling him to purchase land for the lighthouse. Barney got around to it some months later and reported that the owner wanted $50 per acre and that the ship captains and pilots were unhappy because they wanted a light boat off the mouth of the river. Pleasonton responded by telling Barney to acquire the Calvert County land for $50 an acre. In June 1828 Barney purchased two plots of land from Miss Dorcas G. Bourne. One was a two-acre site back from the water to be used for a garden, and the other was a plot nearly 2½ acres in size right at the point.

In the meantime, Barney had received instructions to proceed with getting the construction work underway as soon as he had purchased the land. Pleasonton sent him an advertisement for a 40-foot tower and the standard house, saying he wanted the work completed by the end of the year, because at that time any money not obligated for construction would go into the "sinking fund," which apparently meant back to the general Treasury account, thus requiring another appropriation. Within ten days the advertisement was placed in the newspaper. Several bid on the project, but John Donahoo once again was low bidder. He agreed to build the light tower, the dwelling, and the other structures for $5,685. Pleasonton authorized Barney to enter into a contract with James (or John) Geddes to fit the lantern with the lighting apparatus for $550, although Winslow Lewis had bid $490. By the middle of September, Donahoo had the work underway.[50]

In November Donahoo notified Barney the construction was completed and ready for inspection. By the first of December Barney had written Pleasonton that he expected to hear any day that the lighting apparatus was in place and a keeper needed to be appointed. Pleasonton was several weeks ahead of Barney, having sent a list of eleven applicants for the position to the president on November 12. He recommended James Somerville. President Adams agreed, and within a few days of receiving Barney's letter, Pleasonton was able to respond that the keeper would be Somerville and he would receive $350 per annum.[51] Unquestionably the lighthouse went into service some time in December 1828.

The last lighthouse erected in this group was the one at Point Lookout. The 1825 legislation authorizing the lighthouse called for "a small beacon light." The appropriation was small also, just $1,800. "Beacon light" was a term Barney did not understand, and he asked for a definition. Pleasonton replied that it was "in all respects similar to a lighthouse." Barney visited Point Lookout and suggested the light be placed right at the point.

Late in the spring of 1826 Pleasonton directed Barney to purchase a site for the lighthouse at no more than $50 per acre. Barney later said he had selected an acre of land on "a bleak sand point without the least particle of vegetation and utterly useless for any other purpose" and two acres about 200 yards away for a garden. The land, he said, was "hardly tillable." When approached to sell the property, the owner would not accept $50 an acre, and Barney asked the state legislature to appoint a commission to assess and value the site. The commissioners met and valued the three acres at $1,100. When he learned of their decision, Barney was upset and recommended to Pleasonton that either the decision be appealed or Congress be asked to repeal the law authorizing the lighthouse. Pleasonton, with the permission of the secretary of the Treasury, took the latter course and the money went to the surplus fund. Pleasonton later said that if Congress still wanted to erect a lighthouse at Point Lookout, he recommended an appropriation of $6,500. Congress authorized the structure in May 1828, but provided only $4,500 to erect it.[52]

Congress had spoken, and Pleasonton told Barney that if the owner still wanted the amount the commissioners had awarded him, Barney would have to pay it. Thinking the funds for the work at Point Lookout also included the $1,800 previously appropriated, Pleasonton asked Barney to build a tower and dwelling similar to those on Pooles Island. He quickly found out that only $4,500 was available to erect the light station and to pay for the land. He scaled down his plan, telling Barney to build a structure that would combine the tower and the dwelling—a structure similar to the one erected at Fog Point.

Barney contacted Jenifer Taylor, owner of the property, and found he would not sell at the price the commissioners had awarded. Taylor, however, said he would sell the land for $500, if he were to be appointed lightkeeper. He had approached Pleasonton some time earlier with the proposition and been told it "would not for one moment be entertained by the government." It would be tantamount to selling the office to him, Pleasonton explained.

Pleasonton instructed Barney to offer Taylor the sum the state had awarded him for the land. If he refused to execute a deed, then Barney was to "tender or make payment" of the money to Taylor. The government would then be able to go ahead with construction of the lighthouse, Pleasonton elaborated, because Maryland law provided that tendering the money vested the title in the United States without a deed.

Barney did not act, however, for 1828 was an election year and a new president was elected—Andrew Jackson—which meant a change in the very political office of collector of customs in Maryland as well as other ports in the United States.[53] Barney's successor was Dabney S. Carr.

Pleasonton had sent the land purchase money to Barney and had a hard time retrieving it. Anxious to move ahead rapidly with the construction work, he wrote to the new collector and superintendent of lighthouses, asking him to find out what action Barney had taken on the purchase and to get the money from him. Carr was then to go to Point Lookout and execute the purchase. Barney did not respond, so Pleasonton asked the secretary of the Treasury to send $1,150 to Carr so he could buy the land. Finally, in September, Carr saw Taylor, the landowner, who declined to sign a deed. At this point Pleasonton had to backtrack, and he sent Carr a copy of the letter he had written to Barney about tendering or making payment and instructed him to be governed by it.

Meanwhile Congress was getting impatient and passed a resolution inquiring why the Point Lookout lighthouse had not been erected. Pleasonton responded by recounting the tale of past events and assuring Congress the new naval offi-

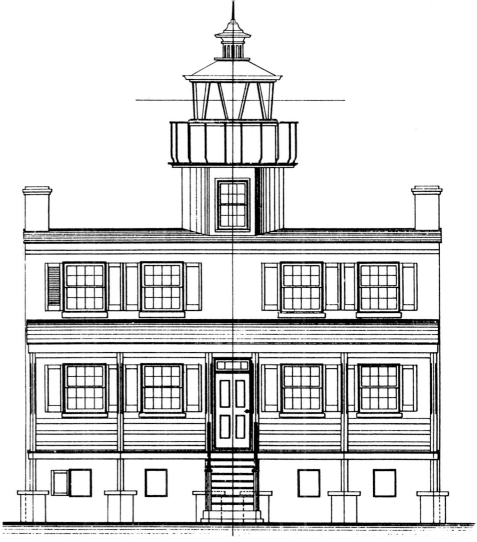

The Point Lookout lighthouse, at the northern entrance to the Potomac River, was authorized in 1825 as a "small beacon light," but a small appropriation and squabbles with the landowner sidetracked the project for several years. With a $4,500 appropriation for both land and lighthouse in 1828, the final specifications called for the tower and dwelling to be combined.

(Front elevation plan 1888, National Archives, Philadelphia)

cer was moving on obtaining the land and getting the lighthouse built.

About this time the secretary of the Treasury expressed an interest in testing the use of gas in a lighthouse, and since Point Lookout was to be erected soon, it was deemed a likely test site. Pleasonton accordingly directed Carr to change the advertisement for proposals to build the lighthouse and seek a proposal to install gaslighting and keep it operating in the lighthouse for a year. The advertisement had already been issued, necessitating a separate inquiry to find someone interested in installing the gaslighting. There were several responses, but for some reason the proposed test was dropped, and Pleasonton instructed Carr to enter into a contract with James Geddes to supply the lamps and reflectors. John Donahoo won the job of constructing the lighthouse with his low bid of $3,350.

Little is known about the appearance of the Point Lookout lighthouse in its early days. In 1858 a lighthouse engineer described it as a two-story, yellow brick dwelling containing four rooms and an attached kitchen, with a shingle roof painted red and the tower and lantern on the roof. Despite this description, it is generally thought to have been a one-story or a story-and-

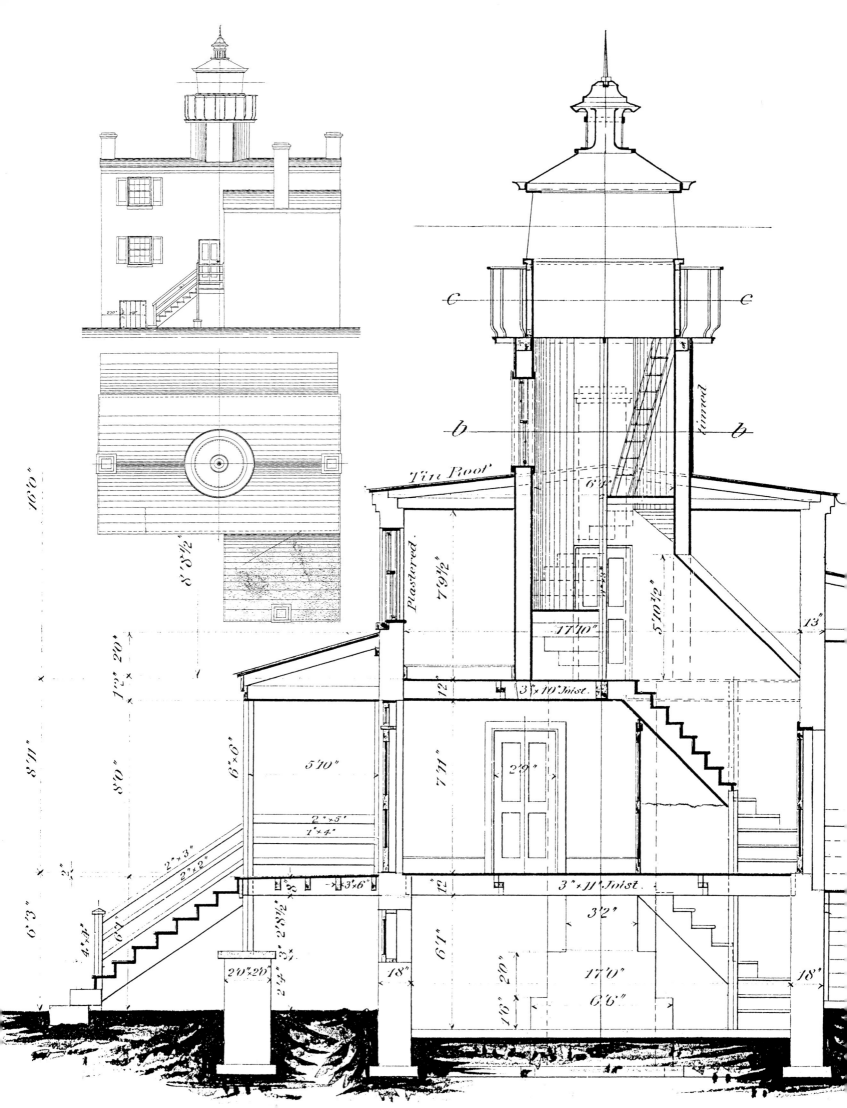

a-half dwelling with a light tower on the roof, an opinion supported by a report prepared in the 1880s that says a second story was being added to the lighthouse. Whatever the size of the structure, the light served to guide ships into the Potomac River and along the western coast of the Chesapeake.

In July James Davis was appointed keeper of the new lighthouse. Donahoo and Geddes did their work, and the lighthouse went into service on September 20, 1830. Davis did not serve long, for he died December 3, 1830. His daughter Ann Davis succeeded him and remained keeper until her death in 1847. At one time Pleasonton referred to her as "one of our best keepers." Pleasonton strongly encouraged the appointment of dependent women of lightkeepers who died in service. He would not appoint a replacement for a just-deceased keeper until he assured himself the widow did not want the job. He articulated

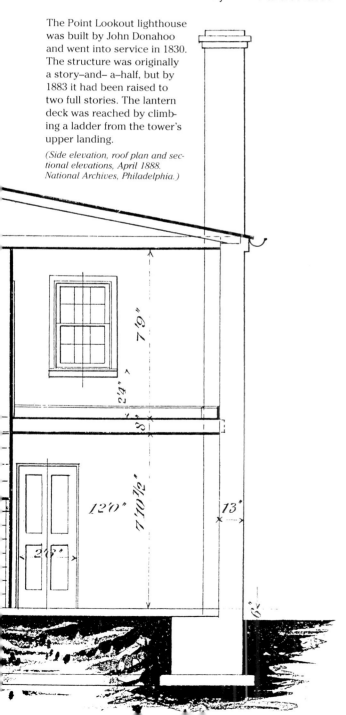

The Point Lookout lighthouse was built by John Donahoo and went into service in 1830. The structure was originally a story–and– a–half, but by 1883 it had been raised to two full stories. The lantern deck was reached by climbing a ladder from the tower's upper landing.

(Side elevation, roof plan and sectional elevations, April 1888. National Archives, Philadelphia.)

this policy in 1851, when he wrote, "So necessary is it that the Lights should be in the hands of experienced keepers that I have, in order to effect that object as far as possible, recommended on the death of a keeper, that his widow, if steady and respectable should be app't to succeed him, and in this way some 30 odd widows have been appointed."[54]

In June 1831 a minor upheaval occurred when it was thought the Point Lookout lantern was made of cast, rather than wrought, iron. Pleasonton was upset and threatened to deduct money from the final payment due Donahoo. Donahoo was able to persuade Pleasonton the lantern was for the most part made of wrought iron—only the sash was of cast iron—and Pleasonton withdrew his threat.[55]

The last string on this package was not tied until two years later, when the government finally received a deed from Taylor on December 13, 1832. Taylor demanded interest on the money owed him because, he argued, such a long time had elapsed between the taking of the land by the government and his receipt of payment. Pleasonton shot back that in view of his recalcitrance in providing a deed he had "no pretense of claim to interest on the money awarded him."[56]

The first ten years of getting lighthouses established in Maryland's waters were successful. A good start had been made, and most of the important places in Maryland's portion of the bay had been lighted. During this period the naval officer and superintendent of lighthouses was William B. Barney, and he deserves credit for his work executing the process from land purchase to final inspection of the new structures. At this time, Pleasonton also contributed much to protecting the bay, exhibiting conscientiousness and imagination that were to fade in later years. Pleasonton gave Barney an easier time than the latter's successors were to experience.

Both Barney and Pleasonton recognized a good contractor. They obviously had confidence and faith in John Donahoo's ability and honesty. Little today is known about Donahoo, but he played an important part in building lighthouses during this period, a role he was to continue in subsequent years. One measuring stick we have for evaluating the man is what he built. Donahoo built well, and his structures lasted. None of them crumbled because of shoddy workmanship or poor materials. Those that have not survived either succumbed to erosion or were torn down.

Thanks to the work of these men, by 1830 lighthouses were scattered about Maryland's portion of the bay from its northernmost area to the southern line.

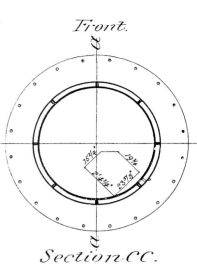

Front.

Section CC.

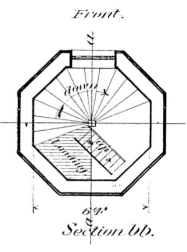

Front.

Section bb.

"The first ten years of getting lighthouses established in Maryland's waters were successful... Pleasonton also contributed much to protecting the bay, exhibiting conscientiousness and imagination that were to fade in later years."

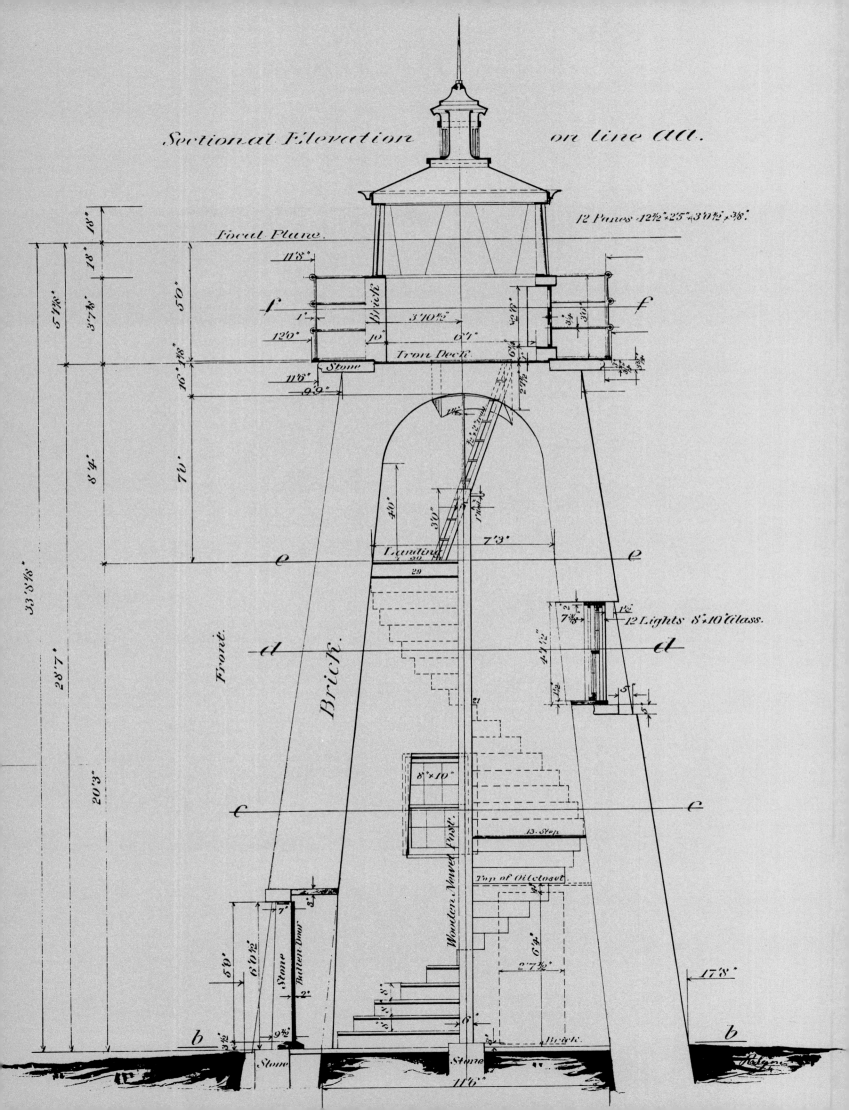

Sectional Elevation on line AA.

Focal Plane.

12 Panes 12½"×25"×30½"×⅜".

Brick

Iron Deck.

Stone

Front.

Brick.

Landing

12 Lights 8"×10" Glass.

Wooden Newel Post.

13. Step

Top of Oil closet.

Stone

Batten Door

Stone

Stone

Brick

Chapter 2

More Lights and the End of an Era

1831-1852

During the first decade Congress was responsible for aids to navigation for Maryland waters, nine lighthouses and three lightboats entered service. All but two of the lighthouses were the traditional short stone towers with the keeper's dwelling nearby. In contrast, the years between 1831 and 1852 saw only eight lighthouses and one new light vessel come on line, with five of these lighthouses being wooden story-and-a-half dwellings surmounted by a tower and the lantern. These latter ones were less expensive.

In 1831 Congress authorized lighthouses at Lazaretto Point at the entrance to Baltimore Harbor and on Turkey Point at the mouth of the Elk River in the upper reaches of the Chesapeake. The secretary of the Treasury was allowed some discretion in selecting a site for the light at Baltimore harbor; he was to choose between Lazaretto Point and Fort McHenry. At the request of Pleasonton, Dabney Carr, Barney's successor as naval officer, looked at the two sites Congress had mentioned and chose Lazaretto Point. Apparently Carr's decision was primarily based on the possibility of reusing one of the old buildings at the lazaretto—a hospital for treating contagious diseases—for the keeper's dwelling. With the savings this would engender, the project could stay within the $2,500 Congress had provided, which was only enough to erect the light tower and supply the lighting apparatus of eleven lamps and reflectors. The land did not cost anything since the government had purchased the site from John O'Donnell in 1804.

Pleasonton agreed with Carr's selection, as did the secretary of the Treasury, and in April, less than six weeks after the legislation was passed, Pleasonton instructed Carr to advertise for proposals to erect a light tower. The successful bidder was John Donahoo, who built the structure for $2,100.[1] The tower was completed and the lighting system installed in the fall of 1831. In early November William Shaw was appointed keeper. In March 1832 Pleasonton wrote that the light had been exhibited for the first time in 1831, although the local superintendent of lighthouses had not reported the exact date.[2]

The brick tower, according to an 1858 report, was 30 feet from base to coping with walls $3\frac{1}{2}$ feet thick at the base and 1 foot 10 inches at the coping or top. The diameter was 11 feet 6 inches at the base and 7 feet at the top. Though originally equipped with eleven lamps and reflectors, by 1858 the tower had a fourth-order lens that gave off a fixed white light with the focal plane 35 feet above sea level. The circular lantern, 6 feet across, was made of iron.

In 1836 the keeper's house, which had been converted from a building on the lazaretto property, was damaged in a fire that destroyed the hospital. After an inspection was made, Pleasonton decided to erect new quarters on a standard plan, using what brick could be salvaged from the dwelling and hospital. In 1858 the keeper's quarters were described as a two-story brick building painted white with a shingle roof. The first and second floors contained five rooms each and the attic two rooms. The dwelling's outside dimensions were 20 feet by 35 feet with an addition of 12 feet x 13 feet.[3]

Money was appropriated for one last lighthouse in Maryland while Barney was still in office—Clay Island in Tangier Sound at the eastern side of the entrance to Fishing Bay. This

Congress had authorized a lighthouse for Clay Island in 1828, but the project was stalled for years, while the Lazaretto Point lighthouse moved briskly to completion – authorized, constructed and lit in 1831. Built by John Donahoo, the brick tower cost $2,100.

(1883 elevation courtesy of George [Bud] Nixon, Rukert Terminals Collection)

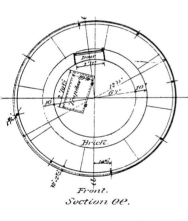

Tall masts shared the Baltimore skyline with industrial smoke stacks in this A. Hoen & Co. engraving (c.1870) of Locust Point (*left*) and Canton. The Lazaretto lighthouse and its fog bell tower are visible, along with a seawall built to control erosion. Strategically located at the entrance to Baltimore Harbor, the Lazaretto lighthouse sat across the river from Fort McHenry.

(T. Edward Hambleton Collection, Peale Museum, Baltimore City Life Museums; Detail: The New Topographical Atlas....MHT Library)

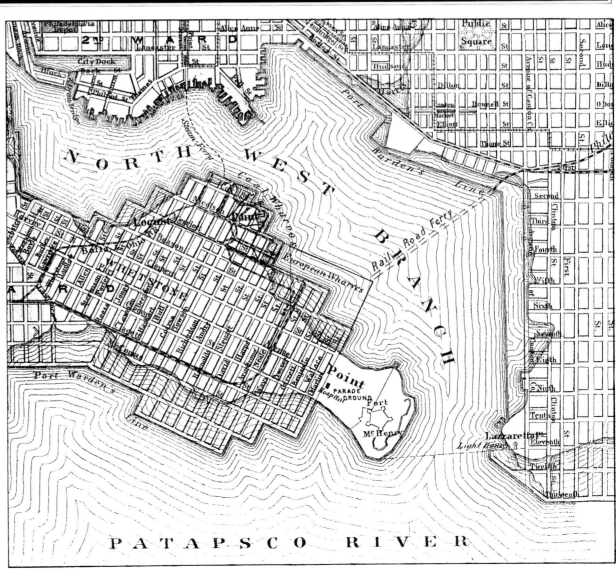

point was also at the western side of the entrance to the Nanticoke River. Congress provided $6,500 for the establishment of this lighthouse in the same act that contained the last appropriation for the Point Lookout lighthouse.

Pleasonton was anxious to get the lighthouse built and pressed Barney to move ahead with purchasing the land for it. Barney seemed to drag his feet, and in December 1828 Pleasonton contacted Littleton Dennis Teackle, a person Barney said he did not trust, calling him "a very tricky gentleman." Pleasonton backed away from Teackle when the latter wrote that he would purchase the land on Clay Island and another site for a lighthouse on Little Watts Island, Virginia for $1,000. Pleasonton said it would not be proper to enter into an agreement with a person who did not own the property. He told Barney to determine who the owners were and to purchase the land. Finally, in March Barney wrote Pleasonton that a deed indicated that Job Slocum and George Lake owned Clay Island. The site appeared to be on Lake's portion of the island, and he wanted $500 for the lighthouse site. Pleasonton authorized Barney to purchase the land, but the following January he changed his mind and instructed Naval Officer Carr, Barney's successor, to send the money to the surplus fund. In 1831 Pleasonton recommended to the Ways and

Means Committee of the House of Representatives that efforts to locate a lighthouse on Clay Island be discontinued since it was so difficult to obtain a deed. Congress responded by reviving the appropriation, forcing Pleasonton to "persevere" and acquire the land.[4]

The new collector moved ahead and in October Pleasonton asked the secretary of the Treasury to send Carr $500 to pay for the Clay Island site. Though Job and Ann Slocum and George and Mary Boyson Lake signed the deed on August 26, 1831, for some reason it did not get to Carr until late in February 1832.

When notified of the arrival of the deed, Pleasonton sent Carr an advertisement to publish in the local papers seeking proposals for building the Clay Island lighthouse. Pleasonton wanted the structure completed by October 1. John Donahoo seems to have been the only bidder, but his price was $200 more than the money left, which was $5,400. Consequently, Pleasonton told Carr to ask Donahoo to match the money available. If he would, then Carr was to enter into a contract with him, but if he would not, Carr was to get in touch with Winslow Lewis and see what he would charge to erect the lighthouse. If Donahoo were to do the work, then Carr was to enter into a contract with Bovis and Geddes to supply the lighting apparatus. Donahoo dropped his price

A turn–of–the–century post-card image shows the 1870 Lazaretto Point fog bell and what may be a buoy shed behind the tower. *Below:* Front elevation, 1888.

(Jack Kelbaugh Collection; Ruckert Terminals Collection)

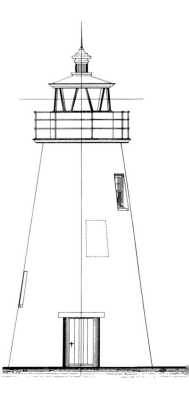

31

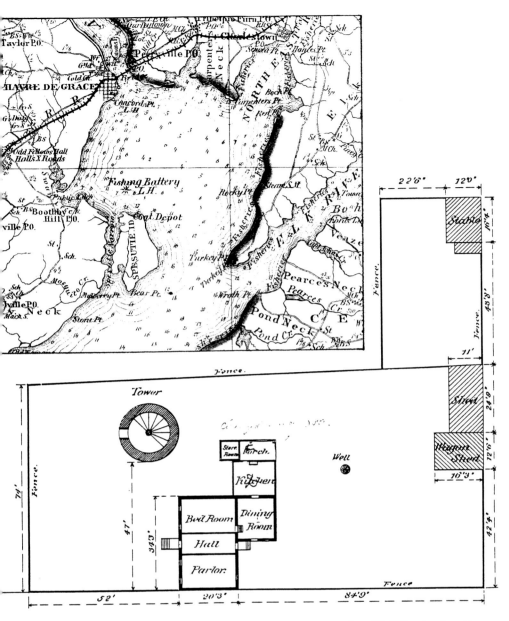

The Turkey Point lighthouse was located atop a high bluff on the point between the Elk and Northeast Rivers. John Donahoo built the tower and story–and–a–half dwelling for $4,355 in 1833. The 1887 survey above shows modifications to the original keeper's house. *Right:* Turkey Point lighthouse, front and sectional elevations, 1905. In 1889 the keeper's house was raised to two stories and a front porch was added.

(The New Topographical Atlas .... MHT Library; 1889, National Archives, Philadelphia)

and built the lighthouse for $5,400, signing the contract August 2, 1832. John Bovis received the contract to install patent lamps and reflectors in the lantern.

The work at Clay Island was completed by October 1, 1832, and Pleasonton wrote the secretary and recommended a keeper be appointed. On October 19 Pleasonton announced that James S. Waller was the keeper of the Clay Island lighthouse. Though it is not known precisely when the lighthouse went into service, most likely it was around the first of November 1832.

In 1858 the *Light List* described the structure as "Light on keeper's dwelling." A plan done in 1857 shows a story-and-a-half dwelling, 32 feet 2 inches by 20 feet 6 inches, with an attached kitchen measuring 13 feet square.[5] It had four rooms, two on each floor. The first floor had a bedroom and a parlor, while the second floor had two bedrooms. The square tower rose out of the center of the dwelling.

The establishment of the Turkey Point lighthouse was more difficult than the Lazaretto Point project, because the government had to obtain the land. From Pleasonton's point of view, Maryland landowners often had an exaggerated idea of the value of their property, and the owner of Turkey Point was no exception. John B. Paca and his wife, Juliana, had heard rumors the government paid high prices for land, so they asked $1,200 for the three to four acres needed for the lighthouse. Pleasonton, who would have paid $100 per acre, thought the Pacas' price was too high and instructed Carr to ask the Maryland legislature to condemn the land. The commission set the land value at $564, which the government paid, and John Paca and his wife signed the deed on December 26, 1832. The deed also provided access to the lighthouse property from the water.

When Carr advertised for proposals to erect the buildings composing the light station, he had only one response—John Donahoo, who said he would do the work for $4,385, $30 more than the money available. Pleasonton wrote to Carr asking him to contact Donahoo and see if he would do the work for $4,355. If Donahoo would, Carr was to contract with him for the work and with James Geddes to supply the lighting system for $419. Donahoo agreed to the price and completed the work in July 1833. Robert Lusby was appointed keeper around August 10, and the lighthouse most likely went into service in the middle of the month.

The brick tower was 31½ feet from its base to the parapet, 16 feet in diameter at the base, and 9 feet 8 inches at the parapet. The walls were 2½ feet thick at the base and 14 inches at the parapet. An interior wooden stairway led from the base to the lantern, which held eleven lamps, each with a fifteen-inch reflector. The brick dwelling was a story-and-a-half structure 34 feet by 20 feet with an attached kitchen.[6]

It was two years after the Turkey Point lighthouse went into service before any action was taken to erect another lighthouse in the Maryland portion of the Chesapeake. In the spring of 1835 the secretary of the Treasury debated whether to station a lightboat at Ragged Point or to build a lighthouse at Piney Point. In late April he decided on the latter course, and Pleasonton wrote to George Brent, collector of customs in Alexandria, Virginia, whom he had decided to make responsible for the lighthouse. He instructed Brent to visit Piney Point, select a site, and purchase the necessary land.

Brent chose a site but found the owner, Henry Suter, opposed to selling it for a lighthouse. Suter

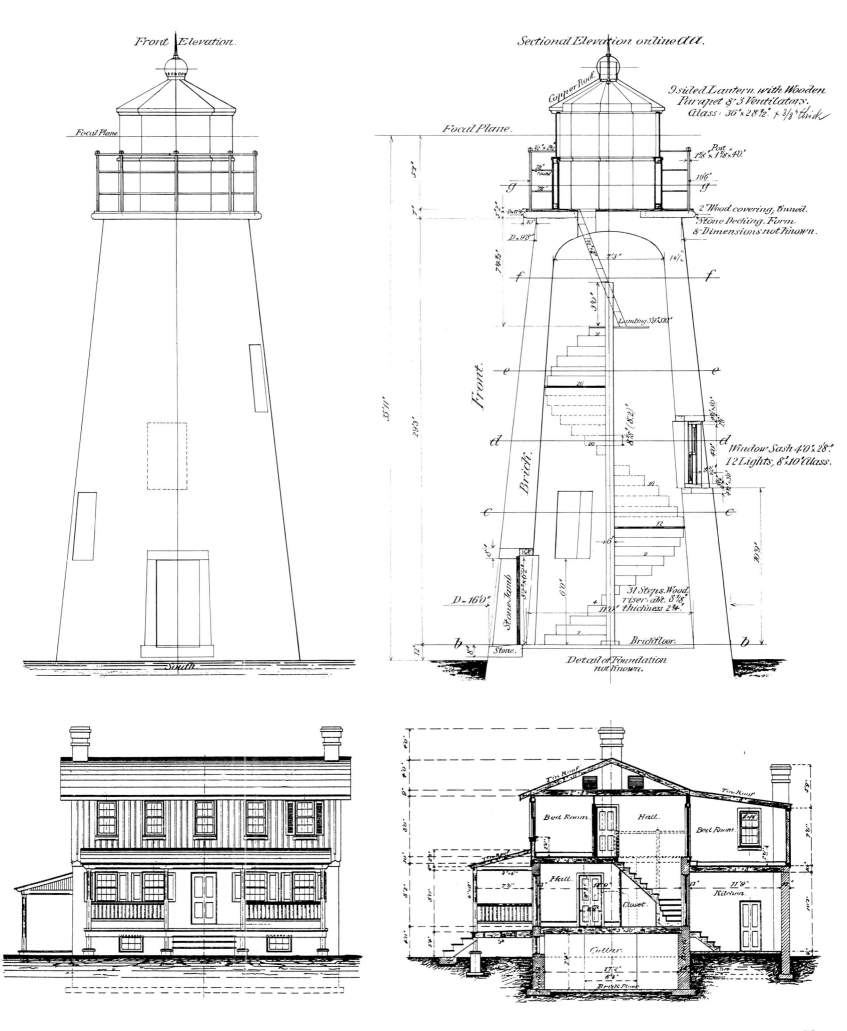

Front Elevation.

Focal Plane.

South.

Sectional Elevation on line AA.

Copper Roof.

Focal Plane.

9 sided Lantern with Wooden
Parapet & 3 Ventilators.
Glass: 36" x 28½", & ⅜" thick.

Post
1⅛" x 1⅛" x 40".

2" Wood covering, tinned.
Stone Decking. Form
& Dimensions not known.

Front.

Brick.

Window Sash 40" x 28",
12 Lights, 8" x 10" Glass.

Landing 3'9"x3'10".

Stone Jamb.

31 Steps. Wood
riser. ht. 8⅛".
thickness 2¾".

Brick floor.

Stone.

Detail of Foundation
not known.

Bed Room.   Hall.   Bed Room.

Tin Roof.   Tin Roof.

Hall.   Kitchen.

Closet.

Cellar.

Brick Floor.

33

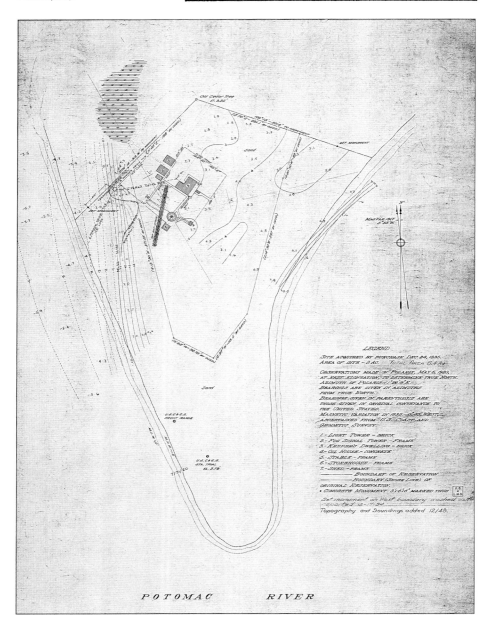

Right: Piney Point, on the Potomac River, was selected as a lighthouse site in 1835, but the property owner, who feared the lighthouse would hurt business at the nearby tavern, delayed the project for months. *Below Right:* The original two–acre Piney Point site purchased by the government on December 24, 1835 is lined off in this 1920 survey.

(The New Topographical Atlas.... MHT Library; National Archives, Philadelphia)

POTOMAC   RIVER

felt such an activity would adversely affect the trade at his nearby tavern, but he said he would sell the property if he could be appointed keeper of the light. Rather than making a high-principled response as he had in the face of such a proposal several years earlier, Pleasonton suggested two courses of action to Brent. One was to go to the legislature and get the land condemned and valued. Since the legislature always awarded more than the land was worth, Pleasonton said, he was reducing the required acreage to two acres. The other possibility would be for Brent to point out to Suter that a lighthouse would attract tavern customers curious about the neighboring structure. If land could not be obtained, the government would cross the river to Ragged Point and put a lightboat there instead. It is not known whether condemnation or persuasion moved Suter to sell, but he and his wife deeded the property to the government on December 24, 1835.

When an advertisement was issued for proposals to build the tower and dwelling, the low bidder was once again John Donahoo, who offered to do the construction work for $3,488 and to fit up the lantern for $400. His bid was accepted, and Pleasonton wrote to him but got no response. A month later Pleasonton suggested that Brent write to Donahoo at Piney Point, where he understood Donahoo had rented a "fishing landing" for the summer. Brent did, and Donahoo responded. By early June Pleasonton was concerned that construction had not begun and told Brent to send someone down to Piney Point to execute the contract with Donahoo.

Donahoo went to work, and two months later Brent reported the lighthouse would be completed by August 20. Pleasonton recommended to the secretary of the Treasury that he appoint Henry Suter as keeper and asked that $3,888 be sent to Brent to pay the contractor. Instead of Suter, however, the secretary appointed Phillip Clark keeper in the middle of September 1836. The lighthouse probably went into service late that month. Donahoo said he lost money on the project because he did extra work, but Pleasonton would not recognize this claim, saying the work was implicit in the contract.[7]

The round, white brick tower Donahoo erected was 26 feet tall from its base to the coping. The walls were 3 feet 10 inches thick at the base and 2 feet 3 inches at the parapet. The interior diameter was 13 feet at the base and 9 feet at the top. Surmounting the tower was the lantern. Today, the bottom half of the lantern, circular and made of cement, appears to be quite old though not original. Access to the lantern was,

and is, by way of a spiral wood stairway inside the tower. The original two-railed iron railing circles the narrow exterior walkway or gallery. Resting on the cement lower half is an octagonal iron lantern with one large pane of glass in each side of the octagon. This type of window indicates this portion was added later, as the old-style lanterns were glazed with small panes in each side.

Donahoo also erected a one-and-a-half story brick dwelling of four rooms with an attached kitchen.[8] Today the structure has two full stories with an enclosed porch extending across its front. The dwelling and the tower were built well, for both are structurally sound and show little evidence of settling or cracking.

Six months after Piney Point went into service, Congress authorized a lighthouse at Sharp's Island and appropriated $5,000 to build it. At this time the Navy commissioners were examining and evaluating the country's lighthouse system. One of their missions was to look at the need for and propriety of building proposed lighthouses. The commissioners agreed that a lighthouse was needed at Sharp's Island on the eastern side of the Chesapeake.

On receiving the Navy report, Pleasonton instructed the recently appointed United States collector of customs, William Frick, to select a

John Donahoo built the round brick Piney Point tower and one–and–a–half–story keeper's house in 1836 for $3,488, also fitting up the lantern for an extra $400. The dwelling was enlarged in May 1884.
(MHT photo by Charity Davidson, 1992)

Left: This 1909 postcard image issued by the adjacent Piney Point Hotel, shows the 1880 fog signal, housed in a 30–foot tower.
(Jack Kelbaugh Collection)

site at Sharp's Island and purchase a few acres. Frick visited the island the last week in July 1837 on a revenue cutter. With the advice of the captain and the pilot of the cutter, he determined that the best location for the lighthouse was "on the extreme north end of the Island, as near as practicable to the shore." He pointed out that because the area was subject to erosion, it would be necessary to set the light tower several hundred yards back from the shore. Four or five acres of woodland would have to be cleared so the light could be seen from the bay.

Pleasonton was considerably upset a month later when he learned the nature of the land would require the purchase of a large tract of ten acres or so. The land had to be acquired, he reasoned, but such a large purchase would not leave enough of the appropriation to build the lighthouse. He decided to obtain four acres of woods at $100 per acre and six acres of cleared land at $50 and then find a plan for a lighthouse and dwelling that could be erected with the remaining money. His first thought was of a concept that had served well in the past when funds were limited—a "Lighthouse and Dwelling house united."

When Frick reported three weeks later that he had bought the ten acres from J. W. and Anne Reynolds for $600, Pleasonton had settled on a course of action. They would erect a tower and dwelling like those at Concord Point in Havre de Grace. Both structures had been built for $4,043, and perhaps a similar price would prevail for the structures on Sharp's Island. He sent Frick a copy of the advertisement and instructed him to publish it and send two copies to the collector in Boston.[9]

Frick received several proposals. Low bidder was Thomas Evans, co-builder of the Bodkin Island lighthouse, and Frick entered into a contract with him for a separate dwelling and tower. Shortly afterwards, a Captain Claxton looked at the Sharp's Island site and urged Pleasonton to erect a combined dwelling and tower made of wood, contending that "within a few years past

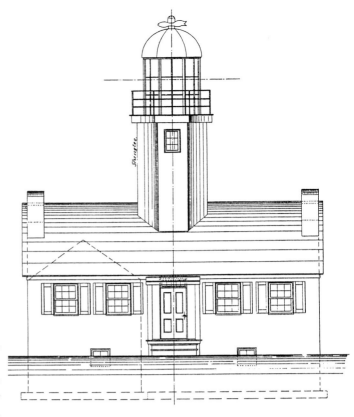

Below: Sharp's Island, located south of Black Walnut Point on Tilghman Island, was known to be subject to erosion. A wooden "unified" tower and dwelling that could be moved inland was built by Thomas Evans in 1838. *Above:* The Greenbury Point Shoal lighthouse, a combined tower and keeper's dwelling at the entrance to Annapolis Harbor, was built by William H. Hooper in 1848.

(Detail: The New Topographical Atlas… MHT Library; Front elevation, 1886. National Archives, Philadelphia)

Eighty acres of the Island have washed away in consequence of the lightness of the soil." Pleasonton instructed Frick to ask Evans if he would surrender his contract and, if so, how much he would charge to build a wooden "unified" lighthouse. Frick was also to ask how much it would cost to put this wooden structure on "wheels" so it could be moved when erosion threatened. Evans responded that he would surrender the contract and erect the combined tower and dwelling "for whatever difference between that and the old plan three disinterested persons may deem right." Pleasonton liked the proposal and directed Frick to prepare estimates for the movable lighthouse.

At this point evidence of steps taken in building the lighthouse at Sharp's Island becomes intermittent, but there is no question that the wooden structure that was built could be moved. When construction was well underway, Pleasonton objected to a proposal Frick made to put up barriers to prevent erosion. He said he had no intention of going to any expense to prevent erosion since the lighthouse had been designed to be moved when the water got near it. Three years later he once again opposed a suggestion to build a breakwater at Sharp's Island, saying he did not understand why such a proposal was being made twenty years before it would be needed, "particularly as the lighthouse here was built of wood, and put upon wheels in order that it might be removed whenever the water encroached upon it."[10]

In June 1838 Pleasonton reported to the secre-

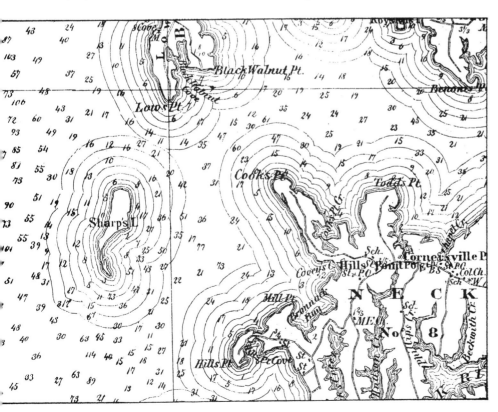

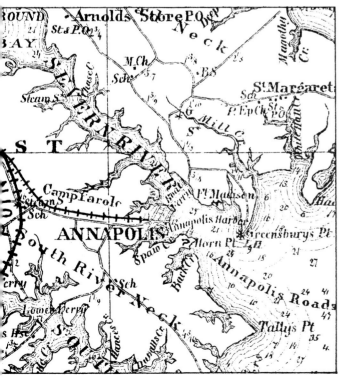

tary that the Sharp's Island lighthouse was nearing completion and would be fitted with the lighting apparatus. The light may not have been exhibited until some time in September, however, since Pleasonton mentioned on September 10, 1838, that the lighthouse needed oil and chimneys for the lamps.[11] It is unlikely a lighthouse would have run out of supplies so quickly, if there had been an earlier delivery of them.

Maryland did not see another new lighthouse until eleven years after the lighting of the Sharp's Island tower. The new structure was built to illuminate the entrance to the Severn River and Annapolis harbor. The secretary of the Treasury had been asked in 1828 to place buoys at Greenbury Point and near Horn Point. Although there was a good channel between these spots, it was difficult to enter unless one knew the river. Congress did not authorize the buoys until 1831, and fifteen more years passed before an effort was made to upgrade these aids to navigation to a lighthouse.

An unusual whale–shaped weather vane topped the Greenbury Point Shoal lantern, adding to the pleasing appearance of the small four-room structure. Presumably some of the eight people pictured above in 1895 lived elsewhere. Buoys had been placed at Greenbury Point and Horn Point in 1831, but entering the channel that led to Annapolis Harbor and the Severn River was still difficult. The Maryland legislature petitioned for a lighthouse in 1846 and Congress appropriated funds for the Greenbury Point beacon in 1847.

(U.S. Coast Guard photo. F. Ross Holland Collection; Detail: The New Topographical Atlas.... MHT Library)

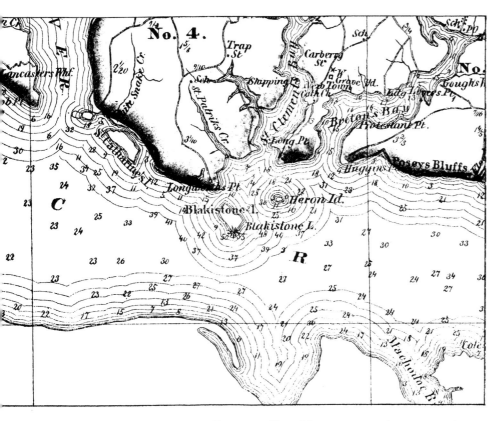

As early as 1843 there had been requests for a lighthouse on Blackistone Island in the Potomac River to guide vessels into St. Clement's Bay. Pleasonton discounted the need for years but Congress authorized a lighthouse for the island in 1848.

(Detail: The New Topographical Atlas.... MHT Library)

Prompted by shipowners and masters of vessels, on March 5, 1846, the Maryland House of Delegates passed a resolution asking Congress for a lighthouse at Greenbury Point. Two days short of a year later, Congress appropriated $3,500 for the project. A week later, Pleasonton asked the new collector of customs, William H. Cole, Jr., to go over to Annapolis, select a site for the lighthouse, and buy a few acres. Cole did not move very fast, and two months later Pleasonton prodded him to display more alacrity and get the site selected and the land purchased.

When he arrived in Annapolis, Cole found that the property owner, Lemuel G. Taylor, did not want a lighthouse at Greenbury Point and had placed the value of four acres at $1,500. Pleasonton instructed Cole to have the state legislature condemn and value the land and cede jurisdiction over it to the federal government. The required legislation was rapidly approved, and the commissioners announced they would meet on March 11, 1848. They awarded the owner $367 for 3¾ acres of land and $133 for a right-of-way to the public road. On hearing this news, Pleasonton decided the right-of-way was not needed as the keeper would have a boat to take him to Annapolis.

Meanwhile, Taylor balked at paying his share of the fee for the commissioners who did the condemnation and valuation and threatened to appeal to a jury. Pleasonton suggested Cole should see the legislators in Annapolis who had an interest in the lighthouse and have them put

pressure on Taylor. Toward the end of April 1848, Taylor accepted the money for the property.[12]

In 1848 Cole entered into a contract with William H. Hooper, the low bidder, to erect the lighthouse. Pleasonton questioned Hooper's reliability because he had failed to finish some work on a city contract. Nonetheless, Hooper's bid of $2,645 to erect the lighthouse and fit it up with lamps and reflectors pleased Pleasonton, and he directed Cole on May 25 to enter into the contract. Hooper was to have the work finished by October 1, 1848. As was becoming regular procedure, a supervisor was hired to be sure the work met the requirements of the contract.

As construction progressed, the overseer became concerned because Hooper was not doing the work in accordance with the contract. Moreover, work was not moving along as fast as it should to meet the deadline. It was apparent in September that Hooper would not be finished by November 1, much less by October 1. By the middle of November, Pleasonton was getting impatient and wrote Cole asking about the status of the work. A few days later Cole sent Pleasonton a letter from Hooper saying the work was complete and the dwelling with its tower rising out of the roof was ready for inspection.

Concerned about the quality of the work, Pleasonton instructed Cole to have a reputable carpenter examine the structure and see if Hooper had followed the contract. The carpenter, Richard C. Murray, certified the lighthouse had been completed satisfactorily. In early December 1848 the secretary of the Treasury appointed Levin Wheeler keeper of the Greenbury Point lighthouse, which in all likelihood went into service shortly afterward.[13]

Wheeler had served nearly thirteen months when he was removed from the position. Joseph Parkinson was then appointed to the job, but he declined, apparently because of the condition of the dwelling. The new collector of customs, George T. Kane, sent R. Swann to examine the building. Swann found the house to be in poor condition—"worthless," he called it—as the doors would not close, the roof leaked, rain came in around the chimneys, and the basement had three to four feet of water in it. Pleasonton instructed Kane to immediately contact the contractor and the carpenter who had certified the work and demand money from them. If they refused to pay, they were to be prosecuted for fraudulent work. Pleasonton could throw a fit of temper over travesties such as this poor workmanship.

To find out precisely what the builder's transgressions were, Kane needed to review the con-

tract. He went to Cole for a copy, but found the former collector of customs had given the only copy to the contractor. When Pleasonton learned of this, he grew angrier, replying, "Mr. Cole's account will probably not be passed at all by the Commissioner of Customs, which will be a deserved punishment, as he will be sued for the money he paid the contractor." Pleasonton had not settled Cole's accounts because he had not sent, as he was required to, a copy of the contract.

Pleasonton directed Kane to send a good carpenter to the lighthouse to assess the problems and give an estimate of the cost of repairs. In April Pleasonton learned that the cost of the work would be around $222. In the meantime, Kane had talked to the certifying carpenter, Richard C. Murray, who had said the work complied with the contract, although that document failed to "call for work essential to the building." It is not known whether Kane demanded payment from the contractor and the carpenter, but most likely he did not. He advertised for bidders to do the repair work, and H. W. S. Evans was low bidder at $130. At this time, a cistern to hold drinking water was installed, although presumably it was not within the scope of Evans's contract. Toward the end of February, Thomas

Morgan was appointed keeper of the Greenbury Point lighthouse.[14]

Located on the north side of the entrance to the Annapolis Roads, the structure at Greenbury Point had a small, wood-shingled light tower on top of the shingled roof of the brick dwelling. The outside dimensions of the story-and-a-half house were 20 feet x 34 feet, and it had four rooms with an attached kitchen.[15]

For some time there had been interest in getting a lighthouse at Blackistone Island, site of the first landing by Leonard Calvert and the Maryland colonists in 1634. The island lay upriver from Piney Point near the entrance to St. Clements Bay. In January 1843 Robert C. Winthrop, chairman of the Committee on Commerce in the House of Representatives, wrote Pleasonton saying Congress had received a petition for a lighthouse on the island. Pleasonton responded to his request for an evaluation saying this was the first he had heard of such a project. He had no knowledge of the site and could "form no opinion in regard to its utility." Three years later a memorial was sent to Congress asking for a lighthouse on Blackistone Island. Pleasonton responded by suggesting any action be postponed because of the greater need for lighthouses in Florida and elsewhere around the

Obtaining the land for the Blackistone Island lighthouse was a time consuming struggle involving ownership squabbles and title disputes. The government finally purchased three acres on the erosion–prone island in 1850. Known as the birthplace of Maryland, a 40–foot cross was erected on the island in 1934 to commemorate the landing of the colonists in 1634. The island is now known by its original name, St. Clement's Island.

(MHT photo by Richard Weeks, 1969)

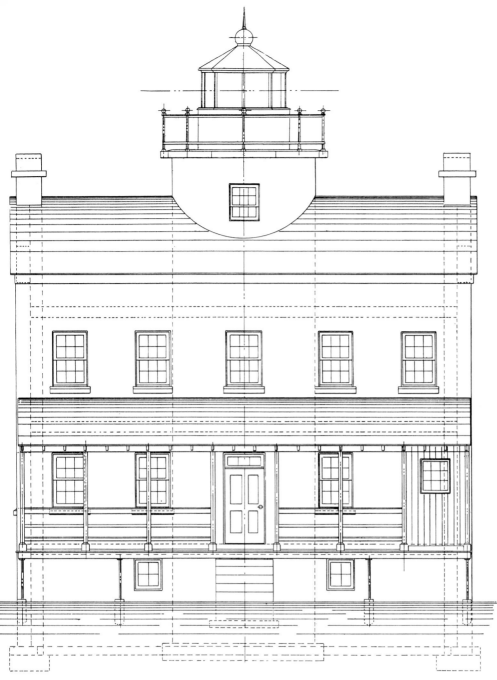

The Blackistone Island light-house, completed by John Donahoo in 1851, was a combined structure: a brick tower surrounded by, and rising through, the two–and–a–half–story brick dwelling.

(1880 front elevation, National Archives, Philadelphia)

country. He added, again, this is "the first time I have even heard that a Light was wanted on Blackistone Island." When the issue surfaced several times in 1848, he said he could not understand the desire for a lighthouse on the site. When a ship leaves Piney Point light the navigator immediately sees the Lower Cedar Point lightboat, he explained, later adding that a light on the island near the Maryland shore would be several miles from the channel, which was close to the Virginia side.[16]

Despite Pleasonton's opposition, the idea of a lighthouse on Blackistone Island would not fade. In August 1848 Congress appropriated $3,500 for a structure on the island. At this time Congress had authorized a number of lighthouses whose usefulness Pleasonton doubted, and he asked the Navy to provide officers to examine these sites, including Blackistone Island. The officers reported back that, indeed, aids to navigation

were needed at all the sites, including Blackistone.

In January 1849 Pleasonton told Edward Green, collector of customs at Alexandria, to secure land for the lighthouse. If the owner was reluctant to sell, Green was to apply to the Maryland legislature for an act of condemnation and valuation. This was to be a course of last resort, however, because of the expense of the process. Green responded that the legislature would not be in session until the following winter. Pleasonton urged him to get in touch with the owner, Dr. Joseph L. McWilliams, and see if he would sell one and one half to two acres for $300. By April Green had reached an agreement with McWilliams, but the owner did not have a clear title. B. G. Harris, the former owner, would not give him one until McWilliams had complied with certain conditions.

In the meantime Green, at Pleasonton's direc-

tion, had hired a lawyer in the area to try to clear up the title. When Joseph Eaches succeeded Green as collector, he took up the task. In May Pleasonton received from the lawyer an extract of a deed from McWilliams, which he sent to the attorney general to determine whether it was valid or not. The attorney general approved the deed as long as there were no encumbrances on the land, evidence that McWilliams was supposed to have supplied previously. Finally, in July, Eaches notified Pleasonton there were no longer any encumbrances on McWilliams's land and the government had clear title to the three acres it wanted.[17]

For the design of the Blackistone lighthouse, Pleasonton had settled on the model of a dwelling with a tower on top. Eaches had ads run in the Alexandria and Baltimore newspapers, and several bidders responded, including veteran builder John Donahoo, who was low bidder at

$3,785. As Pleasonton directed, Eaches entered into a contract with Donahoo, but Eaches refused to go to the island and point out the site for the lighthouse without orders from Pleasonton. Donahoo wrote to Pleasonton urging him to instruct Eaches to accompany him to the site, which Pleasonton did.

In October Donahoo wrote Pleasonton that he had not known a second story was associated with the tower—there was nothing in the ad's specifications about it. Donahoo would charge $700 to build this nine-foot square segment of the tower. Pleasonton realized a mistake had been made—the tower was mentioned in the ad's heading but not in the body of the text. He recommended to Secretary Thomas Corwin that the government pay Donahoo an extra $650 for this work. Including that price, Pleasonton noted, Donahoo's bid would still be lower than the next lowest bidder. The secretary approved.

The lighthouse was built with a spacious front porch and a roof of slate. The front door opened into a hall with a kitchen to the left and a sitting room on the right. In the photo above, looking northwest from the Potomac River, the lighthouse is profiled with the 1881 bell tower to the left.

(St. Clement's Island – Potomac River Museum Collections)

41

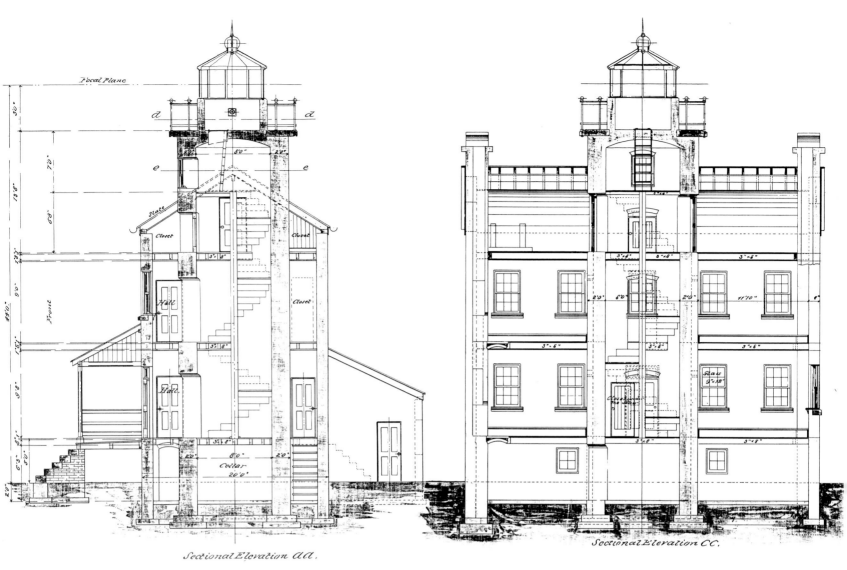

Sectional Elevation AA.

Sectional Elevation CC.

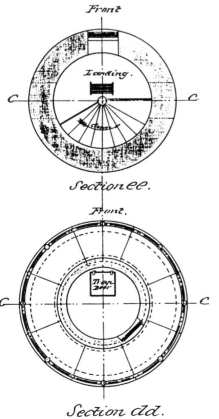

Section CC.

Section AA.

The Blackistone Island tower rose from the ground through the first and second levels of the dwelling house and through the garret to a landing where a ladder and trap door led to the lantern deck. This plan may have influenced the design of the first West Coast lighthouses.

(Plans and sectional elevations, National Archives, Philadelphia)

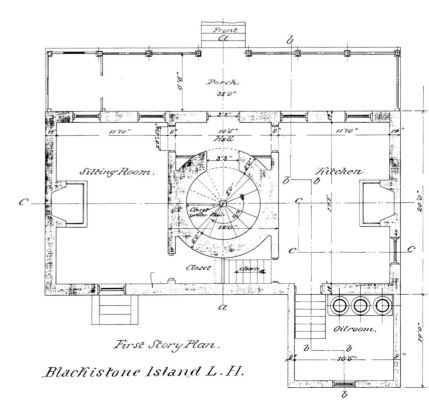

First Story Plan.

Blackistone Island L. H.

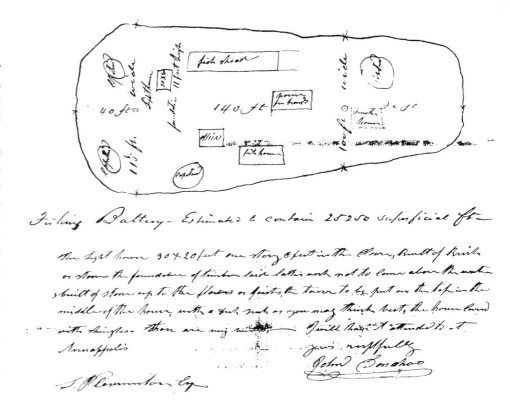

Donahoo completed the lighthouse by early December 1851, and shortly thereafter it was accepted. It probably went into service around the fifteenth of December, with Isaac Wood as keeper.[18]

The lighthouse Donahoo erected was a white brick tower rising from the ground through the dwelling and above the roof. The keeper's house was a two-and-a-half-story unpainted brick structure. It had six rooms, a basement and a roof of slate. A brick porch, for which Donahoo was paid $100 extra, stretched across the front of the dwelling. The outside dimensions were 38 feet x 20 feet.

Nineteenth century documents describe the Blackistone Island facility as a dwelling built around the tower.[19] This design may have been a precursor of the first West Coast lighthouses designed in Washington in 1852. These lighthouses consisted of a story-and-a-half Cape Cod-type dwelling with a masonry tower rising through the center. The tower and the dwelling were separate structures, each able to stand alone.

The last lighthouse in Maryland's portion of the Chesapeake that can be credited to Pleasonton was the lighthouse at Fishing Battery Island. In the upper reaches of the bay about three miles from Havre de Grace, Fishing Battery is a small artificial island at the southwest end of the extensive flats off the mouth of the Susquehanna River. The light, needed to guide vessels to the mouth of the river, would work in conjunction with the Turkey Point and Concord Point lighthouses. Vessels coming from Havre de Grace passed within a half mile of the west side of the island and when abreast of it made a sharp course change. The light would immeasurably benefit vessels traveling at night.

Fishing Battery Island is strongly associated with John Donahoo, the man who built so many of the early lighthouses in Maryland. In addition to his work as a builder, Donahoo was also a fisherman. In the nineteenth century the island was often referred to as Donahoo Battery because at one time he owned the island and had a fishing industry there. Earlier, this two- to three-acre island was known as Edmondson's Island or Shad Battery.

In 1836 Donahoo and his partner, Richard Gale, received permission from the state legislature to add fill to the island. When they began putting it in, other fishing interests complained, saying the fill impeded navigation. Donahoo and Gale fought back, and a court case resulted. In consequence of this, Donahoo and Gale sold the island at a sheriff's sale to Otho Scott and his wife. Donahoo later contended that the Scotts

held the property in trusteeship, but in 1852 the collector of customs in Baltimore reported that no documents could be found supporting that position. Donahoo did lease a piece of the island from Scott for his fishery.[20] It was this series of events that later complicated the establishment of a lighthouse on the island.

In 1851 Congress appropriated $5,000 for the lighthouse on Fishing Battery. Early the following year, Pleasonton directed Collector of Customs Kane to obtain from the state legislature a cession of jurisdiction over the lighthouse site. The legislature responded that it could not cede jurisdiction until the purchase was complete. Pleasonton responded that he did not want condemnation of the land but just a cession of jurisdiction.

Pleasonton was under the impression that Donahoo actually owned the island and Scott held the deed in trust "for the benefit of [Donahoo's] creditors." The fifth auditor instructed the collector to seek out Scott and offer him $200-300 for the site. He felt Scott and Donahoo would be willing to sell the land at a good price since the light would benefit their fisheries. That was wishful thinking, because Scott replied to the collector that he would not take less than $1,000 for the site. Miffed at this response, the fifth auditor recommended to the secretary of the Treasury that Congress be asked to repeal the appropriation, since paying that amount would leave only $4,000 to erect the lighthouse. The secretary approved the action.

At this point Donahoo wrote to Pleasonton, proposing that he acquire the site, build the lighthouse and turn both over to the government

Fishing Battery Island, once known as Donahoo Battery, is strongly associated with the lighthouse builder, who as a major commercial fisherman, once owned it. When Congress appropriated $5,000 in 1851 for a lighthouse at the site, Donahoo's earlier sale of – or continuing interest in – the island complicated matters. Donahoo, in his mid–sixties, finally built the lighthouse, but not exactly to the specifications in the undated note to Stephen Pleasonton, above. His sketch shows a 30 x 20 foot lighthouse among the existing structures, which included "office, house for hands, fish shead and smokehouse."

(Lighthouse Superintendent's Correspondence, Baltimore, 1825–52, R.G. 26, National Archives)

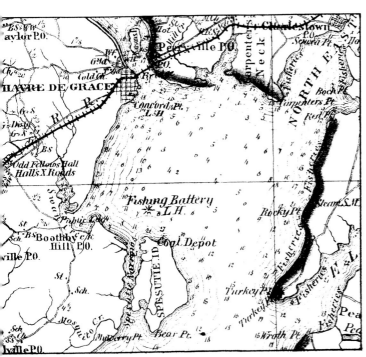

The Fishing Battery lighthouse was needed to guide vessels to the mouth of the Susquehanna River. The light was to work in conjunction with the nearby Turkey Point and Concord Point lighthouses.

(Detail: The New Topographical Atlas.....MHT Library)

A combined light tower and dwelling house, the original structure was a story–and–a– half brick building with the tower on the roof.

(Front elevation, 1889, National Archives, Philadelphia)

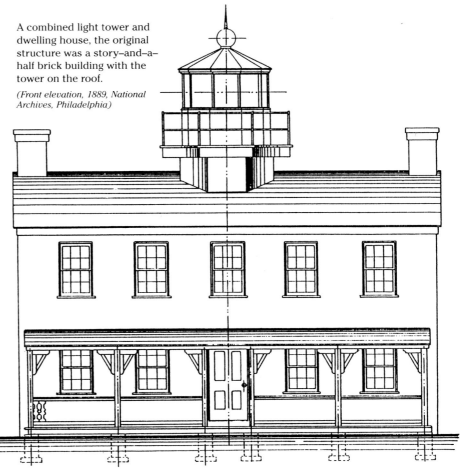

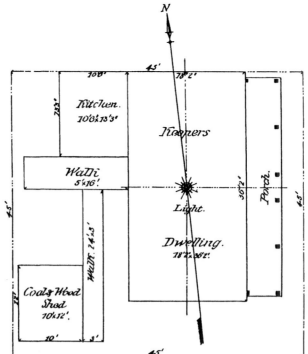

Left: Fishing Battery Island had been the site of commercial fishing operations since the early 1800s. In 1880 the U.S. Bureau of Fisheries leased the majority of the island for "fish cultural operations," crowding the lighthouse and shoreline with wharves and hatchery buildings. The kitchen and coal/wood shed, pictured in the 1887 survey plan, are also visible in the vintage photo.

(Kenneth G. Lay Collection; October 1887 survey, National Archives, Philadelphia)

The brick Fishing Battery structure was raised to two full stories in 1881 and was later altered to accommodate a large lower level storage area, perhaps used for a boat. The photo and elevation on the following pages show the tower and lantern.

(F. Ross Holland photos, 1990)

for the $5,000 appropriation. Pleasonton did not like this idea because it would leave no money for the lighting apparatus, but it did open the door for negotiations. Previously, Donahoo had offered to build the lighthouse for $3,900, but in June 1852 he increased the price to $4,400. Pleasonton responded that if Donahoo would purchase the land, build the lighthouse, and supply the lighting apparatus and oil butts for $4,400 and also provide a deed signed by Scott and himself, he would have a contract. The secretary of the Treasury approved Pleasonton's course, and Donahoo accepted the offer.

By the end of July 1852 Donahoo had turned over to Kane a deed for the site of the lighthouse. So confident was he that the deed would be accepted, Donahoo said he had already laid the foundation and was ready to start building the house. Pleasonton immediately sent the deed to the attorney general for approval, also instructing Kane to send a lawyer to Harford County to ascertain whether Scott and Donahoo had clear title to the land. On August 11, Kane sent Pleasonton the results of the lawyer's investigation.[21] In the meantime, Donahoo was getting anxious

about the status of the deed because he was being dunned by Scott, who wanted his $600. By this time Donahoo had the first tier of joists in place and was beginning the brickwork.

In September the attorney general approved the deed, but there was still one hitch—the Maryland legislature had not yet passed a bill transferring jurisdiction over the land to the federal government. Pleasonton warned Donahoo he could not be paid for the work until the government had jurisdiction.[22] In time, Maryland passed the necessary legislation, the government had a certified statement that two deeds for the land on Fishing Battery Island were registered in the Harford County courthouse, and the structure was finished. The lighthouse went into service in 1853, apparently early in the year as the keeper was appointed on January 7.

The lighthouse was a story-and-a-half brick dwelling measuring 36 feet x 16 feet in plan. Protruding from its shingled roof was a hexagonal wooden tower that supported an old-style lantern equipped with five lamps and five reflectors giving off a fixed white light.

While the land issues at Fishing Battery were being resolved, Pleasonton and Kane became involved in establishing a light in Tangier Sound at the mouth of the Little Annemessex River, which leads to Crisfield. In 1850 Congress had authorized either a lightboat off James Island or a lighthouse on its southwest point, "if the Secretary of the Treasury shall decide that it will answer the purposes of commerce." James Island was also referred to at the time as Janes Island, a name it retained for a number of decades before switching back to James, the name used in the *Light Lists* at least as late as the 1950s. (The current *Light List* uses Janes Island).

"The administration of lighthouses, lightships, and other aids to navigation was passing into the hands of professionals. It was about time, because important technological advances were underway...."

Congress, thinking of the cost of a lightboat, appropriated $8,000 for the lighthouse.[23]

There seemed to be little question what type of aid to navigation the users wanted at this location. Congressman John B. Kerr sent Secretary Corwin two petitions from mariners and navigators who plied the Chesapeake Bay asking that a lightboat be placed near Janes Island. They felt it would be more help in getting by Janes Island Bar than a lighthouse, which would have to be placed some distance from it. One petition bore 61 names and the other 109. Pleasonton wanted another opinion and had Captain Richard Evans of the Baltimore-based revenue cutter visit the area to study the situation. His recommendation was for a light at the southwest point of Janes Island because it would be a more permanent structure.

Kane asked John Done, an unemployed engineer from Somerset County, to go to the island and select a site for the lighthouse. During Done's visit to the area in August 1851, he determined who would use the light and what purpose it would serve. He found two major groups of users: those engaged in the oyster trade, who had boats ranging from sloops of 20 tons to schooners of 125 tons and who transited Tangier Sound and the Little Annemessex River often during the season; and trading vessels that ran between Baltimore and the Pocomoke River area, "of which the number is considerable." A lesser, though still important, group comprised those vessels trading in the Big Annemessex River area.

The greatest hazard to navigation in the area, Done continued, was the bar that makes off from Janes Island "some two miles or more." He reported it as a long, hard spit of sand, exposed at low water but covered at high tide. It was further described as steep on the south side, making navigation by soundings of little help. If a lighthouse were on the island, pilots would have to pass the bar by estimating its length. If they misjudged the distance, their vessels could end up on the bar. Also, the end of the bar marked the point at which vessels changed course going up the sound. This situation, Done added, argued strongly for either a floating light or a lighthouse on the bar as close as possible to its end with a dwelling on the island. He believed a lighthouse on the island "would be of very little utility," except for those boats entering the Little Annemessex River. He strongly recommended a lighthouse on the bar.[24]

Done's report was so lucid and well-reasoned that Pleasonton called a halt to further action on land purchase at Janes Island. He sent the lighthouse recommendation on to Congress, but failed to add that an additional appropriation of $7,000 would be needed to accommodate the $15,000 it would cost to build a lighthouse near the bar's end.[25] Pleasonton then changed his mind again, in response to the results of a land-buying trip Collector Kane had made to Janes Island. Kane had apparently been lobbied by the local citizens and returned with several letters from people who wanted a lightboat. He, therefore, urged Pleasonton to place a floating light off the bar.

Near the end of June 1852 the secretary approved placement of the floating light at Janes Island, and Pleasonton instructed Kane to advertise for proposals to build a 125-ton vessel, 76 feet long on deck with a beam of 21 feet 6 inches, to be completed by November 1. In three weeks Kane had proposals from five bidders. John T. Tardy and Phillip Auld submitted the lowest bid, for $5,990. The lightboat was apparently completed pretty much on time and went into service in 1853, probably in early March.

The vessel was described a few years later as a 137-ton boat of cream color with the station name in black on its sides. It had a cast-iron, octagonal lantern and an 800-pound fog bell that had to be struck by hand. A 2,000-pound mushroom anchor and a 60-fathom riding chain held it on station. A spare anchor was available for emergencies.[26] Although this lightboat went into service after the Lighthouse Board assumed control of aids to navigation, it was Pleasonton's project, his last complete one in Maryland.

The administration of lighthouses, lightships, and other aids to navigation was passing into the hands of professionals. It was about time, because important technological advances were under way and Pleasonton had not altered his organization to take advantage of these or other changes just over the horizon. His method of operation was not geared for a rapid increase in lighthouse construction or for the active role the bureaucrats were to play in proposing and influencing the development of aids to navigation.

Pleasonton had played a reactive role, responding to Congress's authorizations rather than proposing projects. Certainly he had no concept of a system of aids to navigation such as the Lighthouse Board was to develop. Most serious, he stuck with an outmoded lighting system decades after the superiority of a new one had clearly been established.

Pleasonton had been under attack for years, particularly from shipping interests, chambers of commerce, and the Blunt brothers. Edmund and George W. Blunt became Pleasonton's nemesis or "bête noir." Publishers of the *American Coast Pilot*, the brothers acted as the spokesmen for all those who felt the United States's system of aids to navigation was inadequate.

From time to time Congress ordered investigations of the country's lighthouses and studies of aids to navigation used in other countries. Unfortunately, little came of these efforts, mainly, it would appear, because Pleasonton was able to fend off the attacks. Although he was not notoriously bright, he had a wife who was intelligent, witty, and politically active, as well as beautiful, and who entertained well in their home at 21st and F Streets, N.W., in Washington. The Pleasontons, according to a contemporary, "had much influence in the intricacies of the Govt and . . . had great power over the distinguished men by whom the Government was administered."[27]

Although Pleasonton and his congressional allies were able to thwart the assaults made upon his administration of lighthouses over the years, each attack further eroded his control. For example, in 1838 Congress began to give the Army Corps of Engineers an increasing role in the siting, building, and lighting of lighthouses. Although the principal focus of these congressional efforts was not solely the illumination of the lighthouses, other adversaries in the private sector strongly supported equipping American lighthouses with Fresnel lenses. Nonetheless, Pleasonton clung tenaciously to the outdated Argand lamp and parabolic reflector.

In 1851 Congress engaged in a major effort to wrest control of the lighthouse program from Pleasonton. One of the leaders of this movement was Maryland congressman Alexander Evans, who in a speech before the House on March 3, 1851, observed,

> We have been using in this country for several years, a system that has been superseded elsewhere by more refined and appropriate methods. We are still using a system which . . . is a more imperfect system of lighting than any other system in use in any other part of the world. In France, England, Scotland, Belgium, and in Denmark, the method of lighting now in use casts totally into the shade the imperfect kind of reflectors employed in the United States of America. . . .[28]

Evans advocated amending the legislation under consideration to stipulate that "hereafter in all new lighthouses, in all lighthouses requiring new lighting apparatus, and in all lighthouses as yet unsupplied with illuminating apparatus, the lens or Fresnel system shall be adopted, if, in the opinion of the Secretary of the Treasury, the public interest will be subserved thereby." He further proposed an amendment that would set

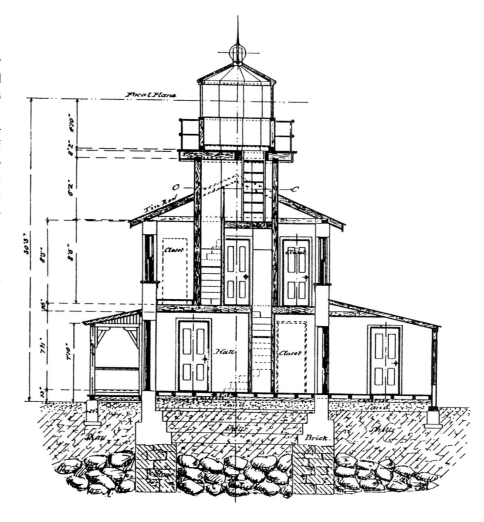

up a body to study the condition of the lighthouse establishment in the United States.

Congress did create in 1851 such a body—an investigatory board composed of military officers and civilian scientists—which conducted a thorough study not only of this country's aids to navigation but also of the newer technology in the field. The resulting 762-page report, issued in 1852, was a damning indictment of Pleasonton's administration. The group recommended that a "Lighthouse Board" be established to administer aids to navigation. Congress created the Lighthouse Board in 1852 and the majority of its first members were those who had served on the investigating body.[29] These individuals received no salary for serving on the board, but performed this duty as an adjunct to their regular jobs. After thirty-two years Pleasonton had lost control of aids to navigation, and Congress authorized the use of the Fresnel lens in all lighthouses in the United States, at first in new ones and old ones needing new lights, and later in all lighthouses.

The world was changing, and the Lighthouse Board would take advantage of advancing technology and bring order and system to the country's lighthouses. More important, the system of aids to navigation the board would establish would be one of the best in the world.

The Fishing Battery Lighthouse, in a sense, symbolized the end of an era. It was the last Maryland lighthouse attributed to the administration of Stephen Pleasonton, who was replaced by the Lighthouse Board in 1852. Fishing Battery was also the last lighthouse built by John Donahoo, who died five years after its completion at the age of 72.

(Elevation, 1889, National Archives; MHT photo by Lillian Wray)

47

Chapter 3

The Lighthouse Board: The Early Years

1852-1872

The Lighthouse Board came on the scene at a propitious time in the development of lighthouse technology, and its engineers and other professionals made the board well-equipped to adapt and use these new methods. Early in its history the board replaced copper-clad buoys with less valuable iron ones and adopted screwpile construction, the Fresnel lens, and the bell buoy — new technologies that improved navigational aids on the Chesapeake and elsewhere.

Screwpile structures, a major innovation developed in England by Alexander Mitchell in the 1830s, were just being introduced in the United States when the Lighthouse Board was formed in 1852. Within several years the board was taking advantage of screwpile and straight-pile construction, as evidenced by this reference in an 1855 report to Congress,

> Light-vessels as aids to navigation, being at best inferior to lights in towers, will, it is hoped, gradually give place to permanent structures upon pile or other proper foundations similar to those erected, in course of erection, or authorized at Minot's Ledge, in Delaware bay, on the coast of Florida, coast of Louisiana, in Chesapeake bay, and in the waters of North Carolina.[1]

This board report specifically mentioned Major Hartman Bache, an engineer who devoted much of his career to work on lighthouses and who had designed and built the first screwpile lighthouse in the country at Brandywine Shoal in Delaware Bay.

The Lighthouse Board discontinued the use of copper-clad wooden buoys, replacing them with iron buoys, which were less expensive to manufacture and lasted much longer. The iron buoys were also less likely to be stolen, as iron was not as valuable as copper. The bell buoy, which had a bell that rang through motion of the buoy, was also introduced at this time.

The most important of the Lighthouse Board's innovations was the introduction of the Fresnel lens on a virtually wholesale basis. The speed of this change was impeded only by the lack of funds, for these lenses were paid for from the board's finite repair and renovation fund. Despite this limitation, the board diligently pursued the course of replacing the Argand lamps and parabolic reflectors in Chesapeake Bay. In fiscal year 1855, fifth-order Fresnel lenses were installed in the lighthouses at Fog Point, Cove Point, Thomas Point, and Piney Point; a fourth-order lens was placed at Lazaretto; and smaller steamer lenses at Greenbury and Concord Points. In fiscal 1857 the light towers at Pooles Island, Turkey Point, Sharp's Island, Fishing Battery, Clay Island, Blackistone Island, and the two at North Point each received a Fresnel lens. The board pointed out the substantial savings in the consumption of oil after these conversions, and within a few years nearly every lighthouse in the country had a Fresnel lens.[2]

The first new structure the Lighthouse Board considered in Maryland was a lighthouse for Seven Foot Knoll, off the entrance to the Patapsco River. In designing for this site the board turned to the new technology.

Agitation for an aid to navigation on Seven Foot Knoll had begun in 1848, when the Maryland legislature passed a resolution asking for a light vessel at the mouth of the Patapsco River. This communication from the state legislature had caught Fifth Auditor Stephen Pleasonton by surprise, drawing a negative reaction from

The Seven Foot Knoll screwpile lighthouse was designed and redesigned several times before construction finally began in 1854. It sat at the mouth of the Patapsco River and replaced Maryland's first lighthouse, Bodkin Island.

(Photo by William Marion Goeshy, c. 1920, MHT Cultural Conservation Program)

The Fresnel lens was introduced in Chesapeake Bay by the Lighthouse Board in 1854. Augustin Fresnel and his successors ultimately made seven sizes, or orders, of the lenses, ranging in size from one foot in diameter to the largest, which was six feet across. A lamp with concentric wicks was used in the lenses and they also varied in size. The large lenses were considered sea coast lights, while the remainder were regarded as river, bay or harbor lights. The first and second–order lenses received large lamps with five wicks, while the third–order lens had three wicks. Lighthouses in Maryland generally used the fourth through sixth–

order lenses. The lucerne, a small covered metal pitcher with a protruding wick, was used to light the concentric wicks of the lamps. This fourth–order Fresnel lens is on display at the U.S.C.G. Training Center in Yorktown, Virginia.

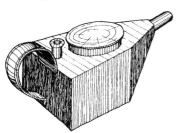

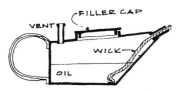

(F. Ross Holland Collection; F. Ross Holland photo, 1988. Drawing by David Battle, F. Ross Holland Collection)

50

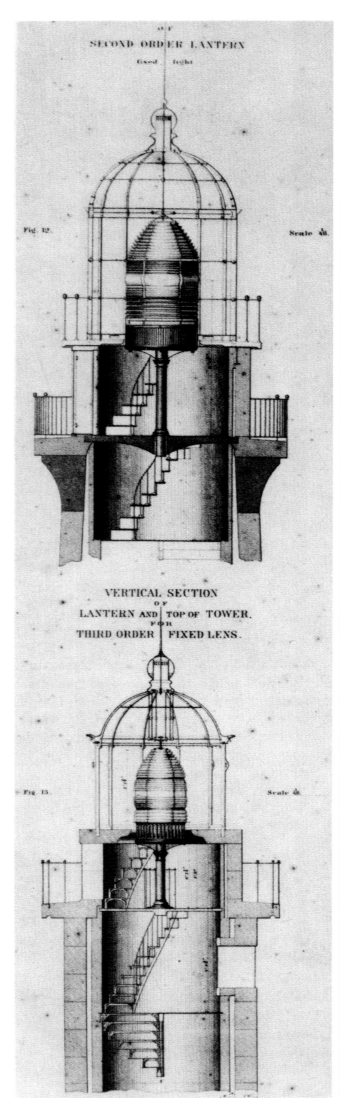

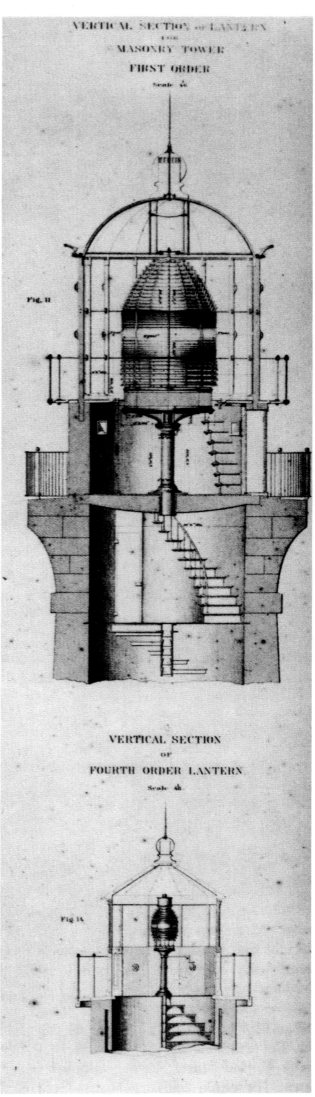

him. In Pleasonton's opinion, the North Point range lights, the Bodkin Island lighthouse, and the buoys up the Patapsco "afford[ed] such security to the trade with Baltimore" that no one before had requested an additional light. Pleasonton had little support for this position, however. In 1850 his representative in Baltimore, Collector of Customs George T. Kane, who also served as superintendent of lighthouses for the district, reported that numerous mariners had approached him urging placement of a floating light at Seven Foot Knoll.

Pleasonton sent engineer B. F. Isherwood, who later achieved fame for his work as chief engineer of the Navy, to evaluate the need for the lighthouse. Isherwood's report reflected the fifth auditor's thinking. When apprised of this evaluation, Collector of Customs Kane responded that navigators and pilots "aver unhesitatingly that this light is as much needed as any other in the Bay." The buoys were useless at night, the seamen said, and there were no good range lights for traversing the channel. Moreover, many vessels had run aground on the shoals.

Pleasonton had continued to resist, saying that putting a light on the shoal would require deactivation of the Bodkin Island lighthouse. By the end of 1851, though, he had realized how strongly merchants and shipowners felt about the need for a light, and he accepted the proposal, which was wise since Congress had already appropriated $27,000 for its completion. Pleasonton enlisted Isherwood to develop a plan to light the shoals.[3] In accepting Isherwood's recommendation for a lighthouse with a second-order Fresnel lens, Pleasonton not only reversed his views about a lighthouse at the site but, more important, he reversed his negative attitude toward Fresnel lenses. Meanwhile, the chairman of the Committee of Commerce in the House of Representatives wrote the secretary of the Treasury asking that an officer of the Revenue Service examine the site and evaluate the need for a lighthouse at Seven Foot Knoll.[4]

While these events were taking place, Merrick & Son of Philadelphia submitted a plan for a screwpile lighthouse at Seven Foot Knoll. Drawn by I. W. P. Lewis, designer of several lighthouses for the Florida Reefs, the plan called for a small, square dwelling with a tower rising through the roof.

Ten months later Lewis submitted another design for a screwpile lighthouse, this time calling for a two-story dwelling with a lantern on top that would be equipped with a third-order lens. The secretary of the Treasury asked the Lighthouse Board to review and comment on these

drawings and specifications. The members responded that as a temporary wooden lighthouse it was all right, but something more imposing and permanent was needed for the "principal guide" for foreign vessels bound for Baltimore. They thought a structure patterned after the Brandywine Shoals lighthouse in Delaware Bay would be appropriate.

In view of the board's comments, Lewis's designs for Seven Foot Knoll did not win the approbation of the secretary of the Treasury, but a design by Theophilus E. Sickels was successful. A civil engineer who apparently had the support of Isherwood, Sickels proposed a building erected on the Pott Pile principle. This would consist of piles that were "hollow cast iron cylinders . . . filled . . . with concrete" and driven into the bottom. A platform on the piles would support a traditional masonry lighthouse, which would have a third-order Fresnel lens. The whole structure would cost $27,000.

In December 1851 the secretary approved entering into a contract with Sickels and with Isherwood as construction supervisor to protect the interests of the government. It was later revealed that Isherwood would also be a surety for the contractor. The collector of customs in Baltimore objected to this arrangement and wrote the fifth auditor saying either Isherwood should not be a surety or he should be replaced as inspector. Pleasonton disagreed, saying the presence of a three-year warranty on the structure should make Isherwood, as a surety, even more concerned with the quality of the contractor's work.[5]

More than eight months after signing the contract, Sickels announced he was ready to start building and asked the government to designate the site. In the meantime, the collector of customs had received word that piles would be useless at Seven Foot Knoll unless they were "driven to a very great depth." In response to the collector's concern, Sickels proposed a modification in the foundation, but the contract expired before the proposal could be fully reviewed by the newly established Lighthouse Board.

When the board did review the project, its members suggested starting over and developing a design for a lighthouse that would work at Seven Foot Knoll. The board's committee on construction, headed by Bvt. Brig. Gen. Joseph Totten, came up with a design that was eventually adopted. The person who actually designed the structure is not known, but it could have been Hartman Bache, who was doing some work in the Chesapeake Bay area at that time. The firm of Murray and Hazelhurst, ironfounders located at

Benjamin Franklin Isherwood, later chief engineer of the U.S. Navy, had recommended that a lighthouse with a second-order Fresnel lens be built at Seven Foot Knoll. After several changes in design, Isherwood was slated to serve as the project's construction supervisor, but the newly established Lighthouse Board started the design process once again. The Board came up with the unusual screwpile design that was eventually used.

(U.S. Naval Institute Photo Library)

The circular Seven Foot Knoll lighthouse was 40 feet in diameter and rested on a foundation of nine iron legs – eight forming an octagon and the ninth in the center. Each was cross–braced and also tied to the center pole. Each leg had a screw–type iron flange on the end that was screwed into the floor of the bay. The round superstructure had sides made of cast–iron plates and a walkway with an iron railing circled it. A gallery with an iron railing surrounded the lantern. Inset: Detail of lightning rod ventilator.

(Left: Photo by Terry Corbett, 1988, courtesy the Empire Construction Co.; inset, F. Ross Holland photo, 1991)

The lighthouse was photographed in 1987 for the Historic American Buildings Survey, a project started in 1933 to preserve America's heritage through graphic and written records of our built environment.

(Photos by Jay L. Baker, Library of Congress, HABS No. MD – 54)

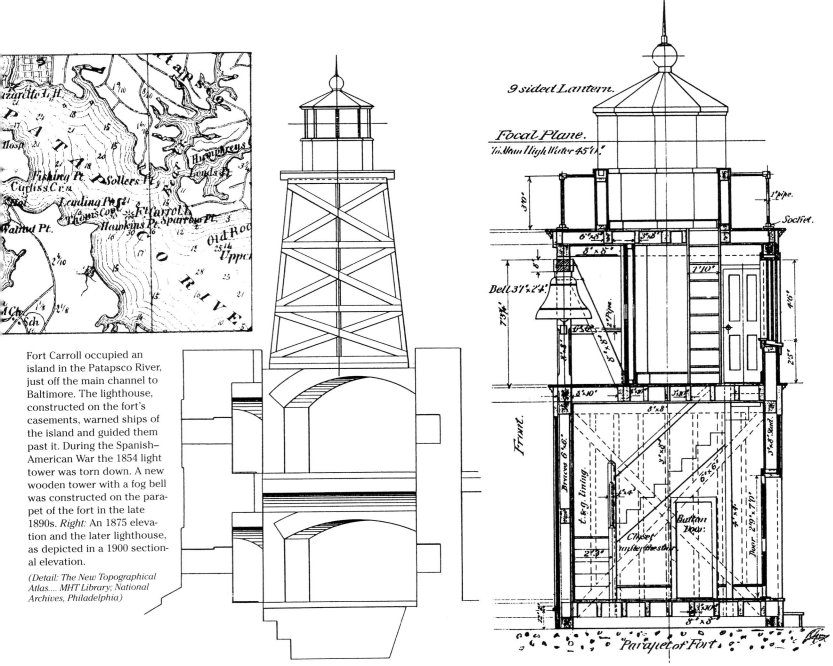

Fort Carroll occupied an island in the Patapsco River, just off the main channel to Baltimore. The lighthouse, constructed on the fort's casements, warned ships of the island and guided them past it. During the Spanish–American War the 1854 light tower was torn down. A new wooden tower with a fog bell was constructed on the parapet of the fort in the late 1890s. *Right:* An 1875 elevation and the later lighthouse, as depicted in a 1900 sectional elevation.

(Detail: The New Topographical Atlas.... MHT Library; National Archives, Philadelphia)

the corner of William and Hughes Streets in Baltimore, supplied the cast iron material for the lighthouse.[6]

Work began on the lighthouse at Seven Foot Knoll in 1854, and by June 30, 1855, it was nearing completion. A later record of the Lighthouse Service reports the Bodkin Island lighthouse, established in 1822, went out of service on January 10, 1856.[7] Since the Bodkin light was to be shut down when Seven Foot Knoll went into service, the first lighting of Seven Foot Knoll must have occurred in January 1856. The new lighthouse was equipped with a fourth-order lens and a fog bell operated by machinery.

The lighthouse finally built at Seven Foot Knoll was a circular structure resting on a foundation of nine iron legs—eight of them placed to form an octagon and the ninth in the center. The legs were iron rods, each cross-braced with those nearest it on either side. Each leg was also

tied to the center pole, forming a sturdy foundation for the dwelling or superstructure. Each leg had a screw-like iron flange on the end that was screwed into the bottom of the bay. This type of foundation would neither sink into the bottom nor pull up easily.

The round superstructure at Seven Foot Knoll, 40 feet in diameter, had sides of cast-iron plates. A walkway with an iron railing circled the dwelling. An iron tower, surmounted by an iron helical bar lantern, rose out of the slightly inclined roof. A gallery with an iron railing circled the lantern. The lighthouse was painted black and its shutters white.[8]

As the Seven Foot Knoll lighthouse was coming into being, two smaller lights went into service on the Chesapeake, at Fort Carroll and Fort Washington.

Fort Carroll sits on an island in the Patapsco River, just off the main channel to the port of Bal-

After 1900 the Fort Carroll lighthouse signalled the turn from the Brewerton Channel into the Fort McHenry Channel, which led to Baltimore Harbor. *Above:* An undated U.S. Coast Guard photo shows the lighthouse with the lens still in the lantern. *Below:* A rare postcard image of Fort Carroll from the water shows the lighthouse between the gun battery and the flagpole. The card was posted in 1910.

(F. Ross Holland Collection; Jack Kelbaugh Collection)

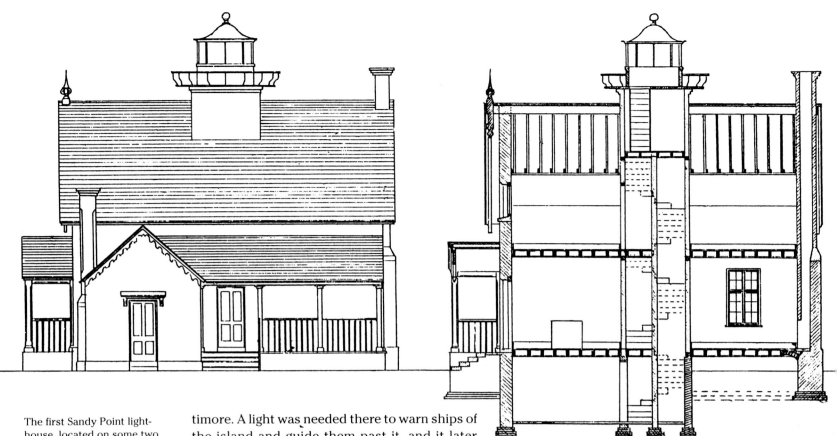

(National Archives, Philadelphia)

The first Sandy Point light-house, located on some two acres north of Annapolis, was a combined structure: a brick tower rose from the ground through the surrounding dwelling's peaked roof. Unlike the simple designs of Maryland's earlier lighthouses, the Sandy Point structure, completed in 1858, sported decoration at the roof line — fanciful early Victorian sawnwork. Side elevation, 1857.

timore. A light was needed there to warn ships of the island and guide them past it, and it later took on the additional duty of signaling the turn from the Brewerton Channel to the Fort McHenry Channel. Building a lighthouse at Fort Carroll was recommended by Captain Henry Brewerton, for whom Brewerton Channel was named. The lighthouse went into service in 1854, equipped with a fifth-order Fresnel lens, which gave off a fixed white light with a focal plane 37 feet above sea level. The tower was a wooden structure, painted brown. The station also had a fog bell, which was apparently located on the parapet of the fort.[9]

Two years after the Fort Carroll light was exhibited for the first time, the Lighthouse Board decided Fort Washington, just south of the nation's capital, should have a light to guide vessels safely through this section of the Potomac River. Since the site was an active fortification, the board had to ask permission of the War Department to erect an aid to navigation. On November 7, 1856, Secretary of War Jefferson Davis gave the Treasury Department permission to establish a lighthouse at the fort on condition it was erected on the wharf and not "within any of the fortifications; and that the light keeper shall be subordinate to the military command of the post and public ground in all that relates to police and discipline." Treasury agreed, and the Lighthouse Board erected a column—later described as an iron post—from which it hung a lens variously referred to as a masthead light, a lens lantern, and a sixth-order lens. It gave off a fixed white light.[10]

The next lighthouse to come on line in Maryland was at Sandy Point, today the anchor site for the west end of the Bay Bridge. Located a few miles north of the entrance to Annapolis, this lighthouse served as a guide to vessels traveling up and down the Chesapeake, warning them of the shoals that made off from this point.

Congress appropriated $8,000 for the lighthouse in 1854, but the time involved in getting jurisdiction from the State of Maryland delayed the start of construction until the summer of 1857. Around this time the Lighthouse Board acquired the land for the light station from Baptist Mezick and his wife, Mary. The site, consisting of a little more than two acres, was about 600 feet north of the point. The land and a right-of-way over the Mezicks' land to the county road cost the government $526.

The Lighthouse Board entered into a contract with W. J. Humes to erect the lighthouse, a story-and-a-half brick structure with a tower rising from the center of its peaked roof. The 31.5-foot by 18.5-foot dwelling had four rooms, an attached kitchen, and a cellar. The main entrance in one gable end was decorated along the roof line with early Victorian sawnwork. This structure was a departure from the simple designs Pleasonton had erected. Nearby was a brick cistern five feet across and five feet deep. The sides of the dwelling were unpainted, but the cast-iron tower that rose through the shingled roof was painted red. The lantern contained a fifth-order lens, which was 50 feet above sea level although only 35 feet above the ground. The characteristic of the light was fixed white varied by flashes. The Sandy Point lighthouse went into service in 1858, early in the year, but the Lighthouse Board did not install a fog bell at the station until 1863.[11]

The Civil War affected lighthouses and lightships considerably from the Potomac River southward. Southern forces deliberately damaged lighthouses and sank or burned lightships to prevent them from assisting the Federal navy. In the early stages of the rebellion, individuals and small local groups disabled lighthouses in the name of patriotism. The keeper of one Florida lighthouse, for example, took out his gun and shot the Fresnel lens before leaving his duty station. Such actions quickly came under the auspices of the military, however, and small parties of soldiers were dispatched to take a specific lighthouse or light vessel out of service. In many cases they went farther than this, applying explosives to the task. Nonetheless, the Confederate government made provisions for the administration of lighthouses that were quite similar to those they had known before the war started.

With few exceptions, actual damage to aids to navigation in the Chesapeake occurred in Virginia's portion of the bay. Only three instances of attack occurred in Maryland waters, all in the Potomac River. For the most part, the Union navy operated in Virginia waters and in the Potomac. The sphere of responsibility of the Potomac Flotilla included a portion of the west coast of the bay to Point Lookout, where a prison held Confederate soldiers.

Some time between April 19 and 24, 1861, Southerners captured the two light vessels at Upper Cedar Point and Lower Cedar Point on the Potomac and burned them, apparently at their moorings. Four others in the Chesapeake between the Potomac River and Hampton Roads were taken about the same time, although two of them were later recaptured. One, the lightship that had been stationed at Smith Point at the mouth of the Potomac, was found in a creek off the Wicomico River. Despite Confederate resistance, a U.S. Navy vessel with troops aboard recaptured the vessel and towed it to Annapolis. Although everything had been removed from it, the boat was still in sound condition.

During the Civil War the lighthouse at Point Lookout was crowded by the radiating wards of the Union's Hammond Hospital. A sprawling, and later infamous, prisoner of war camp was added to the complex in 1863.

(Engraving reproduction courtesy of Elizabeth Hughes)

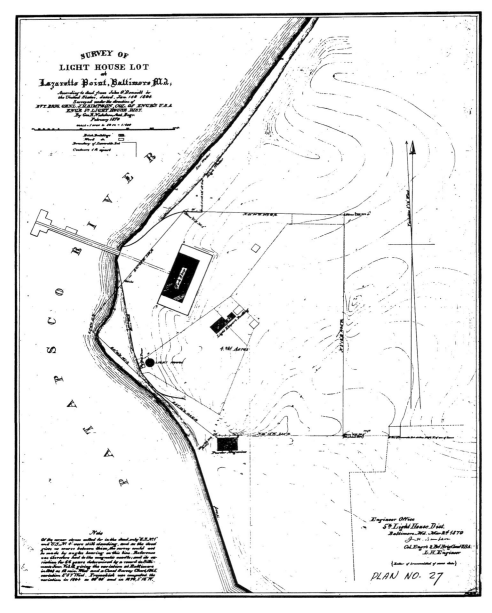

SURVEY OF
LIGHT HOUSE LOT
at
Lazaretto Point, Baltimore Md,

PLAN NO. 27

During the Civil War iron ore was mined on the Lazaretto light station grounds and by the late 1860s a depot for buoy and supply storage had been established at the site. In this 1870 survey the light tower and the keeper's house, which had been rebuilt after a fire in 1858, are shown, along with an enlarged workshop building.

(National Archives, Philadelphia)

Because of the traffic, both civilian and naval, that moved up and down the Potomac River, the Lighthouse Board entered into a contract with a shipbuilder in New Bedford, Massachusetts, to construct two new light vessels to be moored at Upper Cedar Point and Lower Cedar Point. The lightships' arrival in the Potomac was delayed because the contractor had problems paying his bills and liens were filed against him by his creditors, but they were finally placed on station some time before June 1864. Aboard each vessel was a detachment of soldiers to protect it from raiders.

The next, and last, assault upon a Potomac River lighthouse came in May 1864, when a party of Confederates under the leadership of one Goldsmith crossed from Virginia in a small boat and landed at Blackistone Island. The raiders damaged the lantern, destroyed the lens and the lamp, and took away fifteen gallons of oil. Disturbed by this action, the commander of the Potomac Flotilla asked the commanding officer

at Point Lookout to send detachments to guard the Blackistone Island lighthouse and the one at Piney Point. The Lighthouse Board secured another lantern, began repairs on the Blackistone Island lighthouse and soon had it back in service.[12]

In December 1862 the Fifth District asked the board for permission to mine iron ore known to exist on the grounds of the Lazaretto light station. Probably spurred by the needs of war, the board quickly gave permission. By the end of July 1863, the government had entered into a contract with H. W. Ellicott to do the work, and preliminary excavations began shortly thereafter. The government received royalties of $1.56 per ton on the ore. During fiscal year 1864 the company mined "about 700 tons" and paid the government $1,042, all of which went into the general treasury. The mining operation continued for a number of years.

At about the same time, the Fifth District established a lighthouse depot at Lazaretto Point. The Lighthouse Board received permission to take over an old Treasury Department building at the point, although the needs of the military restricted their access at first.[13] The depot was established for the storage of buoys and supplies, but in time the site grew into the principal lighthouse depot for the Fifth District. Beginning in the late 1930s it housed the Lighthouse Service's radio experimentation laboratory.

Throughout the Civil War, the Lighthouse Board struggled to replace damaged aids to navigation, either restoring them or replacing them with temporary lights or markers. These efforts barely scratched the surface of what was needed to return the country's lighthouse system to its pre-war condition. When the war ended, the board began by surveying and assessing the damage that had been done.

In Charleston, South Carolina, the channels had changed dramatically and sunken vessels had to be marked. In the sounds of North Carolina lightships needed to be replaced and lighthouses restored. The tall towers of South Carolina, Georgia, Florida, and the Gulf Coast were seriously damaged. The top of the brick tower at Aransas Pass near Corpus Christi, Texas, had been destroyed. Everywhere the board looked there was devastation. On the positive side, a number of towers in Florida remained intact and could be returned to full operation almost immediately. And, because commercial maritime activity had not been fully restored in southern ports, the board had time to begin by concentrating its efforts on those areas with the greatest need.

The first work undertaken was the installation of a temporary light in places where the aid was missing or required repair. A beacon was placed at the Tybee light tower in Georgia, which had been structurally damaged. A jury-rigged light vessel marked the sunken *USS Wehawken* in South Carolina. Buoy systems were re-established.

Aids to navigation in Virginia's waters suffered as much damage as those in the lower South, but Maryland's lighthouses had been barely touched by the war. The most serious problem for these facilities stemmed not from the war but from erosion.

By 1864 Sharp's Island lighthouse was in imminent danger of being taken by the bay; the district engineer felt the two-story wooden structure with the light on the roof would not last the winter. Erosion had been a threat since Sharp's Island was built. Pleasonton had had the lighthouse placed on "wheels" so it could be moved when water came too close. When the bay had threatened in the late 1840s, he had purchased another site and moved the lighthouse there. This relocation had given the lighthouse nineteen more years of use.

When the second threat came, the Lighthouse Board decided to replace the lighthouse with a screwpile structure and requested the necessary funds from Congress. Congress did not respond, and the Board asked for funds again the next year. The only reason the lighthouse still stood, the Board reported, was that the year had seen "an unusual absence of storm-tides and heavy northwest gales." The bay, it added, was continuing to undermine the bluff and had reached a corner of the lighthouse. This time Congress responded, but before the new work was complete, erosion forced the District to remove the furniture and illuminating apparatus from the original lighthouse. The threat had come quickly, and the island was without a light from November 1-15, 1865. A temporary tripod with a steamer lens on top of it was quickly erected and served until the new lighthouse came on line.

The new light was a hexagonal screwpile structure located one-third mile off the north end of Sharp's Island at the mouth of the Choptank River. Lighted in 1866, probably early in the year, this white lighthouse had a fifth-order lens that gave off a fixed white light to guide vessels up the bay and to the entrance to the river.[14]

The Lighthouse Board next turned its attention to a policy that had been in effect for some time, "to replace the light-vessels, wherever practicable, by permanent structures, because of their greater economy, both in construction and maintenance." The damage done to lightships during the war, particularly in the Chesapeake Bay and the North Carolina sounds, gave the Board an opportunity to implement this policy on a wholesale basis. It was decided to replace the four lightships in Maryland's waters at the same time. These stations were at Hooper Strait (1827), Janes Island (1853), Lower Cedar Point (1864), and Upper Cedar Point (1864).

Hooper Strait received a square screwpile lighthouse, the foundation painted red and the superstructure white. It rested in six feet of water on the shoal on the south side of the channel between Hoopers and Goldsborough islands. The fixed white light from its fifth-order lens guided vessels through the straits and into Tangier Sound. It had a fog bell operated by machinery, striking four times every minute. The Hooper Strait light vessel departed its station after the new lighthouse was lighted on September 14, 1867, and went to Norfolk, where it received a few small repairs before becoming the relief lightship for the District.

On December 16, 1866, the Janes Island lightship was reported to be leaking considerably. The District sent the relief light vessel to take her place so the ship could come to Baltimore for a proper inspection. She was found to be not worth repairing and was stripped of all public property and sold at auction, bringing $518.55. The district relief lightship remained on the Janes Island station until the new lighthouse was completed and lighted on October 7, 1867.

The screwpile structure placed at Janes Island was almost identical to the one at Hooper Strait. The only differences were the roof of the dwelling, which was painted lantern red, and the larger, fourth-order lens. Positioned at the mouth of the Little Annemessex River, its fixed white light served as a guide into the river. When the light was exhibited for the first time, the district inspector, who was present, said, "The light bids fair to become an excellent one . . . ."[15]

The lightships at Upper Cedar Point and Lower Cedar Point were also replaced with square screwpile lighthouses. These structures were identical—each rested on five screwpiles painted brown and had a white superstructure with a lantern red roof and a fifth-order lens that emitted a fixed white light. Over the years as navigational needs changed, the structures were altered somewhat, making them more distinct as new features were introduced in one and not the other. For example, the Lower Cedar Point lighthouse received a fourth-order lens, while the Upper Cedar Point light received a red sector. Both had machinery-operated fog bells, but at

"By 1864 the Sharp's Island lighthouse was in imminent danger of being taken by the bay; the district engineer felt the two-story wooden structure with the light on the top would not last the winter. Erosion had been a threat since Sharp's Island was built."

By 1867 the Lighthouse Board had replaced the four lightships in Maryland waters with square screwpile lighthouses, preferring "permanent structures because of their greater economy, both in construction and maintenance." Wooden vessels with lanterns encircling the masts, the Maryland lightships were less functional than the steel screw *Winter Quarter*, which served the Fifth Lighthouse District from 1934 to 1943. The map shows the upper portion of the District.

(Annual Report 1876, Lighthouse Board. Photo by William Marion Goeshy, c. 1920, MHT Cultural Conservation Program)

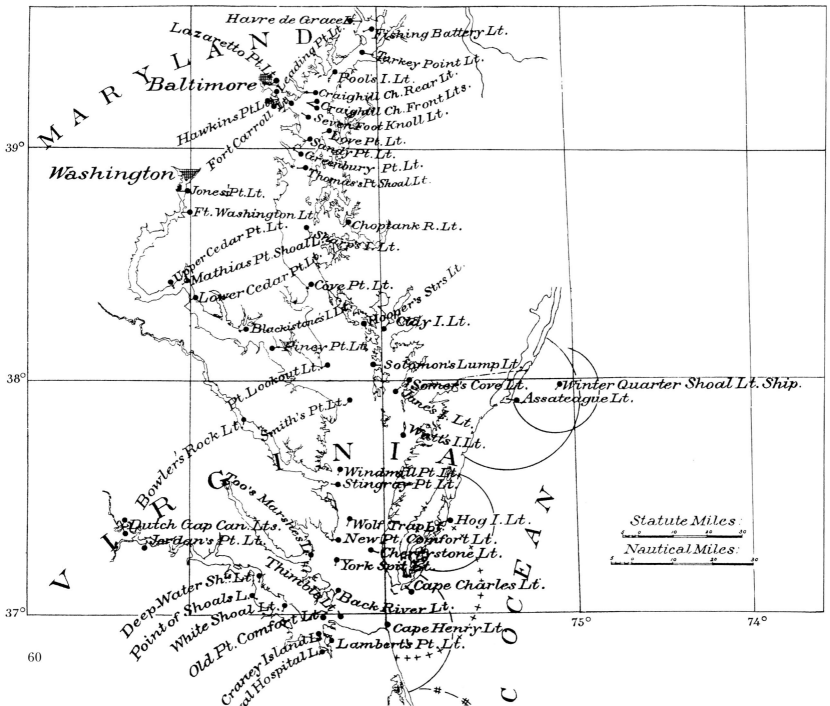

some point, a much larger one was installed at Lower Cedar Point.[16]

When the light was exhibited in the new Lower Cedar Point screwpile lighthouse on August 6, 1867, the light vessel departed for Norfolk, where it was examined, recaulked, and painted yellow. It was assigned to Virginia's York Spit station in October 1867. On July 21, 1867, the day after the new Upper Cedar Point lighthouse went into service, the light vessel went to Norfolk where its sheathing was repaired and its hull painted red. The vessel was towed on August 17, 1867, to Willoughby Spit, Virginia, its new station.[17]

At the same time these lightships were being replaced, another lighthouse was under construction in Maryland. It was located at Somers Cove on the north side of the Little Annemessex River and served as a guide to the harbor at Crisfield. A screwpile structure with a red foundation and a square white dwelling, it was similar to the lighthouses that replaced the lightships. "It is," the Lighthouse Board remarked, "a screwpile structure of the least expensive class." The lighthouse had a sixth-order lens with a fixed white light and a fog bell operated by machinery.[18]

A more important navigational aid was being worked on also at this time—the Brewerton Channel range lights. The purpose of the lights was to guide vessels as they transited Brewerton Channel, especially at night. The North Point range lights guided ships into the Patapsco River, but then there was nothing to help vessels stay in the narrow channel leading to Baltimore Harbor. The Lighthouse Board's 1866 proposal for the lights struck a responsive chord with Congress. Money was provided, and work began in fiscal year 1867. There were to be two structures. The southeast, or front light, was to be placed at Hawkins Point, and the northwest, or rear light, a mile and one eighth away on a bluff at Leading Point. Both sites were on the south side of the Patapsco River a few miles southeast of Curtis Bay.

Work got underway at the just-acquired Hawkins Point site first, mainly because the land at Leading Point had not yet been purchased. The Hawkins Point light was to be a screwpile structure erected offshore in six feet of water. In 1867 the ironwork for the foundation was completed and the construction of the superstructure or dwelling began. On December 16, 1867, William H. Dorsey, Allen G. Dorsey, and Joseph H. and Mary Ann Craggs sold the government a small (100 feet x 400 feet) piece of land at Leading Point for a lighthouse. During fiscal year 1868

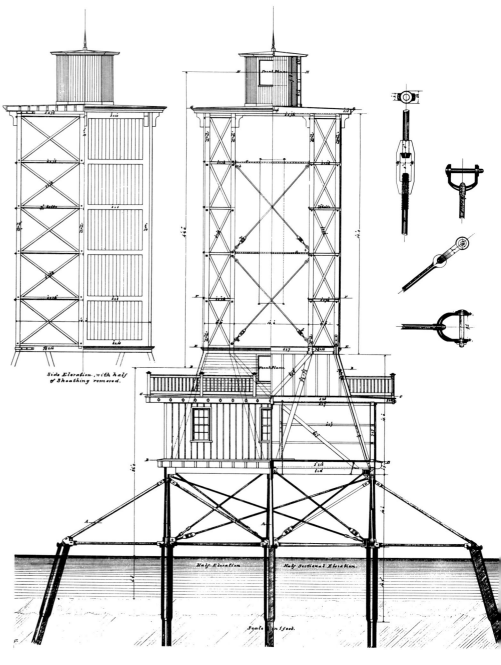

work progressed at both sites, and the Brewerton Channel range lights were first exhibited on November 1, 1868.

The lights bore northwest and southeast from each other, "both being exactly in range with the axis of Brewerton channel." The hexagonal screwpile structure had two lights on it, one 28 feet above water and the other directly over it at 70 feet above water. The rear light, on the bluff at Leading Point, shone from a lantern atop a brick dwelling, and its focal plane was 40 feet above the ground and 70 feet above water. "When a vessel is on the true course coming up or going down the channel," the Lighthouse Board said, "the three lights will be seen in line, one above the other; but whenever this course is departed from, however slightly, to port or starboard, a corresponding change in the positions of the lights will be observed." The lights were pro-

The Hawkins Point lighthouse (the southeast or front light of the Brewerton Channel range) was a hexagonal screwpile structure with two lights, one directly above the other. The Leading Point lighthouse, high on a bluff a mile away, lined up with the other two, helping vessels stay in the narrow channel leading to Baltimore Harbor. Side and half sectional elevations and details of screw couplings, 1867.

(National Archives, Philadelphia)

duced by range lenses equivalent to second-order lenses.[19]

Although recognized as the range lights for Brewerton Channel, these structures were known individually as the Hawkins Point lighthouse and the Leading Point lighthouse until April 1915. On the sixteenth of that month William Raabe, keeper of the Leading Point lighthouse, became keeper of both lighthouses and the lights officially became the Brewerton Channel Front and Rear range lights.[20]

In 1885 this set of range lights was the center of a dispute with the adjacent landowner. Thomas C. Chappell of P. S. Chappell and Son, 8 South Street, Baltimore, laid claim to the Hawkins Point lighthouse. He owned the submerged land on which the lighthouse stood, he said, because the state legislature had granted it to him in 1861. He had built a large chemical works, and he claimed to have a deed that permitted him to extend wharves 1,000 feet from his property, which he wanted to do. He contended the Hawkins Point lighthouse interfered with the use of his property, and he wanted the lighthouse removed. In another letter he said the range light was impeding his development of 6,000 feet of shoreline, since "buildings erected anywhere on the property in the course of the range must necessarily shut it out." He added, "I cannot however permit the Government to use my property and to prevent me from using it." He did, however, say he would accept money to recompense him for the use of his property.

The Board attempted to purchase land to preserve the range between Hawkins Point and Leading Point, but Chappell wanted so much money the Board decided to look into following condemnation procedures through the state.[21] First, they appointed a committee to determine the value of the Hawkins Point property and an easement for the sight line of the light. The committee met, visited the site, and recommended that the government pay Chappell $2,500 if he would recognize that the government owned a two-acre circular site at Hawkins Point and would grant a perpetual easement over his property for the path the range light traveled. Chappell turned down the offer, and in November 1887 the government filed a petition for condemnation in Maryland Circuit Court in Anne Arundel County. Little progress was made on this petition, however, because Chappell was badgering the government attorney with demands for rent payments on the Hawkins Point site.[22]

The case was moved to the United States Circuit Court after Chappell filed an ejectment suit against the keeper of Hawkins Point lighthouse.

The judge held, in the U.S. attorney's words, that the "private interest in the submerged soil at the bottom of the river . . . was subject to the paramount right of the public to use the river for navigation, and of the United States, in the regulation of commerce, to erect thereon such aids to navigation as were reasonably necessary." He added that until the submerged land was actually used by private interests, the United States had the right to use the soil for navigational aids "without the plaintiff's consent, and without compensation." The Board was ecstatic at the ruling, saying it "will effectually dispose of claims for compensation arising from the occupation of the United States of submarine sites for light-houses." The judge allowed the owner $3,500 for the easement, and the Board paid Chappell that amount in 1891 after Congress had appropriated the money.[23]

Some years later, on the morning of March 7, 1913, the *Alum Chine*, a freighter loaded with dynamite for the Panama Canal, exploded and sank in six fathoms of water "directly on the main ship channel" at Hawkins Point. Because the wreck was covered by only twelve feet of water, the Lighthouse Board had a gas buoy placed to mark it. One writer, mindful of the thirty-three persons killed and sixty wounded, described the shipping disaster as the worst Baltimore has ever seen.[24] The freighter took two railroad barges and six boxcars with her to the bottom of the Patapsco. One tug went down while trying to leave the scene. The explosion damaged all three lighthouses in the vicinity—Fort Carroll, Hawkins Point, and Leading Point—blowing in windows and doors and knocking down ceilings. The cost of repairs was estimated at $281.74. To alleviate the greatest concern resulting from the accident—the navigational hazard created by the *Alum Chine*—a contractor was hired to clear the Brewerton Channel of the wreck. It was removed, the Fifth District superintendent reported, "piece by piece as it can be blown apart by small charges of dynamite." The job was done by the fall of 1913.[25]

In 1870 the lightship formerly stationed at Hooper Strait was assigned to Benoni Point to guide traffic up and down the Choptank River and into the other tributaries and harbors in the vicinity. The Lighthouse Board must have intended this as a temporary assignment, for in the same year, Congress appropriated the money needed to erect the Choptank River lighthouse.

The lighthouse the Board decided to build was a screwpile structure similar to the ones built at York Spit and Wolf Trap in Virginia but without four of the fender piles. The site was on a

"In 1885 this set of range lights was the center of a dispute with the adjacent landowner. Thomas C. Chappell ... laid claim to the Hawkins Point lighthouse."

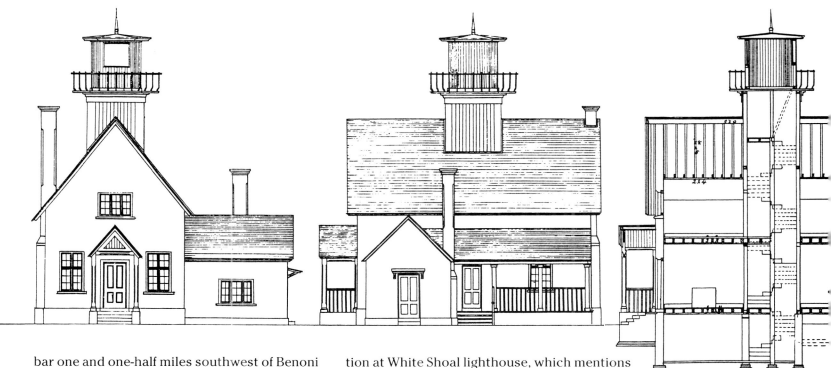

bar one and one-half miles southwest of Benoni Point in eleven feet of water. The lighthouse would mark the entrances into the Choptank, the Tred Avon River, and Island Creek.

After bids had been received from an advertisement, a contract was let in March 1871 to the low bidder, Francis A. Gibbons, who anticipated having the lighthouse completed in October. Construction did not go as rapidly as hoped, however, because of the hardness of the bottom and the contractor's inexperience in this type of construction. The work was finally completed on December 23, and the light was apparently exhibited at that time, since the lightship "was permanently withdrawn." The Board described the Choptank River lighthouse as standing "on ten wooden piles encased in cast iron. Six of the piles form the foundation for the lighthouse proper, the other four being fender piles, serving as ice breakers." The superstructure was a frame building, hexagonal in form, surmounted by a lantern fitted with a sixth-order lens.

Although this lighthouse was referred to in the *Light List* and in official reports as a screwpile lighthouse, the description of wooden piles encased in cast iron does not sound like screwpile construction. A description of construction at the York Spit and Wolf Trap lighthouses sheds some light on this question. At York Spit, the Board reported, it took 243 blows of a 1,600-pound hammer to get the first wood pile to penetrate 20 feet, and at Wolf Trap the wood piles were "covered with cast-iron screw sleeves." This information suggests the wooden piles were driven into the bottom and then cast-iron sleeves were slipped over them and screwed into the bottom. A description of the construc-

tion at White Shoal lighthouse, which mentions the substitution of "a wooden pile covered with a cast-iron screw sleeve for the solid wrought-iron screw-pile," confirms this interpretation.[26] The wooden piles with sleeves were probably adopted because they were less expensive and easier to insert into the bottom of the bay than the iron piles. Also, the cast-iron sleeves were much cheaper than wrought iron but would protect the wood piles from damage by shipworms.

When in 1870 Congress appropriated funds to build a lighthouse at Love Point on Kent Island, it was not the first time interest had been expressed in the site. In 1834 Congress had appropriated $5,500 for a lighthouse here, but Pleasonton had objected to the cost of the land and requested more money. Commissioners appointed by the Maryland legislature to set a value on the property had found the four acres worth $1,000, a sum Pleasonton, who was personally familiar with the island, thought "enormously high." He wrote Congress, saying if they wanted the lighthouse they should appropriate the $1,000 to buy the land.[27] Nothing was done, and the issue faded.

In 1870 Congress reintroduced the idea of a lighthouse at Love Point, and the Lighthouse Board moved quickly to implement the legislation, deciding to erect a screwpile lighthouse in ten feet of water a little off the north end of Kent Island. An advertisement for proposals to build the lighthouse again yielded low bidder Francis A. Gibbons of Baltimore. The Lighthouse Board entered into a contract with him to build the lighthouses at both Love Point and Benoni's Point. By this time in his career, Gibbons had forty-five years of experience in construction.

The brick Leading Point lighthouse, high on a bluff, was a combined structure with the lantern on the roof of the dwelling. The rear, or northwestern, beacon in the three–light Brewerton Channel array had a focal plane 40 feet above the ground and 70 feet above water. The lights were first exhibited on November 1, 1868. Front, side and sectional elevations, 1867.

(National Archives, Philadelphia)

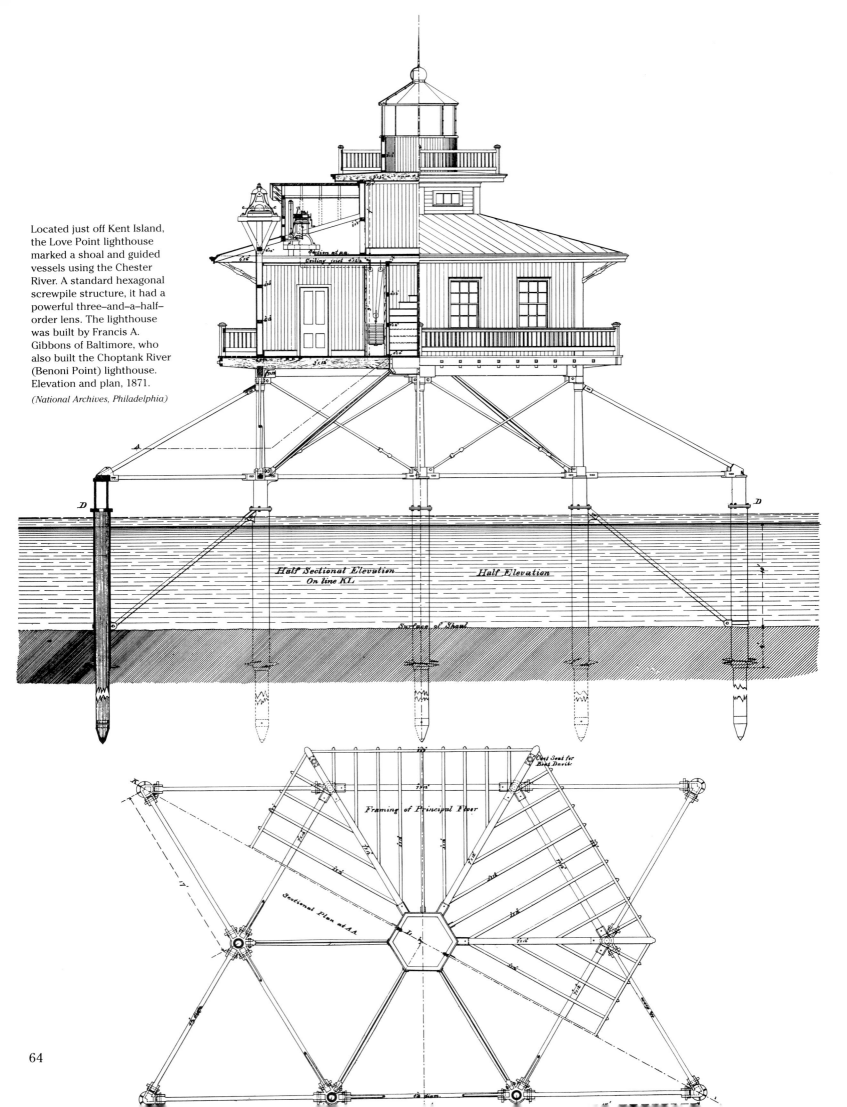

Located just off Kent Island, the Love Point lighthouse marked a shoal and guided vessels using the Chester River. A standard hexagonal screwpile structure, it had a powerful three–and–a–half–order lens. The lighthouse was built by Francis A. Gibbons of Baltimore, who also built the Choptank River (Benoni Point) lighthouse. Elevation and plan, 1871.

(National Archives, Philadelphia)

Half Sectional Elevation On line KL

Half Elevation

Surface of Shoal

Framing of Principal Floor

Sectional Plan at AA

64

Considering this, the Love Point contract was probably his last hurrah, certainly as far as lighthouses were concerned.

Gibbons became involved in lighthouse work in the early 1840s. He apparently got to know Pleasonton and seems to have had a good relationship with him. He occasionally undertook special tasks for the fifth auditor, usually associated with designing or building sea walls and breakwaters to control erosion. Several times he bid on contracts to repair lighthouses and worked on such structures as Point Lookout and Sharp's Island. In 1847 Gibbons erected the Bodie Island lighthouse in North Carolina and in 1848 the Egmont Key lighthouse on the Gulf Coast of Florida. Pleasonton had a high regard for him, saying he "has done some work very faithfully for us."

In 1851 Gibbons and a partner, Francis X. Kelly, obtained the contract to erect the first eight lighthouses on the West Coast of the United States. Gibbons and Kelly obtained a bark, named *Oriole*, purchased materials, hired workers, and sent the vessel to the Pacific coast. With great difficulty and under trying circumstances, including the loss of *Oriole* with half of the materials at the mouth of the Columbia River, the Marylanders managed to get the eight California lighthouses erected by 1854.

After this experience Gibbons apparently did not engage in lighthouse work again until he received the contract to build the Love Point and Choptank River lighthouses. The contract called for work to be finished by October 1, 1871, but Gibbons experienced "unforeseen delays," and the weather turned stormy more frequently than usual, causing further delays. As a result the Love Point work was not finished until August 1, 1872. The light was displayed for the first time on August 15.[28]

Located just off Kent Island and equipped with a machinery-struck fog bell, this lighthouse not only marked the shoal on which it stood but also served as a guide to traffic using the Chester River. It was a standard, hexagonal screwpile lighthouse with an iron foundation painted red and a four-room superstructure painted white with a red roof. What made this lighthouse distinctive was its three-and-one-half order lens, at that time the largest and most powerful lens used in Maryland lighthouses other than the second-order range-type lenses in the Brewerton Channel range lights. The focal plane of the lens was 38 feet above mean high tide. The light was fixed but varied with red flashes to distinguish it from the one across the bay at Sandy Point, which was fixed but varied by white flashes. On November 15, 1875, the lens at Love Point was replaced with one of the fifth-order that gave off a fixed white light. Later it was changed to a flashing light and a red sector was added to cover Swan Point Bar.[29]

Had this lighthouse been built a few years later, it most likely would have been a caisson structure, for it was in an exposed position subject to the dangers of ice floes. Indeed, during its first winter in use, the ice broke not only two of the ice-breaker piles but also two of the legs of the structure, knocking the lighthouse out of service for several days. A $10,000 appropriation repaired the structure and permitted the engineers to place riprap around it, "forming an artificial island." The following year Congress provided $5,000 for additional riprap. It was not too soon, for the winter of 1874-75 was particularly severe, but the Lighthouse Board was happy to note that the Love Point lighthouse "stood the severe test of the winter . . . without damage or material displacement of the stone. It may now be considered secure."[30]

The Lighthouse Board's first twenty years had been a time of testing, particularly of its professionalism. Inheriting a leaky and tattered sailing vessel, the Board turned it into a sturdy steam vessel that could weather any storm. The Board was most severely tested by the Civil War and the devastation it wreaked on aids to navigation in the South, but within two years of the war's end it had restored the system without ignoring the aids in the rest of the country. Ever mindful of the needs of the maritime community, it built on the good things of the past while taking advantage of new technology.

The approach the Board took to operating and maintaining navigational aids is exemplified by its work in the Chesapeake Bay. The Board methodically replaced lamps and reflectors at bay lighthouses with the infinitely superior Fresnel lenses; replaced lightships with offshore lighthouses, at times modifying them to meet conditions encountered in the bay; and, perhaps most importantly, recommmended to Congress where lighthouses and other aids to navigation should be placed and the types that should be used at specific sites.

Generally speaking, the Lighthouse Board's method of operation, although somewhat cumbersome, was effective and professional and generated respect for what the government was doing in this area of responsibility. The harsh criticisms and complaints the fifth auditor had received vanished, and the Lighthouse Board fashioned a lighthouse system and service that did credit to the United States.

"The Board methodically replaced lamps and reflectors at bay lighthouses with the infinitely superior Fresnel lenses and replaced lightships with offshore lighthouses, at times modifying them to meet conditions encountered in the bay...."

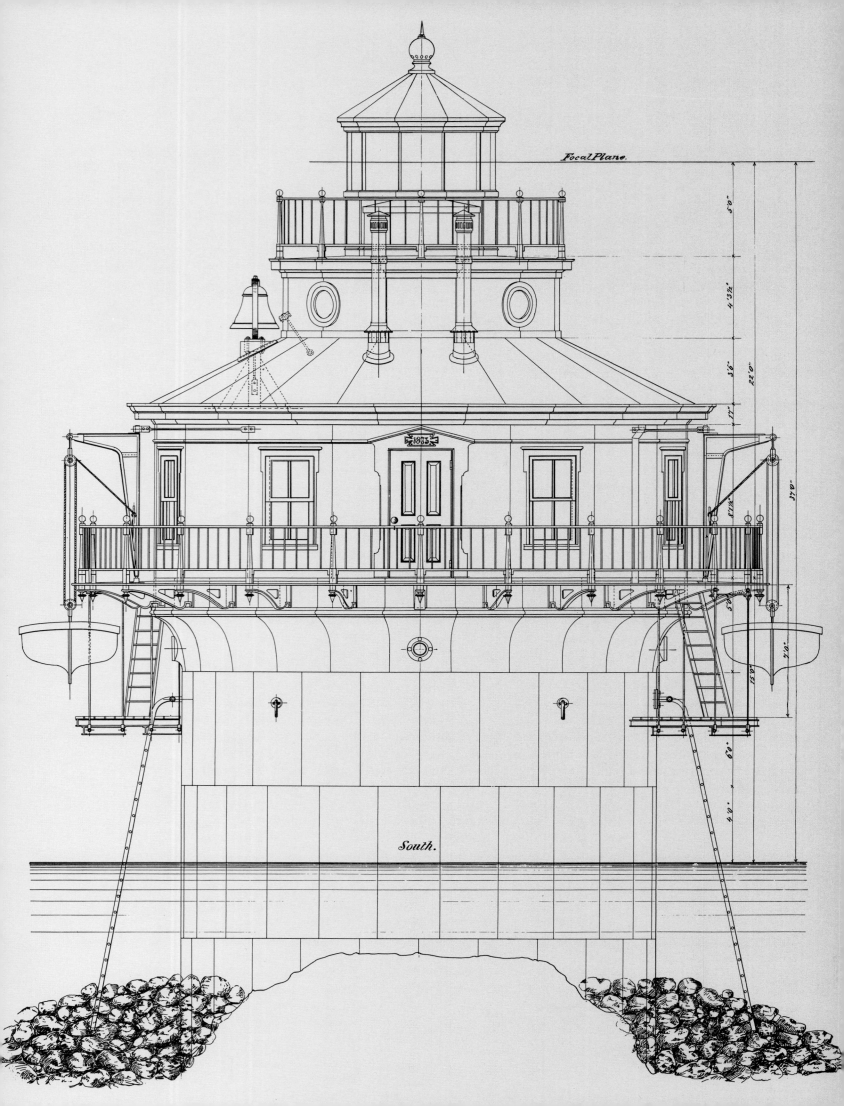

Focal Plane.

South.

1873

Chapter 4

Chesapeake Caissons: A First for the Nation

1873-1910

The 1870s saw the development of a new type of lighthouse that came to be identified strongly with the Chesapeake Bay. The caisson type—like the screwpile structure—was designed to be placed offshore. Because it was sturdier, the caisson eventually replaced screwpile lighthouses at exposed locations in both the Delaware and Chesapeake bays. Today, numerous examples of this style of structure survive from the northern coast of Maine to the lower part of Chesapeake Bay.

Present evidence indicates the first caisson lighthouse in this country went into service in 1873 in the Chesapeake. The last one built was apparently the art moderne Cleveland Ledge lighthouse, erected in Massachusetts in 1943. The only caisson lighthouse built south of Chesapeake Bay was one off the Texas shore marking the Sabine Bank.

At first the caisson was a wood grillage consisting of four layers of 12-inch square timbers built on shore and launched, after which curved plates of iron making a cylinder were bolted onto it. These plates, in courses, had flanges so the metal would fit together smoothly. Weight was placed in the caisson and the whole thus assembled caisson and cylinder floated to the site, where it was sunk and positioned in the bottom. As the structure sank lower and lower, more courses, or sections, of curved metal plate were added to keep the water out of the interior. The caisson and cylinder were usually sunk quite far into the bottom of the bay to give the lighthouse a stable base, and with the wooden portion sunk deep enough in the bay's bottom to be out of reach of shipworms. To lower the tubular structure deeper into the water, workers poured con-

crete and stone into it, and as it sank deeper other workers added more courses of iron plates to contain additional stone and concrete. On this foundation, the builders erected a lighthouse. Later the Lighthouse Board occasionally used caissons made of steel rather than of wood.

The first caisson lighthouse erected in the Chesapeake, and in the nation, was the Craighill Channel range front light. Craighill Channel was named for an Army engineer who did considerable work in the Chesapeake Bay including serving as the Fifth District lighthouse engineer. This channel was used by vessels from the south, for it intersected Brewerton Channel, which led ships through the mouth of the Patapsco River on up to the Fort McHenry Channel, which in turn led to Baltimore harbor. To help vessels stay in these channels, the Lighthouse Board provided range lights. By this time the Brewerton Channel range lights had already been established.

Craighill Channel at this time intersected Brewerton Channel about a mile northeast of Seven Foot Knoll lighthouse and extended southward to the south end of Belvidere Shoal. The channel had been 169 feet wide and generally 21 feet deep, but in 1870 Congress appropriated $50,000 to widen it to 500 feet and to deepen it 22 feet. The enlargement of this channel reflected the growing importance of Baltimore as a port, for the work was done to accommodate the larger vessels calling at the harbor.

Unlike Brewerton Channel, Craighill Channel had no lights to serve as night aids. The north-south orientation of the Chesapeake and the parallel axis of the channel made it necessary to place the range lights, particularly the front one, in the bay. The distance from the channel of locations on shore would have required very power-

The first caisson lighthouse erected in the Chesapeake, and in the nation, was the Craighill Channel range front lighthouse. Introduced in the 1870s, the sturdy caisson lighthouses were designed to be placed offshore, even on soft–bottomed sites, where they proved to be virtually "weatherproof."

(1883 front elevation, National Archives, Philadelphia)

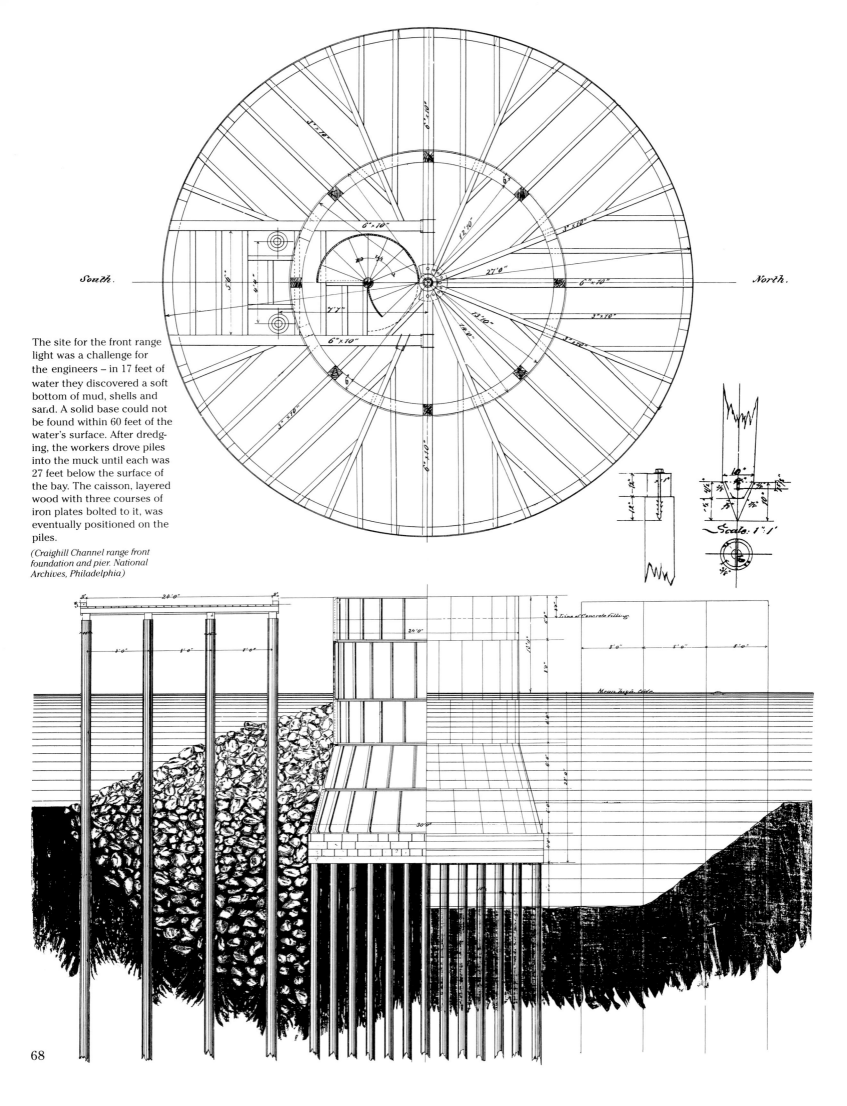

The site for the front range light was a challenge for the engineers – in 17 feet of water they discovered a soft bottom of mud, shells and sand. A solid base could not be found within 60 feet of the water's surface. After dredging, the workers drove piles into the muck until each was 27 feet below the surface of the bay. The caisson, layered wood with three courses of iron plates bolted to it, was eventually positioned on the piles.

(Craighill Channel range front foundation and pier. National Archives, Philadelphia)

South.   North.

The iron cylinder of the Craighill Channel range front lighthouse stood in 14 feet of water and was circled by 5,000 tons of stone to prevent scouring. In 1874 another 675 tons of riprap were added to protect it from moving ice.

(Annual Report 1873, Lighthouse Board. U. S. Coast Guard photo. F. Ross Holland Collection)

Below: The Craighill range lights were needed to help vessels calling at Baltimore stay in the channel, which had been enlarged in 1870. Unlike Brewerton Channel, which it intersected, Craighill had no night aids until the range lights went into service in 1873.

(Photo by F. Ross Holland, 1987)

ful lights for both aids and a tremendous height for the rear light.[1]

The engineers originally thought the front lighthouse should be built on screwpiles, but a winter with particularly heavy ice changed their ideas. They concluded that a stronger structure was needed and settled on a caisson-type lighthouse. At the site, in 17 feet of water, the builders found another surprise—the bottom was a 22-foot layer of mud "so soft . . . that an ordinary pile, stood on end, would penetrate 20 feet under the action of its own weight." Below the mud were layers of sand, mud, and shells. A solid base could not be found within 60 feet of the surface of the bay. The engineers would have to drive piles into the muck until the top of each was 27 feet below the surface of the water. They dredged 10 feet from the bottom and began driving the piles. Once these had been placed, the workers cut off the top of the piles with a circular saw driven by a steam engine. The saw did not permit an even cut and some piles were taller than others. To make a level resting place for the caisson, where necessary, an underwater diver "spiked" chocks of hardwood onto the heads of the shorter piles.

The wood grillage or caisson, made of four layers of 12-inch timbers, arrived from Havre de Grace in early October 1873 with a course of iron plates bolted to it. For safety, the engineers decided to bolt two more courses of plates onto the structure and then, for trim, to pour three feet of concrete into it. Once this work was done, the caisson floated evenly and had a draft of 15 feet. It was moved to the site and placed over the piles, after which 50 to 65 tons of weight (apparently stone) were deposited in the cylinder which slowly sank it to the bottom. This effort was just enough to send it to the bottom where it rested uneasily. A three-foot layer of concrete was required for the caisson to rest firmly on the bottom.

Just before this three-foot layer of concrete was to be poured, it was discovered the caisson was not resting on the piles as precisely as it should. The weight had to be removed, and the caisson brought to the surface. Before the workers repositioned it and lowered it to the bottom again, the engineers placed a 12-foot-square box that was 22 feet tall in the caisson to hold up to 160 tons of gravel. This box was filled to the weight needed to lower the caisson to the piles. Gravel was used because it would be easier to remove if the caisson was not positioned correctly on the piles, allowing it to rise off the bottom so the workers could try again to position it

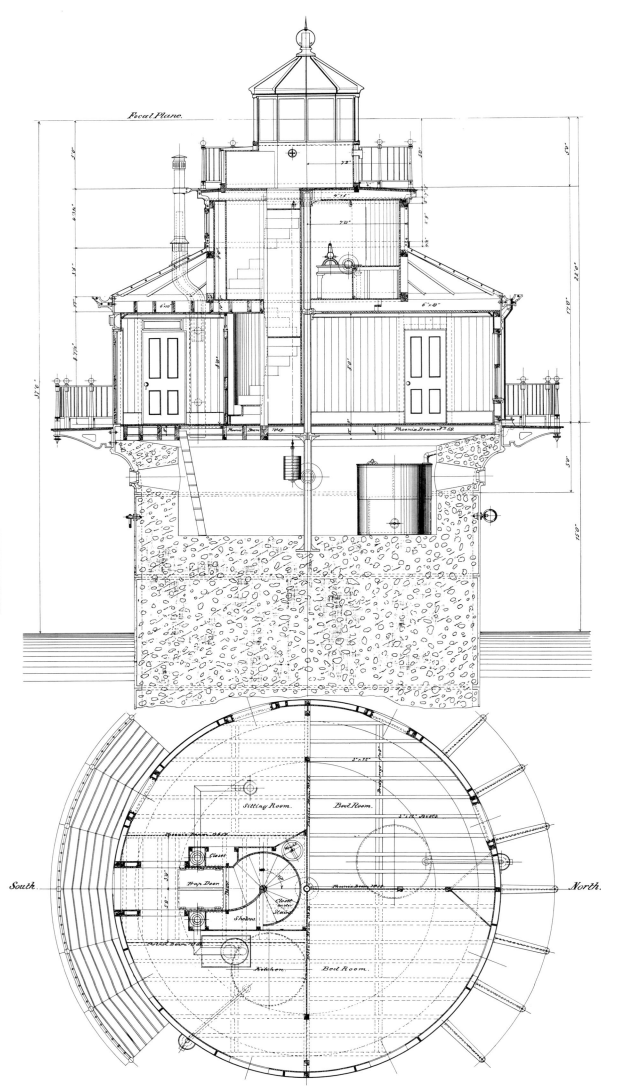

The small lighthouse sitting on the cylinder was a circular iron structure like the one at Seven Foot Knoll. It had four rooms and a watch room between the main floor and the lantern. There were two lights, one for general navigation, and the second, 22 feet above the bay, served as the front range light.

(Photo by F. Ross Holland, 1986. Elevation and floor plan, National Archives, Philadelphia)

satisfactorily. Once the caisson was positioned as the engineers wanted, the workers layered concrete into the structure. The gravel and box were removed and the workers poured concrete into the square void.

After installation of the caisson was completed, workers placed 5,000 tons of stone around the cylinder's base to prevent scouring of the bottom. At low tide this stone pile reached the surface of the water. On top of the cylinder the workers built a temporary wood structure and placed a fourth-order lens in it in order to get the light into operation as soon as possible. The range lights went into service on November 20, 1873.[2]

In October 1874 the iron lighthouse was completed and placed on the foundation, replacing the temporary wood structure. To complete the job, another 675 tons of riprap were dumped around the cylinder. The Lighthouse Board later reported, "The heavy ice of the past winter did no damage to this station, though the locality is one of great exposure."

The iron cylinder of the front Craighill Channel light stood in 14 feet of water. At its lower end, or base, the cylinder was 30 feet across. It tapered to a point 12 feet above the bottom where the cylinder was 24 feet across. At this point the tube ran straight up to the top. Braces fastened to the outside of the cylinder supported the gallery that circled the bottom of the lighthouse. Surmounting the cylinder was the lighthouse, which was shaped like the dwelling on the Seven Foot Knoll lighthouse. This circular iron structure supported the first light, an octagonal lantern that held a fifth-order lens, with a focal plane 39 feet above mean high water. That light was for general navigation in the bay and was visible around the horizon except in the range line and to the north. A second light, 22 feet above the bay, served as the front range light.

The dwelling at the front Craighill Channel light had four living rooms and a watchroom between the first floor and the lantern. Painted brown, it was circled by a walkway enclosed by an iron railing. Two 750-gallon iron water tanks collected run-off from the roof. The cellar contained the oil house and space for storage.[3]

As the front light was going up, other builders worked on the rear light. Its construction was as difficult, though for different reasons. The exact site for the structure had to be determined with great care and in calm weather, for in order for the lights to be an effective aid, they had to be in precise alignment with the comparatively narrow channel. The site selected was 2.4 miles

north of the front range light on a shoal near the south end of Hart Island. After work began, the sandy bottom was found to go down only two feet, below which a layer of mud and sand was followed by another fifteen feet of mud. The engineers realized this site also needed a pile and grillage foundation in order to support the granite piers on which the columns of the superstructure would rest. Because the water was two feet deep at the site, a coffer dam was built to create a dry work area. When the dam was completed, work on the foundation began with the driving of the piles. Several times storms broke the walls of the dam, interrupting work, but by June 1873, the grillage was in place and construction had begun on the piers that formed the foundation of the light tower. In August the piers were completed. The corner columns of the tower arrived about this time from Baltimore, and the laborers anchored them onto the piers.

The Craighill Channel rear lighthouse was located 2.4 miles north of the front range light on a sandy shoal near Hart Island. It also needed a pile and grillage foundation to support the nine piers of Port Deposit granite upon which the dwelling and open–work tower rested.

(Postcard image c. 1895. Jack Kelbaugh Collection)

The Craighill rear light tower was described as "an open frame–work of the form of a frustum of a pyramid of four sides...." The square column that holds the stairway leading to the lantern was surrounded for 73 years by an eight–room dwelling with a tin roof.

(Annual Report 1873, Lighthouse Board. U.S. Coast Guard photo. F. Ross Holland Collection)

Because of the unanticipated expenses involved in erecting these range lights, the appropriation ran out before work was completed on the rear light. As had been done at the front site, a temporary light was placed on the tower, allowing the range lights to go into service on November 20, 1873. As planned, display of the Craighill Channel range lights resulted in the immediate deactivation of the North Point range lights. Meanwhile, Congress appropriated more funds, and the tower of the rear light, with the dwelling nestled at the bottom, was finished in March 1875.[4]

The rear light was set on a foundation of nine piers of Port Deposit granite which rested on the grillage. The Lighthouse Board wanted a strong foundation because "ice is piled up very heavily here sometimes during the winter." The builders erected what was at the time described as "an open frame-work of the form of a frustum of a pyramid of four sides, the corner columns being of cast iron resting on cast-iron disks, which are

anchored to the masonry of the piers." A square column that holds the stairway leading to the lantern was for many years surrounded at the bottom by an eight-room wooden dwelling, which was removed when the light was automated. Surmounting the column is a square lantern that held a fourth-order range lens with a focal plane 105 feet above the bay. A square walkway or gallery surrounds the exterior of the lantern. Another square walkway runs just below the lantern outside the watchroom. The lower half of the light tower is painted white and the upper half brown.[5]

In 1877 M. H. Hill, who owned the land opposite the rear light, filed a suit of ejectment, saying he had rights to the low water point and the light tower. The tower stood at the shallow point, and when the wind occasionally blew the water away, he contended, it was within the low water line and thus on his property. His principal argument was that because the state had given him the right to erect a wharf in the water in front of

The rear light dwelling was razed in 1938, fifteen years after the light was automated. The square stairway tower, now painted brown and white, remains and the light is still active. The square lantern held a fourth-order range lens with a focal plane 105 feet above the bay. The elevation, right, was traced in 1917 from the original drawings.

(F. Ross Holland photo; National Archives, Philadelphia)

his property he could also claim the land under that water. Consequently, Hill believed, the "Light House was erected on soil under water, over all which he had the right to fill or wharf out and therefore was within his 'close.'" The court ruled against him, saying his right was only a potential one to erect a wharf, and since the governor had deeded the land, in this case to the federal government, before he acted on his potential right he had no claim to the piece of property.[6]

On August 21, 1888, a "cyclone" hit the rear light station and ripped off the roof of the house and part of the galvanized covering of the shaft, damaging doors and windows. Repairs to this sturdy structure were accomplished during the following months.

The illuminant of the rear light was changed to acetylene in 1923, when the light was automated. The dwelling lay unused for several years and was the object of vandalism. It was rented to James P. McClurg in 1928 and razed in 1938.[7] The tower remains, and the light is still active.

The success the Lighthouse Board experienced in building the Craighill Channel range front light did not immediately spur the erection of other caisson structures in Chesapeake Bay. The three lighthouses constructed between 1873 and 1882 were of the screwpile type, and for at least two of the locations, that was the most

appropriate type. The exposed position and susceptibility to damage from floating ice at Love Point would have made it a candidate for a caisson lighthouse, but nearly ten years passed before another of this style was built. Then in the early 1880s three were constructed—Sharp's Island, Bloody Point Bar, and Sandy Point Shoal.

Sharp's Island was the second caisson lighthouse erected in the Chesapeake. It was placed on the site of two earlier lighthouses, a "movable" shore lighthouse built in the 1830s and a screwpile structure, both of which had failed. The lighthouse on the shore had succumbed to erosion, and the screwpile lighthouse built to replace it in 1866 was torn from its pilings on February 10, 1881, in an encounter with "a heavy run of ice." It floated away with the keepers still on it, and they stuck with the structure until it ran aground. The two men were later commended for their action.

Deciding that another screwpile lighthouse would probably meet the same fate, the Lighthouse Board determined to put up a more substantial structure—"a cast-iron caisson filled with concrete and surmounted by a tower, also of cast-iron, with a brick lining." Less than a month after the accident, Congress appropriated $35,000 for the new structure. The Board got the new lighthouse underway immediately, entering into a contract with the Builders' Iron Company of Providence, Rhode Island, to manufacture the ironwork.

In August of 1881, the crew went to the site to build the work platform. Meanwhile workers at Oxford, Maryland, were putting together the cedar tank in which the iron caisson would be floated the twelve miles to the site. On September 13, the tank and caisson were launched and towed to the site, where the caisson was separated from the tank and sunk. Workers bolted the second section to the first, and a derrick was erected. The concrete-mixer, boiler, and engine were moved to the work platform, and on September 20, workers began filling the cylinder with concrete. They completed this phase of the work on November 2, at which time the engineers had to suspend work because the ironwork for the tower had not arrived.

Finally, two sections of the tower arrived on November 21. These were immediately towed to the site and placed on the cylinder. On December 6, the remaining ironwork arrived, and by the end of the month it was in place and the conical tower lined with brick. The finish work began but was halted on January 9 because the crew was needed in the southern part of the bay to repair other navigational aids. Enough work had been done to allow the keepers to occupy the station, however, and on February 1, 1882, the light winked on for the first time. Not until May did the crew return to complete the finish work. At this time they also put a roof over the walkway around the tower and installed a water tank.

The Sharp's Island light tower was 37 feet tall and had four rooms. Its fourth-order lens emitted a fixed white light with a focal plane 55 feet above mean low water. The foundation cylinder was 30 feet tall and had a diameter of 30 feet. The lighthouse marked the entrance to the Choptank River and was located so that vessels could take a straight course for the light to the river. It also served as a general aid to bay traffic.[8] Today's charts of Chesapeake Bay do not show Sharp's Island, and the caisson lighthouse stands as a memorial to the lost bit of land.

The second caisson lighthouse in the Chesapeake, the Sharp's Island lighthouse replaced an 1886 screwpile that was torn from its pilings in a storm. (The first beacon was an 1838 "movable" lighthouse built on the island proper.) Completed in 1882, the tower marked the entrance to the Choptank River and today exhibits a decided tilt. The island disappeared about 1940. *Left:* Sharp's Island lighthouse c. 1910, *Below:* Sharp's Island, 1987

(U.S. Coast Guard photo. F. Ross Holland Collection; photo by David Policansky)

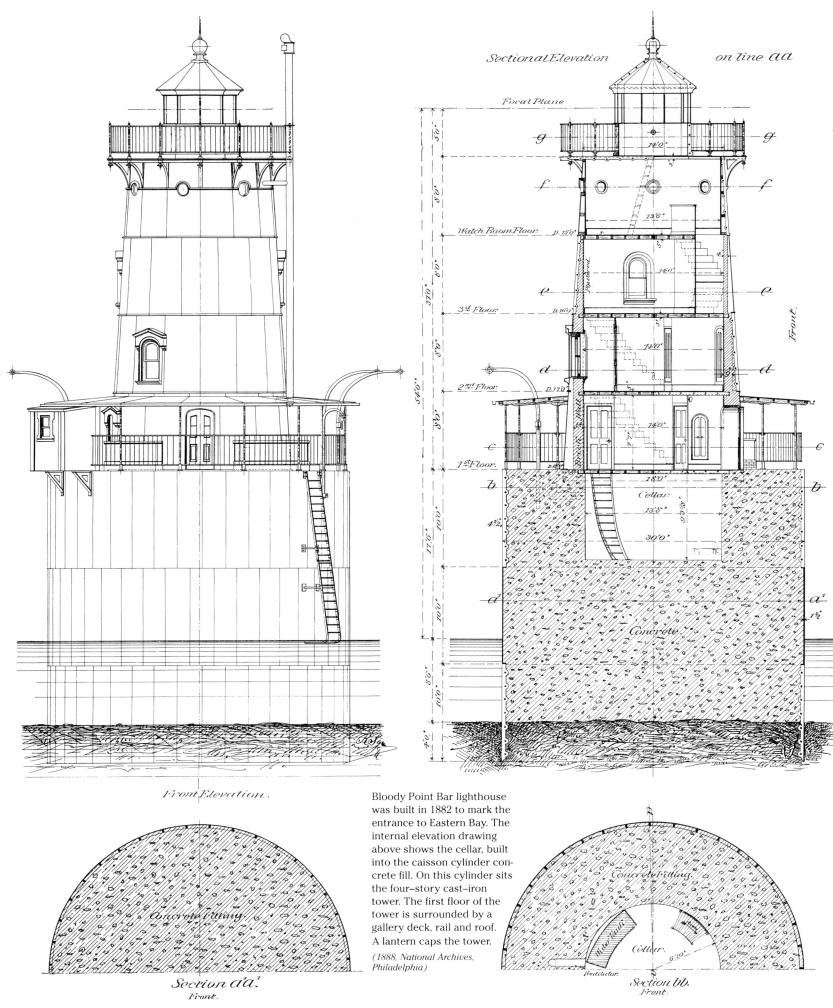

Sectional Elevation *on line aa*

Focal Plane

Watch Room Floor

3d Floor

2nd Floor

1st Floor

Cellar

Concrete

Front.

Front Elevation.

Section aa.
Front.

Section bb.
Front.

Concrete filling.

Concrete filling.

Cellar.

Bloody Point Bar lighthouse was built in 1882 to mark the entrance to Eastern Bay. The internal elevation drawing above shows the cellar, built into the caisson cylinder concrete fill. On this cylinder sits the four–story cast–iron tower. The first floor of the tower is surrounded by a gallery deck, rail and roof. A lantern caps the tower.

(1888, National Archives, Philadelphia)

76

While the Sharp's Island lighthouse was under construction, work was proceeding on the Bloody Point Bar lighthouse at the southern end of Kent Island. A lighthouse was needed at this point to mark the bar and the entrance to Eastern Bay. By February 1882 the iron for construction had been collected and stored at Lazaretto Depot. On June 5, work at the site began, and by the end of the month the working platform was in place with a derrick mast, concrete-mixer, and engine resting on it. In addition, the caisson and the first section had been lowered into position on the bottom and the second section bolted to it.

At this point work was held up for nearly three weeks waiting for the broken stone to arrive. It came on July 18, and the mixing of concrete began. By August 15 the caisson had been filled with over 700 cubic yards of concrete. Work commenced on the conical metal tower, and at the end of August, all of the iron and brickwork and the tower roof had been completed. The woodwork—doors, windows, sash, closets—and the painting were finished during the first week of September. On October 1, 1882, the lighthouse went into service, having cost $25,000. In February a room was added to shelter the fog bell and its striking apparatus. This addition was made at the Sharp's Island lighthouse at about the same time. Bloody Point Bar lighthouse was very similar in appearance to the Sharp's Island light, and the caisson and tower dimensions at each are the same.[9]

The last of the triumvirate of caisson lighthouses erected during the early 1880s was the

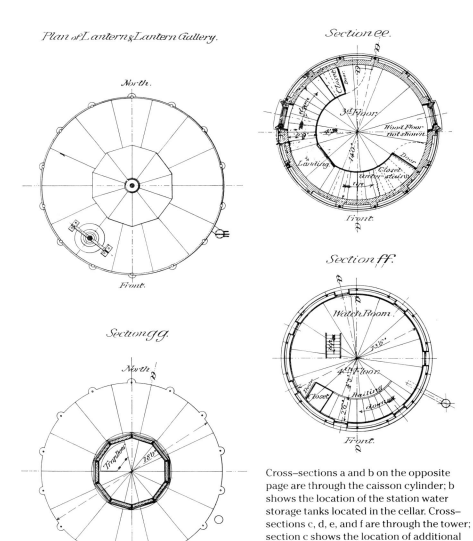

Cross–sections a and b on the opposite page are through the caisson cylinder; b shows the location of the station water storage tanks located in the cellar. Cross–sections c, d, e, and f are through the tower; section c shows the location of additional water storage tanks. Cross–section g is through the lantern. The lantern plan, upper left, shows the location of the fog bell on the lantern gallery deck.

(1888, National Archives, Philadelphia)

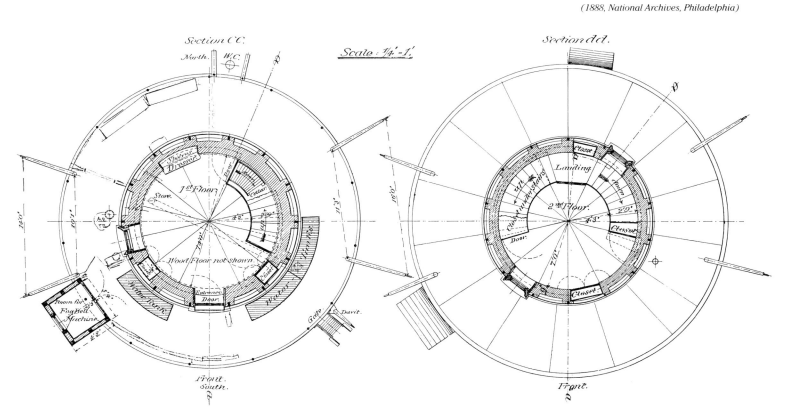

By the late 1870s the lighthouse at Sandy Point on the west side of the Chesapeake Bay had outlived its usefulness. The shoal now extended about a mile from the point and the Lighthouse Board pressed for a caisson lighthouse to be located on the end of the shoal. The caisson, 35 feet in diameter and 32' 6" high, was topped by an octagonal red brick lighthouse with a mansard roof and dormers.

(U.S. Coast Guard photo, c. 1895. F. Ross Holland Collection. Detail: The New Topographical Atlas .... MHT Library)

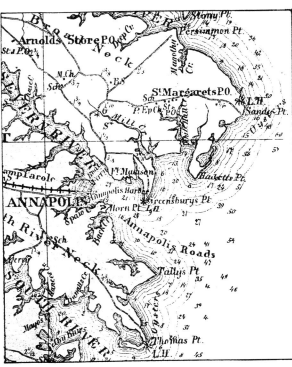

one at Sandy Point. For several years the Lighthouse Board had asked Congress for money to erect a lighthouse to replace the story-and-a-half structure with tower that had been on the shore at Sandy Point since 1858. The lighthouse, the Board contended, was less effective because the channel had moved farther from it. The shoal now extended about a mile from the point, and the fog bell could often not be heard because of the distance. Since this was a turning point for ships going to and from Baltimore, it was a vital location in which to have good and effective aids to navigation.

In August 1882 Congress, perhaps prompted by the Baltimore Board of Trade, which had asked for a change in the light and fog bell at Sandy Point, finally appropriated the $25,000 the Lighthouse Board had requested in its annual report. Congress refused, however, to increase the sum to $40,000 as the Board had requested. The larger sum had been determined necessary to build a sturdier lighthouse for this exposed position. Floating ice would subject the structure to serious shocks in severe winters.

Wanting to move ahead with the lighthouse, the Lighthouse Board decided to make do with the money available by putting in the caisson envisioned but erecting a less expensive light tower. To be located on the shoal, the caisson would be 35 feet in diameter, 32 feet 6 inches high, and filled with concrete. The engineers ordered the iron for the caisson, and in August the crew went out to the site and erected both a working platform and the platform that would hold the caisson before it was lowered into the water. They then shifted the derrick mast, concrete-mixer, and engine to the platform. The workmen put together the first section of the caisson on August 24 and lowered it the next day. On the 27th they added the second section to the first one and lowered the caisson three feet into the sand, leveling it using a water jet and force pump. On the 31st they began mixing concrete, and when they had finished on September 26, the caisson encased 1,000 cubic yards of concrete. In the middle of pouring the concrete the third section of the cylinder was added. As the concrete neared the top, forms were placed to shape the cellar of the keeper's quarters in the top of the cylinder. The day after the concrete work was finished, the masons began erecting the tower, which was to be made almost entirely of brick. The tower was finished on October 9, and the next day workers began putting up the lantern, finishing on the 11th. Though the light was ready to be exhibited on October 18, the Board delayed putting the lighthouse into ser-

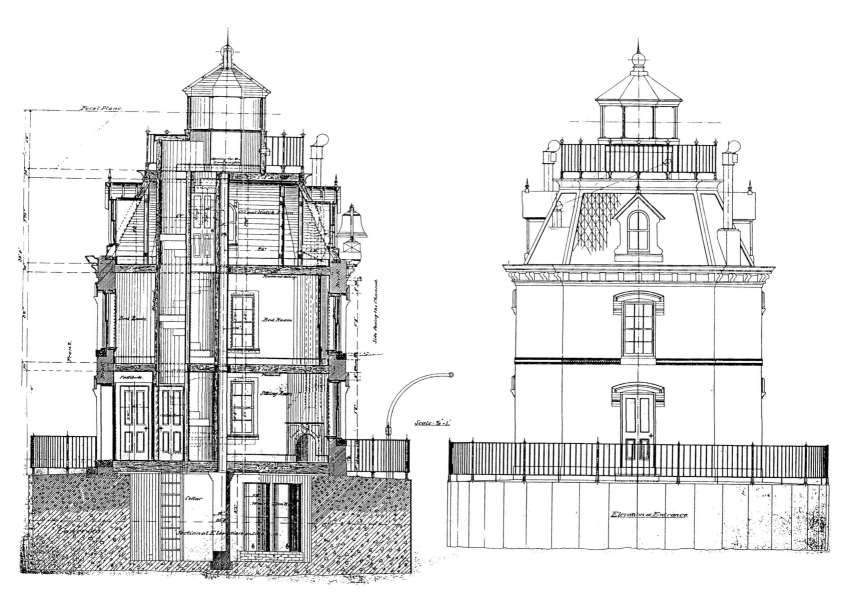

vice until October 30, 1883, because the engineers wanted to give "due notice to mariners."[10]

The lighthouse had a brown cylinder serving as the foundation for an octagonal red brick dwelling with a white mansard roof and dormers. The octagonal fourth-order lantern, resting on the center of the roof, had helical bars or astragals and was fitted with a fourth-order lens.[11]

Eleven years passed before another caisson lighthouse went up in Maryland waters; this time it was located in the southern part of the state at Solomons Lump. Solomons Lump is a shoal that extends out from Smith Island to near the regular channel of Kedges Straits. A buoy placed on the site proved inadequate, and John Donohoo's light at Fog Point, which marked the entrance into Kedges Straits from the bay, was ineffective in guarding vessels against the shoal. The Lighthouse Board, in response to an assessment requested by the House of Representatives, recommended erecting a screwpile lighthouse on Solomons Lump. Since this light would also be effective in guiding vessels into Kedges Straits, it recommended discontinuing Fog Point light when the new light went into service.

Several years passed before Congress appropriated the $15,000 needed for construction. On June 21, 1875, after the site had been selected, construction began on a screwpile lighthouse. A square dwelling sat on five wrought iron piles and had a lantern rising out of the roof. Workers put up the lighthouse in fewer than ninety days, and on September 10, 1875, the keeper displayed the light for the first time.[12]

This lighthouse served until January 1893, when moving ice pushed it over, leaving part of the structure submerged. The following June the Lighthouse Board had all movable property taken away and a lens lantern placed on the wreck, not only to mark it as a hazard but also to provide a temporary substitute for the light. Solomons Lump was such an important light that within two months of the accident Congress appropriated $30,000 to erect a replacement.

The District engineers began developing new plans for a sturdier screwpile structure, but as these neared completion the Lighthouse Board reconsidered, saying they did not wish to risk "the destruction of another light-house by the ice" and would erect instead "a structure which

The Sandy Point Shoal lighthouse (1883) was a three–story dwelling topped by the lantern. The first level contained the entrance to the spiral staircase, a kitchen, pantry and sitting room with a fireplace. The second level contained bedrooms and the third floor housed the watch room.

(Superstructure elevations, 1883. National Archives, Philadelphia)

Following pages:
The Sandy Point Shoal lighthouse welcomes international visitors as a schooner flying the flags of Nova Scotia and Canada sails down the Chesapeake.

(MSA SC – 2796 – 151)

The Solomons Lump Shoal extends out from Smith Island nearly to the channel of Kedges Straits. A screwpile was erected at the site in 1875 and served until 1893 when it was wrecked by ice. Construction of a caisson structure began in April 1895 and the lighthouse went into service in September. Originally there was a white octagonal brick and frame dwelling with the brick light tower built into it. Today only the square light tower stands on the steel caisson and the cast–iron cylinder.

(Photo by F. Ross Holland, 1987)

by its mass and weight could oppose an effective resistance to any movement of ice." The $30,000 appropriation was inadequate to build such a structure, but fortunately Congress approved the use of savings on the Wolf Trap lighthouse in Virginia for work at Solomons Lump. The plans for the new lighthouse were completed in August 1894, after which the Board asked for bids. As was typical at the time, the work was divided into two parts, manufacture and delivery of the ironwork to Lazaretto Depot and erection of the lighthouse.[13]

The contractor for the ironwork, Chamberlin, Delancy and Scott, delivered the material to the Lazaretto Depot in April. On April 1, 1895, the contractor who was to erect the lighthouse, William H. Flaherty, began work on the caisson, which was launched on April 26. The first course of iron plates was installed and 22 inches of concrete poured to provide proper trim for towing the caisson to the site. On May 18, two tugs towing the caisson and a barge and two lighters filled with equipment and materials departed for the site. The ersatz fleet arrived the next day, and by

May 20 the workers had the caisson anchored in position and had begun sinking it. By the last day of the month the structure was at its proper depth, but unfortunately it was not level. The workers were able to straighten it, but in the process the caisson and cylinder sank two and a half feet lower than intended. "To give the structure its proper height above water level," the contractor had to add another course of iron plates to the cylinder. The workers then filled the cylinder with concrete to about six feet above high water level. The cistern and cellar were installed, and the foundation was completed on June 30, 1895.

In less than a month the workers erected the dwelling and tower. Though they were finished by July 26, the lighthouse did not go into service until September 30, 1895. Much of this time was probably consumed in doing the finish work on the tower and installing the lantern and lens.[14]

The Solomons Lump lighthouse was erected on a steel caisson and cast-iron cylinder. Combined, they were 37 feet high. The cylinder at the top was 25 feet across. This concrete and iron foundation supported a brick light tower that was built into the dwelling. The latter was described in 1909 as made of brick, wood, and iron, and in 1950 as a "white, octagonal, frame dwelling." The first floor had one room, the second floor two rooms, and the cellar four rooms. The tower, seven feet across at the base and six feet six inches at the parapet, supported a fifth-order lantern of eight sides. A square gallery surrounded it. Today the dwelling is gone and only the square light tower stands on the foundation.[15]

In 1919 ships' masters and local residents urged that a buoy be placed on Mussel Hole at the entrance to Kedges Straits from Tangier Sound. The Lighthouse Board felt the same objective could be achieved by upgrading Solomons Lump light. At the time the Cherrystone lighthouse in Virginia was being downgraded, so the Board had its fourth-order lens sent to Solomons Lump and the Solomons Lump fifth-order lens returned to Cherrystone.[16]

By 1897 the Lighthouse Board had become concerned about the thirty-mile stretch of shoal water on the east side of the main channel of the bay and the danger it presented to the deeper drafted ships that increasingly plied its waters. The solution the Board recommended was better lighting to help these vessels stay in the channel. It contended that the west side of the channel had high bluffs that were easily seen, but just the opposite was true on the east side. Where the shoals were, the land was low and difficult to see at night. The Board recommended placing a light on this side between Hooper Strait and Tar Bay and urged that an appropriation of $60,000 be made for the lighthouse.

Congress responded and on July 1, 1898, authorized the establishment of a lighthouse at Hooper Island not to exceed $60,000 in cost. The district engineers proceeded to make test borings to find the best site, after which they designed a structure and prepared specifications for contract proposals. The district engineer entered into a contract for $18,955 with the Variety Iron Works Co. of Cleveland for the ironwork. The agreement called for the delivery of the caisson, foundation cylinder, and ironwork for the brick pier by September 13, 1899. A contract was also let to erect the lighthouse.[17]

The ironworks manufacturer delivered the required metal more than a month late, but it turned out to be of little importance, for the contractor who was to erect the Hooper Island lighthouse failed to begin work. The Lighthouse Board rebid the contract in May 1900, and this time it was let to Toomey Brothers of Guilford, Connecticut, for $29,000. Meanwhile, the iron-

The Hooper Island lighthouse, near Hooper Strait on the eastern side of the bay, was built by Toomey Brothers of Connecticut, and went into service in 1902. It rested on a cast–iron cylinder measuring 33 feet across, which expanded into a "trumpet shape at the top." The tower had four stories, a circular watch room on the parapet and the lantern above.

(U.S. Coast Guard photo. F. Ross Holland Collection. Hooper Island sectional elevation, 1898. National Archives, Philadelphia)

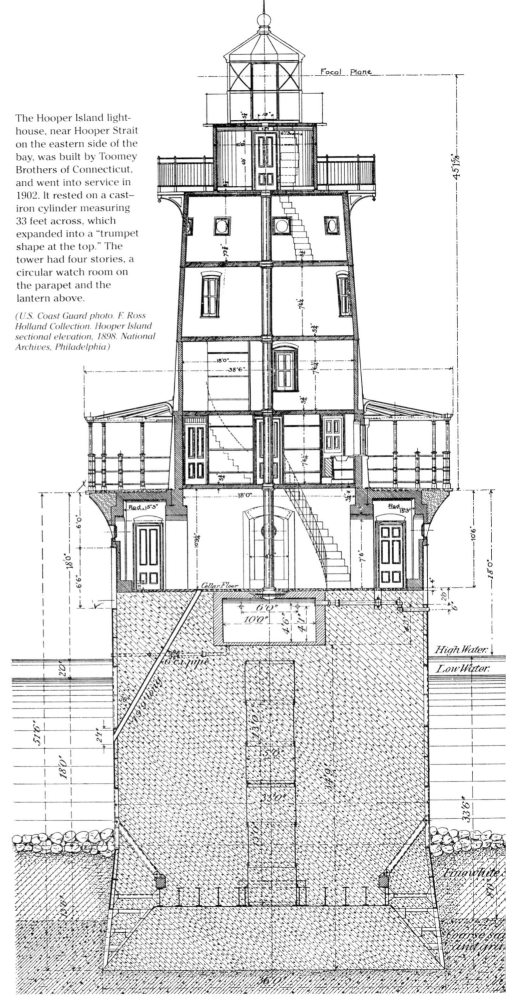

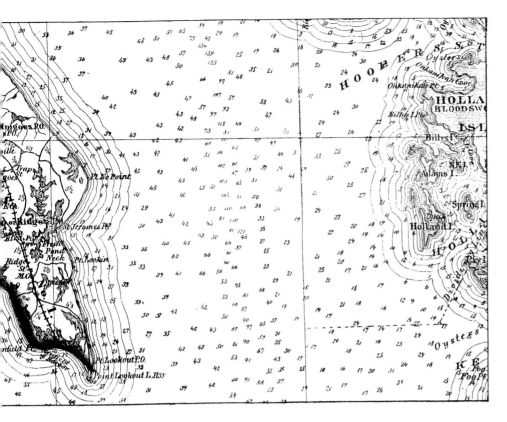

In 1891 the Lighthouse Board proposed a lighthouse for Point No Point, north of Point Lookout. The justification was much the same as it had been for the Hooper Island lighthouse: the danger the 30–mile stretch of shoals posed for the larger vessels that were becoming common in the Chesapeake. In 1901 Congress appropriated funds for the lighthouse.

(Detail: The New Topographical Atlas .... MHT Library)

Opposite page:
The Point No Point construction contract was awarded in 1902 to Toomey Brothers, the firm that had built the Hooper Island lighthouse. Plagued by bad luck, bad weather and construction mishaps, the firm finally completed the work in 1905.

(U.S. Coast Guard photo, 1960. F. Ross Holland Collection)

work contractor had delivered the remaining metal in December 1899.

In early February 1901, at a site on the Baltimore waterfront, the contractor began working on the caisson. Launched on May 21, 1901, this caisson and cylinder were to be put in position by the pneumatic method. For this purpose the caisson had an air shaft, working chamber, and temporary floor in place. The air shaft, located in the center of the caisson, allowed the workmen to get to the very bottom of the caisson to remove the sand, which was done with an air pump. The caisson was towed to the harbor at Mill Creek and the Patuxent River, where the fifth course of plates was added to the cylinder. An equivalent section was added to the air shaft.

On July 6, 1901, the caisson was towed to the site and the work of filling the cylinder with concrete began. Just over a month and 30 feet of concrete later, with the help of the sand pump, the caisson and cylinder had been sunk 5 feet 10 inches into the shoal. The air lock was put into place and the compressor made ready for operation. By August 26 the cutting edge of the cylinder was nearly nine feet below the surface of the shoal, and the concrete filling had reached the 34-foot mark. Five days later, the cutting edge reached 13.5 feet, the desired level. During this period more plates were added to the cylinder, and concrete continued to flow into it. On October 7 workmen finished filling the cylinder, and others began building the wall of the cellar, which was lined with brick. That work was com-

pleted by the 25th, and setting the iron pieces for the tower began. A little more than a month later the builders had the tower up and the lantern, watchroom, and main galleries in place. Interior finish work occupied their time until February 10, 1902, when weather halted all construction. Some riprap had been laid when the cylinder was set, and in April, more was placed around it as further protection against scouring. Toward the end of April the interior work was finished. Fitted with a fourth-order lens emitting a flashing white light, the lighthouse went into service on June 1, 1902.[18]

The new lighthouse rested on a cast-iron cylinder measuring 33 feet across and "expanding to a trumpet shape at the top." The cylinder, which rested on a conical caisson, contained the cellar at its top with cisterns for water below. Brick walls divided the cellar into several compartments for oil, fuel, and provisions. The tower, painted white when it was erected, tapered from 18 feet across at the base to 17 feet at the parapet. It had four stories, with a circular watchroom resting on the parapet and the lantern above. The focal plane of the lens was 63 feet above mean high water. Galleries circled the base of the light tower, the watchroom, and the lantern. A fog bell was installed on the watchroom gallery.[19]

As the Hooper Island light was going up, across the bay another lighthouse was also under construction at contradictorily named Point No Point, six miles north of Point Lookout. In 1891 the Lighthouse Board proposed a light at this place for much the same reasons it used in justifying the Hooper Island lighthouse. It pointed out the 30-mile stretch of shoals and the danger they posed for the larger vessels that were becoming more common on the Chesapeake, and identified the segment of this stretch for which there were no guides. Congress, however, was not stirred by this proposal. The Board repeated its request for the next three years, suggesting in 1894 that in view of the site's exposure to weather, a caisson lighthouse would be required, which would increase the cost estimate from $35,000 to $70,000. When Congress continued to ignore the request, the Board dropped the issue until 1900, when it reiterated its arguments for a lighthouse at Point No Point. This time Congress was swayed, and in March 1901 it appropriated $65,000 for a lighthouse and fog signal.[20]

The district engineer moved fast, and in May 1901 he made test borings to determine "the character of the foundation strata." With this information, he settled on the design of the pro-

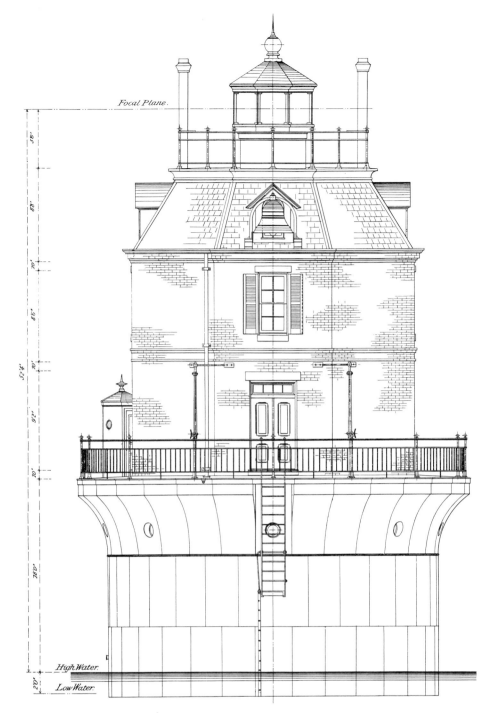

Focal Plane.

High Water.

Low Water.

The 1901 drawing above shows the Point No Point lighthouse exterior but the unusual sectional elevation to the right provides an illustrated construction record of the last months of work, including the note, "Inside of Lantern finished December 24." Although the caption notes that the major work was completed on January 7, 1905, the Point No Point lighthouse did not go into service until April 24, 1905.

(National Archives, Philadelphia)

posed lighthouse, and the district engineer prepared detailed plans and specifications, which were sent out for bid. The bids were received and opened in the middle of December 1901. The low bid for the metalwork was $9,475 and for the erection of the structure, $38,880. The successful bidder for the construction work was again the Connecticut-based firm of Toomey Brothers and Company, who had put up the Hooper Island lighthouse. Like that structure, the Point No Point caisson was to be set at its site pneumatically.

By June 1902 seven courses, or sections, of the cylinder had been finished, as well as much of the other metalwork, including the lantern gallery railing and ladders. Two sections were turned over to Toomey Brothers, who sent them to Solomons Island to be secured to the wood

caisson. In August the construction crew began putting together the wood caisson, which was 32 feet square and 13 feet tall. Two courses of iron plates were bolted to its roof. The bottom of the caisson was the working chamber, and an air shaft had been run to it. Near the end of January 1903, work stopped for the winter.

On March 23, 1903, work resumed. The third course of iron was added to the cylinder, and 12 inches of concrete were poured inside it. On April 3 a tug towed the Point No Point caisson to the construction site. Shortly after its arrival, the working platform collapsed and wrecked the caisson, which turned over, breaking off the second and third courses of plates. A northwest gale was blowing, and it sent the damaged caisson drifting down the bay. The tug took off in pursuit and found it on April 5 near the mouth of the Rappahannock River in Virginia. Taking it in tow, the tug pulled the caisson back to Solomons, where it was flipped back over with the first course of the cylinder up. Workers added two more courses of iron, and on the night of October 21 the cylinder was towed back to the site, where it was quickly positioned on the bottom. On October 23rd about 225 tons of riprap were dumped around the cylinder to prevent scouring.

Workers, meanwhile, began rebuilding the work platform, which also held their quarters, and bolted two more tiers of iron to the cylinder, leaving off a few plates on the fifth course for access. By February, concrete had been poured to three inches above the third course. About that time, disaster again visited the construction site when "a heavy field of moving ice" struck the platform, dumping the air compressor, boiler, iron plates, part of the air shaft, workmen's quarters, tools, and cement into the bay. Fortunately, the cylinder was only slightly damaged. When conditions permitted, the workers began putting up another construction pier and poured more concrete into the cylinder. On June 2 they began sinking the caisson, and by the end of the month it had been sunk 13 feet into the bottom and the sixth course of iron had been added to the cylinder. Adding another course, the workers continued to fill the cylinder, leaving space for two cisterns and a cellar. The cylinder was 30 feet across and 51 feet high, its top 18 feet above the water. Near the top, the cylinder flared out to form a gallery at the base of the lighthouse.

A two-story octagonal brick lighthouse with a mansard roof and dormers was erected on the foundation cylinder. The roof supported an octagonal lantern with a gallery and railing. The lantern was fitted with a fourth-order lens alter-

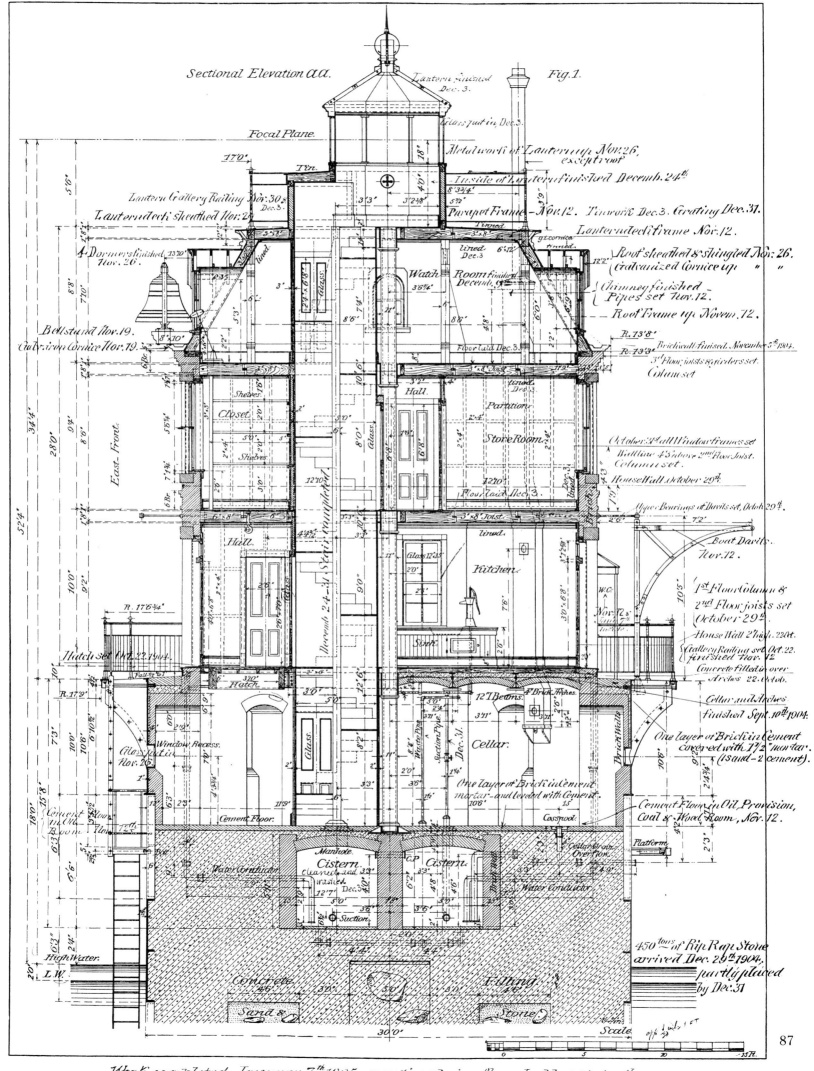

Sectional Elevation a a. Lantern finished Dec. 3. Fig. 1.

87

The tender *Holly*, shown here at Point No Point lighthouse in 1910, was one of the best known government vessels in Chesapeake Bay. A sidewheeler, the tender was commissioned for the lighthouse service in 1881 and for 50 years brought supplies to lighthouses in the Chesapeake, placed and replaced buoys in the bay, repaired and replenished acetylene lights, and performed the myriad duties demanded of light tenders and their crews. Within a few years of *Holly's* launching, President Grover Cleveland "discovered" the tender and later used her for excursions on the bay. *Holly* was one of the last of the sidewheelers to operate in the lighthouse service, retiring from duty in 1913.

(U.S. Coast Guard photo)

CUTOFF CHANNEL,
FRONT BEACON

(North Point Light)

This lighthouse is located off the westerly side of Fort Howard, on the northerly side of the mouth of the Patapsco River. It has a fixed white light visible 10 miles. This lighthouse can be seen from the cars at Jones' Creek, en route to and from Bay Shore Park.

*Could see this from the park where I was today.
V. Maude*

The front beacon of the Craighill Channel upper range, also called the Cut–Off Channel, was built on the foundation of one of the old North Point range lights and was a small brick structure. The keeper's house was on the shore. The Cut–Off Channel was dredged diagonally from Craighill Channel to Brewerton Channel. Ships remained on course in the Cut–Off Channel until a buoy guided them westward to the Brewerton Channel and its range lights, the front one at Hawkins Point and the rear at Leading Point. They continued on course to the Fort Carroll lighthouse and up the Patapsco to Baltimore Harbor.

(Postcard image, c. 1908. Jack Kelbaugh Collection. Map detail: The New Topographical Atlas.... MHT Library)

nately flashing white and red. The new lighthouse went into service on April 24, 1905.[21]

As Point No Point lighthouse was being completed, the last caisson lighthouse to be built in the Chesapeake had just been started. The Lighthouse Board had long wanted another lighthouse along the channels leading to the Patapsco River, but by the time the structure was built, its location and purpose had been changed. In 1890 the Board had wanted the lighthouse near the junction of the Craighill Channel and the Cut-Off Channel because the buoys that mark the turning points are difficult to distinguish, especially for large vessels. Besides this

point of visibility, the Board believed a sturdier, more prominent aid was needed to impress upon navigators the "character of the shoal" as well as to withstand the force of floating ice in winter. Consequently, the structure erected would be expensive—$60,000, the Board advised.

For several years the same request was made, and in August 1894 Congress appropriated the money. In 1895 the Board made borings that revealed the site selected for the lighthouse had 55 feet of soft mud laid over a stratum of sand. This discovery forced a reconsideration of the estimated cost of the lighthouse. First, however, a new site had to be chosen. By this time, the Board's Location Committee had suggested placing the proposed lighthouse at the entrance to Craighill Channel. Harbor improvements contemplated at this time would have altered the entrance to the channel, however, so the Board delayed their re-evaluation of the cost.[22]

In 1896 the "contemplated" improvements became "authorized," and the direction of the entrance to the channel was reconfigured. This shift, the Board reported, required "a corresponding change in the location of the Baltimore light-house, which is intended to mark this entrance." The engineers hoped the move would result in a better building location for the lighthouse. Their test pile "indicated that a safe foundation could be had at considerably less distance below the surface of the shoal than was possible at the location first selected."

With an appropriation of only $60,000 available, the lighthouse builders turned their

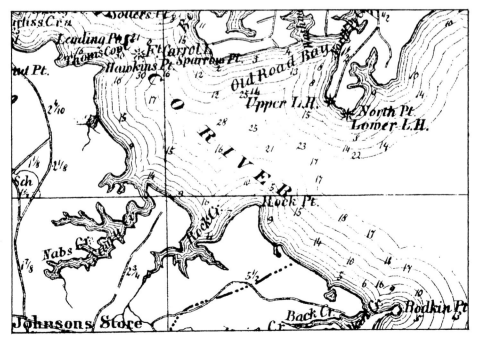

thoughts to a pile structure using disks. A disk, positioned on each of the piles, would help in keeping the pile structure stable. The engineers ordered a pile with a disk, and in September 1898 ran a test at the site. Using suction pumps, they were able to drive the pile and disk only 3 feet 6 inches in two hours. Discouraged, they broke off the tests, and later the Board asked Congress to increase the appropriation to $120,000. In 1902 Congress complied, but with the understanding that "the additional cost for its construction shall not exceed the sum of sixty thousand dollars." Construction was not to be easy, for the crew still had to deal with an overlay of 55 feet of semi-fluid mud. To get a stable foundation it would be necessary to go at least 6 feet 3 inches into the sand.[23]

The construction of the Baltimore lighthouse marked the final step in the development of the avenues to Baltimore harbor. Access to Maryland's most important port began with buoys placed in the Patapsco. Then the Bodkin Island lighthouse was built in 1822, followed in a few months by the range lights at North Point. These lights marked each side of the entrance into the river. In time the lighthouse at Fort Carroll and the range lights at Hawkins Point and Leading Point were added. By the late nineteenth century, channels in the bay had been dredged and defined with buoys until navigators, whether coming from north or south, could follow a channel that led to the entrance of the Patapsco and down the river to the port of Baltimore. The Baltimore lighthouse was the last lighthouse established on these channels.

The Baltimore lighthouse was built to help vessels coming from the south enter Craighill Channel. Once in the channel they followed the Craighill Channel range lights and passed the Baltimore lighthouse to port, staying in the channel until they came to a buoy that marked a turn in it. Ships then altered course and brought the Craighill Channel upper range lights—the front on the foundation of one of the old North Point lighthouses and the rear on Sparrows Point—into alignment, one light directly above the other. As long as the navigator kept the lights aligned, the vessel was in the channel and would pass the Seven Foot Knoll lighthouse on its starboard side.

When the channels were first established, Craighill Channel had continued on to Brewerton Channel, meeting it pretty much perpendicularly. But in the 1880s the New Cut-Off Channel was dredged diagonally from Craighill Channel to Brewerton Channel like the hypotenuse of a right triangle. Ships remained on course in the Cut-Off

Channel until another buoy marked a course alteration to westward, at which point they were guided by the Brewerton Channel range lights—the front at Hawkins Point and the rear at Leading Point. As long as these two lights were aligned, ships were traveling safely up the river in Brewerton Channel. Ships continued on this course to the Fort Carroll lighthouse, which they passed on its starboard side. After 1900 the Fort Carroll light marked the turn into the Fort McHenry Channel, which led to Baltimore harbor. Ships were helped to enter the harbor by a lighthouse at Lazaretto Point, across the entrance from Fort McHenry, and also, since 1913, by a light on a steel skeleton tower, which was boosted to a range light in 1934. Since the late twentieth century, the range lights for these channels have been exhibited twenty-four hours a day.

Vessels coming from the north followed Tolchester Channel to Brewerton Channel, entering it considerably eastward of the point used by vessels coming from the south. These ships fol-

The Craighill Channel upper range rear light is located at Sparrows Point, on the bank of Jones Creek, near Pennwood Wharf. An iron skeleton frame surrounds an inner wooden shaft covered with corrugated iron. A keeper's house was nearby. The range lights were exhibited on January 15, 1886.

(Photo by Robert J. Smith, Jr., courtesy Sparrows Point Division Public Affairs, Bethlehem Steel Corporation)

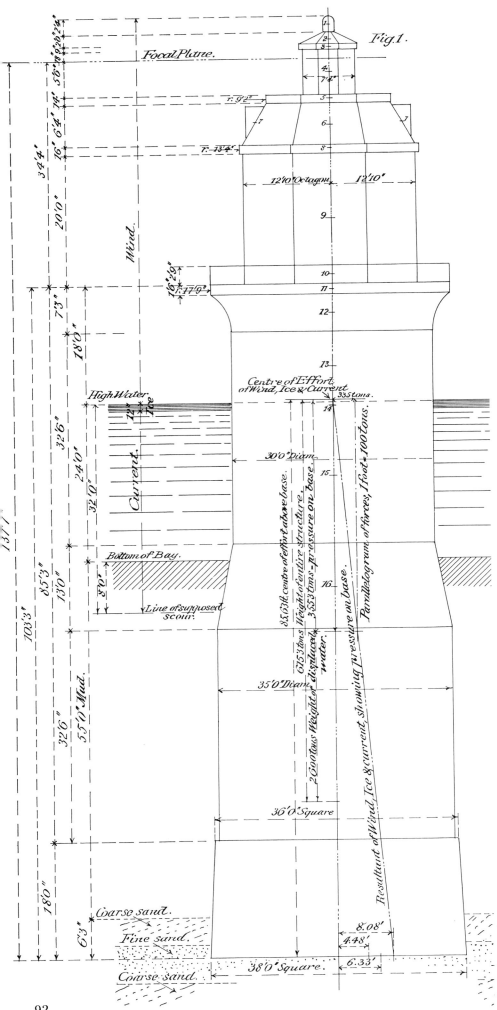

Fig. 1.

lowed the channel into the river and later into Fort McHenry Channel.

These old channels, lined and well-marked with buoys, are still the principal avenues for vessels destined for the Port of Baltimore. Two lighthouses and one set of range lights are no longer part of this system: The Seven Foot Knoll lighthouse has been moved ashore to Baltimore's Inner Harbor, the Fort Carroll lighthouse was deactivated many years ago, and the Lazaretto light went out of service in 1926. The Hawkins Point and Leading Point range lights, later renamed the Brewerton Channel range lights, have been replaced with simpler structures. The Seven Foot Knoll light has been replaced with an automated light erected on the remains of its screwpile foundation. The Baltimore lighthouse remains active, still marking the entrance to Craighill Channel.

Bringing the Baltimore lighthouse to completion was a long and difficult task, and the hardest part came after construction had begun. When Congress appropriated the additional money for a stronger lighthouse in 1902, the district engineer went about drawing plans and specifications for the lighthouse. Two years earlier the Lighthouse Board had written him to say they wanted a lighthouse that would resist "the combined effects of winds, ice, and current." Specifically, the structure would have to resist winds of

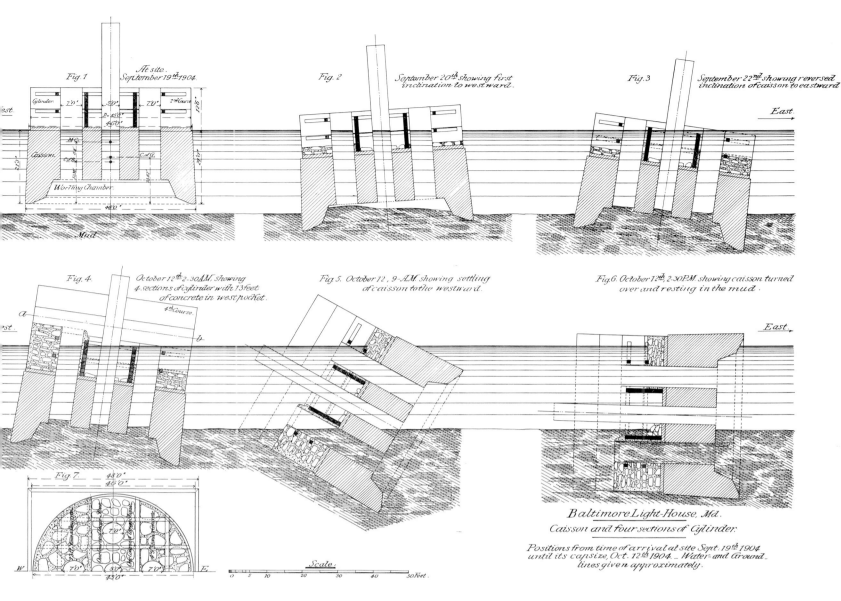

Fig. 1   At site. September 19th 1904.

Fig. 2   September 20th showing first inclination to westward.

Fig. 3   September 22nd showing reversed inclination of caisson to eastward.

Fig. 4.   October 12th 2-30 A.M. showing 4 sections of cylinder with 13 feet of concrete in west pocket.

Fig. 5. October 12, 9-A.M. showing settling of caisson to the westward.

Fig.6. October 12th, 2-30 P.M. showing caisson turned over and resting in the mud.

Fig. 7.

Scale:

Baltimore Light-House, Md.
Caisson and four sections of Cylinder.

Positions from time of arrival at site Sept. 19th 1904 until its capsize, Oct. 12th 1904. — Water- and Ground- lines given approximately.

100 miles per hour, ice pressure of 30,000 pounds per square foot, and a current of three miles per hour. Further, the Board felt the lighthouse should be built by the "pneumatic system of construction." The sum available for the work was $120,000.

In 1902 W. A. Jones, the district engineer, developed a design the Board approved. He moved into the next stage and prepared detailed plans and specifications, which were quickly approved in April 1903. The project was advertised in July, but by August only one bid had been received and it exceeded the construction appropriation by $80,000. Readvertising yielded another bid, and although it, too, exceeded the money available, at $91,900 it was within range of negotiation.

The bidder was William H. Flaherty of Brooklyn, N.Y., who had erected Solomons Lump and Smith Point lighthouses. He proposed to lower the bid to $86,000 if he could use large stones in the concrete and different timbers in the caisson, finish the cellar without brickwork, and reduce

the number of bolts in the caisson. The Board agreed, and the secretary of the Treasury approved this course. Meanwhile, the Atlanta Machine Works of Atlanta, Georgia, had been approved to undertake the metals contract, for which the company received $28,000. The remaining $6,000 was for contingencies.[24]

In early spring Flaherty had assembled material and begun construction of the wooden caisson at the Lazaretto Depot. By the end of June, with twelve courses completed, the wooden caisson was ready for launching and the five steel working shafts were in place. Iron plates for six courses of the cylinder had arrived at the depot. In August the 48-foot-square caisson was launched. Workers added eight more courses of timber to it, bringing the total to twenty, and secured two courses of iron plate.

The caisson was towed to the construction site on September 19 and lowered to the bottom. As it went down, workers added courses of plate iron to the cylinder. Two days after the work had begun, the caisson was eight feet into the mud

Opposite page:
Baltimore lighthouse was once America's only nuclear powered lighthouse. The elevation drawing to the left illustrates that three–fifths of the total structure is underwater. The series of figures above show the position of the caisson and its first four cylinder cast– iron tiers from the time of its arrival to the site on September 19, 1904 until it capsized on October 12, 1904. Note that as the concrete fill is added to the cylinder it inclines in the direction of the most weight; first to the west, then to the east, and finally completely to the west.

(F. Ross Holland photo, 1987; 1899 stability calculation drawing, National Archives, Philadelphia; 1904, National Archives, Philadelphia)

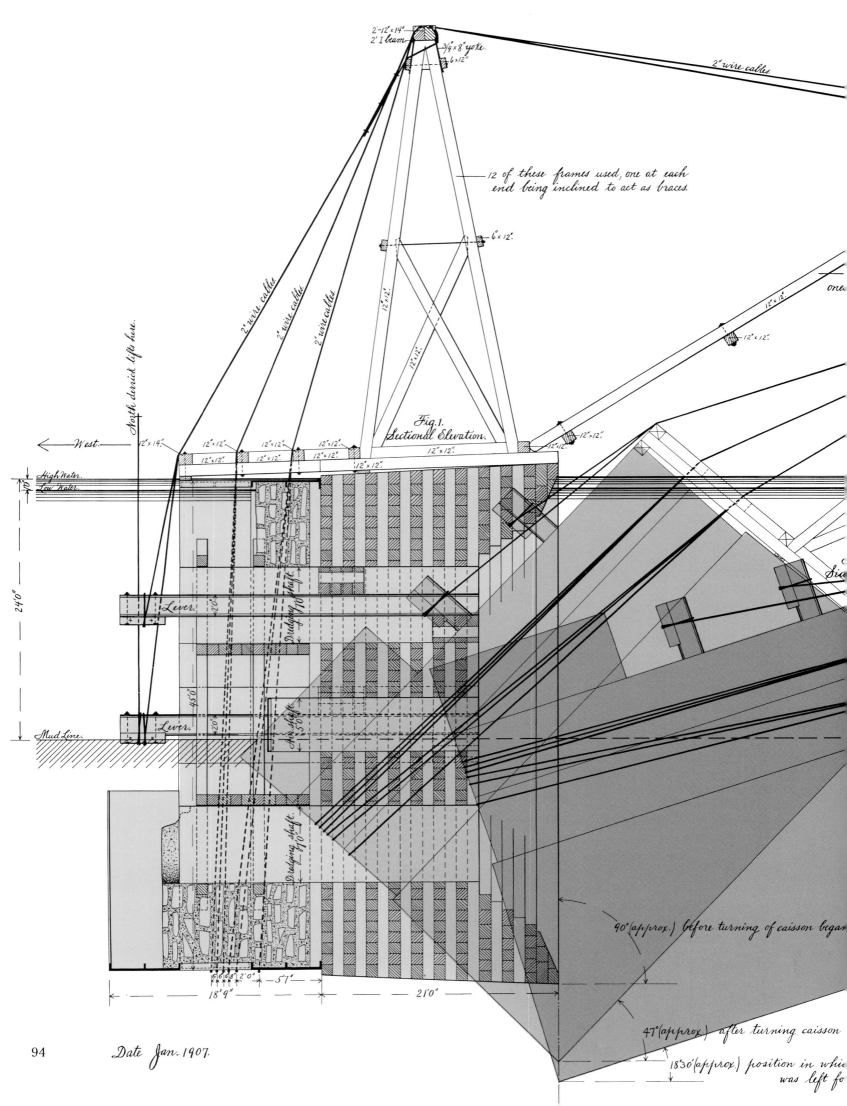

2'-12"×14"
2' I beam
¾×8" yoke.
6"×12".

2" wire cables

12 of these frames used, one at each
end being inclined to act as braces.

6"×12".

12×12'.

12"×12"

12×12'.

one

12"×12"

12"×12"

Fig.1.
Sectional Elevation.

North derrick lifts here.

West.

12"×14"   12"×12"   12"×12"   12"×12"   12"×12".
12"×12".   12"×12".   12"×12".   12"×12".

High Water.
Low Water.

240"

Lever.   20'

Dredging shaft. 10'

450"

Air shaft.
50'

Lever.   20'

Mud Line.

Dredging shaft. 10'

90°(approx.) before turning of caisson began

6"6"6"8" 2'0"   57'

18'9"   21'0"

47°(approx.) after turning caisson

18'30'(approx.) position in whi
was left fo

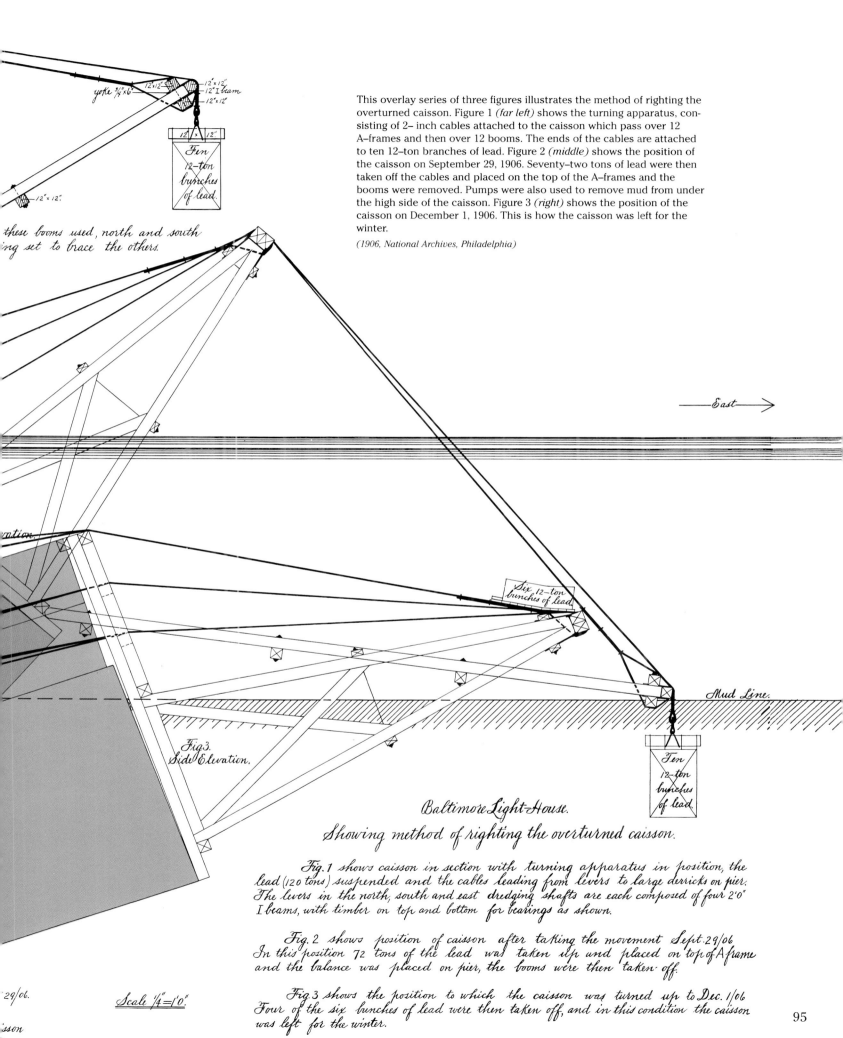

yoke 3/4" x 6"
12" x 12"
12" x 12"
12" I beam
12" x 12"
12" x 12"

Ten 12-ton bunches of lead.

these booms used, north and south
ing set to brace the others.

This overlay series of three figures illustrates the method of righting the overturned caisson. Figure 1 *(far left)* shows the turning apparatus, consisting of 2– inch cables attached to the caisson which pass over 12 A–frames and then over 12 booms. The ends of the cables are attached to ten 12–ton branches of lead. Figure 2 *(middle)* shows the position of the caisson on September 29, 1906. Seventy–two tons of lead were then taken off the cables and placed on the top of the A–frames and the booms were removed. Pumps were also used to remove mud from under the high side of the caisson. Figure 3 *(right)* shows the position of the caisson on December 1, 1906. This is how the caisson was left for the winter.

(1906, National Archives, Philadelphia)

→ *East* →

Six 12-ton bunches of lead

Mud Line.

Fig. 3.
Side Elevation.

Ten 12-ton bunches of lead.

Baltimore Light-House.

Showing method of righting the overturned caisson.

Fig. 1 shows caisson in section with turning apparatus in position, the lead (120 tons) suspended and the cables leading from levers to large derricks on pier. The levers in the north, south and east dredging shafts are each composed of four 2'0" I beams, with timber on top and bottom for bearings as shown.

Fig. 2 shows position of caisson after taking the movement Sept. 29/06. In this position 72 tons of the lead was taken up and placed on top of A frame and the balance was placed on pier, the booms were then taken off.

Fig. 3 shows the position to which the caisson was turned up to Dec. 1/06. Four of the six bunches of lead were then taken off, and in this condition the caisson was left for the winter.

29/06.

Scale 1/4" = 1'0".

isson
r.

No allowance made for any lateral movement that may have taken place at lower cutting edge

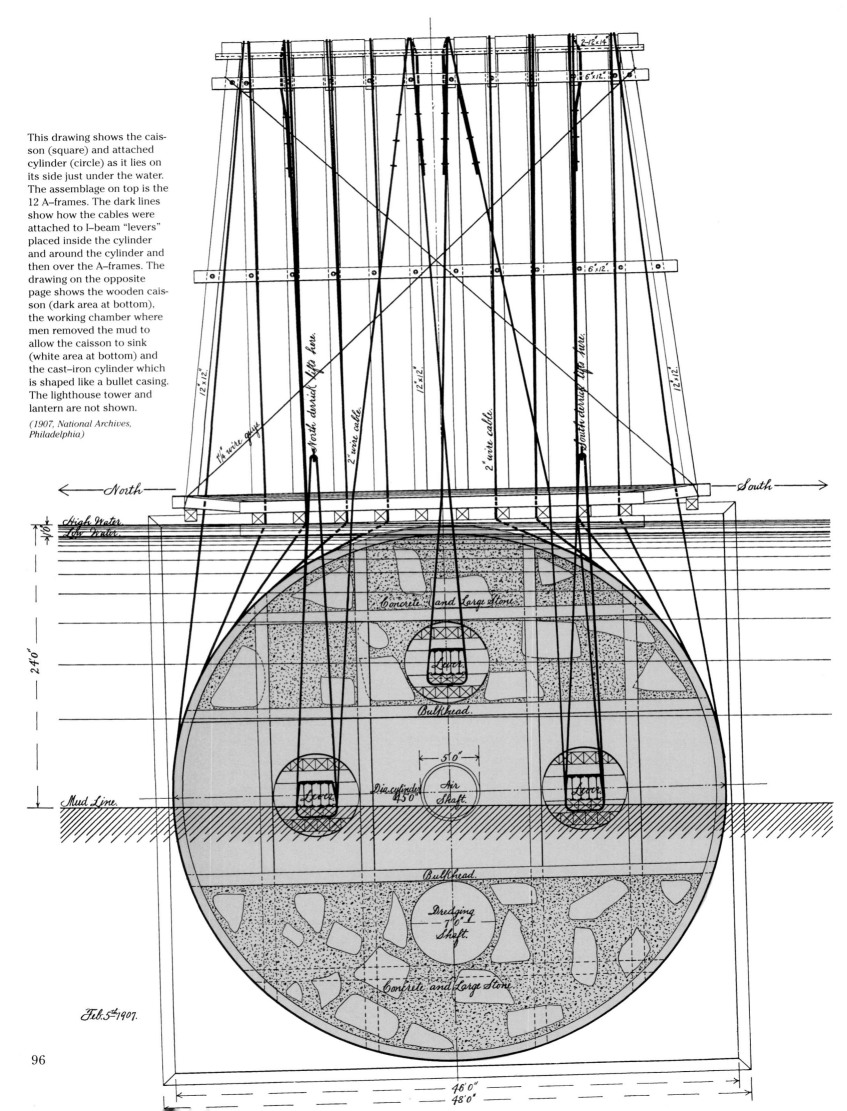

This drawing shows the caisson (square) and attached cylinder (circle) as it lies on its side just under the water. The assemblage on top is the 12 A–frames. The dark lines show how the cables were attached to I–beam "levers" placed inside the cylinder and around the cylinder and then over the A–frames. The drawing on the opposite page shows the wooden caisson (dark area at bottom), the working chamber where men removed the mud to allow the caisson to sink (white area at bottom) and the cast–iron cylinder which is shaped like a bullet casing. The lighthouse tower and lantern are not shown.

(1907, National Archives, Philadelphia)

2–12"×14

6"×12"

6"×12"

12"×12"

12"×12"

12"×12"

12"×12"

1¼" wire guys

North derrick lifts here.

2" wire cable.

2" wire cable.

South derrick lifts here.

← North

South →

High Water.
Low Water.

24'0"

Concrete and Large Stone.

Lever.

Bulkhead.

5'0"

Dia cylinder 45'0"

Air Shaft.

Lever.

Lever.

Mud Line.

Bulkhead.

Dredging 7'6" Shaft.

Concrete and Large Stone.

Feb. 5th 1907.

96

46'0"
48'0"

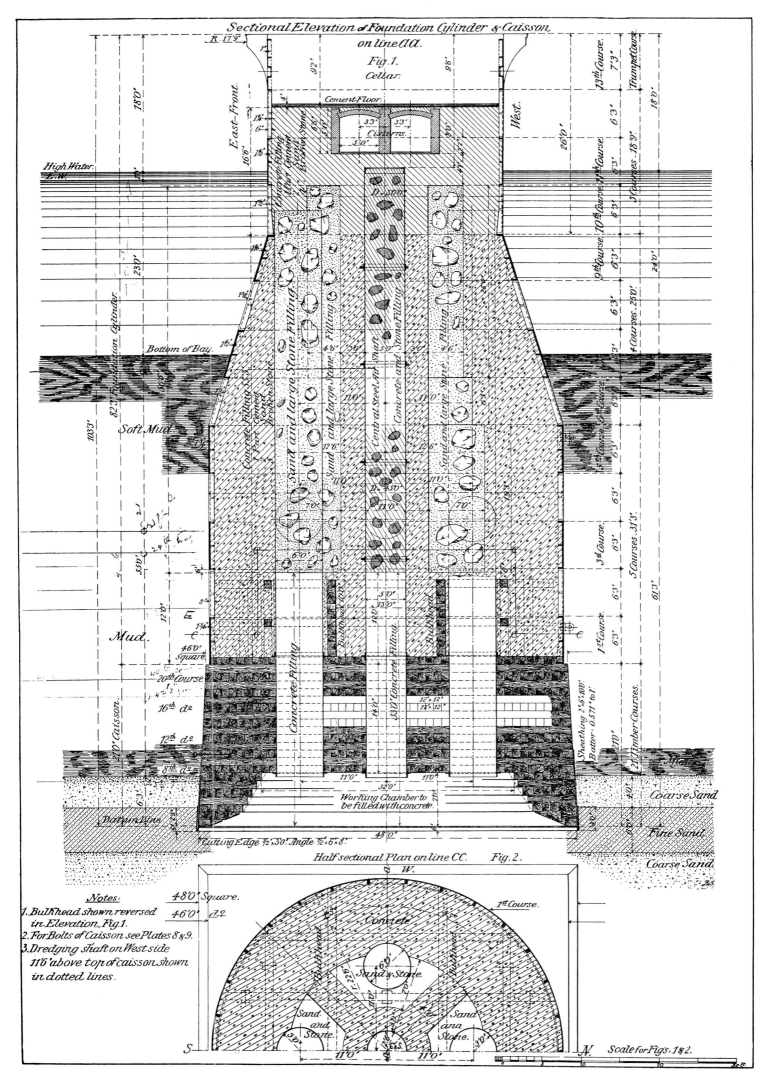

Sectional Elevation of Foundation Cylinder & Caisson, on line AA.

Fig. 1.
Cellar.

Half sectional Plan on line CC. Fig. 2.

Notes:
1. Bulkhead shown reversed in Elevation, Fig. 1.
2. For Bolts of Caisson see Plates 8 & 9.
3. Dredging shaft on West side 116' above top of caisson shown in dotted lines.

97

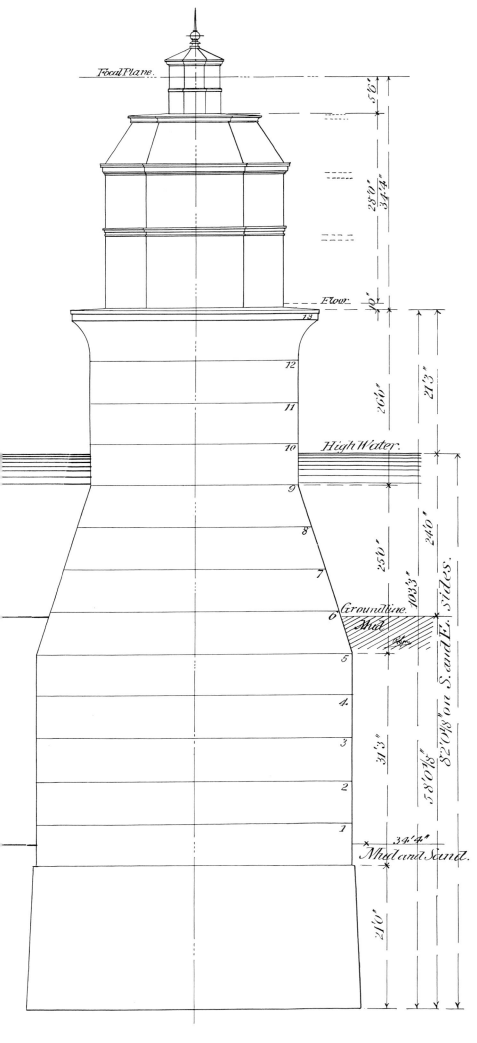

when "heavy seas filled the cylinder" causing it to lean seven feet to one side. On October 7 the contractors added two more courses of iron plating and attempted to bring the cylinder and caisson back to level by putting concrete in the high side. On October 12, a severe storm pushed the cylinder "flat on its side." At this point the contractor ceased operations, saying he would resume in the spring. In writing of the disaster, the *Baltimore American* on October 31, 1904, reported, "The erecting of this lighthouse is conceded to be one of the most difficult undertakings that lighthouse builders have attempted."[25]

By the time spring arrived, Flaherty had defaulted and his company was in the hands of a receiver. Legal maneuvering complicated the situation, and construction did not resume until the fall of 1905, when the contractor's surety, United States Fidelity and Guaranty Co., began work at the site. By December 6, the company had unbolted and removed to the Lazaretto Depot 62 of the 120 plates. Seven were damaged so badly they had to be replaced. By the following year the company had decided to use counterbalancing techniques to right the caisson. To facilitate their efforts, workers erected a U-shaped pier around the caisson to support their housing, storage for equipment and material, ten A-frames, a hoisting machine, three compressors, and a steam engine.

With heavy weights on wire cables strung over the A-frames and booms and the other ends of the cables attached to the caisson, the workers slowly moved the caisson and cylinder 45 degrees toward vertical. At this point, the weights were on the bottom, rendering them ineffective. Adjusting the weights allowed the men to pull the caisson another 10 degrees toward vertical. At this point pumps were used to remove mud from under the high side, and by November 20 the structure was about 17 degrees from vertical. A few days later, with no further movement, work ceased for the season.

When work resumed in April 1907, the company attached the third and fourth courses of iron plates to the cylinder. Placing 80 tons of stone on the high side of the caisson and pumping mud from under the same side brought the structure five feet closer to vertical. At this point the fifth and sixth courses of iron plates were added to the cylinder. About 100 additional tons of stone brought the structure within six feet of vertical. Further work eventually brought caisson and cylinder upright, and the caisson was sunk to 82 feet below sea level.

Filled with stone and concrete, with the basement and water cistern in place, the cylinder

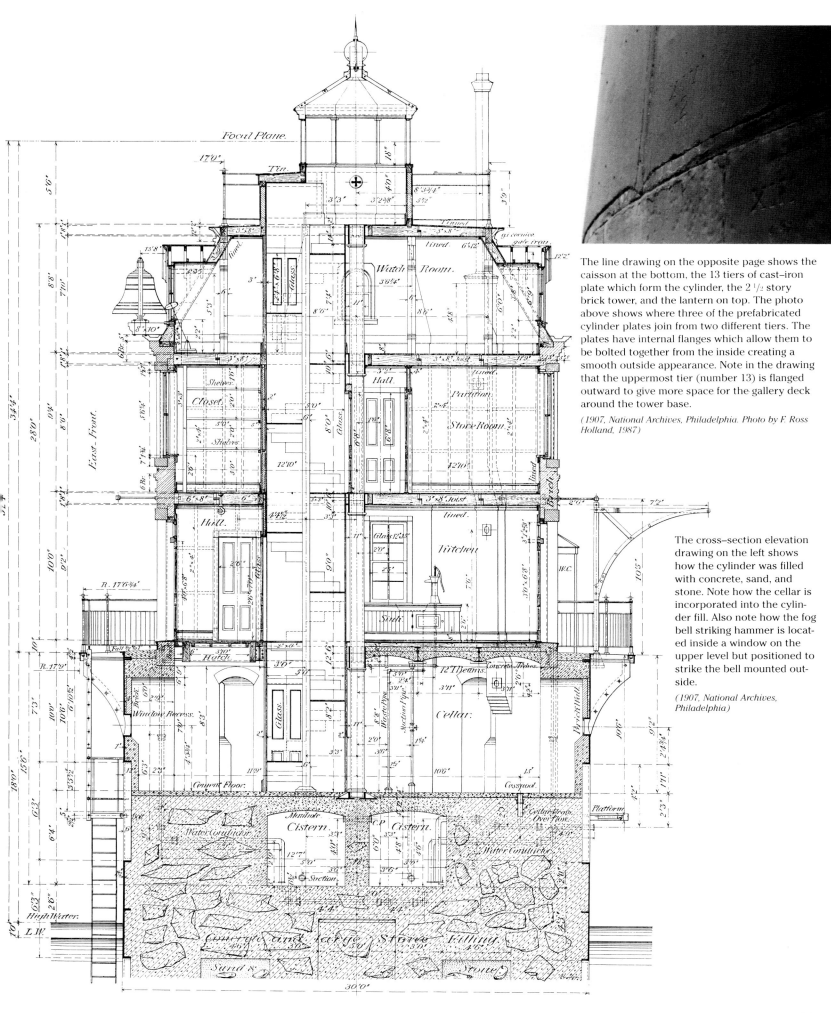

The line drawing on the opposite page shows the caisson at the bottom, the 13 tiers of cast–iron plate which form the cylinder, the 2 1/2 story brick tower, and the lantern on top. The photo above shows where three of the prefabricated cylinder plates join from two different tiers. The plates have internal flanges which allow them to be bolted together from the inside creating a smooth outside appearance. Note in the drawing that the uppermost tier (number 13) is flanged outward to give more space for the gallery deck around the tower base.

(1907, National Archives, Philadelphia. Photo by F. Ross Holland, 1987)

The cross–section elevation drawing on the left shows how the cylinder was filled with concrete, sand, and stone. Note how the cellar is incorporated into the cylinder fill. Also note how the fog bell striking hammer is located inside a window on the upper level but positioned to strike the bell mounted outside.

(1907, National Archives, Philadelphia)

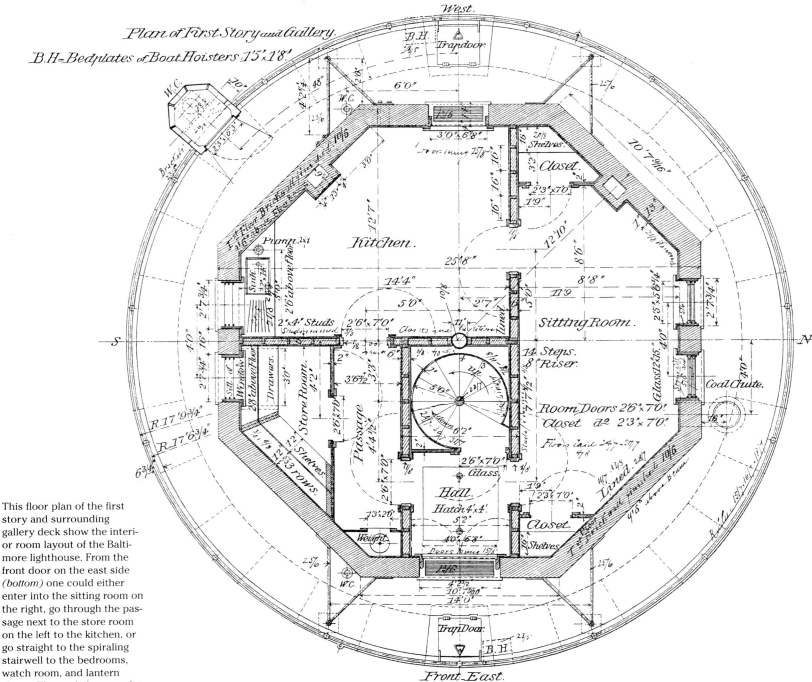

This floor plan of the first story and surrounding gallery deck show the interior room layout of the Baltimore lighthouse. From the front door on the east side (bottom) one could either enter into the sitting room on the right, go through the passage next to the store room on the left to the kitchen, or go straight to the spiraling stairwell to the bedrooms, watch room, and lantern above. The coal chute on the north side of the gallery deck allowed coal from the lighthouse tender to be delivered directly to the coal room in the cellar. Also note that the privy (marked W.C. = water closet) on the southwest side of the gallery deck was a simple straight shot into the Bay.

(1907, National Archives, Philadelphia)

became the foundation for the dwelling. By the end of June 1908, the brickwork was nearly complete, and the covering of the roof was underway. On September 10, 1908, Major W. E. Craighill, Fifth District engineer, notified the Lighthouse Board that United States Fidelity and Guaranty Co. had finished the construction of the Baltimore lighthouse.[26]

The long awaited lighthouse went into service on October 1, 1908. The station had a fog bell, and by 1923 the fog bell had been exchanged for a fog horn.[27]

The caisson of the Baltimore lighthouse rests on ninety-one piles driven into the bottom. It is

positioned 88 feet below high tide. The cast-iron cylinder, painted brown, rises 18 feet out of the water and flares outward at the top. The cylinder is filled with stone and concrete and serves as the foundation of the lighthouse. The upper portion of the cylinder is the basement of the lighthouse, where oil, coal, provisions, and lighthouse equipment were stored. Below the basement is a 3,500-gallon cistern. Portholes spaced around the cylinder admit light and allow ventilation to the basement.

The light gray brick dwelling is octagonal and has a slate-colored mansard roof surmounted by an eight-sided lantern of the fourth-order. The platinum-tipped lightning spindle has a ground wire running from it to the "underside pinnacle on [the] water closet," which was made of cast iron. The dwelling had brown doors and window frames and green shutters. This superstructure, which housed two keepers, has three rooms, a hall, a passageway, and two clothes closets on the first floor; three rooms, a large double closet, two clothes closets, and a hall on the second floor; and a large room on the third floor.

In 1923 the Bureau of Lighthouses decided the illuminant of the fourth-order lens should be changed to acetylene, a move that usually indicated the station was to be automated. Sure enough, on April 19, 1923, the commissioner of lighthouses requested permission of the secretary of Commerce to discontinue the two keepers' positions. The light station was converted to acetylene on May 1, 1923, and on that day the keeper was transferred to Point No Point and the assistant keeper to Seven Foot Knoll, each to an identical post. Responsibility for the upkeep of the Baltimore lighthouse was turned over to the keepers at Sandy Point lighthouse. Because of this added duty, a second assistant keeper was assigned to Sandy Point—the man who had been bumped from the keeper's position at Point No Point. The keeper of the Baltimore lighthouse was a Mr. Midgett, and the keeper of Point No Point lighthouse was also named Midgett. They were undoubtedly related, and one wonders what strains were put on family relations by this change. At the same time the light was automated, the fog horn was discontinued at Baltimore and replaced by a fog bell on Buoy 6C, in the vicinity of the lighthouse.

In May 1964 the Baltimore lighthouse became the world's first atomic-powered lighthouse with the installation of a 2¹/₂-ton atomic-powered generator. After one year, the generator was removed and the lighthouse returned to conventional power.[28]

The caisson lighthouse was the third step—following the lightship and screwpile lighthouse—in the evolution of effective aids to navigation for shoals and similar navigational hazards. Despite its many successes, the design was not the solution for all sites, as the Lighthouse Board found out in the 1890s, when it unsuccessfully tried to erect a caisson structure at the end of Diamond Shoals off Cape Hatteras, N.C.[29] However, for more protected sites, such as those on Chesapeake Bay, the caisson lighthouse was the ultimate solution for soft-bottomed sites.

Caisson lighthouses were very expensive in comparison to other types of structures. The cost, for example, of erecting one could be four

to five times that of building a screwpile lighthouse. At the same time, however, the caisson was much sturdier than the screwpile structure. Not only was it capable of resisting all the Chesapeake could visit upon it, but it was able to survive in areas with even more severe weather. The one caisson lighthouse erected south of Chesapeake Bay—Sabine Bank in Texas—is in an area susceptible to hurricanes and that lighthouse has survived, as have the caisson structures built in northern New England. Of all the traditional screwpile lighthouses erected in Delaware and Chesapeake bays, on the sounds of North Carolina, and on the Gulf Coast, only five have survived and three of those are in museum settings. On the other hand, virtually every one of the caisson lighthouses has survived and still functions as an active aid to navigation. Most important to the story told here, they have served traffic in the bay well.

In May of 1964 the Coast Guard experimented with lighting lighthouses using nuclear power. The chosen test site was Baltimore lighthouse. In the photo above, a 4,600–pound SNAP–7B Strontium–90 powered, 60–watt isotopic fuel cell generator was installed by crane from a Coast Guard buoy tender and passed through the east doorway on a trolley platform. The atomic powered generator, smaller than a 55–gallon drum, was housed in a specially constructed heavy steel box. The test ran for a year and upon completion, the nuclear equipment was removed and nuclear power for an American lighthouse has not been attempted since.

(U.S. Coast Guard photo. F. Ross Holland Collection)

Chapter 5

The Trusty Screwpile: A Bay Tradition

Although caisson lighthouses were erected with regularity after they came to the Chesapeake in 1873, they did not completely replace the screwpile lighthouse as a design for offshore sites. Indeed, after 1873 eleven screwpile lighthouses were erected in Maryland waters.

Generally, the lighthouse builders selected the caisson design for exposed sites likely to get heavy ice during the winter and the screwpile design for more protected sites. There were exceptions, of course. For example, a screwpile design was chosen for the exposed site on Thomas Point Shoal. Over the years the lighthouse was buffeted by ice, a threat revealed by the mounds of stone on the north and south sides of the old structure, dumped there to protect it.

By the last quarter of the nineteenth century, mariners consistently complained about the lighthouse on Thomas Point. Built by John Donohoo in 1825 and rebuilt in 1840, it stood on the point itself, a mile and a quarter back from the end of the shoal it was meant to mark. Vessels in the main channel of the bay that drew more than eight feet of water did not always see the light in time to avoid the shoal. Although the shoal was marked with a buoy, that proved to be an inadequate aid, and, the Board reported in 1872, "it is a matter of frequent occurrence to see vessels ashore there." The location of the lighthouse, the Board added, "is such that little use can be made of it at night, and in times of foggy or thick weather it is utterly useless." The Board believed a lighthouse of the screwpile type placed on the end of the shoal and equipped with a fog bell would better serve the vessels plying the bay. The Board urged the appropriation of $20,000 for a new lighthouse, pointing out that in any case the existing lighthouse needed extensive repairs.

The tower leaked, often flooding the inside and ruining materials. Congress responded quickly to these strong arguments, appropriating the money to replace the lighthouse at Thomas Point with one on the shoal on March 3, 1873.

During the winter of 1872-73, the Love Point lighthouse was damaged so severely that it was out of service for a time and required $10,000 for repairs. In light of this disaster, the Lighthouse Board decided against using the screwpile design at Thomas Point Shoal. It seemed to them that the site demanded a caisson-type lighthouse similar to the one then being erected for the Craighill Channel range front light. The caisson type was more expensive than a screwpile lighthouse, and consequently an additional appropriation of $25,000 was needed.

This request apparently was caught in a directive issued by the House of Representatives asking all government departments to revise their budget estimates. The Lighthouse Board ceased work on plans for a caisson lighthouse at Thomas Point Shoal, opting instead for a sturdier screwpile structure, and asking for $15,000 instead of $25,000. Congress provided the money, and the Board erected a lighthouse resting on 10-inch wrought iron piles. The screwpile lighthouse began operation on November 20, 1875, and the old Thomas Point lighthouse was taken out of service.[1]

Thomas Point Shoal lighthouse was built on piles screwed 11 feet 6 inches into the bottom of the bay. The six-room hexagonal dwelling was painted white and surmounted by an eight-sided fourth-order lantern that contained a three-and-a-half order lens exhibiting "a red flash every 20 seconds." The light's focal plane was 42 feet 6 inches above mean high water. Four iron tanks, each with a capacity of 200 gallons, held water obtained from runoff.[2] Over the years Thomas

The Thomas Point Shoal screwpile lighthouse replaced two earlier towers built on the bluff behind the shoal they were meant to mark. The lighthouse, at the entrance to the South River, began operation on November 20, 1875.

(Photograph by M.E. Warren)

103

The Thomas Point Shoal lighthouse, pictured above, circa 1960, with a Coast Guard crew visible, was protected from floating ice by large deposits of stone and by heavy cast–iron ice breakers. The inset photo shows the lantern's metal ventilator and lightning rod.

(U.S. Coast Guard photo. F. Ross Holland Collection; MHT photos by Mark R. Edwards, 1985)

The lighthouse rests on 10– inch wrought–iron piles which were screwed 11 feet 6 inches into the bottom of the bay. The structural system connection is shown above.

(MHT photo by Mark R. Edwards 1985)

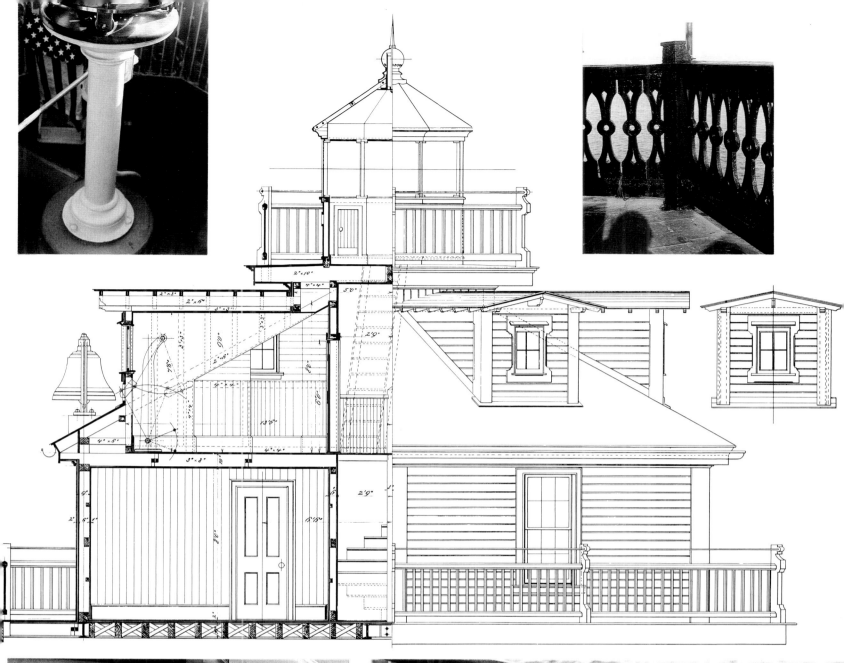

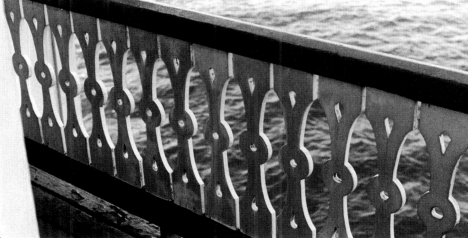

The Thomas Point Shoal hexagonal frame house is surmounted by an eight–sided lantern, circled by a six–sided walkway. The detail photos above show the pedestal supporting the fourth–order Fresnel lens and the Victorian railing on the lantern level. The 1867 sectional elevation shows the interior stairway and ladder leading to the lantern deck. A privy was located on the main deck walkway, which was circled by a Victorian railing.

(MHT photos by Mark R. Edwards, 1985; National Archives, Philadelphia; MHT photos by Mark R. Edwards, 1985)

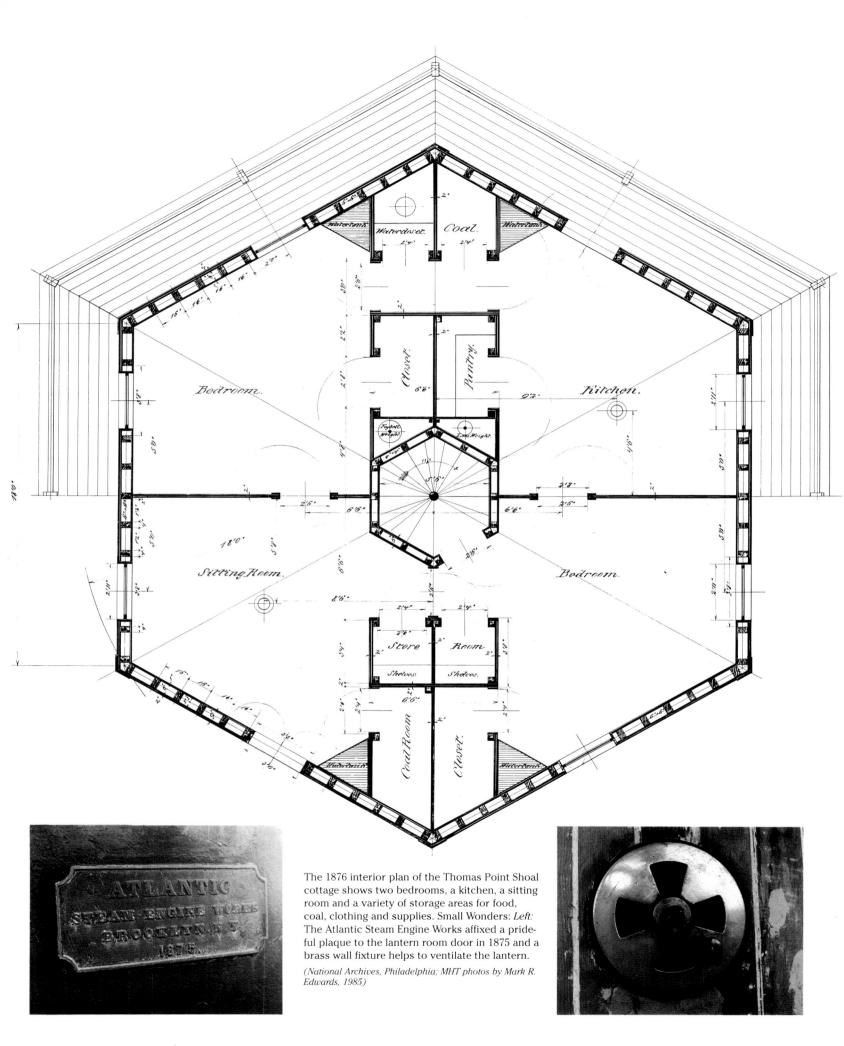

Waterdoset. | Watercloset. | Coal. | Watertank.

Closet. | Pantry. | Kitchen.

Bedroom.

Front Weight | Light Weight

Sitting Room. | Bedroom.

Store | Room

Shelves. | Shelves.

Coal Room | Closet.

Waterdank. | Watertank.

ATLANTIC
STEAM ENGINE WORKS
BROOKLYN, N.Y.
1875.

The 1876 interior plan of the Thomas Point Shoal cottage shows two bedrooms, a kitchen, a sitting room and a variety of storage areas for food, coal, clothing and supplies. Small Wonders: *Left:* The Atlantic Steam Engine Works affixed a prideful plaque to the lantern room door in 1875 and a brass wall fixture helps to ventilate the lantern.

(National Archives, Philadelphia; MHT photos by Mark R. Edwards, 1985)

Point Shoal had fourth-order lenses, sometimes fixed, sometimes flashing. It was automated in 1986, and was the last lighthouse on Chesapeake Bay to have a keeper.

The year after the Thomas Point Shoal lighthouse was completed, another new screwpile went into service in the Potomac River. In June 1872 Congress had appropriated $9,000 for a light in the river at Shipping Point to mark the entrance to the anchorage in Quantico Creek. Apparently this appropriation took the Lighthouse Board by surprise, for when the district engineer and inspector examined the river, they concluded "that a light at Shipping Point [or in the near vicinity] would be of little, if any, use to navigation." Rather, "the place most in need of a lighthouse in the Potomac River," the Board said, "is at or near Matthias [sic] Point," which was twenty-four miles downstream. The Board recommended returning the appropriation for Shipping Point to the Treasury and asked Congress for a new appropriation of $20,000 for the construction of a lighthouse at Mathias Point. This location was near the Virginia side, at the first major bend in the Potomac, opposite the mouth of the Port Tobacco River. At the same time the Board asked for a lighthouse at Port Tobacco Flats, which it considered to be "one of the most difficult places for experienced navigators, who are familiar with the river, to pass at night." The depth of the river changed sharply and abruptly at the flats, and the strong currents tended to set vessels on the shoals. For sailing vessels it was a particularly dangerous stretch. "It is no uncommon sight," the Board elaborated, "to see a vessel aground on these flats. The United States naval steamer *Frolic* went ashore here during the summer of 1873, and remained for some time." The Board recommended an appropriation of $40,000 to build a lighthouse on the flats.

In June 1874 Congress appropriated $40,000 for a lighthouse and day beacon in this section of the Potomac. After careful examination the Lighthouse Board decided to erect the lighthouse at Port Tobacco Flats and the day beacon on the shoal off Mathias Point. The ironwork for the lighthouse was ordered, and a deed from the governor of Maryland indicates it was to be known as Port Tobacco Light Station. At some point, however, the sites were switched, and the lighthouse wound up safely on Maryland's Mathias Point Shoal.

Construction was delayed a year because of more pressing work in other sections of the Fifth District. Work finally began at Mathias Point in late September 1876, and by December 6 the structure was finished. It was a typical Chesa-

peake Bay screwpile lighthouse with a seven-room hexagonal dwelling painted white. The fixed white light of the fifth-order lens was displayed for the first time on December 20, 1876.[3]

Over the years, in addition to this lighthouse and those at Upper Cedar Point and Lower Cedar Point, the Lighthouse Board erected screwpile lighthouses at three other sites in the Potomac River—Cobb Point, Maryland Point, and Ragged Point. The construction of these lighthouses reflects the increased need for aids to navigation caused not only by the increased traffic on the river, but also by an increase in the size and draft of the vessels plying its waters.

In 1885 the Lighthouse Board recommended a lighthouse for Cobb Point, which marks the west side of the entrance into the Wicomico River from the Potomac. Vessels carrying oysters, tobacco, and other products, as well as three steamship lines, made the Wicomico a heavily traveled body of water. It was also attractive because of the good refuge it made from drifting ice and storms. Unfortunately, the river's mouth was nearly closed by bars, and a vessel making the slightest miscalculation would wind up on one of them. A lighthouse was needed, the Board advised, particularly for vessels entering or leaving the river at night. The Board asked Congress for $15,000 to put up the structure.

Receiving no positive response, the Light-

Administrative and jurisdictional problems delayed the construction of the Mathias Point Shoal lighthouse for years, but once work started in September 1876 the screwpile lighthouse on the Potomac River was completed in three months. This January 1948 photo shows a member of the station crew being evacuated from the lighthouse to a waiting Coast Guard cutter during two weeks of severe icing in the Potomac.

(U.S. Coast Guard photo. F. Ross Holland Collection)

The Lighthouse Board had requested a lighthouse for Cobb Point Bar on the Potomac as early as 1875, noting the dangerous entrance to the Wicomico River nearby. Finally authorized in 1887, work on the square screwpile lighthouse began in 1889 when the superstructure was framed at the Lazaretto Depot. The materials and metal work were moved to the site on November 1 and the lighthouse went into service on December 25.

(U.S. Coast Guard photo, March 1918. F. Ross Holland Collection)

house Board repeated its request in 1887. This time Congress authorized the lighthouse and provided the $15,000. The district engineer did not begin work until 1889, by which time the Board had decided to build a screwpile structure. Cobb Point Bar would be built at the same time and with the same plans as the Tangier Sound lighthouse in Virginia. The metal was ordered, and the carpenters framed the superstructures at the Lazaretto Depot. The manufacturer was slow in shipping the metalwork, but finally on November 1, 1889, all the materials were ready to be moved to the site. Work began on November 5, and by the end of the month the Cobb Point lighthouse was complete except for painting.

On December 25, 1889, the Cobb Point Bar

lighthouse exhibited its light for the first time. Its fourth-order lens gave off a fixed white light, with a focal plane 40 feet above water. Five screwpiles supported the square dwelling, which had a square tower supporting the octagonal lantern. The station was equipped with a fog bell operated by machinery.[4]

The next lighthouse to be erected in the Potomac was at Maryland Point, eight or nine miles southwest of Mathias Point. At this point the river makes a sharp right turn to the northwest. In 1887 the Lighthouse Board noted the channel here was narrow and the shoals only ten feet below the surface of the water. With so many deeper drafted vessels on the river, the Board felt a lighthouse was needed at this point and requested funding that year and the next. In 1888 they increased their request to $45,000, explaining that the character of the bottom probably required a caisson lighthouse, and in 1889 they increased it further to $50,000.

Finally, on August 30, 1890, Congress appropriated $50,000 for a lighthouse at Maryland Point. The engineer made boring tests in November, and the Lighthouse Board determined that, "with the bearing surface augmented by disks attached to the piles so as to rest upon the surface of the shoal," a screwpile structure would suffice. Using this construction technique also meant shorter piles could be used.

A contract was let for the ironwork, and it was delivered to Lazaretto Depot in March 1892. Meanwhile, carpenters were putting together the dwelling at the depot, but the press of other work on the bay slowed their work. In July the millwork arrived at the depot and carpenters assembled the framework of the dwelling, after which it was taken apart and packed for shipment to the site. On October 18, after all the material and equipment had been loaded, the tenders *Jessamine* and *Thistle* towed the scows to the construction site. *Jessamine* carried the work party.

At the site the men began putting up the working platform from which they would set the foundation. After all the screwpiles were in place, they slipped the sleeves and disks onto the piles and attached them. The crossbraces, connecting rods, and iron beams to support the dwelling were then fastened to the legs. Around the end of October, with the foundation in place, the crew started to erect the dwelling and raise the light. They completed their work on December 1, and on December 15, 1892, the light was exhibited for the first time.

The Lighthouse Board described the new aid to navigation as follows:

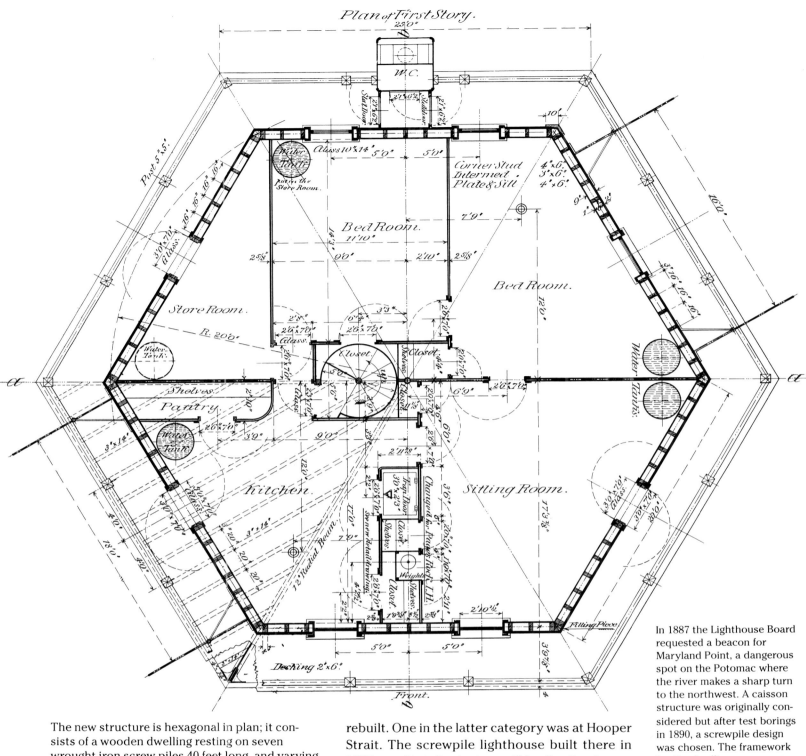

Plan of First Story.

The new structure is hexagonal in plan; it consists of a wooden dwelling resting on seven wrought iron screw piles 40 feet long, and varying in diameter from 7 inches at the top to 10 inches at the bottom or screw end. The piles penetrate 13 feet into the shoal and are provided with circular disks 5 feet in diameter, which rest on the surface of the shoal and augment the bearing capacity of the screws, the shoal being of such a character as to render this provision advisable.

The dwelling had nine rooms and was painted white with a red roof. The lighthouse was equipped with a fourth-order lens that emitted a flashing light and a fog bell operated by machinery.[5]

Meanwhile, out in the bay other screwpile lighthouses were being built, and in some cases

rebuilt. One in the latter category was at Hooper Strait. The screwpile lighthouse built there in 1867 was "totally destroyed" by floating ice on January 11, 1877. The tender sent out to investigate found the wreckage five miles south of the site. The tender's crew was able to recover the lens, the lantern, and some other objects before they had to get out because of the threatening ice. In reporting these events to Congress, the Lighthouse Board requested $20,000 to replace the structure. Congress appropriated the money, which permitted the district engineer to examine the site and do test borings, as well as prepare plans and specifications.

In 1878 work began on the new structure with construction of the frame dwelling at Lazaretto

In 1887 the Lighthouse Board requested a beacon for Maryland Point, a dangerous spot on the Potomac where the river makes a sharp turn to the northwest. A caisson structure was originally considered but after test borings in 1890, a screwpile design was chosen. The framework for the dwelling was assembled at the Lazaretto Depot in early 1892, then taken apart and packed for shipment to a work platform at the site. The light was exhibited on December 15, 1892.

(Maryland Point's first story plan, 1891. National Archives, Philadelphia)

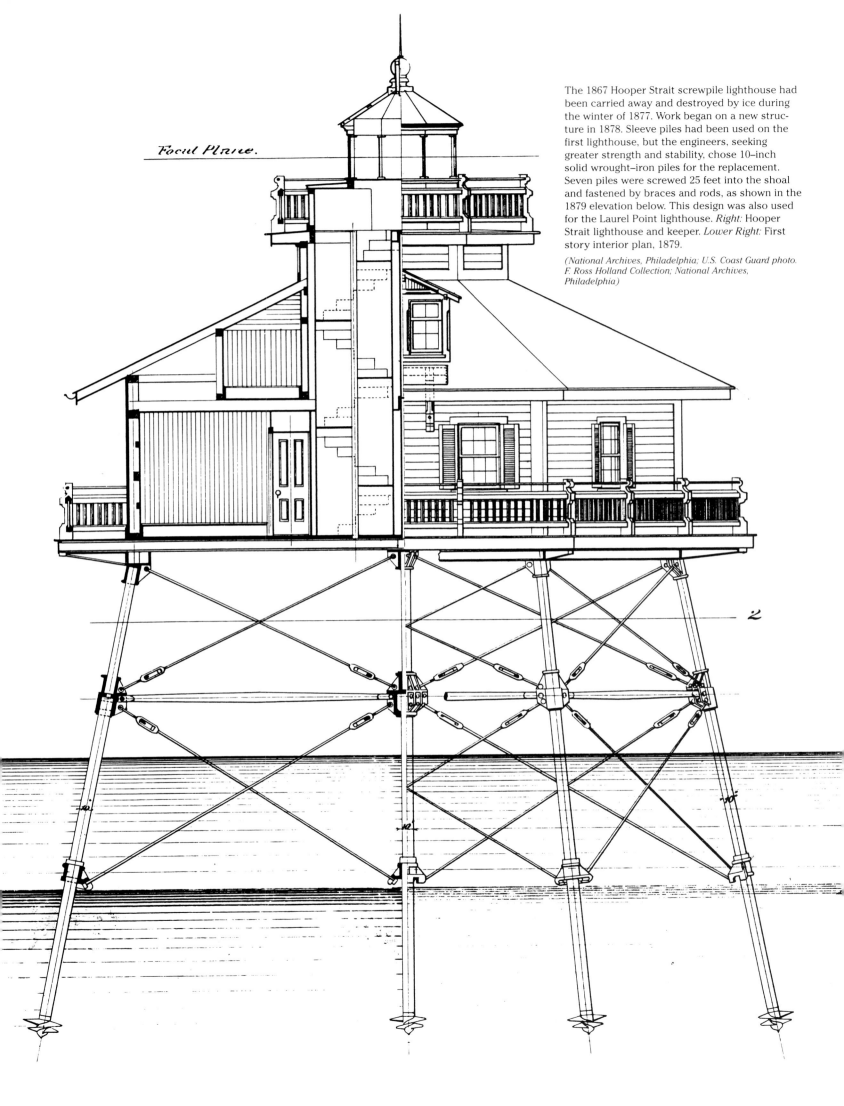

Focal Plane.

The 1867 Hooper Strait screwpile lighthouse had been carried away and destroyed by ice during the winter of 1877. Work began on a new structure in 1878. Sleeve piles had been used on the first lighthouse, but the engineers, seeking greater strength and stability, chose 10–inch solid wrought–iron piles for the replacement. Seven piles were screwed 25 feet into the shoal and fastened by braces and rods, as shown in the 1879 elevation below. This design was also used for the Laurel Point lighthouse. *Right:* Hooper Strait lighthouse and keeper. *Lower Right:* First story interior plan, 1879.

(National Archives, Philadelphia; U.S. Coast Guard photo. F. Ross Holland Collection; National Archives, Philadelphia)

Depot in February. Completed in June, the superstructure was taken down and assembled for shipment to Hooper Strait. When the ironwork arrived from the contractor in September, it was immediately loaded onto a contract vessel with the superstructure and moved to the building site. Workmen had already gone out to erect the work platform, and when the schooner arrived with materials the laborers began setting the foundation.

Sleeve piles had been used on the first Hooper Strait lighthouse, but this time the engineers determined that 10-inch, solid wrought iron piles would give greater strength to the foundation and better resist the buffeting of ice. The workmen and their machinery screwed seven of these piles 25 feet into the shoal and fastened braces and rods to the legs. Once the foundation was in place, they began to erect the hexagonal dwelling. This work was completed in early October, about seven weeks after the first pile had been set. On October 15, 1879, the fixed white light of the fifth-order lens grew brighter as the keeper traced the lucerne around the wick, and the lighthouse was in service.[6]

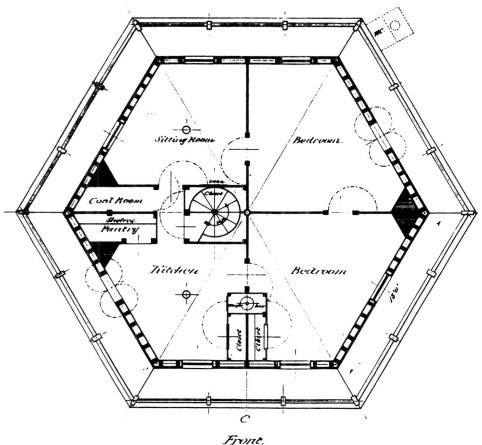

There had been agitation for a lighthouse on Drum Point at the mouth of the Patuxent River since the early 1850s. Vessels had often run aground on the shoal making off from the point and Congress had authorized a lighthouse in 1854. It was almost 40 years before a lighthouse at Drum Point began service however, probably due to difficulties in getting title to the land. The c. 1908 postcard image above shows the lighthouse on the north side of the entrance to the river.

(Jack Kelbaugh Collection)

Four years later, at the mouth of the Patuxent River on the other side of the bay, another screw-pile lighthouse went into operation. Efforts had begun years before to get a lighthouse at Drum Point to guide vessels into the river. The *American Coast Pilot* of 1850 said of the Patuxent: "This is one of the most frequented harbors on the Chesapeake, and it is common with those who seek shelter here, waiting for a fair wind, to remain at anchor until daylight before getting underway." Vessels were advised to guide on Drum Point when entering the harbor, and Lt. A. M. Pennock, an Army engineer detached to the Lighthouse Board, recommended a "small light" here. "Vessels of all classes," he explained, "take advantage of this lee, and in thick weather several have brought up on the spit making off from the point." In August 1854 Congress authorized a lighthouse at Drum Point and provided $5,000 for the work, but construction was not undertaken, apparently because of difficulties obtaining title to the land.[7]

In August 1882, seemingly prompted by a memorial from citizens of the area, Congress authorized range lights for the Patuxent River without consulting the Lighthouse Board. "The

smallness of the appropriation, as well as the absence of necessity for a range here," the Board responded a little tartly, "caused [us] to erect a screw-pile light-house at Drum Point, which answers the present requirements of commerce." Located on the shoal making off from the point on the north side of the river entrance, this hexagonal white lighthouse rested on seven 10-inch, wrought-iron screwpiles. It began service on August 20, 1883, with a fourth-order lens with a focal plane 46 feet above the water.[8]

The next lighthouse to come on line was the one at Great Shoals on the Eastern Shore. In April 1882 the Lighthouse Board, responding to a request from the Maryland General Assembly, recommended construction of a lighthouse at Great Shoals near the mouth of the Wicomico River. The Board told Congress the structure would cost an estimated $15,000. The Committee on Commerce reported out the bill the next month and recommended its passage. In March 1883 Congress authorized the lighthouse and provided the funds. Before the end of the fiscal year in June, borings had been taken at the site and plans and specifications had been developed.

In January 1884 the Fifth District advertised for proposals to manufacture the ironwork for Great Shoals, and the next month work on framing the dwelling began at the Lazaretto Depot. Only a small crew worked on it, and the structure was still only about two-thirds finished by July 1. By July 17, however, it had been completed, disassembled, and shipped with the ironwork to the construction site. On July 19th the workers began screwing the first pile into the bottom. Three days later the foundation was finished, with each pile driven 13 feet into the shoal. On the 26th the frame was put up, and two days later the dwelling was sheathed and weatherboarded. By the end of July the roof was on, the floors laid, the lantern in place, the gallery up, and some of the interior work done. On August 5, 1884, the structure was finished except for painting, and the work platform had been removed. Ten days later, less than a month after its first pile had been set, the Great Shoals lighthouse went into service.

Resting on the screwpile foundation was a square seven-room dwelling painted white. The nine-sided fifth-order lantern held a fifth-order lens that gave off a fixed white light, with the focal plane 37 feet above sea level. The lighthouse had a fog bell, which weighed 1,300 pounds and was operated by machinery. This aid to navigation was intended to guide vessels into the channel leading to the Wicomico River.[9]

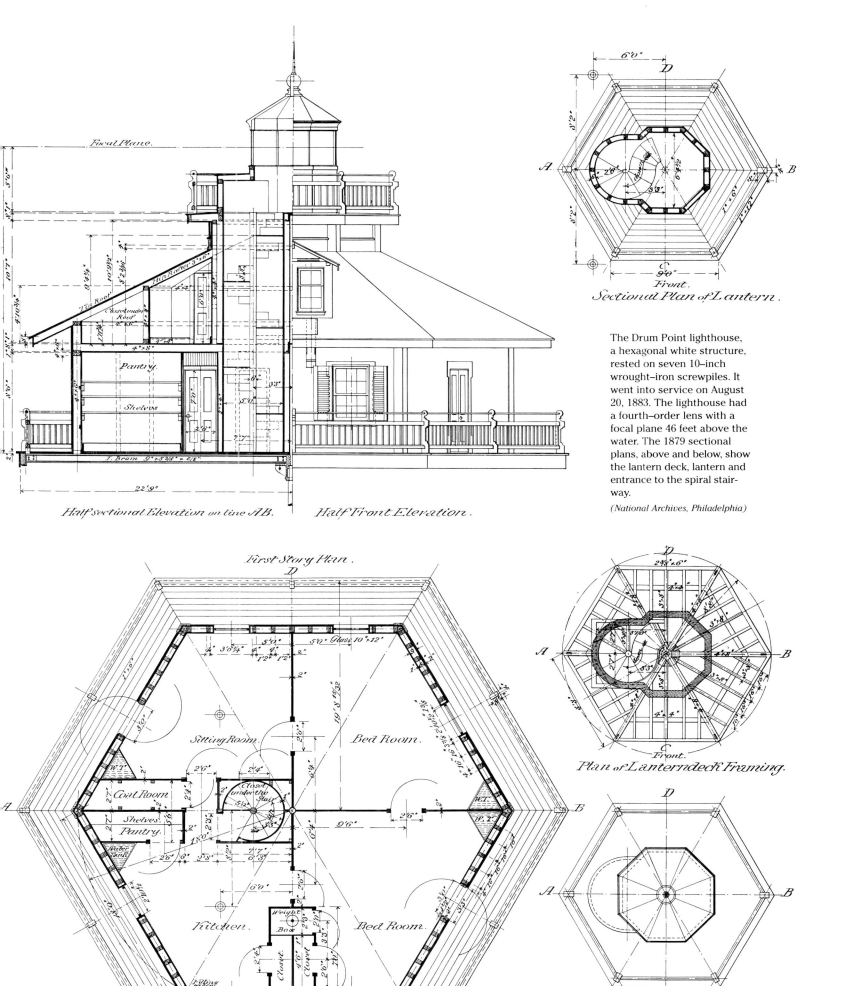

Focal Plane.

Half Sectional Elevation on line AB.   Half Front Elevation.

Sectional Plan of Lantern.

The Drum Point lighthouse, a hexagonal white structure, rested on seven 10-inch wrought-iron screwpiles. It went into service on August 20, 1883. The lighthouse had a fourth-order lens with a focal plane 46 feet above the water. The 1879 sectional plans, above and below, show the lantern deck, lantern and entrance to the spiral stairway.

(National Archives, Philadelphia)

First Story Plan.

Sitting Room.   Bed Room.

Coal Room   Closet under the Stair

Shelves
Pantry

Kitchen.   Bed Room.

Weight Box   Closet   Closet

Front.

Plan of Lanterndeck Framing.

Plan of Lanterndeck & Lantern.

113

Murder in the Lighthouse??

The Holland Island Bar lighthouse was partially prefabricated at the Lazaretto Depot on a 100–foot scow which was towed to the construction site, a shoal north of Smith Island. The lighthouse went into operation on November 25, 1889.

(U.S. Coast Guard photo. F. Ross Holland Collection)

Holland Island Bar File, MHT Cultural Conservation Program, *Keepers and Kin,* oral history collection compiled by Elaine Eff.

A baffling mystery which took place in a Maryland lighthouse involved Keeper Ulman Owens of the Holland Island Bar lighthouse who was found dead in the lighthouse on March 15, 1931. His body was found in his room which was in great disarray. A blood-stained knife lay on the floor. The body was naked, except for a torn shirt, and had many bruises. An area doctor examined the keeper and found no knife wounds. He suggested that Owens died of a heart attack and that bruises had been made by the keeper thrashing around and bumping into the furniture during the heart attack. When he died is not known, but the last entry in the lighthouse log was on March 12.

Some speculated that the keeper had somehow gotten mixed up with rum smugglers. But no one could find any solid evidence to support this contention. The "probable heart attack" theory, though propounded by a coroner's jury, seemed even weaker. Today no one knows who or what killed Keeper Owens, or for what reason. It is one of those mysteries that will never be solved.

In 1888 Congress appropriated $35,000 for a lighthouse off Holland Island, north of Smith Island. It was to be situated on a long, dangerous shoal known as Holland Island Bar. In describing its need, the Lighthouse Board said, "It will be an important guide for both sailing vessels and steamers for a long distance both north and south of Kedges Straits. It will also serve as a guide for vessels seeking an anchorage in Holland's Straits, and when supplied with a red sector it will, with Solomon's Lump light, indicate the channel through Kedges Straits."[10]

The construction of this lighthouse was teamed with that of a similar one going up at the Great Wicomico River in Virginia. The metal for each was bought under the same contract, which was let in February for delivery in August, and carpenters began building both lighthouses at the Lazaretto Depot. The Holland Island Bar lighthouse was to have been built on the depot's old scow, but it was in such terrible condition it could not be used. The depot workers built another scow, 100 feet long and 28 feet wide with a rounded bow to facilitate towing. At the end of the fiscal year, the Board reported that it expected both structures to be ready for shipment to their sites in August 1889.

The Great Wicomico lighthouse was taken to its site first, and after work there was well underway, the material for the Holland Island Bar lighthouse was transported to its construction site, arriving September 20, 1889. The workers began erecting the structure right away, but the weather turned rough and they could do little until October. At that point work speeded up, and by the end of the first week of November the lighthouse was nearly finished. The clean-up work was undertaken, and on November 25, 1889, the Holland Island Bar lighthouse was operating, just two weeks behind the lighthouse at Great Wicomico River.

This screwpile lighthouse was located on the shoal nearly three miles south of Holland Island. Seven piles, each penetrating the shoal 13 feet, formed the foundation. The white hexagonal dwelling supported a black fourth-order lantern fitted with a fourth-order lens, which gave off a fixed white light 42 feet above mean high water. The lighthouse was fitted with a machine-operated fog bell weighing 1,200 pounds.[11]

The last screwpile lighthouse, and last lighthouse, erected in Maryland waters was the one at Ragged Point. The point made off from the west side of the Potomac River, generally opposite Piney Point lighthouse. This point, the Lighthouse Board advocated, needed to "be marked by a light at night and a fog signal during thick weather."

The Lighthouse Board first requested funding for this structure in 1896, but despite yearly requests for an appropriation of $20,000 for the navigational aid, Congress did not provide funds until June 20, 1906, when it authorized the Ragged Point lighthouse and fog signal, to cost no more than $30,000. Ten days later Congress appropriated $15,000 to begin the work. At the same time the Board urged Congress to appropriate the remaining $15,000 to complete the work. For three years, the Board had warned Congress that for six years there had been a steady increase in labor and materials costs.[12]

Congress took the hint, and on March 4, 1907, it appropriated the additional $15,000 to finish the structure. The $30,000, as it turned out, was inadequate to erect "a suitable light and fog-signal" at Ragged Point. Despite its efforts the Board

had been unable to secure a satisfactory bid for the work, "but the lowest received was so high as to show that the light-house could not be built within the amount appropriated." The Board estimated that an additional $15,000 was required. On May 7, 1908, however, Congress appropriated $5,000 which proved satisfactory. A contract was let for the lighthouse and fog bell station, and the work began. On February 26, 1910, the construction was completed.[13]

The fog bell striking apparatus and fourth-order Fresnel lens, from which a flashing white light emanated, were ready for operation. On March 15, 1910, the station went into service. The final cost was $34,223.97.[14]

Although the low, one-story screwpile lighthouses at one time literally dotted Chesapeake Bay and the sounds of North Carolina, very few were built any place else in the country. The screwpile technique was employed elsewhere, such as on the Florida reefs, but the structures were tall towers that in no way resembled the screwpile structures on the Chesapeake.

Only two of the low screwpile structures survive in their original locations: the old Middle Bay lighthouse in Mobile Bay, Alabama, and the Thomas Point Shoal lighthouse near Annapolis. Most of the others were taken down when their lights were automated.

The last lighthouse erected in Maryland waters was at Ragged Point on the Potomac River. Built at a cost of $34,223.97, it went into service on March 15, 1910. It was dismantled in the 1960s.

(U.S. Coast Guard photo, 1912. F. Ross Holland Collection)

The Love Point lighthouse, one of Maryland's early screwpile structures, waged many battles with the winter ice of Chesapeake Bay. After the lighthouse lost two legs in the winter of 1872, riprap was piled around it to form a protective "island." The lighthouse was torn down in 1964, but the riprap island and the remains of the old piles survive and now hold a flashing light.

(Photo by F. Ross Holland, 1987)

The picturesque Somers Cove square screwpile went into service in 1867, guiding vessels to the harbor at Crisfield. The lighthouse was destroyed in the 1930s. Thomas Point Shoal is now Maryland's only screwpile still serving in its original location.

(U.S. Coast Guard photo 1915. F. Ross Holland Collection)

The second Janes Island lighthouse succumbed to ice in 1935, following in the path of its predecessor, which had been taken by ice in January 1879 and replaced with a sturdier screwpile structure in December of the same year. The Somers Cove lighthouse was destroyed in the 1930s after it had been automated. The Choptank River lighthouse, off Benoni's Point, was carried away by ice and the Cherrystone Bar superstructure, in Virginia, was brought over to replace it in 1921. In 1964 this lighthouse was demolished. The Love Point lighthouse was torn down in 1964, eleven years after it was automated. The screwpile foundation still has a light affixed to it. The Mathias Point lighthouse was taken down in 1963 and replaced with a steel tower. The Lower Cedar Point lighthouse burned in December 1893 and was replaced in Septem-

ber 1896. It was once again replaced in 1948, this time by a white skeleton tower which supported both an automated light and fog bell. Today the site is marked by a buoy. The Upper Cedar Point lighthouse was dismantled in 1963 and replaced with a small light on its foundation. Maryland Point lighthouse was taken down in the 1960s. Ragged Point lighthouse was dismantled, apparently also in the 1960s. Great Shoals lighthouse was demolished in 1966. Holland Island Bar lighthouse was mistakenly subjected to rocket fire from naval airplanes in 1957 while still manned; damage was considerable and two keepers were slightly injured. Three years later the structure was dismantled, and the replacement light was automated. Cobb Point Bar lighthouse was dismantled in 1940. Greenbury Point Shoal lighthouse was dismantled in 1934, but its foundation

today has a small light on it. Sharkfin Shoal lighthouse was automated in 1964 and about that time the dwelling was dismantled and a steel skeleton tower placed on the old foundation.[15]

In addition to the Thomas Point Shoal lighthouse, three other Chesapeake screwpile lighthouses survive in museum settings, all in Maryland. The Hooper Strait lighthouse is part of the Chesapeake Bay Maritime Museum in St. Michaels, and Drum Point lighthouse has been moved to the Calvert Marine Museum in Solomons. Both are being preserved as historic structures and are depicted as they would have been when in service. The Seven Foot Knoll lighthouse stands at Baltimore's Inner Harbor, where it is used as office space for the Living Classrooms Foundation.[16]

Low screwpile lighthouses for over 100 years liberally dotted Chesapeake Bay and the sounds of North Carolina, and in much lesser numbers the Gulf of Mexico and Delaware Bay. They disappeared quickly in the 1960s when automation was in full force. Today only five of them survive, but the "romance" of the small structures lives on.

In recent years the design of the screwpile lighthouse has achieved a degree of popularity which is manifested in the design of restaurants, a hotel, inns, and bed and breakfast establishments. Moreover, architects have prepared plans for beachhouses that are near clones of the screwpile lighthouse.

The first Lower Cedar Point screwpile went into service in 1867 but burned in 1893 and was replaced in 1896 by the structure pictured above. In 1948 it also was replaced – by a white skeleton tower with an automated light and fog bell. Today a buoy marks the site.

(U.S. Coast Guard photo 1912. F. Ross Holland Collection)

Chapter 6

Confronting the Bay: Erosion and Growing Pains

Erosion was a problem with Maryland lighthouses from the day the first one was built. In 1822, the year Bodkin Island lighthouse went into service at the mouth of the Patapsco, Lewis Brantz and James Gibson reported that it was threatened by erosion and urged that something be done to protect it. The following year the naval officer for the Port of Baltimore, after reviewing a study of conditions at Bodkin Island and North Point, recommended building a wall at each site to halt the erosion. In August 1823 a wall was placed at Bodkin Island, with two feet underground and four feet above ground. The wall held, and it was not until 1842, after a serious storm, that it needed repairs.[1]

North Point was threatened several times by erosion. In 1836 an earlier wall had to be repaired. By 1851 the bluff near the lighthouse was eroding, and collector of customs George P. Kane proposed building breakwaters to protect the structure. The following year he found erosion about to claim an important section of the government property. The record does not reveal what was done about these threats, although Kane drafted advertisements for proposals to build a "jettee."[2]

More serious erosion occurred at Thomas Point and at Cove Point. The light tower at Thomas Point had been built in 1825 on a high bank, 100 feet from its edge, but as time went by, the bay crept closer to the structure, eating away at the base of the bluff. Placing stone at the site had not impeded the advance of the water, and by 1837 Pleasonton had concluded that placing more stone would be too expensive. It would be more economical to move the lighthouse when the water advanced closer in two or three years. By 1838 the edge of the bank had moved to within fifteen feet of the light tower. Two years later,

when it was just a few feet from the tower, Pleasonton sought Winslow Lewis's advice.

Lewis visited the site and told Pleasonton the tower must be moved immediately. He proposed relocating it to just behind the keeper's dwelling and raising the tower three feet so the light would clear the chimney of the house. He proposed to perform the work for $2,000, using the materials of the old tower and obtaining any new materials required. Pleasonton agreed, and directed the collector of customs to enter into a contract with Lewis, who said he would finish the work by September 1, 1840. Nearly a year later, someone recommended protecting the site with a stone breakwater. Pleasonton commented unfavorably on the recommendation, saying stone had not worked in the past. If the dwelling was threatened, he responded, it could be moved.[3]

The solution at Thomas Point was relatively simple compared to that undertaken at Cove Point, where Pleasonton elected to fight the erosion. In 1831 the keeper of the Cove Point lighthouse, Dr. Walter Wyville, told Pleasonton the bay was encroaching on the lighthouse, endangering it. He suggested installing two rows of pilings driven fifteen feet into the sandbar. Pleasonton liked the idea and instructed the collector of customs to have it done. When Pleasonton learned the cost of the work a few weeks later, however, he directed that brush and stone be placed around the lighthouse to protect it until spring, when the conditions could be examined and a proper course determined. The records are silent until 1837 when Pleasonton visited the site and expressed the view that stone should be placed to prevent the water from "molesting" the foundation of the tower. This was apparently done, but the stone piles were subsequently destroyed by storms.

The saddest story of erosion at a Maryland lighthouse – mainly because it didn't have to happen – is the tangled tale of ecological disaster, bureaucratic paper shuffling and corporate insensitivity that led to the ruin of the Cedar Point lighthouse on the south side of the entrance to the Patuxent River.

(Photo by A. Aubrey Bodine. Peale Museum, Baltimore City Life Museums: The A. Aubrey Bodine Photographic Collection)

Maryland's first lighthouse, Bodkin Island, was quickly threatened by erosion. In 1922, the year it went into service, officials were calling for protective measures and a four–foot wall was placed around it in 1823. Abandoned in 1856 and destroyed in a storm in 1914, both the lighthouse and the island have vanished.

(MSA SC 1887 – 32)

In 1841 Pleasonton suggested driving piles between the water and the lighthouse and boarding up the openings with heavy planks. He felt this solution would not only stop erosion but would also collect sand. A few months later he sent I. W. P. Lewis, an engineer and nephew of Winslow Lewis, to look at the erosion problem and see what could be done to inhibit it. Lewis offered a plan that would cost $5,000, a price that must have caused the blood to drain from Pleasonton's face. He turned to others, including Winslow Lewis, for advice. In July 1842 he decided to put in groins. The work was done by Winslow Lewis, who was low bidder on the project. After the groins, made of piles and planking, had been put in and survived a winter, Pleasonton received a report that they were living up to

expectations. Within three years, however, a number of the piles and much of the planking had to be replaced. Repairs were made, but by the next year all of the work had been undone by the weather. In 1846 a major repair effort was undertaken, for which F. A. Gibbons was the low bidder. In 1850 John Hance, the newly appointed keeper, reported that the groins "have been much injured by worms" and needed to be replaced. At this point, Pleasonton decided not to rebuild them, but rather to fill cribs with stone and float them to Cove Point. The wood would eventually disappear, but the stone would remain.[4] The records do not show whether this work was undertaken.

Under the 1846 contract that allowed for the repair of groins at Cove Point, Gibbons was also to repair the groins at Point Lookout. By 1847 the seawall there was in need of considerable work. Three years later Pleasonton directed that four or five additional groins be placed at Point Lookout, in an attempt to halt erosion at the worst points. Similar to those built elsewhere, the groins consisted of 10-inch piles with three-inch planking between them. The person doing the work did not agree with Pleasonton that groins were needed. Instead, he wanted to repair the stone wall that had been partially undermined in 1850 and was in danger of deteriorating further. A breakwater located about eight feet in front of the wall had sunk considerably,[5] also contributing to the deterioration of the wall. The record of what was eventually done is not available, but, whatever it was, it was sufficient, for the lighthouse still stands and the shoreline at this point is well protected from the forces of erosion.

Virtually surrounded by water on three sides, the Point Lookout lighthouse went into service in 1830 on a tip of land that was eroding badly. A seawall was built, but it needed repair by 1847 as did the protective groins which had been added. The banks of the lighthouse complex were later stabilized with riprap.

(U.S. Coast Guard photo, 1930. F. Ross Holland Collection. Far right: Photo by F. Ross Holland, 1987)

When Pleasonton heard of the erosion potential on Sharp's Island, which was caused by the "lightness of the soil," he elected to build a combined wooden tower and dwelling on "wheels" that could be moved as the land eroded. With this view, he never considered or undertook any erosion control on this island. By 1864 the lighthouse was in imminent danger of being destroyed by encroachment from the bay. By the following year, the bay had reached the corner of the structure, forcing the Lighthouse Board to abandon it. The island was without a light for two weeks before a temporary one could be erected. Congress finally appropriated the money needed for a new lighthouse, a screwpile one, which was built and lighted in 1866.[6]

The stone breakwater built at Fog Point on Smith Island in 1837 was not effective, and by 1843 it was being labeled "remains." This destruction was due in great part to the encroachment of

As early as 1831, Pleasonton and a succession of builders and engineers began an ambitious program to halt erosion at Cove Point. Piles of brush and stone, groins and finally more stones were tried. More modern solutions to the problem can be seen in the U.S. Coast Guard photo above.

(F. Ross Holland Collection)

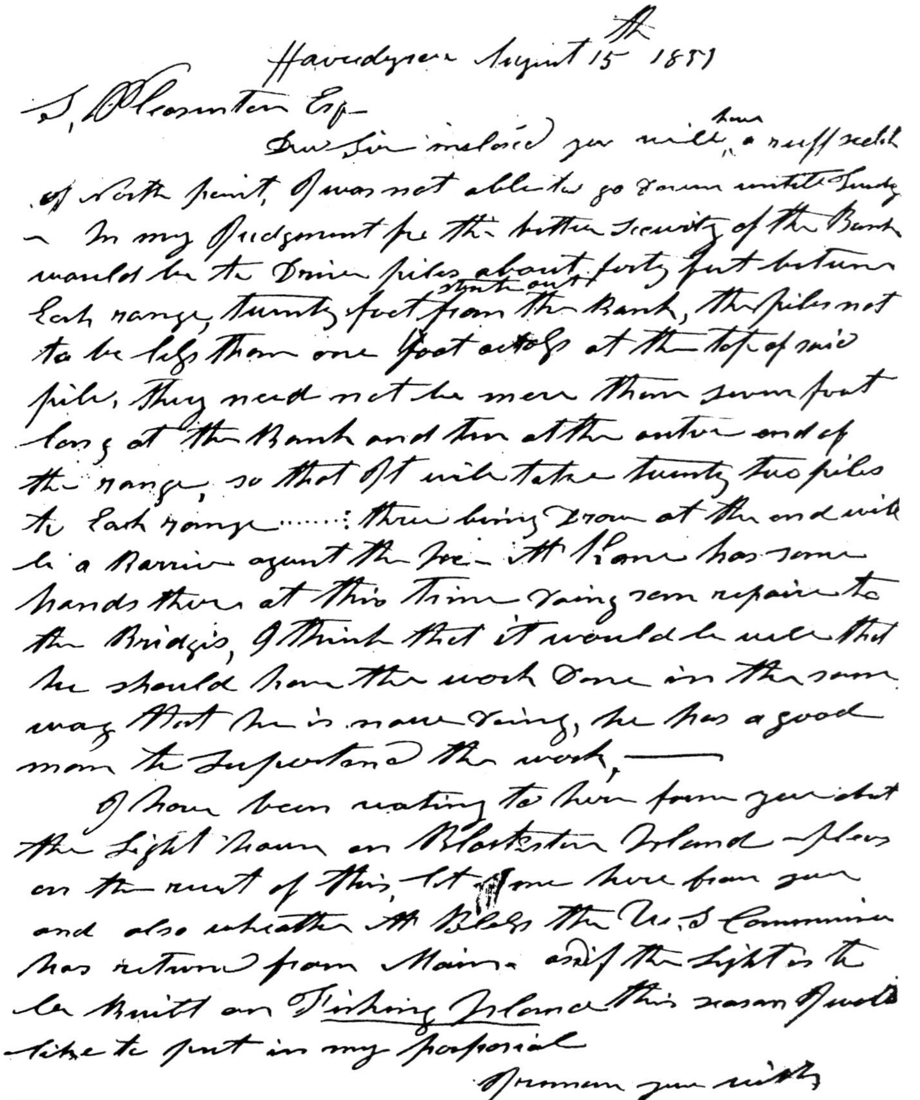

[Handwritten letter, transcribed at right]

Havre degrace
August 15th 1851

S. Pleasanton Esq.

Dear Sir inclosed you will have a ruff scetch of North Point, I was not able to go down until Tuesday - In my judgement for the better security of the Banks would be to Drive piles about forty feet between each range, twenty feet straight out from the Banks, the piles not to be less than one foot across at the top of said pile, they need not be more than seven foot long at the bank and ten at the outer end of the range, so that It will take twenty two piles to each range..: three being down at the end will be a barrier against the ice - Mr. ? has some hands there at this time doing some repair to the bridges, I think that it would be well that he should have the work done in the same way that he is now doing, he has a good man to superintend the work.

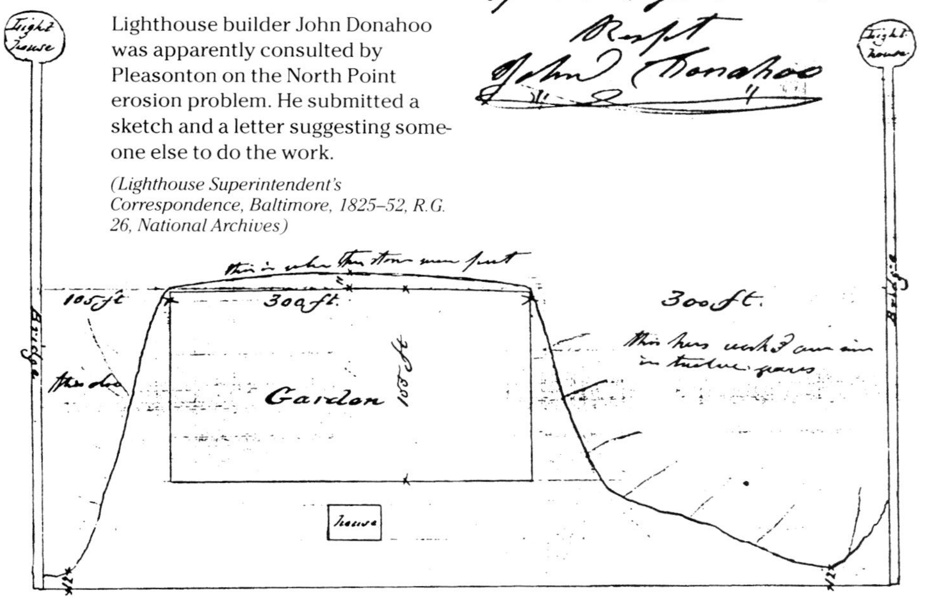

Lighthouse builder John Donahoo was apparently consulted by Pleasonton on the North Point erosion problem. He submitted a sketch and a letter suggesting someone else to do the work.

(Lighthouse Superintendent's Correspondence, Baltimore, 1825–52, R.G. 26, National Archives)

1843 and was hired three years later to repair it. Repaired again in 1848, the wall was in need of further work two years later.[7]

The Lazaretto lighthouse faced erosion problems in 1837, just six years after its construction, prompting Pleasonton to wonder why it had been placed so close to the shore. His first response was to move the lighthouse, which he told the collector of customs to do. Tear down the old tower, he directed, and rebuild it some distance away. If that would not be feasible, Pleasonton proposed building a lighthouse that could be moved. It "can be set near the edge of the Bank and removed as often as is necessary with very little expense," he noted, "the first cost will be but a few hundred dollars."[8] He included a drawing, which unfortunately has been lost.

In response to Pleasonton's letter, William Frick, the collector of customs at that time, expressed his concern about the Lazaretto light and the rapidly encroaching water. The previous fall, he reported, the water was "ten to twelve yards from the base of the tower" and by May it had reached it. Frick suggested building a curved wall five feet high about eight feet in front of the light tower, and estimated it would cost $200. Apparently Pleasonton agreed, and in November 1837 Frick reported that the semicircular stone wall had been built and the foundation was considered "perfectly safe for years to come." Nonetheless, by 1842 Frick's wall needed shoring up.

When Pleasonton sought advice from a Major Turnbull of the Corps of Engineers, he was advised to replace Frick's wall with a stone wall set in hydraulic cement and measuring six feet high, six feet across at the base and three feet wide at the top. After the job had been advertised, a contract was let to Gibbons to put up the wall. Pleasonton at this time again proposed

the bay in the winter of 1842-43. Pleasonton proposed replacing the breakwater with a 300-foot wall made of a row of wood piles "close together and filled in on the land side with stones or earth." In a few weeks Pleasonton had developed his idea to a wall of stone "laid in the best Hydraulic cement." F. A. Gibbons built this wall in

moving the lighthouse or building a new tower of wood. Perhaps the latter option was a reference to his movable lighthouse. Three years later the new wall needed shoring, and Pleasonton said that sheet piling would be more effective than the additional stone Collector Kane recommended. Others also advised Pleasonton to use stone, but he stuck to a pile solution. In July 1851 a representative for Kane examined the site and suggested putting up a wall three feet high with a five-foot base in front of the existing wall.[9]

Pleasonton generally did not like constructing breakwaters or seawalls. It was his opinion that moving a lighthouse was "more economical." Despite this attitude, he moved only two of the lighthouses in Maryland, although all but two under his control were seriously threatened by erosion. He preferred sheet-piling over stone for halting the encroachment of the water because it was less expensive. Nevertheless, he put in a lot of stone breakwaters and seawalls, mainly because everyone else said stone was more effective. The few trained engineers from whom he sought advice, such as Benjamin Isherwood

and Major Turnbull, particularly advocated the use of stone. This opinion was supported by the collectors of customs and the captains of the revenue cutter whom he occasionally sent to inspect lighthouse sites and render advice on erosion problems.[10]

Two of the last three lighthouses in Maryland to succumb to the threat of erosion were those at Greenbury Point in Annapolis Harbor and at Sharkfin Shoal off Clay Island, which is north of Bloodsworth Island. In 1878 the Lighthouse Board *Annual Report* noted that Greenbury Point was eroding and eventually the lighthouse would be taken. The report also pointed out that the light was of little use because it was barely distinguishable from the lights of the Naval Academy. Though the Board asked for no appropriation at that time, it did remark that "a screw-pile structure on the end of the shoal would be of much greater value than the present light."

In 1879 the Board again mentioned the threat to the lighthouse and the light's shortcoming, this time recommending an appropriation of $25,000 for a lighthouse on Greenbury Point

Built in 1848 near Annapolis Harbor, the Greenbury Point lighthouse was threatened by erosion and of little use 30 years later. Since the light could barely be distinguished from lights at the U.S. Naval Academy, the Lighthouse Board finally received funds in 1889 to build a screwpile on the nearby shoal. When it was completed in 1891 the old lighthouse became a day-marker – and apparently a turn–of–the–century picnic site.

(U.S. Naval Institute Photo Library)

123

Shoal. The Board repeated this request for several years, and in 1889 Congress finally appropriated the money. An equal amount was appropriated for the Sharkfin Shoal light, which was to replace the lighthouse on Clay Island. The island was being washed away and the threatened lighthouse required so many repairs that the work would be tantamount to rebuilding it. In addition, a light at Sharkfin Shoal would be of greater service than one on Clay Island.[11]

The Board decided to erect similar lighthouses at the two points and to follow parallel construction processes, so that a report on the status of one was a report on the other. In February 1890 contracts for the ironwork were let, and by July the construction of the two superstructures was well underway at Lazaretto Depot in Baltimore. By the end of June 1891, the superstructures were finished and ready for transportation to the sites. The Board decided to send the Sharkfin Shoal dwelling out first, and to have it lighted by September 15, 1891. Installation of the superstructure for the Greenbury Point Shoal would begin once its twin was in service.[12]

These plans went slightly awry before the Sharkfin Shoal construction began, however. The Board decided that the lighthouse site should be changed to one of greater utility to the mariner. By the time the engineers had located a new site two miles southwest of the old lighthouse, made the necessary test borings, and obtained jurisdiction over the property from the legislature, December was upon them, and it was too late to begin construction.

In the meantime, the district engineer had shifted construction efforts to Greenbury Point Shoal, and on July 28, 1891, work began on the foundation. The workers driving the piles found that the soil was not firm enough to give good support to the foundation. The lighthouse builders had faced this problem before at a site in North Carolina and decided to use the same solution. They obtained cast-iron disks "of as great diameter as the spaces between the parts of the ironwork would allow." They attached cast-iron sleeves to the disks and slipped the sleeves and disks onto the piles, forcing them down "until the disks had obtained a solid bearing on the shoal." The sleeves were then bolted to the piles. This effort took about six weeks, and in the middle of September the builders were able to adjust the sleeves and disks and put the braces and cross-bars in place, completing the foundation. The dwelling was built, and this part of the work was completed by October 8. Two men were left to paint the structure and take down the construction platform. The new light-

Opposite page:
The Sharkfin Shoal screwpile replaced the 1832 lighthouse on Clay Island in Tangier Sound, a dwelling with the tower on the roof. The island was washing away, so a site on the shoal southwest of the old lighthouse was chosen in 1891. Originally planned as a parallel construction project with Greenbury Point Shoal, the two superstructures were completed at Lazaretto Depot in 1891, but a site change delayed the construction at Sharkfin Shoal. The lighthouse, with its fourth–order lens, went into service on August 1, 1892 and the Clay Island beacon was discontinued.

(U.S. Coast Guard photo. F. Ross Holland Collection)

house went into service on the night of November 15, 1891. At the same time the old one was discontinued, but it was left in place as a daymark.[13]

The new lighthouse on Greenbury Point Shoal rested on seven screwpiles. Its hexagonal six-room dwelling was topped by a fourth- order lantern of eight sides holding a fourth-order Fresnel lens, which emitted a fixed white light whose focal plane was 39 feet above mean high water. The lighthouse also had a fog bell.[14]

It was not until the May following the lighting of the Greenbury Point Shoal lighthouse that work resumed on the lighthouse at Sharkfin Shoal. On June 3, after the tools, machinery, and equipment for construction were loaded onto scows, the tender towed the materials to the site, where "the platform for setting the ironwork was put up and the shears, engine, and boiler were adjusted." The screwpiles and other pieces of the foundation were put in place and the erection of the superstructure was begun. By the end

of June all the exterior work was complete, and during July partitions were constructed and the structure painted, inside and out. All the work was completed by the end of July, and on August 1, 1892, the light of the new structure was exhibited for the first time.[15] Despite its delayed schedule, it looked like its sister lighthouse at Annapolis Harbor.

Another type of erosion that threatened Maryland lighthouses was found at the bottom of the bay. This undersea erosion caused scouring, or

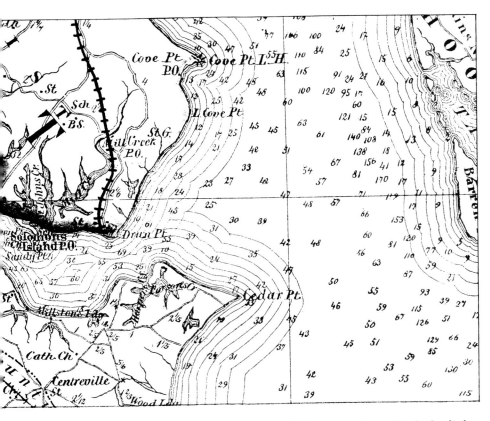

A lighthouse for Cedar Point, at the south side of the entrance to the Patuxent River, had been discussed as early as 1825. The Lighthouse Board began a sustained effort to obtain a fog signal and lighthouse in 1888 and in 1894 received an appropriation of $25,000. One–and–a–half acres of land were purchased in 1894 and work on the structures began in May 1896. The light station was completed in October. By 1907 erosion had become a problem.

(Detail: A New Topographical Atlas.... MHT Library)

washing away, of the ground on which the lighthouse rested. A number of caisson-type lighthouses were affected by this problem, which caused both Sharp's Island and Bloody Point Bar lighthouses to tilt. Righting them was a difficult task, and stone had to be placed on the scoured side of each to prevent further damage.

The saddest story of erosion among Maryland's lighthouses—mainly because it didn't have to happen—is that of Cedar Point light on the south side of the entrance to the Patuxent River. A lighthouse at the point had been talked about for a long time, beginning at least as early as 1825. In 1826 the Maryland legislature approved ceding jurisdiction over the land at Cedar Point to the federal government. Nothing came of this attempt, however, probably because Pleasonton felt the new lighthouse at Cove Point was sufficient to satisfy the needs of navigation for that section of the coast.

The first sustained effort to get a lighthouse at Cedar Point began in 1888. In that year the Lighthouse Board recommended the establishment of one, reporting to Congress that

> the harbor at the mouth of the Patuxent River is the best on the western side of Chesapeake Bay. Vessels about to enter this harbor from the south pass close to Cedar Point, where the water is deep near the shore. In thick weather sounding is no safeguard, as the change from deep to shoal water is abrupt. The establishment of a light and fog signal on Cedar Point would also be of much value to the general navigation of the bay, as most vessels pass near this point.

Congress did not respond to this recommendation, and the Lighthouse Board repeated it in its *Annual Report* for four years before Congress finally appropriated $25,000 for a lighthouse and fog signal at Cedar Point.[16]

In March 1894 the Lighthouse Board purchased from the Patuxent Cedar Point Company of Baltimore about one-and-a-half acres of land at a cost of $5,000. Plans were drawn for the new lighthouse, and a contract was let for erecting the lighthouse and appurtenant structures. Work began on May 7, 1896, and by the end of the fiscal year, June 30, the concrete foundation of the lighthouse had been completed and the framing on the dwelling begun. The concrete foundation for the oil house was laid and its rafters put in place. The outhouse received its brick foundation, and the fog bell tower and boathouse were nearing completion. The Board expected to have the work on the light station finished within three months.

On September 20, the contractor completed the construction of the lighthouse and the subsidiary structures. The district engineer installed a fourth-order revolving lens in the light tower and a bell in the 35-foot-tall wooden fog bell tower. A brick walkway 12 feet long connected the fog bell tower to the dwelling. The light station went into service on October 31, 1896.

The cottage-style, brick-and-wood dwelling was three stories tall, the first story being the basement. The light tower rose from one corner of the roof and supported the iron lantern. The lantern's ventilator ball stood fifty feet above the ground, and the lens gave off a red light that flashed every five seconds. The first floor of the fog bell tower was a summer kitchen, and the second had two storerooms. A brick oil house, a frame boathouse, and a privy completed the station.[17]

The Cedar Point lighthouse served quietly and effectively in its early years. About the only excitement the keeper had was in 1903, when the steamer *Moore and Brady*, owned by Bramble, Harrington and Company, was wrecked at Cedar Point. The keeper provided food and lodging for the captain and crew, but when he attempted to contact the company for reimbursement of his expenses he had difficulty getting in touch with the owners. The district office, based in Baltimore, took up the keeper's cause but also had problems contacting the owners.[18] The records do not reveal if the keeper was repaid or not.

Erosion does not seem to have been a problem at Cedar Point until 1907, when the district engineer noted the land had shrunk since 1894 and flooded during storms. He recommended

laying a rubble wall containing 500 cubic yards of stone, and this was done in the summer of 1907. The work was inadequate, however, and in February 1908 another 200 cubic yards were added.

About a year later District Engineer W. E. Craighill visited the site to see if the gravel operations at Cedar Point, approved probably around 1907, were damaging the station. He noted that the firm doing the offshore dredging, the New York, Philadelphia, and Norfolk R.R. Company based in Cape Charles, Virginia, intended to secure 600,000 yards of gravel, 200 feet from the land. He concluded that the work was doing no harm to the lighthouse site.[19] Interestingly, over a decade later Joseph J. Hock, vice president of the Arundel Corporation, blamed the erosion damage around the lighthouse on the railway company, saying, after it had promised not to dig gravel within 200 feet of the lighthouse shore, "digging

the gravel off shore will not injure the shore in any way." He went on to say, "what has injured the shore, is that a permit was granted the N.Y. P. & N. R. R. some years ago to dig sand and gravel for ballast in car floats and in doing this practically all of our shores as well as the lighthouse shore has been ruined."[20]

In the fall of 1912 the keeper, Loch W. Humphreys, notified the district office that a storm had swept the area and caused the beach on the south side of the lighthouse to erode enormously. The boardwalk connecting the oil house and bell tower had been washed away, and he feared for the safety of the bell tower, as three feet of its foundation had already been exposed. Within a month, the district had mobilized a crew and dispatched it to Cedar Point, where the men began installing piles and sheeting while waiting for rock to arrive to build a

By 1915 the Cedar Point bell tower and the cottage–style brick and wood dwelling with its square light tower rising from the roof had been circled by a protective seawall. Erosion control had begun in 1907 with a rubble wall, and then a jetty to protect the south and east shores, followed in 1914 by groins to protect the north beach.

(U.S. Navy photo, c. 1918)

127

"Meanwhile, the Arundel Sand and Gravel Company continued to excavate gravel just west of the boundary line of the light station, although they apparently were fully aware the north beach would soon vanish."

jetty. Completed on November 22, this work was done to "protect the south and east shore from washing."[21]

A year later the Lighthouse Service's chief construction engineer, H. B. Bowerman, inspected this work and was pleased to find it holding and the beach building out toward the end of the jetties. The wall on the south side was in very good condition and was trapping sand, raising it above the level of sand on the inside. The water at very high tide flowed behind this wall and dumped sand on the inside. There would be a substantial increase in the amount of sand trapped, Bowerman noted, "were it not for the continued removal of the beach just west of the wall by the Arundel Sand and Gravel Co."

The threat of erosion at Cedar Point now came from the north, where the shoreline was "being pushed in on the station." The Arundel Sand and Gravel Company of Baltimore had recognized that the inlet on this side was widening and placed an old scow on each side of it. These did not stop the erosion, however, and at the time of Bowerman's visit the shoreline had moved about 400 feet past the scow toward the light station. The water was rapidly eating away the north beach as well, which would sever the lighthouse from the mainland. The keeper told Bowerman that at the rate the erosion had taken place in the past two months, the water would reach the northern boundary in six months. To stave off this encroachment, Bowerman recommended installation of groins on the north beach. Meanwhile, the Arundel Sand and Gravel Company continued to excavate gravel just west of the boundary line of the light station, although they apparently were fully aware the north beach would soon vanish.

In the autumn of 1914, the district put in the recommended groins, and the district superintendent reported they had started to build up the beach. Bowerman, apparently in response to the keeper's report that a gale had done some injury to a groin and washed the sea over all the beach, visited the site in January 1915. He reported that all the new groins, except No. 1, were "standing very well." Only the middle section of No. 1 was still in place. The opening in the north spit had widened, but he found no evidence of a break in the south spit. He recommended at this time the construction of a concrete wall around the light station.[22]

R. L. Hankinson, Fifth District superintendent, visited the site in October 1916 and found the groins, jetties, and seawall holding. However, he noted, if the Arundel Sand and Gravel Company began operations again, it would have a deleterious effect on the structures that the Lighthouse Service had put in place to protect the island from erosion.

The Lighthouse Service had been trying for some time to get a handle on the problem caused by the dredging at Cedar Point but with a notable lack of success. The Corps of Engineers, from whom the sand and gravel company had obtained a permit to do the dredging, was of little help. The Corps did not feel its authority to protect navigation could be used to accomplish another objective indirectly.

A solicitor of the Department of Commerce felt there were numerous precedents prohibiting a property owner from doing something on his property that would have a damaging effect on neighboring property. This opinion was sent to the Department of Justice with a request for the attorney general to take the requisite action. Apparently nothing was done, for nothing in the correspondence indicates what happened to the request. Five years later, employees of the Bureau of Lighthouses could remember the request had been made, but could not remember what action, if any, had resulted from the letter.[23]

The Arundel Sand and Gravel Company did not conduct dredging operations constantly, but started up about every four to six years. It was these periods of activity that galvanized the Bureau of Lighthouses to action. One such time occurred in the summer of 1920. Keeper W. S. Stinchcomb notified District Superintendent H. D. King that a crew from the sand and gravel company was at the site dredging gravel about "one hundred strides" from the light station and planned to take several schooner loads. King wrote to the company, "This letter will serve notice . . . that the Lighthouse Service interposes objection to the removal of gravel from this vicinity and will hold persons or corporations responsible for the same liability for any damages that may result to the Lighthouse property." Joseph J. Hock, vice president of the company, responded that he would instruct his men to stay clear of the lighthouse when dredging offshore, adding that digging offshore would not damage the shoreline. The shore had been damaged some years earlier, he said, by the sand and gravel operation of the New York, Philadelphia and Norfolk R. R., when ". . . all of our shores as well as the lighthouse shore [had] been ruined." King wrote back that he disagreed with Hock's conclusion and that he wanted it on record that he protested "the digging of any gravel at any point which may have the slightest tendency to cut into the already slender spit connecting the lighthouse with the solid mainland." At the same time he instructed Keeper Stinchcomb to keep an eye on the gravel operations and to let him know what was happening.[24]

In September the keeper notified King that the same person who had been dredging gravel earlier was now digging about 100 yards from the lighthouse. At the request of the keeper, the manager of the company's local farm told the crew to cease digging, but they refused to heed him. Over a month later King wrote to the Arundel Corporation, as it was now known, to rein in the crew and live up to their agreement. Hock, in response, sent a representative to talk to King. The Arundel official told King that only a small amount of gravel had been removed, but he had instructed the crew to cease operations at the site. Hock later reassured King that before beginning large-scale operations "we will go in this matter fully with you."

King's understanding from Hock and his emissary was that the company would not dig for gravel at present, but that they did not give up their rights to undertaking a large-scale operation in the future. Recognizing the company's rights and having the full assurance of Hock that discussions would take place before operations began, King recommended to the commissioner "that this informal understanding be accepted as satisfactory for the present." The commissioner approved the recommendation. Interestingly, King added that the question in time could become academic, as he believed it was doubtful the light station could be protected from the "encroachment of the sea." In his opinion, he commented, a gas-powered bell buoy would probably be a better aid than the lighthouse.[25]

In this afterthought, King reached the heart of the issue. The work of the Arundel Corporation was not the sole cause of the erosion that threatened the lighthouse. The natural erosion caused by the bay waters was very much in action at Cedar Point. Nonetheless, the technological development in erosion control at that time probably could have permitted the Lighthouse Service to save the light station as had been done at Cove Point and Point Lookout. However, the Arundel Corporation's gravel operation exacerbated the condition, ultimately making it impossible to save either the land or the light.

In the spring of 1924 Joseph J. Hock, now president of the Arundel Corporation, notified King that the company planned to resume operations and wanted "to cancel the obligation we assumed in our letter." He added that meanwhile "we will agree not to load any schooners or barges from this deposit and we will notify you before we send equipment to Cedar Point." A

week earlier the district office had received a letter from the keeper at Cedar Point reporting that the schooner *Smith J. Martin*, Capt. L. B. Kelly in command, "was loading gravel from the beach within 150 yards of Cedar Point Light Station." F. C. Hingsburg, the district's first assistant superintendent, dispatched Hock's communication to Washington. He reminded the commissioner of the June 6, 1914, opinion of the departmental solicitor and urged that the Department of Commerce seek to enjoin the company "from removing large quantities of sand and gravel from the narrow spit at Cedar Point which will cause injury to the Lighthouse Reservation." He also recommended that the Commerce Department ask the War Department not to issue a permit for dredging at Cedar Point.[26]

The Commerce Department, responding to a request from the commissioner's office, asked the Justice Department in June 1924 to get an injunction prohibiting Arundel Corporation's sand and gravel operations at Cedar Point. At the same time the department asked the War Department not to grant a permit for dredging "in the immediate vicinity of the Cedar Point Light Station." When a response had not come a month later, a Bureau of Lighthouses official telephoned the Justice Department. He was told that the department first had to determine if it had issued a permit. No response had come from the War Department, but they would prod them to expedite a reply. Within a few days, both Justice and Commerce received notice from the War Department that no permit had been issued and none would be issued for the vicinity of the Cedar Point Light Station "unless after reference to your Department of any case in question, a waiver of objection is received, or the opinion established that the permit will not be contrary to the interests of your Department." The Department of Justice replied that it recommended the Bureau of Lighthouses work with the War Department to get a satisfactory permit.[27]

In August 1924 the War Department received a request from the Arundel Corporation to dredge at Cedar Point, and near the end of August the permit was sent to the Department of Commerce for review. The chart accompanying the proposed permit showed a radius of 1/4 mile around the lighthouse reservation defining the proposed protective zone. When King reviewed the document, he felt the radius was inadequate to protect the light station, and he recommended that sand and gravel operations be allowed no closer than 1,000 yards from the southwest corner of the lighthouse reservation. The recommendation was passed up the line and over to the War

"In September the keeper notified King that the same person who had been dredging gravel earlier was now digging about 100 yards from the lighthouse. At the request of the keeper, the manager of the company's local farm told the crew to cease digging, but they refused to heed him."

129

"For two days in November a 'terrific' southeast gale poured water over the spit that connected the lighthouse reservation to the mainland. Keeper Gary E. Powell speculated that if the next wind came again from the south '...we will be Cedar Point Island light'."

Department, where it was accepted and incorporated into the permit.[28]

Erosion did no damage at Cedar Point Light Station during the next year, but it returned in full force in late fall 1925. For two days in November a "terrific" southeast gale poured water over the spit that connected the lighthouse reservation to the mainland. Keeper Gary E. Powell speculated that if the next wind came again from the south "... we will be Cedar Point Island Light"; if the next wind came from the north, it would probably cause a buildup of sand in places where it had washed away. An engineer in the district office agreed with his assessment and advised doing nothing at that time, thinking a north wind would likely come. The next wind came from the south, but it was fortunately a moderate one and only covered about a 50-foot stretch of the spit. In early December another storm struck, causing further damage to the spit. Keeper Powell reported "... it is going fast, water is now across it and only a normal tide." Water six to ten inches deep was in the yard, nearly to the lighthouse on the north and east sides.

District Superintendent King was distressed at this news, particularly since work to guard against further damage at Cedar Point would be expensive and most likely not permanent. The Lighthouse Service had poured considerable money into the station for erosion control in the past. If nothing was done, he believed, as the keeper did, the station would soon be on an island. At the same time, he recognized the lighthouse was relatively modern, in excellent condition and served "its purpose admirably." The light was no longer just a harbor light, but had also become a main channel light as the Lighthouse Board had predicted it would in 1888. In recognition of its new status, King recommended the light be made brighter by changing it from red to white. He resurrected a former suggestion as well: Perhaps now was the time to consider replacing the light with a first class gas and whistling buoy or gas and bell buoy. But his heart was obviously not in this recommendation, for King urged that F. C. Hingsburg be consulted for his opinions, because he had served in the district and had recently visited the lighthouse.[29]

Just a few days after sending his letter, King received a communication from Joseph J. Hock announcing that the Arundel Corporation planned "to take some gravel from our Cedar Point property, possibly two or three small schooner loads per month, of about 50 tons each, within 75 to 150 feet of the lighthouse. We feel certain that this will in no way effect your property at the lighthouse." The gravel, he

added, would be obtained with shovels, not dredging equipment.[30] The only land the Arundel Corporation owned that was within 75 to 150 feet of the lighthouse was the thin spit of land that connected the lighthouse reservation and the mainland.

King responded by sending Hock copies of Keeper Powell's last two reports on the recent erosion at the site and objecting to Hock's statement that work within 75 to 150 feet of the lighthouse would not be injurious to government property. In support of King, George R. Putnam, the commissioner, wrote to Hock expressing views similar to King's and adding that the company's permit prohibited them from removing sand or gravel within 1,000 yards of the southwest corner of the lighthouse reservation. On the file copies Putnam noted that Hock had said the sand and gravel would be obtained with shovels. He asked King to check with the district office of the Corps of Engineers to ascertain whether the War Department would have jurisdiction if the gravel were removed by shovel rather than with dredging equipment. King did, and in a separate letter to Commissioner Putnam, expressed the view that past decisions had defined navigable waters as measured to the high water mark and any sand or gravel removed below this mark and within 75 to 150 feet of the lighthouse "would be clearly within the navigable waters of the United States." King later received a response to his question from the district engineer of the Corps of Engineers, who wrote, "The removing of sand or gravel above the high water line and not altering or modifying the shore line would exclude action by this department."[31]

These findings quickly became academic, when Hock replied to Putnam's letter, saying,

> We beg to acknowledge receipt of your letter of the 15th instant . . . and in reply beg to advise you that we purchased the property in 1909, and have been carrying same since at a great expense to us for the express purpose of dredging sand and gravel. We cannot see how you can consistently ask us to keep carrying this property without netting us a revenue for the purpose which we purchased same, in order to protect the lighthouse which can be protected by riprapping. You certainly protect all of your other lighthouses that are out in the water and there is no reason that we can see why you should throw the burden upon us in order to protect this one.

Hock added that he wanted to cooperate and not damage the lighthouse property but could not agree with Putnam's statement "that by taking 100 to 150 tons per month from the shore line above the high water line [we] will endanger

Tragedy at Cedar Point: Edgar's Tale

MRS. DARE:
"You had to go through Cedar Point Farm and then you walk right down to the water's edge, you know, and then there was a long walk up to the lighthouse. We used to go down there and have all our Sunday School picnics down there every summer. We used to have a time up at that beach. From there up to the lighthouse, it was, I guess, about two blocks.

"...After my mother died, see, my father got married again. We children, she left twelve children at her bedside when she died. We just had to scatter and get on ... Mr. Willis [the lighthouse keeper] took my little brother Edgar Taylor. He was going to learn him to be a lighthouse tender, and he took him in down there...Just helping with the light, you know, and so on, cleaning the lights and keeping the place clean and doing what he was doing then, cleaning the stables out and all....

"They were taking [the horses]them across the creek. It was blowing real hard, a March day, and he loaded this guy up, he and Mr. Willis did. Edgar was going to push it, push it across this little creek that come in from the Patuxent River. He was going to push it across there and unload it and then come back. He got right in the channel of this little stream that was going in and he lost control of the boat. It was right heavy. He was a good swimmer. He'd swim anywhere. He had trouble and he couldn't get the boat to push it right, and Mr. Willis saw that he was in trouble and he started to him from the shore in a rowboat. He got near to him and he looked, and Edgar had ran in the other end of the boat, trying to push it. Mr. Willis gave two or three more strokes in the rowboat, and he turned around and looked and never saw nothing. Everything was gone...he was about halfway across the thing when this happened. Of course, he had gum boots, long gum boots, and they say they was what held him down, that he couldn't swim with them on and he couldn't get them off under the water."

DR. EFF:
"I thought that Cedar Point light was connected by a causeway onto the mainland. I thought you could walk. I thought it was connected by land."

MRS. DARE:
"Well, it was at one time, but then it's all washed away now. The river took it all away."

—MYRTLE TAYLOR DARE

Mrs. Myrtle Taylor Dare was interviewed in St. Mary's County, Maryland in 1990 by Elaine Eff, Maryland Historical Trust Cultural Conservation Program, for the oral history project *Keepers and Kin: Maryland Lighthouses of the Chesapeake Bay.* Mrs. Dare was 94 years old at the time of the taping.

---

your lighthouse." Moreover, the War Department had told the company it did not need a permit since the removal was to occur above the high water line.[32]

The statement about not needing a permit was chilling to both King and Putnam, particularly to King, who knew it was true and that it would lead to what he feared most—the company taking the gravel from the thin spit that was the last connection the lighthouse reservation had to the mainland. This removal would lead to a permanent breach of the spit, making the reservation an island. "In my opinion," he said, "this is the end and aim of the Arundel Corporation, for once this neck of land has been cut the abandonment of the lighthouse reservation becomes inevitable in the course of a comparatively short time." The Arundel Corporation would then have a free hand "to proceed with the work of extensive gravel deposits in this vicinity." On receiving King's assessment of the situation, Putnam wrote the secretary asking for the case to be referred to the departmental solicitor "for such action or advice as may be deemed appropriate."[33]

On January 6, 1926, the acting secretary of Commerce sent a request to the attorney general asking that injunction proceedings be undertaken against the sand and gravel company. The Department of Justice responded, saying it was not clear on what basis the Commerce Department thought the company could be enjoined from obtaining gravel above the high water mark. It also asked why the Bureau of Lighthouses had not acquired the land by purchase or condemnation in view of the grave danger to government property. In answer to this communication from the Department of Justice, the acting solicitor at the Commerce Department prepared virtually the same report as that put together when the department had asked for an injunction against Arundel Corporation a year and a half earlier. In transmitting the report to the Department of Justice, the acting secretary of Commerce said the Bureau of Lighhouses would consider purchasing the land if the effort to get an injunction failed.[34]

For all practical purposes the clash between the Bureau of Lighthouses and the Arundel Corporation ended on February 25, 1926, when Keeper Powell wrote:

I regret to have to report to you the fact that beach was torn and destroyed today during S. E. gale the worst storm since I have been here, entire beach during height of storm under water except about 50 ft. from wall and it about 10 ft. wide, at 9 p. m. there is a channel about 100 feet wide about 150 yds. from sta. over my hip boots, and I am afraid it will never fill in again as I write water is running like a mill race through same, wind now S. W.[35]

"On January 6, 1926, the acting secretary of Commerce sent a request to the attorney general asking that injunction proceedings be undertaken against the sand and gravel company. The Department of Justice responded, saying it was not clear on what basis the Commerce department thought the company could be enjoined from obtaining gravel above the high water mark."

"In June a 'heavy south wind' washed water across the length of the neck up to the woods on the mainland. At the same time another gravel crew began operations on the inside or mainland shore of the neck."

Opposite page:
The three–story Cedar Point lighthouse was also a stylish home with two full porches affording a view of both the land and the water. A decorative sunburst on each of the gabled ends accented the design elements below the lantern deck. The photo at left was taken by William Marion Goeshy, a veteran Maryland lighthouse keeper, and it shows his young wife, Beatrice, on the waterside porch steps in the early 1930s.

(Goeshy Gould Collection. MHT Cultural Conservation Program)

He added that the beach was "stripped clean" and the opening seemed to be "widening all the time."

King did not want to decommission the Cedar Point lighthouse immediately, but he knew a change in aids to navigation there was in the offing. In anticipation, he wrote to various maritime organizations, such as steamship companies and pilots' organizations, asking their assessment of the value of the present aid and whether a modern gas and bell buoy would be as useful as the lighthouse. He said that much money had already been spent trying to protect the lighthouse from erosion and that an assessment was being made of the cost of further work to protect the site—money that could be more effectively applied to other projects. He assured the addressees there was no existing plan to put the lighthouse out of service. Early responses indicated that masters of vessels would accept the change to a gas and bell buoy.[36]

In early March King dispatched assistant superintendent T. S. Johnson to Cedar Point to assess the situation. Johnson found conditions not quite as bad as Keeper Powell had reported during the storm. The spit of land connecting the light station to the mainland was only a narrow neck, and its lowest point was submerged about one foot at mean high tide; consequently, there was no "immediate danger of the keeper being cut off from communication with the mainland." Johnson recommended against doing anything to protect the spit, since whatever was done would be expensive and would have to be done on Arundel Corporation property. He also found that the sheet piling under the seawall had been riddled by shipworms, placing a portion of the wall in immediate danger of collapse with much of the remainder likely to fall in a year or two. He felt the station could be operated by a keeper for an indefinite period, but he recommended removing the keeper when he could no longer communicate with the mainland safely. At that time he thought the light should be automated with acetylene and a Dalen sun valve which was light-sensitive and turned the gas off in the morning and back on in the evening. He also urged that the keeper be furnished with a skiff in case the beach washed away.[37]

Two days after Johnson left, a schooner arrived at Cedar Point carrying a crew to remove gravel. The skipper, Capt. Kelly, had in his pocket a copy of the U.S. engineer's letter dealing with removing gravel above the high water mark. He talked to Keeper Powell, who showed him the thin strip connecting the lighthouse reservation to the mainland. Kelly, concluding that gravel should not be removed from the slowly eroding beach, set up operations 700 to 800 yards west of the lighthouse, closer to the mainland and well into a wooded area.

Powell left the lighthouse to telephone in a report of the resumption of gravel removal. He waited until 4:30 p.m. for an answer that never came and then hurried back. As he crossed the thin neck of land to the light station, he noted that water was running a foot deep across a forty-foot swath of the neck. Before a stiff southern wind the tide continued to rise, and Powell estimated that by 8:00 p.m. the swath had widened to 100 feet. Early the next morning the keeper's two sons had to wade through knee-deep water for 200 feet to traverse the neck. Later that day Powell reported, "It is not a case of beach being clear of water during ebb tide, it is a perfect channel, and as south winds continue it hourly gets worse."

On March 8, 1926, King wrote to the commissioner and recommended dropping the injunction proceedings against the Arundel Corporation, since the sand and gravel company had selected a site for their operation that would not damage the light station. Commissioner Putnam replied that a recent storm had severely damaged the neck connecting the light station to the mainland, but that erecting protective works would cost more than the Bureau of Lighthouses was willing to spend. He pushed King's request up the bureaucratic line, and on April 1, 1926, the Justice Department notified the secretary of Commerce that it would take no further action on the injunction.[38]

With the Bureau of Lighthouses unwilling to expend the large amount of money required to build adequate protective works, the condition of the light station steadily declined. In June a "heavy south wind" washed water across the length of the neck up to the woods on the mainland. At the same time another gravel crew began operations on the inside or mainland shore of the neck. Powell felt work should be stopped since the gravel at that location was "the foundation of [the] inside end of beach." In late August a gale from the east swept the area, washing water off the neck from the light station to a point about twenty-five yards into the woods. The Bureau of Lighthouses once again considered undertaking major work to protect the light station from erosion and once again rejected the proposal.

Around the middle of November 1926 a southeast gale—the worst Keeper Powell had seen in his thirty-five years of experience on the water—swept Cedar Point. The water washed over the

Located at the edge of what is now the Naval Air Station Patuxent River complex, the Cedar Point lighthouse has served as a landmark symbol for the Navy base, with its image incorporated into the station logo. When the old structure was battered by hurricanes in the 1970s, the Friends of the Cedar Point Lighthouse initiated efforts to save the lantern, which was moved to the Naval Air Test and Evaluation Museum grounds in 1983.

(MHT photo, c.1970)

woods, uprooting a number of the big pines. Powell saw seven or eight down and others drifting away during the day. Because of the downed pines, the beach was seventy-five yards longer. The damage from this storm appears to support the assessment he had made in June of the effect of the gravel operation.

The station was also damaged in the November storm. A log tore the gate off its hinges, and the station boat was lost. At the height of the gale the yard was under two to three feet of water, and when this receded the basement of the dwelling was flooded with eighteen inches of water. Water had washed over the wall, flooding the bell tower, and water and wind had deposited ten to fifteen tons of sand in front of the barn. By eight o'clock in the evening 250 feet of the neck was covered with two to three feet of water.

In January 1927 Powell sent a more hopeful report. Winds from the south had pushed sand

over the neck, where it settled. The beach was nearly back to its former size, and he felt that in the absence of high tides and heavy storms the "beach has a chance of building up higher than it ever was." In April King visited the station and found the condition of the land bridge more promising. What concerned him was that the riprap at the seawall was failing and the sheet pile foundation of the wall was exposed one to two feet around the station.[39]

About this time King's thoughts crystallized on the course of action that should be taken. He wanted to save the Cedar Point lighthouse by building "defensive works" around its reservation without worrying about saving the neck that connected it to the mainland. His plan, he estimated, would cost $15,000. The proposal did not get a happy reception in Washington; virtually everyone who reviewed it responded negatively, due in part to its cost. Also, the idea of a gas buoy and bell, suggested several years earlier, had lodged firmly in their minds.

Meanwhile, at the light station a little sand had built up at some places and washed away at others, but the seawalls continued to deteriorate fairly rapidly. King suggested to the commissioner that if the Bureau felt the gas buoy and bell was the best solution, it should be tested while the "defensive works" at the station still held. Then, if the buoy did not work, there would still be time to implement his proposal. The commissioner agreed and instructed King to submit a proposal to test the buoy and discontinue the light station. King proposed using a type D gas and bell buoy, which had just been received from the General Depot and was being used in the district as a relief buoy. He said it would be available toward the end of July and proposed starting the test on August 1 and running it for a year. He also recommended retaining the keeper at Cedar Point until the test was completed to protect the property from vandalism.[40]

Commissioner Putnam approved the proposal, and on August 1 the Cedar Point light station went out of service and the new buoy, positioned about 1,150 yards and bearing 75 degrees from the lighthouse, took its place. Within a few days King received a letter from Capt. W. C. Almy, master of the steamer *State of Maryland*, praising the new buoy. King sent a copy to Putnam.

Storms continued to batter the light station, eroding the beaches and contributing to the collapse of the seawalls and riprap. After three storms in October, the neck connecting the station to the mainland was covered with water at all tides and the station was so damaged that Superintendent King feared for the the safety of

Keeper Powell and his family. King recommended closing the station and moving the keeper and his family by November 30, 1927. The Washington office approved, but it is not clear whether Powell left the station at that time, for he later sent several communications to King that were datelined from Cedar Point.

The grounding of the *Mary M.* prompted several complaints about the new buoy. The vessel was an oil burner with a length of 64 feet and a beam of 18 feet. Her skipper, Capt. Greenwell of Hollywood, Maryland, was working the vessel close to shore in a thick fog, when it ran aground near the north jetty at Cedar Point. Fortunately, the grounding occurred at "very low" tide and Capt. Greenwell was able to work the vessel off at high tide.[41]

Capt. L. F. Miles of Pearson, Maryland, wrote to King that it was "an act of Providence" that the *Mary M.* did not have a more serious accident. He thought the lighthouse should be put back into service, citing his belief that all the captains who entered the Patuxent found the buoy useful only in fair weather. King responded that the buoy with bell fully satisfied the needs of those vessels plying the main channel. He recognized, however, that the buoy failed to serve the traffic sailing close to shore and that the concrete wall and stone jetties off Cedar Point were a hazard to this traffic in foggy weather. King recommended putting either a gong buoy "just off the point, as close in as the depth of water will permit, or an unwatched acetylene light on the extreme point of the seawall." Small craft should be considered, King added, but "the experience of the past six months does not, in my opinion, indicate any necessity for the reestablishment of the light station."[42]

At this point it was apparent that the service was not going to reestablish the station, for it would require too much money to make it safe from the elements. Despite the protests of Congressman Stephen Gambrill, who submitted a petition signed by twenty-six masters of vessels asking for the resurrection of the lighthouse, Commissioner Putnam moved ahead with making a decision on King's proposals, including one made in February to sell the light station. He concluded that the light station should be sold except for a 10' x 10' plot of land adjacent to the seawall, where the service would erect a skeleton tower to hold an acetylene light. The Arundel Corporation purchased the rest of the property, paying $2,100 for land and appurtenances, which it officially acquired on July 6, 1928.[43] This price was less than half what the Bureau had paid for the land in 1894.

As time went on more sophisticated means of protecting sites from erosion were developed, and lighthouses in Maryland no longer succumbed to the encroachment of the bay. Threatened lighthouses on the shore—particularly Point Lookout and Cove Point—are well protected, their coasts armored with steel sheet piling and large stone riprap. For caisson lighthouses, still occasionally damaged by scouring, the Coast Guard adds stone at the base of structures having problems.

Growing Pains

As aids to navigation increased in the Chesapeake and operations became more complex, the Lighthouse Board found it needed a depot or storage area in the bay. In 1863 Commodore W. B. Shubrick, chairman of the Lighthouse Board, told his boss, Secretary of the Treasury William Seward, that the Lighthouse Establishment needed a storage area in the Fifth District for supplies, buoys, and other equipment. He asked if the Treasury Department's vacant building at Lazaretto Point could be turned over to the Lighthouse Board. The land area was part of the five acres the federal government had purchased in 1804 from John O'Donnell, first developer of the Canton area, for a lazaretto or fever house for smallpox victims. After checking with local federal representatives, the secretary agreed the Lighthouse Board could take over the structure.

By mid-September 1863, the dilapidated wharf at Lazaretto Point had been rebuilt, the building repaired, and the lighthouse depot put into operation. The keeper of the Lazaretto lighthouse added storekeeping to his duties, for which his salary was increased from $350 to $500 per year.[44]

The depot was not immediately of significant use to the district, for the military took over a major portion of it to store ordnance, but even after the Civil War the depot did not prosper. In 1870 the Board reported that space for storage of buoys in the district was inadequate because only a few buoys for the upper Chesapeake and its tributaries could be stored at Lazaretto. The Board acquired a lot at Portsmouth, Virginia, which it hoped to use as a central depot for light vessels and buoys.

In 1871 the Lazaretto Depot, which had been neglected, received extensive repairs to the workshop, wharf, and seawall. At Portsmouth a new wharf was built and the lot enclosed with a

In 1883 the Point Lookout
light station, located between
the principal Chesapeake
depots at Lazaretto Point
and Portsmouth, Virginia,
assumed an additional func-
tion as a buoy depot. The
new depot's first wharf, 65
feet long, was replaced in
1890 by a 365–foot structure
that broadened as it ap-
proached the buoy and coal
sheds. A new tramway to
help move buoys and sup-
plies of coal to the water was
also added. Note the 1872
fog bell tower visible to the
south of the lighthouse.

(Photos, c. 1900, National
Archives)

fence. Skids on which buoys could be repaired
were placed about the yard. Two buoy depots
were evolving, one serving the northern part of
the bay and the other serving the southern portion. The Lazaretto Depot also became a manu-
facturing shop, for in 1872 it began producing the
framework for screwpile lighthouses and in 1873,
a number of spar buoys and sinkers and two iron
beacons. Portsmouth Depot focused primarily
on buoys, housing the principal supply and man-
ufacturing most of the spar buoys in the district.
It also stored the district coal and emergency
supplies.[45]

By 1877 Portsmouth was the largest depot in
the district, but Lazaretto was more diverse in its
activities. Screwpile lighthouses and caissons
were built there and the first courses of metal
plates were attached to caissons before they

were floated out to the sites. Staff at the depot
kept enough spare buoys on hand to serve the
needs of the upper Chesapeake and Baltimore,
and beginning in 1879 coal was stored there for
district tenders.

In 1882 a new buoy shed 100 feet long and 40
feet wide was built at the Portsmouth Depot, and
the old shed was extended 50 feet to match the
new one. The following year the Lighthouse
Board abandoned the idea of getting land for a
new wharf at Portsmouth. Finding the Army
would be willing to let them have a site with "sufficient frontage on deep water" at Fort Monroe,
the Board asked for an appropriation of $10,000
to establish the new station, including construction of a new wharf. After the depot had moved,
the Portsmouth site could be sold for more than
it would cost to establish the new depot. Con-

The Attack of the Buffeting Buoys

"When we moved from Piney Point to Point Lookout in '31, in August—I can remember it right now, 23rd, 1933—we had a terrible flood and storm. The whole Point, you might say, was on the water, and those buoys were on the racks on the Bay side. Those things got 50, 60 feet long, great big things, that big around, with iron on the bottom of them, and they got floating between those buoy sheds and the lighthouse. They would come down there and hit that lighthouse and it was knocking the corner right out of the building, right apart—with those things floating down through there from the tide—I mean, just like ramrods. We kids got out there, and when they'd come down through there, we'd steer them and let them go on by so they wouldn't tear the lighthouse down. That was a bad flood."

—Herbert Yeatman

gress responded positively, and the Lighthouse Board began work on the new site in 1884. Fortunately, only planning had been done, for when the engineers surveyed the Fort Monroe site they found it unsatisfactory for a depot. The Board decided to rehabilitate the old site and rebuild the dilapidated wharf.

Meanwhile, the Lazaretto Depot, after years of waiting, finally got a new wharf. Completed in January 1884, it was opened to use after the area around it had been dredged and the old wharf torn down. The addition of storage facilities and reconstruction of the seawall put the depot into excellent condition.

In 1883 the Board determined that the great distance between Lazaretto and Portsmouth was delaying buoy work, necessitating a buoy depot between the two principal depots. The site selected for the new depot was Point Lookout light station at the mouth of the Potomac River. The engineers built a wharf 65 feet long and 35 feet wide and a standard 100' x 40' buoy shed. The wharf's piles were sheathed in metal to protect them from shipworms. In 1884 a tramway was built at Point Lookout to facilitate moving supplies and buoys from the buoy shed and the coal shed to the water.[46] Within a few years the other two depots in the bay had tramways also.

During this period Lazaretto Depot was a bustling place. Customs inspectors occupied about a third of the upper floor of the main building. The increasing work of the district kept craftsmen and laborers busy, and dock space was getting crowded again. Portsmouth was also busy but had a more serious dock shortage, requiring a new wharf for which Congress

Herbert Yeatman was born in 1918 a few miles from the Drum Point Lighthouse where his father had also served as keeper. He was interviewed by Elaine Eff, Maryland Historical Trust Cultural Conservation Program, in 1990 for the oral history project *Keepers and Kin: Maryland Lighthouses of the Chesapeake Bay.*

seemed reluctant to appropriate the funds. Point Lookout was more fortunate, for in 1890 money was provided to complete a new wharf and tear down the old one. As in the past, the piles were sheathed in metal. The new wharf was 365 feet long and 15½ feet wide, gradually broadening as it neared the buoy and coal sheds. New railing for the tramway was also put in place.

In 1892 the Portsmouth Depot was finally able to acquire additional land. The depot property, which bordered on the Elizabeth River, then comprised the area on the river bounded by Randolph, First, and Henry Streets. Although the depot itself was not in good condition and virtually all of the structures needed repair, six years passed before any funds were available to do this work and build a new wharf.

In the meantime, another buoy depot was added to the bay, at the old naval proving grounds opposite Annapolis. In 1896 the Navy transferred the land to the Lighthouse Board. The wharf was rebuilt, a tramway was laid, and the depot went into service.[47]

The Annapolis Depot was responsible for buoys between Sandy Point and the Patuxent River. Point Lookout concerned itself with the middle section of the bay and its tributaries. Portsmouth handled the lower section of the bay and kept the supplies for all of the Fifth District. The Lazaretto Depot was responsible for buoys and appendages—mooring anchors, chains, etc.— for the upper part of the bay and continued to be the base for constructing lighthouses. It had workshops for the "preparation of material and preliminary work of construction," as well as for repair work on aids to navigation.[48]

In July 1914, when the Lazaretto lighthouse and fog signal were electrified, power was also brought to the depot. Power machinery was introduced to speed up carpentry work for boats and lighthouse repairs. The depot was deeply involved in all construction and repairs in the district, especially on vessels. The Fifth District had six tenders, eleven light vessels, and about 300 small boats, each of which received repairs from time to time at the Lazaretto Depot. Work on buoys continued to be a considerable part of the depot's workload.

In 1916 a visitor remarked on the congestion at Lazaretto Depot caused by buoys awaiting repairs and the lack of equipment to handle them. The basic problem seemed to stem from the crowded conditions caused by industrial development at Canton. Only six feet from the buoy shed stood a fertilizer plant owned by the American Agriculture Chemical Company. Such plants were susceptible to sudden fire, and in

1911 a fire occurred, lasting all day and well into the night. Fortunately, it was confined to the plant, but men had to stand by, ready to move the scow and pile driver should they be threatened. Two years later another fire broke out in the plant, and this time Lightship No. 52 and the tender Woodbine were in some danger, although fortunately they escaped damage.[49]

The Lazaretto Depot's location in a physically close community had other drawbacks. After the United States's entry into World War I, nearby manufactories hired night watchmen to prevent sabotage. The Lighthouse Service already had a keeper living on the grounds and a night watchman, but companies in the area were vocally critical of the Bureau for not hiring more guards. The district felt sufficiently pressured to hire another guard.[50]

In 1921, probably at the instigation of the Bureau, House Resolution 14899 was passed, calling for expansion and improvement of the Portsmouth Depot. Representative Coady, from Baltimore, was concerned over this move and talked to lighthouse commissioner George R. Putnam, expressing concern that Lazaretto Depot would be closed. Putnam assured him there would always be some sort of activity there because of the importance of the port of Baltimore, the large number of buoys in the upper Chesapeake, and the presence of ship repair facilities in Baltimore, where many lighthouse vessels came for repair and overhaul. He did say the Service had discussed locating district headquarters outside of Baltimore in a more central location. The Fifth District included a good portion of North Carolina, making Norfolk near the middle. He added that only a few jobs were associated with that office, and its space would be quickly filled by other government agencies.

A number of positions were transferred to Portsmouth in 1921, although district headquarters remained in Baltimore. In 1934 the Bureau reorganized and transferred its remaining construction activities from Lazaretto to Portsmouth. Five boatbuilders, three machinists, a woodworker, and a helper-leader were transferred. Lazaretto retained eleven positions—the keeper, two watchmen, a checker, a machinist, a chauffeur, and five laborers and one laborer-leader. On January 23, 1935, the district superintendent wrote the commissioner that the transfer had been completed.[51] By 1938 district headquarters had moved to Norfolk.

That same year the Bureau decided to move its radio laboratory from Detroit to "a more convenient location." It had been established there in 1934 because of the presence of personnel experienced in radio work as well as the marine activities of the Lighthouse Service. Staff at the facility repaired equipment, modernized the radiobeacon, and tested and experimented with new radio aids such as ultrahigh frequency, radiophones, radio control, and improved radio direction finders. Friction developed between the laboratory and the Eleventh District office, and by 1938 the radio lab was looking for a new home. A new building going up at Lazaretto looked like the answer to their wishes. They liked Baltimore because it was becoming a center for radio transmitter manufacture. Bendix Corporation was already there, and Westinghouse's radio plant was relocating to Baltimore. The factories would be both a source for contracting some of the lab's work and a place where materials could be obtained.

The senior radio engineer, L. M. Harding, made a case for the move to Baltimore, and everyone agreed with it. The Fifth District pointed out it would be more efficient for the laboratory to be close to the Washington Office, and the Eleventh District said moving the radio lab would be a source of considerable relief.[52] The real source of conflict between that district office and the lab seems to have been more than just workload. Perhaps it stemmed from the eternal conflict between the old and the new.

During his career George R. Putnam, longtime commissioner of lighthouses, promoted the adaptation of radio to aids to navigation. When he retired in 1935, Putnam considered the introduction of radio into the work of the Lighthouse Service as one his two proudest achievements.

By 1938, on the eve of the radio lab's move to Baltimore, radio was playing an important part in assisting navigators in their work. The Service had 144 radiobeacon stations along the coasts of the continental United States and its territories. Located at light stations and on lightships, these beacons gave out a signal, each distinctive, with a range of 200 miles or more. The beacons could be picked up by vessels with a radio direction finder and operated continuously during fog and for two ten-minute periods per hour in clear weather. With ninety-two radiobeacon stations in operation, the use of the radio telephone was growing. The technology permitted the Lighthouse Service to communicate with remote stations and vessels and provided important weather information.

Ninety-one light stations and vessels had both the radio and sound fog signal. This combination was useful when a vessel was close enough to hear the fog signal, for both the radio signal and

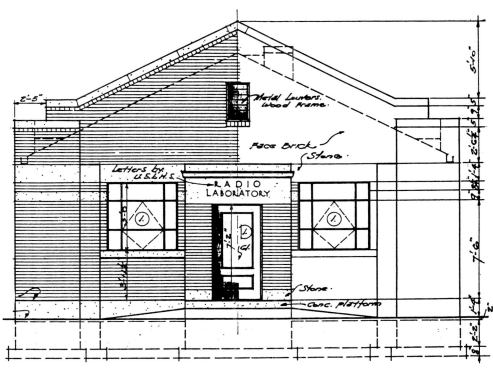

the fog signal were emitted at the same time and timing the difference between receipt of the radio signal and the sound of the fog horn allowed the navigator to determine the ship's distance from the station.

In 1938 the use of radio for remote control was being developed. Two stations and one vessel could be operated by remote control, eliminating the need for keepers. The radio laboratory had been doing research and development in this area and put together several apparatuses on which potential manufacturers could bid. In addition, the lab worked to improve and refine the types of radio signal apparatus to improve the navigational help they offered.[53]

The Lighthouse Service decided that the new building planned for Lazaretto Depot could not be adapted to include the needs of the radio laboratory, so the Washington office provided funds to erect a special building for the lab. A contract for $14,494 was let in August 1938 to Avon Construction Company of Baltimore. In the process of excavating the foundation, the builders uncovered "considerable brickwork" from the old Lazaretto light tower at the southwest corner of the new building.

By the middle of November the laboratory building was nearing completion and the administrative paperwork to transfer the lab's personnel from Detroit to Baltimore was underway. The move was to begin on February 2, and all employees were to be available and at work on February 13, 1939, in Baltimore.[54]

Moving the radio laboratory to Baltimore was the last significant act in the Fifth District before the Lighthouse Service was absorbed by the Coast Guard. It is appropriate that it was an action looking to the future.

By the 1930s the development and refinement of radio aids to navigation had become an important part of the work of the Lighthouse Service. In 1938 the Service decided to move its radio laboratory from Detroit to Baltimore, which was becoming a center for radio transmitter manufacture. Although a new building was already in the planning stages for the Lazaretto Depot, funds were appropriated for a special building for the laboratory which opened at the Lazaretto site on February 1939. During its construction workers uncovered brickwork from the old lighthouse tower, which had been torn down in 1926.

(National Archives, Philadelphia)

Chapter 7

Keeping the Lights

"You need big families in a lighthouse so you can entertain each other, I guess,

because it is kind of lonely. You're off on the last end of nowhere. Only one way you go –

you go up the road. You don't go down the road there, because there's nowhere to go."

—HERBERT YEATMAN*

In general, lighthouse keepers are thought of as duty-bound professionals, but as far as the Chesapeake Bay is concerned, this view did not have much basis in truth until the 1870s. By that time political affiliation as a qualification for the position of keeper had waned, and more and more new keepers were transferred from positions at other light stations. A career service had begun to develop. This trend grew rapidly after 1883, the year the classified civil service was brought into being and hiring government employees on merit became a policy.

Lighthouse keeping evolved into a profession in three stages. During the first stage, from the beginning of government administration until about 1852, those who administered aids to navigation knew little about lighthouses and their operation. The second period began with the founding of the Lighthouse Board in 1852. The military officers and civilian scientists then in control of aids to navigation instituted requirements of discipline and professionalism for the employees of the lighthouse system. The third phase emerged in 1910, when Congress again placed aids to navigation in the hands of civilians, many of whom were career government employees. The new Bureau of Lighthouses maintained the standards of discipline and professionalism of the system and also began to give public credit to those who engaged in rescues in addition to maintaining a good light.

When aids to navigation were controlled by the commissioner of revenue and the fifth auditor of the Treasury, politics played a strong role in the appointment and dismissal of keepers. In a significant number of cases, a keeper's appointment year and removal year coincided with the advent of a new administration. A lengthy but incomplete list of Maryland keepers appointed between 1821 and 1852 reveals a striking number of hirings and dismissals clustered around 1841, 1845, and 1849, the years in which William Henry Harrison, James K. Polk, and Zachary Taylor were inaugurated.

Surviving references for those seeking a lighthouse keeper's position often emphasize the individual's political affiliation. In 1844 William T. Leonard wrote the secretary of the Treasury urging that William Thompson be given the keeper's job at Clay Island. Thompson, he said, was an older but good and honest man who no longer could do hard work but was a "consistent disciple of the Jeffersonian faith." The Matthews brothers of Port Tobacco wrote the secretary telling how pleased they were with the appointment of James H. Morgan, "a devoted Whig," as keeper of the Lower Cedar Point lightboat. In seeking the support of John C. Rives for the position of keeper of the Upper Cedar Point lightboat, Charles J. Lancaster noted that he had been captain of a coasting vessel and had "voted the Democratic Ticket for 35 years."

When Stephen Pleasonton's nominee for the Piney Point lighthouse was rejected in February 1841, he expressed his disappointment to the Alexandria collector of customs in a letter. It would "be proper," he added, "to notify Mr. Heard [the new appointee] that under the circumstances of the case, he cannot, if he accepts, expect to be continued in the place longer than the new administrations shall come into office." In this case, Henry J. Heard was fortunate, remaining at the lighthouse until 1845, when Zachary Taylor came into office.

Sometimes appointments were terminated for political reasons even within a party, as Edward Lucas discovered. William Henry Harrison

Political appointees, politicians, probably a scoundrel or two, heroes, widows and daughters of keepers, old soldiers, adventurers, civil servants, active duty Coast Guardsmen – all were part of the unique cast of characters who served more than 160 years as the keepers of Maryland's lighthouses. Photographed in July of 1885, this unknown keeper of the Bloody Point Bar lighthouse basks in the sun, jaunty in his isolation at the southern end of Kent Island.

(U.S. Coast Guard photo. F. Ross Holland Collection)

*Son of William Yeatman, veteran Southern Maryland lighthouse keeper, Herbert Yeatman was interviewed in 1990 for the MHT Cultural Conservation Program.

An artist created this tranquil engraving captioned, "Interior of an east coast lighthouse" for *St. Nicholas Magazine*. While Maryland lighthouse families lived relatively normal lives, those in remote locations often sent their school–aged children to "board" with a relative for the academic year. Tenders delivered supplies, but most light stations on land contained large garden plots and food was carefully preserved for the winter. Perhaps the romantic window garden, pictured at left, contained more than flowers.

(F. Ross Holland Collection)

appointed Lucas keeper of Bodkin Island lighthouse, but he was removed from the job when Vice President John Tyler succeeded to the presidency after Harrison's death.

Congressional district lines had to be observed in making appointments. When Congressman John Taliaferro suggested a keeper for the soon-to-be-activated lighthouse at Cove Point in 1828, Pleasonton quickly informed him that the policy was to appoint a keeper from the district in which the lighthouse was located. Cove Point was in Congressman Dorsey's district, he added. In 1828 Baltimore Naval Officer Barney stated that he discouraged applicants for keeper's positions who did not live in the district of the lighthouse.

On occasion appointees were active politicians. The first keeper of the North Point range lights, Capt. Solomon Frazier was a member of the state legislature. When completion of the light was delayed, he asked for permission to serve until the legislative term ended the following January. Pleasonton granted this request with the understanding that Frazier would not receive any money as keeper while he served in the legislature.[1]

Usually the local collector of customs or naval officer submitted a list of potential keepers with his preferred candidate mentioned first.

The list then went to the fifth auditor, who usually agreed with it and forwarded it to the secretary of the Treasury. Until the mid-1830s the secretary sent the list on to the White House, where the president of the United States selected the appointee. After the mid-1830s, the secretary made the selection.

Lighthouse keeping in the first half of the nineteenth century was not a difficult job, and many people sought the position for just that reason. An applicant for the Thomas Point lighthouse in 1844 said he was a veteran of the War of 1812 and had fallen on hard times. He was growing older and had a family to support. He felt he should replace the present keeper, who, in addition to having certain moral deficiencies, was strong and healthy and had only a wife to care for. The implication was that this individual could more readily find work elsewhere. An applicant who had lost his vessel to an ice breaker asked the secretary for a keeper's position because his "afflictions" did not permit him to do hard work. In 1849 Levi Cathell of Baltimore wrote directly to the new president, Zachary Taylor, asking to be made keeper of the Lazaretto lighthouse. He said he was old and infirm and had a wife and nine children.[2]

When a keeper was appointed, little guidance was given about performing the tasks of the position. Pleasonton's instructions were limited to telling the district superintendent to inform the new keeper he was to remain at the lighthouse and attend personally to the duties of keeping the light. The keepers may have received some verbal information from the collector of customs, who also served as district superintendent of lighthouses. However, William H. Glover, who became keeper of Bodkin Island light in 1849, said he received no instructions before taking charge of the lighthouse.

In 1828 Pleasonton told Naval Officer Barney, "In reply to your enquiry respecting instructions to the keepers of the floating lights, whatever may be necessary, the superintendents give themselves." This lack of instruction applied to shore-based keepers also. In 1835 Pleasonton issued a one-page list of directions to the keepers, admonishing them to keep lamps burning from sunset to sunrise and to trim the wick every four hours to keep them "exactly even on top." Lamps and reflectors were to be kept clean at all times. Careful records were to be kept of oil received and used. The keeper was not to sell liquor on lighthouse grounds, nor was he to leave the lighthouse without permission of the district superintendent. All communication with the fifth auditor, was to be through the district superintendent.[3]

Pleasonton was solicitous of widows or dependents of deceased keepers and would invariably give them the opportunity to succeed their husband or father. Capt. John Gray, of Bodkin Island, died in August 1822, and William B. Barney strongly recommended that his widow, Araminta, be appointed keeper. Pleasonton endorsed Barney's letter and forwarded it to President James Monroe. The president was not as enthusiastic and responded, "Let her to continue for the present, that the subject may be further considered." The following January he declined to appoint her, saying, "if she will get some male friend of hers to accept the appointment nominally, suffer her to do the duties of Keeper and ascribe the compensation [I] will confer the appointment on him." Mrs. Gray's nephew, Mark W. Foreman, agreed to accept the appointment, and the lady became the sub-rosa keeper. Barney later reported she performed extraordinarily well. By November she had remarried and approached Barney about having her new husband, an alien, appointed keeper. Barney informed her an alien could not be appointed, and at the end of the year she departed the light station. Phillip Marshall became keeper January 1, 1824.[4]

Pleasonton's other appointments of widows

Josephine McWilliams Freeman, one of a number of female keepers on Chesapeake Bay, succeeded her father at Blackistone Island in 1875 and served until 1911. (Dr. Joseph McWilliams hadn't died: he owned the island and was reportedly very busy turning it into a vacation site featuring a steamboat landing and a hotel.)

(Photo courtesy of Josephine Freeman Mattingly. St. Clement's Island – Potomac River Museum Collections)

and dependents followed a more traditional course. In October 1834 David Riley, keeper of North Point, died. His widow was appointed in his stead and was still serving in 1845. Ann Davis was appointed keeper when her father, the Point Lookout keeper, died. By 1838 she had, according to Pleasonton, a reputation as "one of our best keepers." She died in office in February 1847. Mrs. Rosanna Tatham succeeded her husband around 1846 and served as keeper of Bodkin Island until she resigned in 1849. Mrs. M. Nuthall was appointed keeper of Piney Point in 1850 after her husband, John, died. She served until 1861, when she was removed. Mrs. Elizabeth Lusby was appointed keeper of Turkey Point on her husband's death in 1844 and served until she died in 1861. Mrs. Harriet Valliant became keeper of Sharp's Island in 1851, when her husband died.

Pleasonton stated in 1851, "So necessary is it that the Lights should be in the hands of experienced keepers that I have, in order to effect that object as far as possible, recommended on the death of a keeper that his widow, if steady and respectable should be appointed to succeed him, and in this way some 30 odd widows have been appointed." In one instance he appointed a woman as keeper of a Maryland lighthouse although she apparently was not a widow, cer-

Maryland's best–known female lighthouse keeper was Fannie Mae Salter, the long-time keeper at Turkey Point. In 1990 one of Mrs. Salter's children, Olga Crouch, was interviewed about her mother's life: "When I was sixteen, we came up here. Then after Dad died, the next year... I married. We lived with Mama to help her keep her light... She wanted to stay here and she wanted to do her best... Mama, she would start out in a terrible thunderstorm to go down to the bell house and start the bell... She missed my dad, but her work was a big thing to her." Mrs. Salter had a garden, reared her children and raised turkeys on the isolated bluff.

(Photos c. 1935, courtesy of the descendants of Fannie Mae Salter. MHT Cultural Conservation Program)

tainly not of the outgoing keeper. In October 1845 Mrs. Charlotte Suter succeeded Henry J. Heard at Piney Point. She was removed in May of the following year.[5]

The Lighthouse Board had a policy against appointing female lighthouse keepers, at least without the permission of the Board. Despite this attitude, the personnel records of the period 1852-1910 show the Board not only did not remove female keepers appointed under the fifth auditor but themselves appointed a number of women to serve as keepers and assistant keepers. Indeed, Piney Point lighthouse had two female keepers in a row in the 1870s, Elizabeth C. Wilson and Mrs. Helen C. Dune. The Board often appointed widows to keeper positions, and wives often worked as assistant keepers while their husbands were keepers.[6] The women were generally paid the regular rate for their work, although on occasion, when wives wanted to live with their husbands at isolated light stations, they were listed as assistant keeper but not paid.

The policies of the Bureau of Lighthouses regarding women were similar to those of the Lighthouse Board, even to taking advantage of free help. Mrs. James L. Weems served as assistant keeper at Drum Point without pay so she could live at this screwpile lighthouse with her husband.[7] The last female civilian lighthouse keeper in Chesapeake Bay was Mrs. Fannie May Salter, at Turkey Point. She retired in 1947, having served twenty-two years after her husband had died.

The Lighthouse Board sometimes allowed wives to visit their keeper husbands for short periods during the summer months, but the Board members were more rigid than the Bureau of Lighthouses in giving permission for these visits. For example, they did not think it advisable to let wives and families visit keepers at facilities with an assistant keeper. After 1910 the Bureau allowed families to live at or visit the "water stations" with the permission of the district superintendent. There was danger on the water, however, a fact tragically underscored when the family of Keeper L. E. Tillett of the Lower Cedar Point light station visited him in September 1920 and a child drowned. The family had been given the required permission, and district superintendent H. D. King feared the commissioner might decide to prohibit future family visits to lighthouses. He urged the commissioner to continue permitting family visits during the summer months, under the conditions already in effect. Ultimately Commissioner Putnam agreed with King and allowed the visits to continue.[8]

Though Pleasonton's attitude about women

was reasonably enlightened, his attitude toward blacks was probably typical of the day. He had an exceedingly low opinion of their ability and character and did not want blacks employed in lighthouses or on lightboats, except as cooks for lightboat crews. Before the regulation on this subject was issued, Pleasonton wrote, many lightboat captains "were in the habit of employing negro crews, . . . generally slaves belonging to themselves. It was obvious that the public property ought not to be entrusted to people of this class, who are irresponsible, and are always careless of what is committed to them, nor could a discrimination be made between the free and the slave. It was thought indispensible therefore to prohibit their employment in any of the Boats, with the single exception of a cook, and this exception was made because white male cooks are not easily to be obtained." Pleasonton believed in strict adherence to the regulation against black crewmen, even to the point of paying seamen more than the prevailing rate in order to get whites.[9]

This policy was not continued under the Lighthouse Board or the Bureau of Lighthouses, though there must have been a transition. At the time of the Civil War, the Board required special permission to hire blacks, and some were employed during this period. This hiring practice may have been a temporary policy that applied only in the war zone.

Though neither the Board nor the Bureau kept records about the race of its employees, the 1870

Fannie Mae Salter climbed the Turkey Point tower with fuel for "her" light until she was sixty years old. The lighthouse was converted to electricity in 1942 but the lens still needed to be spotless. After Mrs. Salter's retirement in 1947 at the age of 65, the light was automated.

(U.S. Coast Guard photo. F. Ross Holland Collection)

After the turn of the century, family visits to the "water stations" could be scheduled for the summer months if permission was granted by the district superintendent. Unfortunately the visits could be dangerous for small children. In 1920 a child drowned while visiting the Lower Cedar Point lighthouse and Herbert Yeatman relates a close call at Point No Point *below*.

(Point No Point lighthouse photo, 1918, F. Ross Holland Collection)

"When my father was at No Point lighthouse, my sister went out there to get up in the lighthouse, and she fell off the ladder, overboard, and she was wearing these little full skirts. The air caught under it and she was floating down the bay. My father had to jump overboard and catch her and bring her back. She thought that was the greatest thing in the world, floating down the bay, didn't realize she was getting ready to drown. . . She must have been four or five years old at that time, but she can still remember it."

—HERBERT YEATMAN

146

report of inspections in the Fifth District noted that the Lower Cedar Point lighthouse had a "colored" keeper and assistant keeper. The former was named Robert Darnell and the latter John F. Parker; both were listed as "young."[10] Despite the presence of these two men, it appears as if the employees of the Lighthouse Board and the Bureau of Lighthouses in Maryland were nearly all white.

Applicants to tend lighthouses were always numerous. Activation of a new lighthouse, death of a keeper, even rumor of a death or a dismissal, generated a spate of letters from office seekers. In one instance, when Pleasonton heard the North Point keeper had died, he asked for information from the district superintendent, who replied, "Such a report was circulated here two weeks since principally by a Captain Fox, who was desirous of obtaining the situation."[11] Many letters were simply from unemployed persons seeking jobs, often at a specific lighthouse.

Many of the keepers selected during the period of patronage turned out to be marginal, and some were of even lesser quality. A few were competent and conscientious keepers. Winslow Lewis, designer of the lighting system used in the lighthouses at that time and a builder of lighthouses, remarked, "Government have heretofore been rather unfortunate in their selection of keepers for Light Houses in the Chesapeak."[12]

Pleasonton was aware of the poor keepers and often erupted at their delinquencies. When the Piney Point keeper did not seek another contractor for a serious erosion problem when the one employed for the work did not show up, Pleasonton observed, "Such an embecile ought not to remain there." He found the district superintendent at fault, as well, because when he learned the work was not under way, the superintendent did not go to the site and prod the keeper to action.[13]

The many legitimate complaints made about the performance of lighthouse keepers centered, as might be expected, on how the light was kept. In 1827 Naval Officer Barney reported that the lights at North Point were poorly kept and the station had "become a disgrace to any keeper." He added, "In fact whether from the infirmity of age, sickness or indolence, the keeper appears perfectly indifferent to his duty, and things are going the wrong way very fast." A year later Barney wrote to Pleasonton, sending an anonymous letter he had received complaining how poor the North Point range lights were, with the western being out more often than the eastern one at North Point. During this period he despatched a letter to Pleasonton citing the number of com-

plaints he had received about the keeper and, apparently, about the poor quality of the light at North Point.[14] In 1838 Winslow Lewis complained of the poor condition of the lighting apparatus at Piney Point and the failure of the keeper to keep it properly clean. Two years later Pleasonton heard "verbally" that the light was badly tended at Piney Point and frequently went out before daylight. Moreover, the keeper was often away from the lighthouse, leaving the station "in the care of a negro woman or boy." In view of Pleasonton's attitude about those of African descent, the last statement must have caused his blood pressure to rise. In 1843 Captain Prince of the revenue cutter *Wolcott* said Piney Point "is indifferently kept, and requires repairs." A month later Capt. Jonathan Howland, the supplier of oil to the nation's lighthouses, reported the lighting apparatus at Piney Point was dirty and in terrible condition—the reflectors were covered with soot or lamp black, and the lamps had been burning without tubes though a dozen were on hand. In 1849 the district superintendent received complaints about the light at Cove Point being "too feeble . . . for its location." In the same year Pleasonton received a verbal report that on at least one evening both lights were out at North Point.

By this time Pleasonton had long since abandoned the position of Thomas Jefferson, who had said, "I think the keepers of lighthouses should be dismissed for small degrees of remissness, because of the calamities which even these produce." Instead, in response to the complaints he received, Pleasonton took cautious action, instructing the district superintendent to inspect the stations and talk to local people, as well as to ship's masters who passed the lighthouses frequently, about the quality of light and, if necessary, to obtain written statements.[15]

Lightboats came in for their share of complaints, which were usually directed at the keeper rather than the crew. Finding qualified seamen to serve as crew for the light vessels was difficult, and in order to hire crew, it was necessary to pay them merchant marine wages. In the beginning, lightboat keepers hired their own crew and were given the money to pay them. Many of these keepers, according to a report in 1838, hired local people, most of whom were farmers.

This hiring procedure was open to cheating by less than honest keepers. In 1828 Seaman John J. Graves accused Capt. Fox, keeper of the Hooper Strait lightboat, of paying the seamen $10 per month each while charging the government regular seaman's wages, which were $16 per month.

Lurching off the Lightship

"Most of the time at night he would tell me all these stories of the experiences that he'd had on lighthouses, and he had lived or had been stationed on the lightships for years and years and years. One time he stayed out on the lightships for nine months, and he came ashore and he had all of his paychecks in his pocket, and he had such wobbly legs, he sat on the curb and the police picked him up and said he was a drunk. He wasn't a drunk. They tested him and found out that he wasn't a drunk. He said, 'Where can I go to have these checks cashed?' And they said, 'Your best bet will be the Red Cross.' So he went to the Red Cross and got his checks cashed."

—BEATRICE GOESHY GOULD

Beatrice Goeshy Gould married William Marion Goeshy in 1930 and spent her "honeymoon year" at the Drum Point Lighthouse. Keeper Goeshy served in lightships, at the Craighill Channel Range and at Piney Point. In a 1990 interview with Elaine Eff, Maryland Historical Trust Cultural Conservation Program, Mrs. Gould recalled that her husband served for 30 years and died on the day that he was to retire.

"After he [my father] left Seven Foot Knoll, he transferred down to Point No Point lighthouse.... It's in the bay about four miles, something like that, offshore. Anyway, he was stationed out there. Oh, this must have been about 1912, '15, along in there.

"Anyway, one time while he was out there, the whole bay froze over and he was stranded out there for so long, a month or so, and couldn't get ashore, and he ran out of food. So he takes the shelves out of the closets and all, and builds a little scow, enough to float him if he broke through [the ice] walking ashore, and he walked on shore with that little rig. He didn't break through or drown or anything, naturally."

—HERBERT YEATMAN

Naval Officer Barney said that Fox's response, when apprised of this charge, "remove[s] from my mind every idea of his culpability."[16] It would be interesting to know what the other seamen had to say about this charge.

In 1838 Captain Webster, of the revenue cutter then based in Chesapeake Bay, charged that many keepers of lightboats—particularly, it seemed, in Virginia waters—had not been paying their crews all the money due them. The upshot of an investigation by the Norfolk collector of customs was to have the collectors, in their capacity as district superintendents of lighthouses, hire and pay the seamen. On his appointment as keeper of the Lower Cedar Point lightboat in April 1845, Thomas Shorter was informed he would neither hire nor pay the seamen. He wrote Pleasonton that people had been writing disparagingly of him because the local collectors hired and paid the crew, a responsibility he should have. Pleasonton, sugar-coating his response somewhat, replied that some years back the collectors had been given the responsibility of hiring and paying the crew because keepers had been employing unfit seamen who often left the vessel during the day, leaving only "negro boys" to protect it. Whether these rumors were true or not, he went on, was of small consequence since it was best to take precautions. "If this regulation cannot be carried out," he added, "I shall recommend to Congress to substitute Lighthouses for these vessels, as answering a better purpose at less than one-half the expense." A few months later Pleasonton heard that Shorter had told his crew their wages were to be reduced to $10 dollars a month. They had been getting $22, which included $7 for rations. Pleasonton immediately wrote to the acting collector, who was filling in for the ill regular one, informing him it was the collector's responsibility to hire the seamen and pay them. He was not, Pleasonton added, to rely on the keepers to hire and pay seamen. This distrust probably influenced Pleasonton to contract with a supplier to provide rations for those stationed on lightboats, rather than giving the personnel an allowance.[17]

Failure of keepers and crews to obtain permission when leaving a lightboat was prevalent throughout the country, but particularly so in Chesapeake Bay. Unquestionably, it happened more often than is evident from the surviving correspondence, since many no doubt were not caught. Lightboats were located in isolated places and were not closely supervised by the distant collectors of customs. Complaints about Maryland keepers leaving light vessels at night

or during the day were received more often than they should have been, but the situation is understandable when political appointees with no sense of service were running the vessels. Also, it appears these political appointees had some protection, for if charges were lodged against an individual, he would be investigated by the collector of customs, another political appointee, most likely of similar political persuasion. As described above, the seaman's charges against Capt. Fox, keeper of the Hooper Strait lightboat, were dismissed by the local collector of customs after he received a written explanation from Fox. No other investigation was undertaken.

In 1841 a person signing himself Capt. Francis Keeyes wrote of the keeper's neglect of the Upper Cedar Point light vessel. Pleasonton directed the district superintendent to investigate and report if the keeper, James H. Neale, "is constantly in the vessel at night attending to his duty, or whether he leaves it in charge of a white man and a lame black man as stated in the letter." At the same time he reminded the superintendent that it was his responsibility to hire the seamen. For his dereliction, Neale was instructed to stay aboard the lightboat at night; if he did not, he would be removed. At the same time, Minchen Lloyd, keeper of the Lower Cedar Point light vessel, was accused of being absent from the lightboat and virtually confessed to the fact. He received the same punishment as Neale. Henry Shenton, keeper of the Hooper Strait lightboat in the late 1840s, justified his absences from the vessel on the basis that past keepers had done it. Pleasonton instructed the district superintendent to tell Shenton to stay aboard the boat, making his absences few and short, otherwise he would be removed. All of these keepers received, at best, a slap on the wrist for their derelictions.

The keeper of the Upper Cedar Point lightboat, Thomas Lloyd, was caught with his absences exposed in the spring of 1849, when the *John Emory*, a schooner, ran into the lightboat, damaging the vessel and its lantern. Lloyd and his crew were not aboard at the time. An investigation by the district superintendent revealed that Lloyd was never aboard more than once a week and "never at night." On receiving the report, Pleasonton recommended Lloyd's removal to the secretary of the Treasury. In less than two weeks, a new keeper, James H. Neale, was named to replace him.[18]

George W. Keene, keeper at Hooper Strait, was the subject of accusations that he absented himself from the lightboat two to three weeks at a time, leaving no one in charge, and that he was constantly drunk, unfit for duty, and disagreeable as a supervisor. The accusers, the three crew members, even asked that he be discharged. The collector of customs informed Keene and asked him to answer the charges. Keene termed all the charges false, but dealt in detail only with the accusation of being away from the vessel. He said he had been away visiting an ill sister "who died yesterday." On his departure, Keene said, he left the mate and all the crew, as well as Capt. A. H. Pritchell, whom he had hired to take his place.[19] When he received the response, the collector bundled up all the papers associated with the issue and mailed them off to the secretary of the Treasury with the recommendation that nothing be done until he could investigate further, adding he felt the lightboat was in good hands. Further action on this case was perhaps lost in the investigation of 1851 which led to the establishment in 1852 of the Lighthouse Board.

Many complaints were made about lighthouses and lighthouse keepers, but not all of them were justified; some were obviously sent by people who hoped to dislodge a keeper to get his job. It is difficult to view the record today and state with assurance which complaints were legitimate and which were sent with ulterior motives. One view is to reject the anonymous ones and generally to accept those that came from knowledgeable people, such as the oil contractor, the captains of the revenue cutters, and, with caution, such people as Winslow Lewis and John Donahoo.

Though Pleasonton could become infuriated with keepers when they did something wrong, he nevertheless had a deep concern for their living conditions and welfare. In 1835, when it became necessary to build a new keeper's dwelling at Cape Henry, he remarked to the district superintendent, "If there is not a Porch to the house, one ought to be added for the comfort of the family, in that warm and exposed situation."[20] This concern was not uncommon for him, and several times he reminded the collector of customs that a porch should be included in new construction.

The managers of the resort adjacent to the Piney Point lighthouse complained in 1839 of the keeper's cow grazing on their property. Pleasonton instructed the district superintendent to go to the site and make some sort of settlement whereby the keeper could have pasturage on the property or access to it. He made it clear he wanted no settlement that would force the keeper to get rid of his cow, since that would deprive his family of the milk. In 1845 Pleasonton authorized the purchase of a cookstove for the Pooles

Island keeper's dwelling because it was for the comfort of the keeper and his family.

Pleasonton's attitude about the welfare of the keepers may have mellowed over the years. The surviving records generally indicate that during his early years as the administrator of lighthouses he was quite strict about spending money on any items for them. In 1829 he refused to pay for cookstoves for the Bodkin Island and Fog Point lighthouses, saying keepers were not allowed such stoves and furniture. About the middle of the 1830s he began to authorize the supply of two cords of wood annually at the lighthouses. Although it was his policy to purchase boats only for lighthouses on islands, Pleasonton could be persuaded by district superintendents to authorize a boat for a mainland lighthouse if their justification was reasonably strong. Over the years he shifted his attitude, and it became even easier for keepers to obtain a boat.[21]

Keeper Leonard Staubley was photographed in uniform in front of his Blackistone Island lighthouse in 1927. Prior to 1880 keepers wore civilian clothes, but in 1884 the Lighthouse Board mandated a dark blue jersey or flannel uniform with cap, vest, double-breasted coat and trousers. Captain Staubley served from 1912 to 1917, returning from World War I to serve again as keeper from 1920 to 1932 when the station was closed.

(St. Clement's Island – Potomac River Museum Collections)

From 1882 until 1917 a Scottish immigrant, Captain Stephen Andrew Cohee, *(right)*, manned the lighthouse at Pooles Island, an isolated site in the upper bay. Over the course of 35 years he buried a wife, Anna, took a second, Agnes, and gave his seven children, and later his grandchildren, the run of the island with a pack of water dogs. One son, Bill, educated himself by reading near the oil lamps in the lantern of the lighthouse, according to Peg Cohee, who married the keeper's grandson. Gladys Cohee *(right)* posed on the beach near a towering pile of ice, while grandson Steve, who lived on the island with his parents from 1912 to 1917 is surrounded by puppies and chickens.

(Photos courtesy of Mrs. Stephen William Cohee)

Pay for working in a lighthouse did not increase much for nearly a hundred years after the first Maryland lighthouse was lit. The early lightkeepers in Maryland received $350 per year, the lowest amount paid keepers in the young United States. At that time the ceiling was $400 annually, enacted by Congress. For more isolated locations, such as Clay and Pooles Islands, the pay increased $50. The highest paid keeper for many years was the one at North Point, who received $600 a year because of having to tend two lighthouses. After 1831 when the fog bell was installed, the Pooles Island keeper received an additional $60 per year.

In 1915 the keeper of Leading Point lighthouse received $520 per year, a sum that increased to $676 when he was given the added duty of tending both of the Brewerton Channel range lights.[22] This amount was just $76 more than Solomon Frazier had received in 1823 for tending the range lights at North Point. At this time the commissioner of lighthouses received $5,000, while his top assistants took in $4,000 each per year.

A decided improvement in the welfare of the keepers came in 1918, when a retirement system went into effect for field personnel such as lightkeepers and light vessel employees. Two years later, the retirement system was expanded to cover "most of the other persons in this Service excepted from the special [1918] law."[23]

Pleasonton turned a deaf ear to keepers who claimed reimbursement for something they had done at a light station without proper authority, no matter how useful their actions may have been. When Benjamin Mead was removed as keeper of Thomas Point lighthouse in 1835, he claimed payment for a stable and smokehouse he had erected while at the station. Because the work had not been authorized, Pleasonton denied the claim. In 1849 Ezekial Morrison filed a claim for $15 he spent whitewashing the light and bell towers at Pooles Island. Pleasonton denied this claim on grounds that the keeper had done the painting himself; if he had gotten someone else to do it, Pleasonton would have honored the claim with a proper receipt. In 1830 Mrs. Hester Fox claimed $15 for a roundhouse her husband had erected on the Hooper Strait light vessel. Pleasonton refused the claim but offered to let her have the roundhouse, if she wanted it.[24]

The Cohees kept chickens and hogs for winter meals and in the summer months the four girls "fished" for perch by scooping them up in peach baskets. They reportedly used a garden rake to catch crabs. Keeper Cohee supplemented his income by catching rockfish and selling them in the Chesapeake City markets. Agnes Cohee made most of the children's clothes and the captain bought their shoes during his twice–yearly boat and buggy trips to "town." He measured the children's feet with a forsythia switch to be sure he would buy the right size.

(Photo courtesy Mrs. Stephen William Cohee. Interview notes, Teresa Kaltenbacher, 1996)

Floating ice was a menace that the keepers of both lightboats and screwpile lighthouses had to contend with. Built in 1875, the Thomas Point Shoal lighthouse was battered by moving ice two years later and was soon guarded by piles of stone and cast–iron ice breakers.

(MHT photo by Mark R. Edwards, 1985)

In the early days of navigational aids in Maryland the threat of greatest concern to the lighthouse keepers was erosion, but for the lightboats the most important was floating ice. To avoid the damage ice could cause, Pleasonton had the light vessels brought into port during the period when ice was most likely to be a problem—generally about December 15 to February 1. The specific dates were determined each year by Pleasonton. If a keeper sought refuge at other times, he was lashed with the sharp side of Pleasonton's tongue. In January 1850 George W. Keene, keeper of the Hooper Strait lightboat, felt threatened by increasing ice at the vessel's station and moved the boat to the safety of a nearby creek. Pleasonton was upset when he heard and threatened to have Keene removed. Keene, however, escaped punishment. Pleasonton learned

the lightboat keeper had not received his notice about moving lightboats prior to seeking refuge. In addition, Keene had found the ice was getting thick and feared the vessel would become caught in it, doing injury to it and keeping him from getting medical help for a crew member who was near death.

Ice was later a great threat to keepers manning the screwpile lighthouses. Floating ice is not a problem in Chesapeake Bay every year, but it comes every so often, and in the late nineteenth and early twentieth centuries screwpile lighthouses made especially vulnerable targets. The first victim was the first screwpile lighthouse erected in the bay. Ice overturned the Pungoteague lighthouse in 1856, just short of completion of its first year. Fortunately, Pungoteague's lantern and lens were saved. In January 1877 ice pushed over the first Hooper Strait lighthouse. The wooden superstructure drifted for five miles before it fetched up on the shore. Two years later the Janes (James) Island lighthouse was demolished by ice. Three years after that, ice tore the Sharp's Island lighthouse from its screwpiles, and the two keepers rode the structure until it grounded, an action for which they were commended by the Lighthouse Board. In 1893 ice pushed over the Solomons Lump lighthouse, leaving it partially submerged.[25] Virtually all of the other screwpile lighthouses were buffeted more than once by floating ice and had to be repaired when warm weather returned. Fortunately, none of these accidents or ice-buffetings caused serious injury or death to any lightkeepers, but unquestionably it caused them, at the least, some anxious moments.

Over the years the Lighthouse Board tried several techniques to keep ice away from the lighthouses. They first attempted to fend it off with a barrier of poles screwed into the bottom on the sides of the lighthouse that caught the normal currents of the bay. These were not effective and the Board began dumping heavy stone where the poles had been. These stones worked quite well, although the individual deposits had to be replenished every so often. Piles of stone can still be seen on the north and south sides of the Thomas Point Shoal lighthouse.

Ice continued to wreak havoc in the Chesapeake. In January 1918, particularly severe weather—the worst since 1856—struck most of the country, especially affecting Chesapeake Bay and the sounds of North Carolina. As a consequence, the Lighthouse Service reported, "by far the most serious and widespread destruction [occurred] in Chesapeake Bay and the sounds of

North Carolina, where upwards of 125 lights of all classes have been badly damaged or destroyed." "The ice," the Service added, "has not only caused the complete destruction of many unwatched lights, but has also swept away or seriously injured a number of attended light-houses, particularly those on pile foundations." Several lightships in the southern part of the bay were dragged from their stations and seriously damaged. A tug and a tender continued moving about the bay to see that the keepers had enough food and to assess the damage done to the structures. The harsh weather continued into March, doing more damage to aids, including nearly destroying the Old Plantation Flats screwpile lighthouse in Virginia. Drifting ice struck the Greenbury Point Shoal lighthouse, causing the lens to fall off its pedestal. Two panes in the lantern broke, Keeper John Berentson reported, and "everything in the house was upset except the stove and water tanks."[26]

In February 1920 the keeper and assistant keeper abandoned the Maryland Point light-house because of heavy running ice. They feared for their safety, especially when they could not keep a fire in the stove or operate the light and fog bell. They returned after five days to find no damage to the structure but some to the riprap.[27]

Storms and the possibility of fire were also potential threats to Maryland lighthouses. On the whole, screwpile lighthouses held up quite well when a severe storm swept the bay. A few structures were damaged, but most were quickly repaired. On August 23, 1933, a storm did "considerable damage" to the Drum Point lighthouse. Waves fifteen feet high swept the lower deck of this screwpile lighthouse and pushed a tree against the legs of the foundation. The tree remained there and caught other driftwood the storm brought. The sea flooded the lower floor, and a gaff on the davit broke and dumped the station's motorboat into the bay, where sand filled it. The same storm lashed the Point No Point caisson lighthouse and broke porthole glass, flooding the cellar. Salt water filled the station's water tanks, and the sailboat was ripped from the davits and drifted away.[28] This storm

Ice also caused trouble at land-based lighthouses. The keeper at the Concord Point light station must have had great difficulty in getting to the lantern from his distant dwelling during the ice gorge of 1904.

(Postcard image, Kenneth G. Lay Collection)

A Wild and Stormy Struggle

The most daring rescue in the history of Maryland's lighthouses was undertaken by Keeper Thomas J. Steinhise of the Seven Foot Knoll lighthouse. On the night of August 20, 1933, the tugboat *Point Breeze*, caught in a northeaster, began taking on water. At 12:30 a.m. on the 21st the captain ordered the crew to abandon ship. Meanwhile, he fired flares that fortunately attracted the attention of Steinhise. The keeper decided the vessel was in serious trouble and lowered the station's motor boat into the water. With waves breaking over his small craft and interfering with the operation of the engine he made his way to the desperate seamen who were calling to him from all directions. He retrieved five of the crew from the bay and also the body of the tug's chief engineer. The captain, chief mate, and the captain's young son stayed aboard the tug and were subsequently rescued by another tug. Steinhise, in the meantime, made his way back to the lighthouse where he took aboard the five who were alive and the body of the chief engineer. Here he rendered first aid to the injured.

L.M. Hopkins, superintendent of the 5th Lighthouse District, which embraced Chesapeake Bay, urged that the secretary of Commerce send a letter of commendation to Steinhise and recommended he also be given a life saving medal, later refining that recommendation to a gold life saving medal. The secretary quickly dispatched a letter to Keeper Steinhise praising him for his actions. The Committee on Life Saving Medals evaluated Steinhise's actions on the night of August 20 and 21, 1933, and concluded the standards called for the keeper to receive a silver medal. This prized award was presented to Keeper Steinhise in January 1936.

Seven Foot Knoll File, Lighthouses of the Chesapeake Bay, Maryland Historical Trust Cultural Conservation Program, *Keepers and Kin,* oral history collection compiled by Elaine Eff.

Maryland's lighthouse keepers were sometimes rescuers *(above)* and at other times were rescued. In this undated winter photo a formidable rescue party poses in front of the nation's first caisson lighthouse, the ice–bound Craighill Channel range front lighthouse. The object lying on the ice may be a physician's bag.

(MSA SC 2117 – 152)

also injured the Thomas Point Shoal lighthouse and the rear light for Craighill Channel.

The most serious fire in a Maryland lighthouse occurred at Lower Cedar Point in 1894. The screwpile lighthouse was completely destroyed and had to be rebuilt. The investigators were never able to determine the cause of the conflagration. Running a close second to this incident was the gutting by fire of the Bloody Point Bar caisson lighthouse in 1960. Only one of the two Coast Guardsmen was burned, and he only slightly. In 1929 Keeper H. C. Sterling accidentally set the Solomons Lump lighthouse on fire while burning off paint that covered rotten wood. He was able to put out the flames quickly with a fire extinguisher. At the Hooper Island lighthouse the year before, the incandescent oil vapor lamp had caught on fire, damaging several prisms and two center rings of the lens. The lens had to be removed and replaced by a lens on hand, which had been made of spare parts in the district depot.[29]

Lighthouse keepers and lightboat tender crews rescued people in distress on the bay under the fifth auditor and the Lighthouse Board—far more under the latter than the former—but this part of their work was emphasized more under the Bureau of Lighthouses. The Bureau took pride in this duty of its employees and recorded their deeds in the *Lighthouse Service Bulletin*, a monthly, in-house publication that briefly chronicled activities of the Service. In a section on personnel, the *Bulletin* mentioned keepers and incidents in which they were involved, usually rescues or assistance to boaters. The earliest entry for a Maryland keeper commended Henry C. Wingate of Piney Point "for rendering assistance to a schooner which had run aground." William H. Davis, Jr., keeper of the Lazaretto Point Depot, was commended for "the precautions he took to prevent the spread of a fire to the Lazaretto Point Lighthouse Depot." The notations were unfortunately brief. For example, the *Bulletin* reported only that keeper Thomas Jacobson of Point Lookout gave assistance to "the occupants of U.S. Navy Hydroplane C-1, which was disabled in the water, and towed the boat to shore." The more detailed official report of this incident reveals the plane landed three miles northeast of the lighthouse and Jacobson went to its assistance in the station sailboat, towing the plane to the river (southwest) side of the station, and hauling it up on shore. In addition, he provided quarters for the aviators who spent two nights with him before they were able to get their plane operating again.[30]

Types of assistance rendered by lightkeepers over the years ran the gamut of problems mariners and others could run into on the bay. Reported incidents included helping occupants of a disabled motorboat get to safety, helping a launch get off a bar, participating in the rescue of a man overboard from a steamer, furnishing food and assistance to two oystermen whose canoe overturned in winter, rescuing two men in a skiff caught in drift ice and providing food and shelter for them for nearly a week, assisting fishermen lost in a fog, and towing disabled boats to where they could be repaired.

Some rescues had rather unusual features. A. J. Simpson, keeper of Blackistone Island, assisted "five occupants of a sailboat, which was drifting toward a deep hole of whirlpools." One afternoon in August 1919, Keeper G. M. Willis of Point Lookout "rescued three persons from drowning, recovered the body of another person who had drowned, and endeavored to recover the bodies of two other persons." In his report of the accident, H. D. King, the district superintendent of lighthouses, said, "It is considered that the services rendered in the saving of life on this occasion constitutes a case of actual heroism." In May 1923 Keeper C. W. Salter of Turkey Point "rendered assistance to a barge which was being towed by a motor boat that became disabled." This was another instance in which the official report is more interesting and enlightening than the cryptic *Bulletin* listing. The barge was an auction boat billed as a "Floating Department Store Loaded with Bankrupt Merchandise." It carried men's, women's, and children's clothing and shoes. The motorboat towing the barge became disabled, and Keeper Salter saw the barge was about to be caught in a strong northwest wind. He used the light station's boat to tow the barge to safety under Turkey Point. The dry goods on board were valued at $25,000.[31]

The assistance the keepers provided to those who ran into misfortune was a service those who used the bay came to appreciate. Being caught on a foggy night on the water with no food and inadequate clothing and then stumbling across a lighthouse where the keepers not only rendered assistance, but provided food and shelter for the night filled many with gratitude. In 1936, when the Bureau of Lighthouses contemplated automating the Seven Foot Knoll lighthouse, the district superintendent objected to the proposal, "stating it would be strenuously opposed by local people, particularly because of life saving work in the past by these keepers."[32] This refrain was to be heard often over the next three or four decades as the Bureau, and later the Coast

Maryland lighthouse keepers intervened in many incidents on the water. Henry Wingate of the Piney Point lighthouse saved a schooner that had run aground, Thomas Jacobson of Point Lookout towed a U.S. Navy hydroplane back to safety at the lighthouse and Clarence W. Salter of Turkey Point rescued a floating department store. The "store" was an auction boat, a barge loaded with dry goods valued at $25,000. When the motorboat pulling the barge became disabled, Salter towed the barge to safety in the station boat. An experienced keeper in Virginia, Salter died shortly after going to Turkey Point and was succeeded by his widow, Fannie Mae. At left he is pictured in Virginia waters c. 1910.

(Photo courtesy of the descendants of Fannie Mae Salter. MHT Cultural Conservation Program)

Because of the many services rendered by keepers to those in danger on the bay, the district superintendent objected strongly when the Bureau of Lighthouses first mentioned automating the Seven Foot Knoll lighthouse in 1936. The lighthouse was automated in 1948 and the modern plastic lens shown above was in place when the lighthouse was photographed in 1987 for the Historic American Buildings Survey.

(Photo by Jay L. Baker, Library of Congress, HABS No. MD–54)

Guard, automated lighthouses. It indicates how firmly this aspect of the work of the lightkeepers had become implanted in the public mind.

In effect, the elimination of lightkeepers began in 1902 when the Lighthouse Board converted the lighting apparatus in a channel light in Mobile Bay, Alabama. The conversion was the installation of an acetylene lamp which automatically turned off in the morning and on again at sunset.[33]

Later acetylene lamps began to be used at other small lights in the country and then in lighthouses. Baltimore lighthouse, marking the entrance to the Craighill Channel, was automated with acetylene in 1923. Electricity moved automation along, but the final push came in the 1960s when the Coast Guard undertook a program to automate all lighthouses, using for the most part optics made of acrylic. These optics did not have a light that reached as far as did the Fresnel lenses, but for a place such as Chesapeake Bay these new lights were quite acceptable.

Members of a Coast Guard Aids to Navigation Team are the "keepers" now at the Craighill Channel upper range rear light. Boatswain's Mate 2nd Class Robert Tallmann (right) and Seaman Cary Marshall visit the lighthouse every six months to replace lights and to clean the lens and windows. The Coast Guardsmen are stationed at the Curtis Bay Coast Guard Yard.

(Photo by Robert J. Smith, Jr., courtesy Sparrows Point Division Public Affairs, Bethlehem Steel Corporation)

Modern plastic lenses in many sizes, such as those pictured above, helped make wholesale lighthouse automation possible. By the 1960s fewer than 60 U.S. lighthouses had keepers and by 1990 they were virtually all gone. Maryland's last keeper left the Thomas Point Shoal lighthouse in 1986.

(Photo by F. Ross Holland)

The last lighthouse in Maryland's waters to be automated was the Thomas Point Shoal lighthouse in 1986. The keeper locked up the lighthouse and departed. Thenceforth the light would be maintained by an Aids to Navigation Team (ANT). The members of the team visit the lighthouse on a quarterly basis and examine the structure and the light, making whatever repairs and adjustments the lighting apparatus needs, including replacing burned out bulbs. Structural repairs are to be left to work crews. The ANTs are the new lighthouse keepers.

Chapter 8

Legacy of the Lighthouses: Challenge and Change

The first aids to navigation built in Maryland were the conical masonry tower, the lightship, and the house with a light on the roof. Over time many lighthouses either fell victim to erosion or became outdated and were taken out of service, sometimes to be replaced by another style lighthouse in a different location. A number of the earliest lighthouses have survived, however, and some are still active.

Two lighthouse structures that still stand, although they were abandoned long ago, are found on Pooles Island and Fishing Battery Island. The Pooles Island lighthouse was updated from time to time to meet changing conditions and to take advantage of technological improvements, particularly in lighting. In 1857 it received one of the new Fresnel lenses of the fourth-order and ten years later, a modern lantern. In 1894 ruby panels were placed on two sectors of the lantern to create a red light that would mark a course change to the eastward.

In 1913 steamship companies began to complain about the lighting around Pooles Island, saying their vessels, particularly those coming from the Chesapeake and Delaware Canal, often ran aground. Congressman Frank O. Smith was aboard a steamer that ran ashore on Pooles Island, and he complained that the shoal off the south end of the island was "one of the most treacherous . . . I have ever seen." He urged that a range light be placed on the lower end of the island. The Bureau of Lighthouses agreed, and the district inspector attempted to acquire land for the lights. Unfortunately, the owner, whose overseer was not on friendly terms with the lighthouse keeper, made demands the inspector felt the Lighthouse Service could not meet. Congressman J. Charles Linthicum appealed to the district inspector and the landowner to come to

terms. They finally did, and the range lights were built, coming into service on September 14, 1914.

During World War I the Army established a new artillery proving ground east of Baltimore along the bay and condemned Pooles Island for inclusion in the complex it named Aberdeen. The Army wanted the three lights on Pooles Island moved or automated because artillery firing was to take place nearby. The Bureau agreed to automate the lights and persuaded the Army to pay for the cost of the work. The range lights were equipped with strong stake lights, and the lighthouse received an acetylene burner for the fourth-order lens. On June 12, 1918, the Pooles Island keeper, Amasa J. Simpson, was transferred to Blackistone Island. In 1939 the Pooles Island lighthouse went out of service, and the tower became a day mark. All that is left at the original site is the light tower, which appears to be structurally sound.[1] The nearby keeper's house was destroyed long ago, but ruined sections of a curved brick wall litter the beach, possibly remnants of the circular oilhouse.

Major stabilization and restoration efforts are underway, which include repointing mortar joint failures and cracks on the tower, fabricating new wooden windows and wire-brushing and painting the cast-iron lantern.

Spearheaded by the U.S. Army's Cultural Resource Office, Directorate of Safety, Health and Environment at Aberdeen Proving Ground, the effort has produced results - and partnerships. Volunteers from APG have stripped the tower of its beard of vines and have removed dirt and debris from inside the tower. An Army lead abatement team has repaired the lantern and cleaned the stone tower of organic residue. A U.S. Coast Guard Reserve lighthouse maintenance unit stationed in Baltimore will perform the mortar repair as part of its active-duty

The fourth lighthouse constructed in Maryland, Pooles Island was authorized during the administration of the fifth president of the United States. Built by John Donahoo and Simon Frieze in 1825, the tower is being carefully restored by its owner, the U.S. Army Garrison at Aberdeen Proving Ground. The oldest standing lighthouse in Maryland, the Pooles Island tower has now been cleaned of its destructive beard of vines, shown approaching the lantern in the 1987 photo at left. While currently off–limits to visitors for safety reasons, the lighthouse remains a safely isolated symbol of a distant past – a time when the waterways of a new nation were both information highway and super–highway.

(Photo by F. Ross Holland)

Following pages:
Pooles Island Panorama – Past and Present

The large photo, above left, shows the abandoned Pooles Island light station in 1928. The keeper's house was demolished in the 1930s. *(Above)* Pooles Island received the first fog signal in the Chesapeake in 1828. The wooden bell tower above, pictured c. 1910, replaced it. Home is where the family gathers, and in the case of Keeper Stephen Andrew Cohee, they gathered on the lighthouse steps – as did the family dog. *(Left)* Only traces of the lighthouse's white–washed steps are visible in this 1996 photo but restoration is gradually giving the lighthouse back its former dignity. During Captain Cohee's 35–year tenure the light station became a complex with many outbuildings, including a chicken house, stables, a boat house, sheds and an oilhouse. The large keeper's dwelling was adjacent to a 200–acre privately owned farm, which produced choice peaches, prized and costly in the markets of Baltimore. The photo, far left, taken from the gallery deck of the lighthouse, shows the famous orchard behind the keeper's house.

(U.S. Coast Guard photo; Photos courtesy of Mrs. Stephen William Cohee; MHT photos by Lillian Wray; Photos, c.1915, courtesy Mrs, Stephen William Cohee)

163

assignment. APG public works carpenters will handcraft traditional six-over-six wooden windows, and the contractor who painted the Concord Point lighthouse has volunteered his services for the Pooles Island tower.

Already nominated by the U.S. Army for inclusion on the National Register of Historic Places, the lighthouse is unlikely to become a tourist attraction anytime soon. But as part of its proactive cultural resource program, APG hopes to eventually arrange scheduled visits to the lighthouse for the general public.

The Fishing Battery lighthouse, on an island in the northern Chesapeake near Havre de Grace, had a somewhat different career and fate. This story-and-a-half brick house with a lantern on its roof went into service in 1853. Two years later it received a sixth-order Fresnel lens, and in 1864, a new modern lantern. Workers raised the structure to two stories in 1881 to secure more room in the dwelling.

In 1880 the Bureau of Fisheries leased the remainder of Fishing Battery Island for "fish cultural operations." The Bureau purchased its part of the island in July 1891 for $15,000. By 1911 the fisheries personnel had left the island, and the lightkeeper was responsible for their structures. Looking after them became an onerous chore for him, and at the prodding of the Bureau of Lighthouses, the Fisheries Bureau agreed to pay the keeper $5 a month.

In 1917 the Bureau of Lighthouses had the Fishing Battery light converted to acetylene and recommended discontinuing the keeper's position. In 1921 the Bureau of Fisheries wanted to sell its land and suggested the Bureau of Lighthouses might want to sell its property at the same time. This idea appealed to the Bureau, which had just received a report from the District stating that the automated lighthouse needed repairs. The Bureau responded positively to this suggestion but said it wanted to keep a twelve-foot-square piece of land for a skeleton tower to support the light. Although the island ultimately was not sold, the Bureau of Lighthouses did erect the steel skeleton tower and moved the light to the top of it.

In the 1920s and early 1930s, the old lighthouse received a reprieve when it was leased for duck hunting and fishing. By 1938, however, it had become a dilapidated victim of vandalism. The District recommended razing the old structure, burning the flammable material, and leaving the bricks in a pile, but this plan was never carried out. Perhaps the lighthouse became lost in larger issues that grew out of the reorganization that transferred responsibility for aids to

navigation to the Coast Guard less than a year later.

In 1942 Executive Order 9185 transferred the island to the Department of the Interior to become part of the Susquehanna National Wildlife Refuge. This refuge was later abolished, and Fishing Battery Island was transferred to Blackwater National Wildlife Refuge.[2] The lighthouse lay idle, attracting little attention until the late 1980s, when a group of interested citizens, members of the Battery Island Preservation Society, Inc., became concerned about the historic lighthouse and began to stabilize it. Considering the long period of neglect it experienced, and the extensive repairs the lighthouse needs, the building is, nevertheless, in remarkable condition and is restorable.

Although the Society does not own the lighthouse, and vandalism and neglect have taken a heavy toll on the old structure, the volunteers continue to raise money for the long-anticipated restoration through such projects as the annual Havre de Grace Seafood Festival, jointly sponsored with the city's Maritime Museum.

In 1996 the Fishing Battery lighthouse was declared "excess to the needs of the Coast Guard" paving the way for transfer to another governmental agency or to an "interested party." The most recent Coast Guard property survey, conducted by a civil engineering team in 1994, found that the foundation was not structurally sound, contributing to an overall rating of "poor condition."

The 17th lighthouse built in Maryland, the last of "Donahoo's Dozen" and one of only two sur-

Built in 1853 by John Donahoo, the Fishing Battery lighthouse is one of only two surviving Maryland lighthouses that combine the keeper's dwelling and the light tower. (The other is at Point Lookout.) Essentially abandoned since the 1930s when it was considered for demolition, vandalism and neglect may soon do what the Bureau of Lighthouses didn't.

(Photo by F. Ross Holland)

The Blackistone Island lighthouse, opposite page, completed by John Donahoo in 1851, was very similar to Fishing Battery, except it was built as a two–and–a–half–story structure. Decommissioned in 1931, the lighthouse stood abandoned and deteriorating until a fire of unknown origin reduced it to a charred ruin in 1956. The remains were later demolished.

(St. Clements Island – Potomac River Museum Collections)

Continued on page 178

to #178

In 1921 the Bureau of Lighthouses erected a 38–foot steel skeleton tower behind the Fishing Battery lighthouse and automated the light. Now solar powered, the light is still active. *(Below)* In recent years members of the Battery Island Preservation Society, Inc., have attempted to stabilize the lighthouse for preservation, but their work has been consistently vandalized.

(Photos by F. Ross Holland, 1990)

Long a mecca for commercial fishermen, Fishing Battery Island in its heyday was a bustling place, crowded with boats and buildings. The U.S. Bureau of Fisheries leased the island for "fish cultural operations" in 1880 and later purchased the majority of it. A boat basin, a hatchery, storage buildings, a fish basin, staff residences and a mess hall were all in place by 1887, six years after the lighthouse had been raised to two full stories.

(Photo, c. 1890; Kenneth G. Lay Collection)

A Moving Experience

There is much more than meets the eye in this tranquil waterfront scene at St. Michaels, Maryland. What man creates sometimes needs to be recreated – rescued, restored and repositioned so that past history can become living history, available to all who want to experience it.

The Hooper Strait lighthouse (*left*) is one of three Maryland screwpile lighthouses that were moved between 1966 and 1988 to new locations where they can be visited by the public. In the following photo essays their dramatic moves, all initially delayed by bad weather, are detailed. The lighthouses did not give up their grip on the bay easily, and none were powder puffs – especially the Seven Foot Knoll lighthouse which tested a derrick at 220 tons. Nor were they free to good homes, although they all got one and the presence of each has been felt in their new communities.

The Chesapeake Bay Maritime Museum now runs a popular summer "Lighthouse Overnights" program in the Hooper Strait lighthouse that lets children, accompanied by an adult, experience the life of a lighthouse keeper from 5 p.m. until 7 a.m.

Calvert Marine Museum called upon the community for help after the Drum Point lighthouse was moved to the complex in Solomons. Calvert County residents proudly supplied the living quarters with all the needed period furnishings – everything from a former keeper's best china to a pot–bellied stove.

The Seven Foot Knoll lighthouse, on Pier 5 in Baltimore, welcomes visitors and is headquarters for the Living Classrooms Foundation.

The 1985 Chesapeake Bay Maritime Museum photo at left shows the Hooper Strait lighthouse, the bugeye *Edna E. Lockwood,* and the Point Lookout fog tower, moved to the complex in 1968.
(MHT photo by Eric Ledbetter)

Narrow, crooked Hooper Strait was marked by a lightship in 1828, a square screwpile lighthouse in 1867 and a new hexagonal screwpile structure in 1879 after the first one was destroyed by ice floes in 1877. The Hooper Strait lighthouse was manned for 75 years, was automated in 1954 and by the 1960s was an unattractive nuisance. The Coast Guard declared it surplus in 1966 and the new Chesapeake Bay Maritime Museum rallied funding and support to buy it. When negotiations were completed in October 1966, construction of a new foundation of steel pipe piles began on the museum grounds, upper left. Too large to move in one piece, the lighthouse was cut in half horizontally, just below the roof line and below the first–level framing. The two pieces were loaded by crane onto a barge on November 6 and the lighthouse, pulled by a tugboat, began its 60–mile trip up the Chesapeake. Crowds cheered the next day as the lighthouse was reassembled *(above)* on a firm foundation and with a new mission.

(All photos, Chesapeake Bay Maritime Museum. Left, CBMM photo by C.C.Harris, 1968)

171

When the crew of a vessel on the Chesapeake couldn't see a familiar light beacon because of inclement weather, they heard a fog signal, usually a bell. Point Lookout lighthouse received a tall wooden fog tower in 1872 to serve both bay traffic and mariners turning into the Potomac River. Struck by machinery, the bronze bell was housed in a frame structure near the lighthouse. But after the buoy and coal sheds were built in the early 1880s, the sound of the bell was blocked: the sheds were taller than the tower. A new three–story tower was built in 1888, attached to the east end of the coal shed and the bell was moved there. At left, two young ladies, relatives of the keeper, sat on the tower steps for a photographer in 1910. The tower was not needed at Point Lookout by the 1960s because of a new offshore tower with an automatic light and horn. In 1968 the tower was detatched from the coal shed, loaded onto a flatbed and taken to the Chesapeake Bay Maritime Museum. A crane repositioned the tower, thirty– six feet high and 9 feet square and its 1000–pound bell.

(Photo above, MHT Cultural Conservation Program, others Chesapeake Bay Maritime Museum)

When it went into service in 1883 the Drum Point lighthouse was 120 feet offshore and stood in ten feet of water. By 1931 when keeper William Marion Goeshy photographed his bride Beatrice *(right)* swimming, years of silting had pushed the shoreline close to the lighthouse.

(Photo above, Goeshy Gould Collection, MHT Cultural Conservation Program.)

By the early 1960s when it was automated, the lighthouse was high and dry at low tide. Abandoned by the Coast Guard in 1962 and turned over to the State of Maryland, the lighthouse deteriorated even as the Calvert County Historical Society fought to acquire and restore it. In 1973 the group succeeded in listing it on the National Register of Historic Places. In 1974 they learned they could have the lighthouse but not the land, so plans were made to move the lighthouse, by now fire– damaged and with no remaining doors, to the Calvert Marine Museum. The lighthouse was to be moved in one piece and in February 1975 workers began preparing a new foundation. In March, a barge and tug reached the lighthouse and a crew with cutting torches began work on the screwpiles, but were forced away by bad weather. They returned on March 22, and a steam crane hoisted the 41–ton lighthouse, secured by cables, into the air where it dangled *(left and above)*. Two tugs brought it upriver where a large crowd waited to see it settled on its new foundation – finally safe and ready for restoration.

(All photos, Calvert Marine Museum)

The first screwpile lighthouse in Maryland waters, Seven Foot Knoll, outlasted every one that followed, except Thomas Point Shoal, still at its original site. Seven Foot Knoll replaced Maryland's first lighthouse, Bodkin Island, and went into sevice in 1856. But by the 1980s it too was replaced – by a steel tower – and its future was bleak. Signed over to the City of Baltimore in the late 1980s it was slated to be moved to Pier 5 and restored – if it could be transported. The engineering staff of the Empire Construction Company spent months devising a plan which became operational on October 11, 1988, a cold, windy day. A team of divers first cut the iron pilings that screwed the lighthouse to the floor of the bay. Then a massive crane, called "The Samson", which sits atop a barge, slowly hoisted the 220–ton lighthouse and started upriver, heading under the Key Bridge – a tricky maneuver – and into the Inner Harbor. Now home to the Living Classrooms Foundation, the lighthouse also welcomes tourists.

(All photos by Terry Corbett 1988, courtesy the Empire Construction Company)

Built by John Donahoo in 1831, the Lazaretto Point lighthouse, only 34–feet high, was torn down in 1926 and replaced by a steel skeleton tower, tall enough for vessels to spot on the crowded Canton waterfront. After 59 years the landmark was reborn when a privately funded replica was built to honor Norman G. Rukert, late owner of Rukert Terminals Corporation, which occupies the site of the former lighthouse reservation. Not a tourist attraction, the lighthouse is at the end of a busy working pier, but is visible from Ft. McHenry.

(F. Ross Holland photo, 1991)

viving Maryland examples of the lighthouse with the tower on the roof, Fishing Battery may be doomed - a victim of vandalism, inaction and bureaucracy.

The Lazaretto Point lighthouse, built by John Donahoo in 1831, was one of those that outlived its usefulness and was torn down. After a bout with erosion from which it emerged victorious, the lighthouse continued quietly to play its role in guiding ships to Baltimore harbor. The first change in the light came on January 1, 1870, when a 400-lb. fog bell went into service and the light was changed from white to red. This change was necessary because it was difficult to distinguish the light of the lighthouse from the lights emanating from iron furnaces and a rolling mill behind it.

Although the red light at Lazaretto Point solved the problem for a few years, it was not a permanent solution, for by 1883, the maritime community was complaining to the Lighthouse Board. Mariners said "buildings in the neighborhood belonging to private parties" obstructed the light. The Board had a tall mast erected just behind the lighthouse and placed a red light on it that rose above the obstructions. Around this time the arrival of several chemical plants roughened the neighborhood. "The gases," the Board lamented, "from the numerous chemical works in the immediate vicinity destroyed the paint, and even the whitewash, soon after it was put on."[3]

The next year, in 1884, the Board found the new light did not reach above all the obstructions and decided to move the mast 78 feet nearer the river channel. A few years later it discontinued the mast light and changed the tower light to a flashing one, beginning December 10, 1888.

In 1892 the station received an iron oil house and a 30' x 13' 7" structure with a shingle roof, which served as a summer kitchen and fuel storehouse.[4] We can speculate what OSHA's reaction would have been to that arrangement, if the agency had existed in those days.

In 1914 the District recommended changing the Lazaretto Point light from flashing to fixed red. The Bureau contemplated doing away with it all together, but the District, although it had originally proposed this action, was opposed to the idea. Moreover, the maritime community strongly felt the Lazaretto lighthouse should remain. The fog signal, which became electrically operated in 1914, was of special importance to navigators.

In July 1914, the District proposed hiring a night watchman and giving that person responsibility for the lighthouse and the fog signal. The Bureau approved this action within the month. At about the same time, the district superintendent recommended replacing the rotating fourth-order lens with a three-and-a-half- order fixed lens. This change was suggested for purely practical reasons, for there was such a lens in stock and obtaining another fourth-order lens would have required an expenditure. The larger lens was installed, but by November 1920 the light was considered of "very little importance."[5]

By 1926 factories and warehouses on the Canton waterfront were so numerous they obscured the Lazaretto light, and the Bureau of Lighthouses had little choice but to abandon the old tower. In its place the Bureau erected a steel skeleton tower, taller than its predecessor, on the wharf at the foot of Clinton Street. On September 27, 1926, the new, fixed white light went into service. The next day workmen began tearing down the old masonry tower. Several people contacted the district office complaining about the change. The district superintendent thought the complaints originated "from a former asst. Kpr, now active in East Balto. political circles."[6] These comments did not deter the Bureau of Lighthouses, and the old light tower disappeared.

In 1985 the landmark was reborn, when a local port businessman took 19th-century specifications obtained at the National Archives to a 20th-century architectural firm and said," Build us the Lazaretto light." Dedicated to the memory of the late Norman G. Rukert Sr., an avid historian and owner of the 17-acre Rukert Terminals Corp., the replica was planned and underwritten by his son and nephew. The new structure sits on a working pier and is neither an aid to navigation nor a tourist attraction. It is rather a quiet tribute to a man who loved the old Baltimore waterfront and who had talked for years of rebuilding the old lighthouse himself.

Two lighthouses similar to the one that had been at Lazaretto have had a happier fate—Concord Point and Turkey Point. The Concord Point

lighthouse, located in Havre de Grace, where its builder, John Donahoo lived and worked, served the traffic in the northern reaches of the bay. In 1838 the light tower received a coat of Roman cement, and seven years later Pleasonton ordered a coat of "the best hydraulic cement" to be plastered over the tower and then white-washed. In 1858 the inspector reported the tower had recently received a sixth-order steamer lens. The whitewashed stone keeper's dwelling, 34' 6"x 20' 6" in plan, was one-and-a-half stories tall and had four rooms, plus an attached kitchen. By 1909 it had grown to six rooms and a kitchen, with a stable and coalhouse on the grounds. All of the 43,000-square-foot dwelling site not occupied by structures was cultivated as a garden. Ten years later the district superintendent described the dwelling site as "improved by an eight room two-story dwelling with a front porch and cellar, size in plan approximately 34' 5" x 40'; a frame storehouse 14' x 40'; walks, outbuildings, etc., all in a good state of repair."[7]

In 1918 the Concord Point keeper, Henry O'Neill, decided to retire, and the Bureau of Lighthouses felt it was a good time to automate the light. Electric lines had reached the town, and the district proposed converting the light to

A Havre de Grace landmark since its construction in 1827, the Concord Point lighthouse continues to be a symbol of service to the community, as interpreted in the official patch worn by the EMS ambulance attendants in the city. The tower had been electrified and was unmanned when the photo below was taken in 1933.
(MHT photo by David Tillman; Kenneth G. Lay Collection)

Restoration is underway at the Concord Point keeper's house, shown above, c. 1910, surrounded by flood waters. The dwelling has now been stabilized and non–historic additions are being removed. Blocks of the Port Deposit granite used to construct the walls of the house are visible at left.

(Kenneth G. Lay Collection; Photo by William L. McIntyre, 1996)

electricity, but when it was discovered that electric current was unreliable locally, the proposal was changed to acetylene to implement automation. O'Neill wanted to remain in the keeper's house and agreed to give the light the little attention it required in exchange for his continued occupancy of the residence. The Bureau of Lighthouses abolished the keeper's position, effective January 15, 1919. O'Neill did not complete quite a year of retirement, for he died on December 12, 1919. His son, Harry, wanted to stay in the dwelling and look after the light, and he was supported in this effort by his nephew, Millard E. Tydings. Then a lawyer in the area, Tydings asked that his uncle be allowed to live on the site until the old structure was sold. The Bureau of Lighthouses agreed.

In 1920 the Bureau began action to sell the keeper's house to the highest bidder. The sale was advertised in the newspaper, but the Bureau received only one bid, and that was from Michael Fahey of Havre de Grace, who offered $4,000. The district superintendent accepted this bid, and on May 15, 1920, forwarded Fahey's check to the commissioner for transfer to the Treasury. A few days later, Superintendent King wrote the commissioner that Harry F. O'Neill's services would be terminated on May 31, 1920. Seven years later, with electric power improved, the Bureau converted the tower's light to electricity.[8]

The tower has been turned over to the town

of Havre de Grace, which has leased it to the Friends of Concord Point Lighthouse Inc.. This non-profit organization maintains and interprets the historic structure and has turned its attention to the restoration of the keeper's dwelling, known locally as the O'Neill House. The house has experienced many uses—saloon, restaurant, reputedly a bordello at one time—and has had many additions. Restoring it will not be an easy task, but work began in 1989 with grants from the National Park Service's Lighthouse Preservation Fund and the Maryland Historical Trust. The building has since been stabilized, and the removal of non-historic additions is underway. The Friends organization hopes to develop the building into a museum and interpretive center.

Across the bay on Elk Neck, and high on a bluff, the Turkey Point lighthouse successfully guided the fishing traffic about that section of the bay, as well as ships to and from the Chesapeake and Delaware Canal. In 1855, in keeping with its charge to improve the navigational lights of the country, the Lighthouse Board installed a fourth-order Fresnel lens in the old-style lantern of the tower. Usually these lanterns were not satisfactory for use with the new lenses, and the Board tried for some time to get an appropriation to replace the lantern with a newer one. Finally, in 1867, a "new and improved lantern" was installed. In April 1888 the effectiveness of the station was improved by the addition of a 1,200-lb. fog bell struck by machinery.

In 1889 the keeper's dwelling at Turkey Point was raised to two stories, and a new front porch was built. In 1933 the lamp in the lens was changed from oil to incandescent oil vapor, and in 1942 the station was converted to electricity. When the last keeper, Mrs. C. W. Salter, retired in 1947, the lighthouse was automated. Later, the dwelling and outbuildings were taken down, probably in the 1970's. Mrs. Salter was the last female civilian keeper in Chesapeake Bay and may have been the last one in the country.[9] The light, located in what is now Elk Neck State Park, is still active although it has been obscured by trees from time to time. Near the old tower a sharp-eyed observer recently noted a remnant of the flag pole, a cut-off pipe set in cement. The base bears a scrawled line cut into the cement long ago when it was wet... "Fannie Salter, August 1940."

Down the bay near Maryland's southern border, three lighthouses of the early period have survived: Piney Point on the Potomac River, Point Lookout at the mouth of the Potomac, and Cove Point about five miles north of the Patuxent River.

Fannie Mae Salter, keeper at Turkey Point, welcomed electricity to the light station in 1942, holding one of the new electric lightbulbs in her right hand for photographers. In her left is the incandescent oil vapor lamp which was "new" to Turkey Point in 1933. After Mrs. Salter's retirement and automation, both in 1947, the keeper's house, *(above)* was taken down.

(U.S. Coast Guard photo; Photo courtesy of the descendants of Fannie Mae Salter. MHT Cultural Conservation Program)

The Piney Point lighthouse
was threatened by erosion in
1837 and again in 1848.
Groins were added in 1850
and later expanded. The 1952
photo above shows the light
station reservation and the
1880 fog bell tower which
was destroyed by a storm in
1965. There were more trees
and fewer outbuildings in
1912, when the photo at right
was taken.

*(U.S. Coast Guard photos. F. Ross
Holland Collection)*

PUBLISHED BY LEWIS M. THAYER, WASHINGTON, D. C. COPYRIGHTED 1906

Tourists from the famous Piney Point Hotel, adjacent to the light station, were often photographed in front of the lighthouse, as shown in the 1906 promotional postcard at left. Not always friendly neighbors, the resort had complained vigorously about the keeper's wandering livestock in 1839. The Fifth Auditor even became involved in the dispute which was finally settled diplomatically by Keeper Phillip Clark.

(Jack Kelbaugh Collection)

Within a year of its lighting in 1836, the Piney Point lighthouse faced an erosion problem that threatened the foundation of the light tower. Pleasonton instructed the Alexandria collector of customs, who was responsible for aids to navigation in the Potomac, to place watling around the foundation and to apply a coat of hydraulic cement to the tower.

In 1838 it was discovered that the wrong reflectors had been placed on three lamps in the Piney Point lantern. Pleasonton tended to be more lenient with people he liked, and John Donahoo, who had built the lighthouse, was one of his favorites. Saying too much time had passed to force the contractor to supply the correct reflectors, Pleasonton directed George Brent, the collector, to order three lamps and reflectors from Winslow Lewis at a cost of $305.

A few months later Lewis complained the keeper was not keeping the lighting apparatus clean, which prompted Pleasonton to have the collector admonish the keeper, telling him he would be removed if further complaints were heard. Lewis also mentioned that the vane did not turn to let the smoke out of the lantern and there were no ventilator holes at the bottom of the lantern. Each octagon of copper, he said, should have a hole in it with a copper slide to open and close it. Pleasonton instructed Brent to have the vane repaired and the holes put in the copper.[10]

In 1839 the major problem at Piney Point was the wandering of the keeper's cow and hogs. The animals repeatedly trespassed on the land of the neighboring Pavillion Company, a resort development. Pleasonton instructed Brent to resolve the problem in person, for he wanted the keeper to have the cow for milk for his family. The keeper, Phillip Clark, wrote Pleasonton asking that he be permitted to settle the problem directly with the company. Pleasonton agreed, with the stipulation that the permit guarantee the keeper a 25-foot right-of-way across company land to get his animals to pasturage or otherwise permit him to keep the cow.[11] The records do not indicate what solution was found, but certainly some accommodation was made since the issue was not brought up again during Clark's tenure.

In March 1840 Pleasonton was again told that Clark was negligent in his responsibilities, particularly in tending the light. Pleasonton directed Brent to investigate and especially to ask masters of ships what they knew about the light and the keeper. It is not known what sort of report Brent filed, but less than a year later a new keeper, Henry J. Heard, was appointed to Piney Point. Pleasonton was disappointed at this selection because he had been pushing a Mr. Hammond for the position, a man who would have been acceptable to the Pavillion Company. Also, Heard used an uncommon amount of oil, which he blamed on leaky casks. The former keeper's records indicated he had also used an excessive amount. Nonetheless, Pleasonton felt Heard appeared to be a careless person, so he wrote to the secretary of the Treasury that he was unqual-

Now a part of the St. Clement's Island – Potomac River Museum, the Piney Point Lighthouse and Park offers special programs for groups of school children and is a popular destination for tourists. Pictorial exhibit panels relate the history of the lighthouse.

(St. Clement's Island – Potomac River Museum photo by Michael Humphries)

183

"Stabilization and rehabilitation of the Piney Point lighthouse have been on–going for several years. Bricks on the exterior of the tower have been repointed, the lantern deck has been stabilized and extensive moisture control measures are planned for the interior of the structure .... listed on the National Register of Historic Places in 1976."

ified and recommended Captain John Wilson. Wilson had been recommended by a number of local people, including the Pavillion Company, but Heard was not removed.

In May 1843, Captain Howland of the contract supply vessel complained severely of the manner in which Heard kept the lighting apparatus, saying the reflectors were covered with soot and the lamps had been burning without their glass chimneys. Some months later Captain Prince of the revenue cutter *Wolcott* reported the lighthouse was "indifferently kept." Despite these charges, Heard continued to hold onto his job. The following year, neighbors reported the keeper's stock was trespassing on their land. Finally, in the fall of 1845, Heard was removed as keeper and Mrs. Charlotte Suter appointed in his place. Mrs. Suter did not serve long, however, for in May 1846 she was removed and William B. Taylor took over as lighthouse keeper.[12]

In 1848 erosion once again threatened the lighthouse foundation, and Pleasonton directed that it be protected "by turning the creek and watling the shore." He instructed the keepers to hire a Mr. Bennett to do the work. When Bennett failed to do the job, Pleasonton wrote a scathing letter to the collector of customs in Alexandria, saying Taylor should have hired someone else. Now, he added, the erosion will continue through the winter months "and will require ten times the sum to secure it from further damage." Pleasonton blamed the collector as well, saying when he saw the work was not being done, he should have gone down to Piney Point and prodded the keeper to action.

It did not take a keeper with a towering intellect to figure out when his job was in danger. A petition, probably instigated by Taylor, from ship's captains, pilots, and local residents, went to the secretary of the Treasury urging that the keeper be retained since he kept a good light and had the confidence of the maritime community. The petition had little effect, and in May 1849 John W. Nuthall was appointed the new keeper of the Piney Point lighthouse. In the meantime, Pleasonton had suggested putting up a post and rail fence and placing watling between the rails. This work apparently was never done, for a month later Pleasonton instructed the collector of customs to have groins put in to protect the lighthouse grounds. These were completed in February 1850.

A postscript to this incident is that Nuthall did not serve long as keeper, dying in July 1850. On the strong recommendation of Pleasonton, the secretary replaced him with his widow.[13]

In June 1855 the old reflector system of lights, which consisted of ten lamps each with a 15-inch reflector, was replaced at Piney Point with a fifth-order Fresnel lens. The lighthouse did not receive a new-style lantern until 1864. In 1880 the station received a fog signal, a bell struck by machinery. Its housing was a tower 30 feet tall. In May 1884 the dwelling was enlarged by the addition of one story. By 1920 the station consisted of the tower, keeper's dwelling, concrete oil house, frame stable, frame shed, and fog signal tower.[14]

Decommissioned in 1964 and listed on the National Register of Historic Places in June 1976, the Piney Point lighthouse moved closer to its new "career" as landmark site and heritage museum. In the 1980s the Coast Guard transferred ownership of the old light station to St. Mary's County. Now a part of the St. Clement's Island-Potomac River Museum, the Piney Point Lighthouse and Park, dedicated in 1995, occupies a six-acre site featuring outdoor exhibits, picnic areas and a boardwalk that connects the historic buildings with the new museum .

Stabilization and rehabilitation of the lighthouse have been on-going for several years. Bricks on the exterior of the tower have been repointed, the lantern deck has been stabilized and extensive moisture control measures are planned for the interior of the structure.

Point Lookout lighthouse, located on the north side of the mouth of the Potomac River, had a different history, becoming in time a buoy depot as well. Ann Davis, who became keeper in December of 1830 upon the death of the first keeper, her father, remained at the task and achieved a fine reputation. She served until her death in 1847 and was replaced by William Wood in February. Wood was not as successful as Miss Davis, and two years later the collector of customs replaced him with William P. Baxter. At that point some of Wood's delinquencies came out. He was short fifty-six gallons of oil and twenty-nine panes of glass. He blamed the loss of oil on a cat falling into it and drowning, remaining there, unknown to him, for a long time until the "oil Smelt so Bad" he could not use it. He lost the glass, he said, when he was "handling wood [and] A stick fell . . . and Broke 29." Keeper Baxter reported that Wood had used up virtually all the supplies at the station. He found the oil almost gone, which fact forced him to light only half the lamps. All the "reflecting glass" was broken except for three panes. (It is not known whether "reflecting glass" referred to the reflectors or to the panes of glass used in the lantern.) In any case, Baxter said he could get by for awhile without the other supplies, but he needed the oil and the glass right away.[15]

The Lighthouses of Sharp's Island

MARCH 1837
The Sharp's Island light-house was authorized.

JULY 1837
A site was selected on the north end of Sharp's Island and ten acres of land were purchased. Fifth Auditor Pleasonton decided to build a lighthouse that was a dwelling with a tower on the roof. The "unified" lighthouse would be on "wheels" so it could be moved when it was threatened by erosion.

SEPTEMBER 1838
The lighthouse was completed and lighted.

LATE 1848
The lighthouse was moved inland to a new site.

NOVEMBER 1, 1865
The first lighthouse was taken by erosion.

NOVEMBER 15, 1865
A steamer lens was put into service as a temporary light.

EARLY 1866
A new screwpile light-house went into service. It was located at the mouth of the Choptank River, 1/3 mile off the north end of Sharp's Island.

FEBRUARY 10, 1881
Ice tore the lighthouse from its foundation and the wooden structure drifted away with the two keepers aboard. It fetched up on the shore and the keepers and some items

from the house were rescued. The keepers were commended for remaining with the light.

MARCH 3, 1881
Recognizing the importance of this light, Congress appropriated $35,000 for an iron caisson lighthouse.

AUGUST 28, 1881
A construction crew arrived on site to build the offshore work platform.

SEPTEMBER 13, 1881
Workers at Oxford, Md. completed the caisson, which was then floated to the construction site twelve miles away.

FEBRUARY 1, 1882
The lighthouse was completed and its fourth-order lens lighted.

1973-1976
Battered by heavy moving

ice, the light tower began to lean.

JULY 22, 1982
The lighthouse was listed on the National Register of Historic Places.

MARCH 21, 1996
In the weekly supplement to the "Local Notice to Mariners" the U.S. Coast Guard sought comment on discontinuing the Sharp's Island lighthouse and replacing it with "an adjacent light of lesser height

and/or lesser nominal range."

FEBRUARY 6, 1996
The Star Democrat, Easton, Md. published the first story on the Coast Guard deliberations, unleashing a public outcry and follow-on stories in a number of national publications.

SUMMER 1996
A U.S. Coast Guard civil engineering unit began a cost analysis to see if it is feasible to stabilize the lighthouse in its tilted position. The Chesapeake Bay Maritime Museum, with guaranteed funding for moving costs, requested that the Coast Guard donate the lighthouse.

In 1872 the Lighthouse Board began installing a "large fog-bell" at Point Lookout to serve both passing bay traffic and those navigators turning into the Potomac River. Struck by machinery, the bronze bell was installed on a red "frame detached from the house" and put into operation on November 2, 1872.

In 1883 workers removed the old roof from the dwelling and raised the structure one story to give the keepers more room. They put a new tin roof on and plastered the three new rooms. At

the same time a buoy depot, to be administered by the lighthouse keeper, was established at Point Lookout to serve the central part of the district. The depot created a problem, though. In a few years the Lighthouse Board was receiving complaints that the fog bell could not be heard. Determining that the new coal and buoy sheds, which were higher than the bell tower, were blocking the sound, the Board had a new frame tower erected in 1888 in front of the coal shed and moved the fog bell there. At the same time,

The Sharp's Island survey map was drawn in May 1848, the year the light-house was moved inland. The island consisted of about 400 acres then. The "new light" was added to the map in 1866. Always prone to erosion, Sharp's Island vanished about 1940.

(U.S. Coast Surveys 1803-1846, Register 251, MHT Library. Photo, F. Ross Holland)

The remote Point Lookout lighthouse, pictured in an early 19th century lithograph above, has had some unusual neighbors since its founding in 1860, notably the infamous Civil War prison camp and the Point Lookout resort. The lighthouse received additional responsibilities as a depot in 1883, and the lighthouse was enlarged. The roof was raised one story, giving the keepers three new rooms. It was converted to double keeper's quarters in 1928.

(Lithograph, courtesy Calvert Marine Museum. Photo, c.1910, MHT Cultural Conservation Program)

The Point Lookout light-house, painted by U.S. Navy and community volunteers in 1996, has outlived its neighbor, the once proud and famous Point Lookout Hotel. Friction developed in the 1930s when the resort at Point Lookout wanted to land excursionists at the light-house wharf. The Bureau of Lighthouses denied permission, but in 1933 the Point Lookout Hotel advertised that a trip would land at the wharf. Angry officials in the Bureau permitted the landing, but flatly refused to consider others. With the advent of improved roads the hotel flourished for several more decades.

(Top, U.S. Navy photo; inset photo, Point Lookout Hotel 1929, MHT Library; photo by Ross Kimmel, c. 1989, prior to demolition of the hotel. MHT Library)

Opposite page:
The last screwpile lighthouse on Chesapeake Bay, the 1875 Thomas Point Shoal lighthouse was manned until 1986. Still active as an aid to navigation and listed on the National Register of Historic Places, Thomas Point Shoal has become a symbol of Maryland's maritime heritage.

(F. Ross Holland Collection)

The Cedar Point lighthouse, long in ruins, was dismantled in its 100th year but large architectural elements salvaged by the Navy and given to nearby museums will keep memories of the old lighthouse alive. The Calvert Marine Museum received the decorative sunbursts on the gabled ends of the lighthouse and plans call for the Piney Point Lighthouse and Park to receive the lantern, now on the grounds of the Naval Air Test and Evaluation Museum.

(U.S. Navy photo 1996)

the station received a new summer kitchen and a new stable. Six years later an iron oil house was added.[16]

The dwelling went through a major renovation in 1927 and 1928, when it was converted to a double keepers' quarters. The work to be done was summed up in these specifications:

> The rear wing of present dwelling is to be torn down and rebuilt of frame, remove present roof and cover entire building with a hip roof covered with red hexagonal asbestos shingles laid French method, exterior walls both brick and wood to be covered with galvanized metal lath and stuccoed with cement plaster. Partitions to be rearranged and the present stairway to be removed and new stairways to be built to allow private entrance to each apartment on all floors. The plaster of all interior walls and ceilings to be removed and covered with wallboard.

In addition, all flooring was to be replaced with new material, a new hot water heating system installed, a concrete foundation poured to support the new addition, the cellar cemented over with six inches of concrete, and a new chimney built.[17] This work pretty well changed the dwelling to its present appearance.

In the 1930s several companies wanted to use the buoy depot's long wharf to land passengers visiting resort developments at Point Lookout. In 1930, when the Point Lookout Development Company requested permission to land at the wharf, the Bureau was strongly opposed to its use by others because this activity would interfere with the loading and unloading of buoys, coal and other government activities. As a result, the company was denied permission to tie up there.

But in 1933, the owners of the hotel at Point Lookout advertised that its boat would land excursionists at the lighthouse wharf. The Bureau was not happy about this announcement but permitted the steamship to land once, telling the company it would not give permission in the future. The company asked to be allowed to land people there until it could build its own wharf, but the Bureau said no. The amusement company countered by getting Senator Millard E. Tydings and several congressmen to put pressure on the Bureau of Lighthouses. Nonetheless, Commissioner Putnam stood firm and said the Bureau would not depart from its policy.[18]

The lighthouse continued in service until 1966 and is located on what is now U.S. Navy property, an annex to the Naval Air Station Patuxent River.

While the lighthouse is not open to the public, any boaters who regularly see it from the water will notice the 1996 facelift, courtesy of volunteers from NAS Pax River and the local community. The Point Lookout lighthouse and a local beach were chosen as community fix-up projects through Christmas in April USA, a national volunteer service organization with a local chapter in St. Mary's County. More than eighty workers spent two days scraping, priming and painting under the watchful eyes of team leaders and a museum professional.

Up the coast and four miles north of the Patuxent River is Cove Point. The lighthouse there went into service in 1828 and has served well through the years. In 1857 a fourth-order Fresnel lens replaced the lamps and reflectors. Though now automated, the light still guides vessels along that section of the bay. The houses at the light station serve as quarters for several Coast Guard personnel who work at nearby stations.

The Cove Point station has had a fog signal for many years, the first in 1834. This bell lasted until 1858, when it was considered worn out and was replaced by a new bell and striking apparatus. In 1880 the first of a series of bell towers was built. Fashioned at the Lazaretto Depot, the first tower lasted seven years before it had to be replaced. Eleven years later, in 1898, an iron fog

Maryland's first permanent keeper, Captain John Gray of Bodkin Island, would never have dreamed in 1822 of a lighthouse without its keeper, much less of a 1,000 watt lamp like this one at the Craighill Channel upper range rear lighthouse. A stand–by lamp is placed with it on an automatic turret. When one light goes out, the other swings around in its place. But the futuristic technology of the present has its roots deep in the past, with a mission that never changes – safe passage for mariners.

(Photo by Robert J. Smith, Jr., courtesy Sparrows Point Division Public Affairs, Bethlehem Steel Corporation)

bell tower, a square pyramidal structure 31 feet tall, was installed. This tower was removed in the spring of 1901 and replaced with another wood frame structure, this time on a brick foundation. This tower held a second class Daboll trumpet fog signal. The old fog bell, attached to a support on the roof, was retained for emergency use.[19] Although there could be many reasons for the frequency with which the Cove Point bell tower was replaced, the records offer few clues. A likely reason was the change in fog signal equipment, such as the shift from the fog bell to a trumpet signal.

Repairs to the structures at the Cove Point station were made from time to time as needed. In 1883 the dwelling was raised to a two-story building, which gave three additional rooms. "With the enlargement," the Board said, "the station has six good rooms and a good basement or cellar, and is in excellent order."[20]

Through its early years the light station faced constant threats from erosion, and this menace continued into the latter half of the nineteenth century. In more recent years the danger has been lessened with the use of steel sheet piling and large stones.[21]

The history of lighthouses in Maryland is that

of continual progress in the development of a first class system of aids to navigation. Fifth Auditor Pleasonton built all of the shore-based lighthouses and thus laid the foundation for an adequate system. With the exception of those taken by erosion and later replaced with offshore lights, all the lighthouses of this period—thanks in great part to builder John Donahoo—still stand.

On the foundation of these early structures, the Lighthouse Board built an infinitely superior array of lights by using a lighting system much better than the one Pleasonton had used. The Board brought new technology, both in lighting and structures, to aids to navigation. Most important, it brought in professionals to improve the aids and train the keepers. The Board instilled discipline with surprise inspections and provided training, detailed information, and recognition for its employees. As a result of this attitude, the Board developed pride in the work of the keepers and a career for them. It also recognized their service with awards for heroism.

The Bureau of Lighthouses did not build any major lighthouses in Maryland, but it carried on the policies of the Lighthouse Board and solidified the organization's sense of service. It began to call itself the Lighthouse Service and continued to recognize keepers who had rendered assistance to those in danger on the bay. Commissioner Putnam and his subordinates softened some of the more rigid policies of the Board, such as making it easier for families to visit keepers of offshore lights, but they continued the high standards the Lighthouse Board had set. The Bureau greatly expanded aids to navigation and, like its predecessor, took advantage of advancing technology to improve their effectiveness. It was fitting that at its end the Lighthouse Service was expanding research in the use of radio for its duties.

The Coast Guard, formed in 1915 by the amalgamation of the Life Saving Service and the Revenue Cutter Service, took over the Bureau of Lighthouses in 1939. The Coast Guard continued the standards of the past, and over the years, as its predecessors had done, took advantage of new technology. The latest innovation is the use of solar-powered acrylic lenses to automate lighthouses. All of Maryland's active lighthouses are now automated, the offshore ones accessible by boat, although visiting them is not permitted.

The surviving lighthouses and the records of their administration since 1822 provide touchstones to the past. They illumine not only the evolution of navigational aids but the proud growth of maritime activity in Maryland.

Notes

CHAPTER 1

1. D. Alan Stevenson, *The World's Lighthouses Before 1820* (London: Oxford University Press, 1959), pp. 8-13.

2. Francis Ross Holland, Jr., *America's Lighthouses: An Illustrated History* (New York: Dover Publications, 1988), pp. 13-14.

3. George Weiss, *The Lighthouse Service: Its History, Activities and Organization* (Baltimore: Johns Hopkins Press, 1926), pp. 4-5 and 10.

4. Lighthouse Board, *Laws of the United States Relating to the Establishment, Support, and Management of the Light-houses, Light-vessels, Monuments, Beaches, Spindles, Buoys, and Public Piers of the United States from August 7, 1789, to March 3, 1855* (Washington: A. O. P. Nicholson, public printer, 1855), p. 51.

5. Fifth Auditor's Office, Lighthouse Letters, v. 5 (May 27, 1817-Dec. 12, 1821), p. 281, Record Group 26, National Archives.

Henceforth, unless otherwise indicated, all manuscript sources cited are from Record Group 26.

6. Weiss, *Lighthouse Service*, p. 4; Fifth Auditor's Office, Lighthouse Letters, v. 20 (July 17, 1844-June 9, 1845), p. 339, RG 26, National Archives.

7. Lewis Brantz later became the first president of the Philadelphia, Wilmington and Baltimore Railroad; he died in 1838. Fifth Auditor's Office, Lighthouse Letters, v. 5, pp. 127-29; and Peter J. Guthorn, *United States Coastal Charts, 1783-1861* (Exton, Pa.: Scheffer Publishing, c. 1984), p. 82.

8. Brantz to Samuel Smith, Baltimore, July 20, and August 25, 1819, Lighthouse Superintendent's Correspondence, Baltimore, 1819-24 (henceforth cited as LSCB); and Fifth Auditor's Office, Lighthouse Letters, v. 5, pp. 127-29. The latter reference will hereafter be cited as Lighthouse Letters.

9. Brantz to Smith, Baltimore, Nov. ?, 1819, LSCB, 1819-24.

10. Brantz to Smith, Baltimore, April 16 and June 28, 1819, LSCB, 1819-24.

11. Brantz to Smith, Baltimore, Sept. 24, 1819, LSCB, 1819-24.

12. Henry B. Latrobe to Brantz, Baltimore, Oct. 30, 1819, LSCB, 1819-24.

13. William B. Barney to Stephen Pleasonton, Baltimore, June 5 and 19, 1820, and Jan. 10, 1821, LSCB, 1819-24; and Lighthouse Letters, v. 5, pp. 347, 363-64, 372-73. The remainder of Bodkin Island was purchased on July 8, 1822, from Henry C. and Elizabeth Dunbar for $225. See Site File, Bodkin Island, RG 26.

14. This shed, some years later, was to evolve into the major lighthouse depot for the Fifth Lighthouse District. Barney to Pleasonton, Baltimore, March 17, 1821, LSCB, 1819-24.

15. Yernell & Macguire to Barney, Baltimore, April 3, 1821, and Barney to Pleasonton, Baltimore, April 4 and 10, 1821, LSCB, 1819-24.

16. Barney to Pleasonton, Baltimore, April 10, June 2, Aug. 3 and 13, and Sept. 7, 1821, LSCB, 1819-24; and Lighthouse Letters, v. 5, p. 384.

17. Barney to Pleasonton, Baltimore, September 13, 1821, LSCB, 1819-24.

18. Barney to Pleasonton, Baltimore, Sept. 27 (2 letters), Nov. 15 and Dec. 15, 1821, and Winslow Lewis to Superintendent of Bodkin Island lighthouse, Boston, Sept. 15, 1821, LSCB, 1819-24.

19. Lighthouse Letters, v. 5, pp. 372-73, 376. Congress appropriated a total of $22,200 for the lighthouses at Bodkin Island and North Point. On March 3, 1819, it provided $9,000; on May 15, 1820, $6,600; and on April 30, 1822, another $6,600. See Lighthouse Board, *Laws*, pp. 51, 55, 56.

20. Lighthouse Letters, v. 5, p. 436; and Barney to Pleasonton, Baltimore, Sept. 13 and 21, 1821, LSCB, 1819-24.

21. Lighthouse Letters, v. 5, pp. 460, 467, 471; Barney to Pleasonton, Baltimore, Nov. 15, 1821, and Thomas Evans and William Coppeck to Pleasonton, Baltimore, Dec. 8, 1821, LSCB, 1819-24.

22. Barney to Pleasonton, Baltimore, April 10, May 11, June 15, July 5, July 9, August 2, 1822, LSCB, 1819-24; and Lighthouse Letters, v. 5, pp. 514-15. The keeper of the North Point lighthouse was to be Solomon Frazier who was a member of the Maryland legislature. He asked, since the lighthouse was not complete, to continue being a member of the legislature until the session ended in January 1822. Pleasonton agreed, saying Frazier was not to be paid while attending the legislature. See Barney to Pleasonton, Baltimore, Dec. 15, 1821, LSCB, 1819-24, and Lighthouse Letters, v. 5, p. 518.

23. Barney to Pleasonton, Baltimore, July 5 and 9, 1822, LSCB, 1819-24; and Lighthouse Letters, v. 5, pp. 514-18.

24. Barney to Pleasonton, Baltimore, Aug. 6, 9, 14, and 27, Sept. 11, and Nov. 14, 1822, LSCB, 1819-24. The readvertisement for bidders called for the tower to be a round lighthouse built of stone with a stone foundation in five feet of water and four feet above high tide. The tower was to rise 35 feet above the foundation, and the walls were to be three feet thick at the base and 20 inches at the top. The top of the tower would be capped with a soapstone deck. "On one side of the deck to be a scuttle door to enter the lantern of the same dimensions as that of the eastern lighthouse; the frame of which to extend down the whole thickness of the arch, to be of cast iron, and the door and iron frame covered with copper, thirty ounces to the square foot; with an iron handle on the upper, and a bolt on the lower side, and good wrought iron hinges." The circular stairway would be constructed of dressed stone, and an iron ladder from the platform at the top of the stairs would lead to the lantern. The lantern would be octagonal with an iron frame. One-half inch anchor posts would extend five feet down into the stonework. "The height and diameter of the lantern to be sufficient to admit an iron sash in each octagon to contain twenty-one squares, eleven by nine; eighteen of which to be glazed with the best double glass from the Boston manufactory; the other three squares or lower tier to be of sheet copper thirty ounces to the square foot." One of the octagons was to contain an iron door covered with copper. On the top of the dome would be a ventilator. The foundation was to be built in a coffer dam. A footbridge would connect the light tower and the shore.

25. Barney to Pleasonton, Baltimore, Nov. 7 and 26, and Dec. 17, 1822, and Jan. 10, 1823, LSCB, 1819-24.

26. Barney to Pleasonton, Baltimore, Jan. 19 and 24, 1823, LSCB, 1819-26; Barney to Pleasonton, Baltimore, Jan. 25, 1823, LSCB 1819-24. For information on David Melville see Sarah C. Gleason, *Kindly Lights: A History of the Lighthouses of Southern New England* (Boston: Beacon Press, C. 1991), 61-77.

27. Barney to Pleasonton, Baltimore, Jan. 24 and 25, 1823, w/attachment, LSCB, 1819-24, and Note, Pleasonton to Sec. of the Treasury transmitting letter of Solomon Frazier, Dec. 5, 1822, in Early L. H. Correspondence, Misc., 1821-1825.

28. Barney to Pleasonton, Baltimore, Sept 29, 1823, LSCB, 1819-24.

29. Note, Pleasonton to [Secretary of the Treasury], Dec. 5, 1822, w/attachment, Early Lighthouse Correspondence, Misc., 1821-25.

30. Brantz to Pleasonton, Baltimore, June 12, 1823, LSCB, 1819-24.

31. Lighthouse Board, *Laws*, p. 63; Barney to Pleasonton, Baltimore, Dec. 22, 1823, LSCB, 1819-24.

32. Barney to Pleasonton, Baltimore, July 26, Aug. 15 and 31, and Dec. 30, 1824, and Bid of Joshua Turner, Thomas Point lighthouse, Feb. 15, 1825, w/enclosure, LSCB, 1825-52.

33. Barney to Pleasonton, Feb. 17, 1825, LSCB, 1825-52.

34. Barney to Pleasonton, Baltimore, Feb. 18 and 23, 1825, LSCB, 1825-52.

35. Barney to Pleasonton, Baltimore, Oct. 3 and Dec. 30, 1825, LSCB, 1825-52. The tower Donahoo erected had to be rebuilt some years later, but not because of poor construction, as one writer has stated, rather due to the fact that erosion threatened the structure and it was taken down and rebuilt at a safer location.

36. Barney to Pleasonton, Baltimore, Aug. 18, 1825, LSCB, 1825-52; and Robert Mills, *The American Pharos or Lighthouse Guide* (Washington: Thompson and Homans, 1832), p.77.

37. Barney to Pleasonton, Baltimore, Dec. 30, 1824, LSCB, 1819-24; and Site File, Pooles Island.

38. Barney to Pleasonton, Baltimore, March 18, Oct. 3 and Nov. 29, 1825, LSCB, 1825-52. Donahoo and Frieze also painted the Thomas Point and Pooles Island light towers with Roman cement. See Nov. 29 letter.

39. Lighthouse Letters, v. 7 (March 1, 1828-April 1, 1829), pp. 276 and 320; Barney to Pleasonton, Baltimore, Nov. 12, 1828, w/attachment, LSCB, 1825-52. In 1828 a fog bell was installed at Beavertail lighthouse in Rhode Island. It was small and ineffective and was in service only four years. See Gleason, *Kindly Lights*, p. 75.

40. Lighthouse Letters, v. 7, p. 403, v. 8 (April 4, 1829-July 12, 1831), pp. 438 and 494, and v. 9 (July 12, 1831-May 6, 1833), p. 294; Barney to Pleasonton, Baltimore, Sept. 22 and Dec. 16, 1828 and March 16, 1829, LSCB, 1825-52.

41. Lighthouse Board, *Laws*, pp. 73, 75.

42. Site File, Havre de Grace; Barney to Pleasonton, Baltimore, June 13 and 29, 1826, LSCB, 1825-52; Lighthouse Letters, v. 7, pp. 55-56, 134, 157, and 162.

43. Barney to Pleasonton, Baltimore, June 18, Aug. 28, Nov. 2, Dec. 3, 1827, and April 4, 1829, LSCB, 1825-52; Lighthouse Letters, v. 7, pp. 171, 229, 244, and ltr. dated Nov. 3, 1827.

44. Barney to Pleasonton, Baltimore, June 13, 1826, May 3, June 15, Sept. 11, and Dec. 1, 1827, LSCB, 1825-52; Lighthouse Letters, v. 7, pp. 39, 55-56, 74, 171, 180, 215, 231, 232, 235, 245, 275.

45. Willard Flint, *Lightships of the United States Government* (Washington: U.S. Coast Guard, 1989), Index 050 and Index 051; Lighthouse Letters, v. 12 (Feb. 15, 1837-Dec. 30, 1837), pp. 170-71, 331, v. 13 (Jan. 1, 1838-October 17, 1838), p. 408, and v. 14 (Oct. 17, 1838-Aug. 22, 1839), p. 21, 284.

46. Lighthouse Board, *Laws*, p. 73.

47. Site File, Fog Point; Barney to Pleasonton, Baltimore, Jan. 8, Aug. 14 (w/attachments), and Sept. 15 (w/attachments), 1826, and March 17, 1827, LSCB, 1825-52; and Lighthouse Letters, v. 7, pp. 76, 85, and 123. The Fog Point design was not unique, and had been used previously by Winslow Lewis and others.

48. Barney to Pleasonton, Baltimore, March 20 and 31, April 16 and 18 (2 letters), Aug. 27, Sept. 15 and 24, 1827, June 25, 1828, and June 18, 1829, and Winslow Lewis to Barney, New York, April 8, 1827, LSCB, 1825-52; Lighthouse Letters, v. 7, pp. 158, 226 and 334; *20th Congress, 1st Sess., House Doc. No. 185*, p. [13] (Serial # 173).

49. Lighthouse Board, *Laws*, pp. 65-66, 78; Barney to Stephen Pleasonton, Baltimore, Dec. 27, 1825, LSCB, 1825-52.

50. Site File, Cove Point; Barney to Pleasonton, Baltimore, Oct. 13, 1826, June 27, July 7, 22 and 23, and Sept. 19, 1828, LSCB, 1825-52; Lighthouse Letters, v. 7, pp. 94, 165-66, 259, 330, 345, and 370. There is an indication that the advertisement called for the light tower to be erected on piles. See Lighthouse Letters, v. 7, p. 330.

51. Barney to Pleasonton, Baltimore, Nov. 11 (two letters) and Dec. 1, 1828, LSCB, 1825-52 ; and Lighthouse Letters, v. 7, pp. 387 and 399.

52. Barney to Pleasonton, Baltimore, Dec. 27, 1825 and Oct. 7, 1826, and Barney to E. J. Millard, Baltimore, Oct. 13, 1826, LSCB, 1825-52; and Lighthouse Letters, v. 7, pp. 25, 46, 93, and 277; Lighthouse Board, Laws, pp. 65-66, 79-80.

53. Barney to Pleasonton, Baltimore, Sept. 16, 1828, LSCB, 1825-52; Lighthouse Letters, v. 7, pp. 329-30, 332, 371, 402.

54. Barney to Pleasonton, Baltimore, Sept. 21, 1829, LSCB, 1825-52; Lighthouse Letters, v. 8, pp. 36-37, 39, 42, 111, 182, 187, 193, 201, 209, 246, 261, 271, 363, 407, v. 9 (July 12, 1831-May 6, 1833), p.306, v. 13 (Jan. 1, 1838-Oct. 17, 1838), p. 460, v. 22 (April 27, 1846-Dec. 14, 1846), p. 509.

55. Lighthouse Letters, v. 8, pp. 502-503, and v. 9, p. 11.

56. Lighthouse Letters, v. 9, pp. 143-44, 373-74.

CHAPTER 2

1. Robert de Gast, The Lighthouses of the Chesapeake (Baltimore and London: The Johns Hopkins University Press, 1973), p. 161.

2. Lazaretto Site File; Note from Stephen Pleasonton, April 19, 1831, Early Lighthouse Correspondence, Misc., 1830-39; Lighthouse Letters, v. 8, pp. 425, 457, 494, and v. 9, pp. 3, 41, 78, 171.

3. "Descriptive List of Lighthouses, 5th District," v. 1, 1858, p. 218; Lighthouse Board, "Inspection Book, 5th District," 1867, Report #18; R. Lyons to Pleasonton, Baltimore, April 12 and 18 and Sept 17, 1836, LSCB, 1825-52; and Lighthouse Letters, v. 11 (June 10, 1835-Feb. 15, 1837), pp. 90, 249, 263, and 324.

4. Barney to Pleasonton, Baltimore, Dec. 12, 1828 and March 16, 1829, LSCB, 1825-1852; and Lighthouse Letters, v. 7, pp. 319-20, 373-74, 402, and v. 8, pp. 2, 22-23, 378, 385, 457.

5. Site File, Clay Island; Lighthouse Letters, v. 9, pp. 76, 145, 148, 167, 188, 308, 313; and "Descriptive List of Lighthouses, 5th District," v. 1, 1858," p. 138; and 22nd Cong., 2nd Sess., House Doc. No. 108, p. 4 (Serial # 234).

6. Turkey Point Site File; Lighthouse Letters, v. 8, p. 425, v. 9, pp. 4, 145, 148, 150, 208, 294-95, 378, and v. 10 (May 7, 1833-June 9, 1835), pp. 34, 50, 57; "Descriptive List of Lighthouses, 5th District," v. 2, 1858.

7. Piney Point Site File; Lighthouse Letters, v. 10, pp. 421-22, 441-42, and v. 11, pp. 204, 246-247, 253, 301, 361-62, 365, 388, 390, 399-400.

8. "Descriptive List of Lighthouses, 5th District," v. 2, 1858, and Lighthouse Board, "Inspection Book, 5th District," 1867.

9. Sharp's Island Site File; Lighthouse Letters, v. 12, pp. 188-89, 233-34, 284; William Frick to Pleasonton, Baltimore, Aug. 1, 26, 30, Dec. 22, 1837, LSCB, 1825-52.

10. Frick to Pleasonton, Baltimore, Oct. 2, 1837, LSCB, 1825-52; Lighthouse Letters, v. 12, pp. 341, 396, v. 13, pp. 8-9, 16-17, 24, 67, 200, 317, and v. 17 (July 21, 1841-July 12, 1842), p. 37. Just what "wheels" were used and how they worked is not known. Perhaps some day a researcher will come across a description of this lighthouse.

11. Lighthouse Letters, v. 13, pp. 253-54, 460.

12. Greenbury Point and Greenbury Shoals Site File; James Bayle to Richard Rush, Annapolis, Feb. 5, 1828, Early Lighthouse Correspondence, Misc., 1826-29; Lighthouse Letters, v. 23 (March 2, 1847-July 24, 1847), pp. 34, 86, v. 24 (July 24, 1847-Jan. 11, 1848), pp. 54, 442-49, v. 25 (Jan. 12, 1848-Aug. 1, 1848), pp. 1, 72, 173, 236-38, 244, 284-85. 29th Cong., 1st Sess., House Doc. No. 177 (Serial No. 485), p. 1.

13. Lighthouse Letters, v. 25, pp. 295-96, 353-54, v. 26 (Aug. 1, 1848-Dec. 22, 1848), pp. 240, 273-74, 291, 395, 407-409, 418, 444, and v. 29 (Jan. 25, 1850-Feb. 18, 1851), p. 30.

14. Lighthouse Letters, v. 29, pp. 14, 30, 33-34, 37-38, 64, 152-53, 161, 192; George T. Kane to Pleasonton, Baltimore, Feb. 7 w/attachment, Feb. 11, April 11, May 4, 1850, LSCB, 1825-52.

15. "Descriptive List of Lighthouses, 5th District," v. 1, 1858.

16. Lighthouse Letters, v. 18 (July 13, 1842-Aug. 26, 1843), p. 237, v. 21, p. 455, and v. 25, pp. 147, 336.

17. Lighthouse Letters, v. 26, pp. 483-84, v. 27 (Dec. 22, 1848-May 12, 1849), pp. 76, 87, 260; v. 28, pp. 252-53, v. 29, pp. 59, 115-16, 197-98, 320, and v. 30 (Feb. 18, 1851-Feb. 28, 1852), pp. 57, 296-97; Lighthouse Board, Laws Relating to Lighthouses, p. 134.

18. Lighthouse Letters, v. 30, pp. 296-97, 364, 366, 404, 475, 477, 511, 517, 567.

19. "Descriptive List of Lighthouses, 5th District," v. II, 1858, p. 98; and Lighthouse Board, "Inspection Book, 5th District," 1867, Report # 12.

20. Battery Island Site File.

21. Lighthouse Letters, v. 30, pp. 510, 708, and v. 31 (March 1, 1852-Oct. 15, 1852), pp. 9, 63, 123, 134, 177, 203, 219, 229, 237, 265, 354-55, 372; Kane to Pleasonton, Baltimore, March 4, April 24, May 8, July 31, and Aug. 5 and 11, 1852, John Donahoo to Pleasonton, Havre de Grace, June 3 and 15, Sept. 13, 1852, Thomas Corwin to Pleasonton, [Washington], June 5, 1852, and William L. Hodge to Pleasonton, [Washington], June 19 1852, LSCB, 1825-52.

22. Donahoo to Kane, Havre de Grace, Aug. 26 and 27, 1852, and Kane to Pleasonton, Baltimore, Sept. 7, 1852, LSCB, 1825-52; and Lighthouse Letters, v. 31, p.416.

23. Lighthouse Board, Laws Relating to Lighthouses, p. 149; 32nd Cong., 2nd Sess., Sen. Exec. Doc. No. 22 (Serial # 662), p. 86.

24. John Bozman Kerr to Thomas Corwin, House of Representatives, Feb. 24, 1851, and Kane to Pleasonton, Baltimore, March 24, July 14 and 21, and Aug. 18 w/attachment and notations, 1851, LSCB, 1825-52; Lighthouse Letters, v. 30, pp. 15-16, 62-63; Pleasonton to Thomas Corwin, Treasury Dept., April 2, 1852, and John H. Done to Kane, Princess Anne, Md., Aug. 14, 1851, Dept. of the Treasury, "Lighthouse Letters, 1851-52, Series P," p. 437, 438. The last entry is hereafter cited as "Lighthouse Letters, Series P."

25. Pleasonton to David L Seymour, Treasury Dept., Feb. 6, 1852, LSCB, 1825-1852.

26. Pleasonton to Corwin, Treasury Dept., April 2, 1852, "Lighthouse Letters, Series P," 1851-52, p.437; Fifth Auditor's Office, Lighthouse Letters, v. 31, pp. 227, 248; Kane to Pleasonton, Baltimore, July 1 w/attached contract, and 22, 1852, Lighthouse Superintendent's Correspondence, Baltimore, 1825-52; "Descriptive List of Light Vessels, 5th District", 1858, p. 46; and Flint, Lightships of the U.S. Government, Index 049.

27. William James Morgan, et al., eds., Autobiography of Rear Admiral Charles Wilkes, U.S. Navy, 1798-1877 (Washington: Government Printing Office, 1978), p. 317.

28. Congressional Globe, 31st Cong., 2nd Sess., v. XXIII (Washington: 1851), p. 397.

29. Congressional Globe, 31st Cong., 2nd Sess., v. XXIII, pp. 397-98. For the report of the investigating board see 32nd Cong., 1st Sess., Sen. Exec. Doc. No. 28 (Serial #617).

CHAPTER 3

1. 34th Cong., 1st and 2nd Sess., 1855-1856, Sen. Exec. Docs. (Serial # 814), pp. 253-254.

2. 34th Cong., 1st Sess., House Exec. Doc. No. 10 (Serial # 846), pp. 356-57; 34th Cong., 1st and 2nd Sess., Sen. Exec. Docs. (Serial # 814), pp. 251-54; 34th Cong., 3rd Sess., Sen. Exec. Doc. No. 3 (Serial #874). p. 600.

3. Lighthouse Letters, v. 25, pp. 147-48, and v. 29, pp. 144, 242, 255, 590, and 631; and George T. Kane to Pleasonton, Baltimore, May 31, June 6 and 13, 1850, LSCB, 1825-52.

4. Pleasonton to Corwin, Dec. 19, 1850, "Lighthouse Letters, Series P," 1850, pp. 222, 223, and 1851-52, p. 1.

5. Merrick & Son to Corwin, Philadelphia, undated, "Lighthouse Letters, Series P," 1850, pp. 216-18; John Martin to Corwin, Washington, Jan. 4, 1851, p. 231, Note, Corwin to Mr. Harrington, May 28, [1851], p. 219; Specifications, Screw Pile Lighthouse, Seven Foot Knoll, p. 337, all in "Lighthouse Letters, Series P," 1851-1852; Lighthouse Letters, v. 29, p. 632, and v. 30, pp. 581-82, 648; B. F. Isherwood to Pleasonton, Washington, Dec. 16, 1851; Kane to Pleasonton, Baltimore, Jan. 27, Feb. 11, Sept. 6, 10 and 17, 1852, LSCB, 1825-52; Compilation of Public Documents and Extracts . . . Relating to Lighthouses . . . 1789-1871 (Washington, G. P. O, 1871), pp. 780-82.

6. 33rd Cong., 1st Sess., Doc. No. 2 (Serial # 694), p. 184; 34th Cong., 1st Sess., Doc. No. 10, p. 357; 34th Cong., 1st and 2nd Sessions, Sen. Exec. Doc., p. 261; 34th Cong., 3rd Sess., Sen. Exec. Doc. No. 3, p. 600; Maryland Historical Trust, State Historic Site Inventory Form: Seven Foot Knoll Lighthouse, in MHT library.

7. Robert de Gast, The Lighthouses of the Chesapeake (Baltimore and London: The Johns Hopkins University, 1973), p. 160.

8. "Descriptive List of Lighthouses," 5th District, v. 1, 1858, Seven Foot Knoll.

9. Lighthouse Board, Descriptive List of Lighthouses, 5th District, 1858, p. 212; Lighthouse Board, "Inspection Book," Fifth District, Report no. 22; Site File, Fort Carroll; 33rd Cong., 2nd Sess., Doc. No. 2 (Serial # 749), p. 318.

10. Site File, Fort Washington; "Descriptive List of Lighthouses, 5th District," v. II, 1858, p. 106.

11. Site File B, Sandy Point; "Descriptive List of Lighthouses," Fifth District, v. 1, 1858, p. 188; Lighthouse Board, "Inspection Book, Fifth District," 1867, Report no. 19; Lighthouse Board, Index Slips, Sandy Point, March 10, 1858; 35th Cong., 2nd Sess., Sen. Exec. Doc. No. 2 (Serial # 979), p. 284; Lighthouse Board, Light List, 1866 (Washington: G. P. O., 1866), pp. 42-43; Lighthouse Board, Annual Report, 1863, p. 156. Plan, Sandy Point lighthouse, August 7, 1857, No. 1S, Folder MD-41, National Archives, Philadelphia Branch.

12. 37th Cong., 2nd Sess., Sen. Exec. Doc. No. 2 (Serial # 1121), pp. 204-205; 38th Cong., 2nd Sess., House Doc. No. 3 (Serial # 1222), p. 167; Official Records of the Union and Confederate Navies in the War of the Rebellion, Series I, V. 5, pp. 433-34; Official Records, Navy, Series I, v. 4, pp.468-69.

13. 38th Cong., 1st Sess., House Exec. Doc. No. 3 (Serial # 1186), pp. 156 and 160; 38th Cong., 2nd Sess., House Doc. No. 3, pp. 167-68; W. B. Shubrick to S. P. Chase, Treasury Dept. May 19, July 31 and Sept. 16, 1863, all in "Lighthouse Letters, Series P, 1862-64."

14. 39th Cong., 1st Sess., House Exec. Doc. No. 3 (Serial # 1254), p. 195; 39th Cong. 2nd Sess, House Exec. Doc. No. 4 (Serial # 1287), p.217; Lighthouse Board, Light List, 1873, pp. 64-65; Lighthouse Letters, v. 25 (Jan. 12, 1848-Aug. 1, 1848), pp. 126-28, 143, 173, 204-205, 265-66, 435-36; v. 26 (Aug. 1, 1848-Dec. 22, 1848), pp. 44 and 59; Lighthouse Board, "Inspection Book, 5th Dist.," 1867, Report # 17.

15. Lighthouse Board, "Inspection Book, 5th District," 1867, Report # 32 and Report # 31; Lighthouse Board, Annual Report, 1867, pp. 23-24.

16. Lighthouse Board, Annual Report, 1867, p. 21; Lighthouse Board, Light List, 1873, pp. 64-67; Lighthouse Board, "Inspection Book, 5th District," 1867, Reports # 9, 19, 31 and 32; Lighthouse Board, Form 60, Upper Cedar Point Light Station, June 21, 1909, and Form 60, Lower Cedar Point, June 18, 1909.

17. Lighthouse Board, "Inspection Book, 5th District," 1867, Report # 9 and Report # 10. Lighthouse Board, Annual Report, 1867, pp. 23-24; Flint, Lightships and Lightship Stations of the U. S., Index 049, and Lightvessels, pp. 21, 24 and 25.

18. See Somers Cove in Lighthouse Board, "Inspection Book, 5th District," 1870; Lighthouse Board, Annual Report, 1867, p. 22; Lighthouse Board, Light List, 1873, pp. 64-65.

19. Lighthouse Board, Annual Report, 1867, pp. 22,

1868, p. 47-48 and *1869*, p. 45; Lighthouse Board, *Light List,1868*, pp. 66-67; Site File, Brewerton Channel Range Rear.

20. George C. Havenner to Commissioner of Lighthouses, [Washington], April 7, 1915 and H. D. King to Commissioner, Baltimore, April 17, 1915, File 2307E, CBL, 1911-1939.

21. Thomas C. Chappell to Chief Inspector of Lighthouses, Baltimore, Oct. 5 and Nov. 2, 1885, and C. S. Fairchild to S. C. Rowan, Washington, July, 1886, Site File, Hawkins Point; Lighthouse Board, *Annual Report, 1886*, p. 49.

22. Lighthouse Board, *Annual Report, 1887*, p. 48, and *1888*, p. 84.

23. C. S. Fairchild to S. C. Rowan, Washington, July 8, 1886, and O. W. Chapman to Secretary of the Treasury, Washington, August 17, 1889, Site File, Hawkins Point; Lighthouse Board, *Annual Report, 1889*, p. 92, *1890*, p.100, and *1891*, p. 90. Chappell did not accept this ruling gracefully. He continued filing appeals over the years, apparently the last being in 1914 when he filed suit through the Court of Claims. See Thomas C. Chappell, Petition, Court of Claims, [Aug. 1914] and Hankinson to Commissioner, Baltimore, Sept. 12, 1914, File 2307E, CBL, 1911-1939.

24. Robert C. Keith, *Baltimore Harbor: A Picture History* (Baltimore: Ocean World Publishing Co., 1982), p. 27.

25. Note of Telephone call from Ruland, March 7, 1913, Ruland, "Recommendation as to Aids to Navigation," March 10, 1913, Ruland to Commissioner, Baltimore, March 28 and July 19, 1913, all in File 2307E, Correspondence, Bureau of Lighthouses, 1911-1939; Keith, *Baltimore Harbor: A Picture History*, p. 27.

26. Lighthouse Board, *Annual Report, 1870*, pp. 33-34, *1871*, p. 30, *1872*, pp. 40-41; Lighthouse Board, *Light List, 1872*, pp. 34-35.

27. Site File, Love Point; Report of Commissioners to Assess and Value Land for Love Point Lighthouse, certified May 14, 1835, LSCB, 1825-52; Lighthouse Letters, v. 10, pp. 233, 317-18, and 465, v. 11, pp. 133 and 164.

28. Lighthouse Board, *Annual Report, 1870*, p. 34, *1871*, p. 30, and *1872*, p. 41; F. A. Gibbons to Pleasonton, Baltimore, Aug. 15, 1849, LSCB, 1825-52; Lighthouse Letters, v. 19, pp. 177-178, 226, v. 20, pp. 62, 85, and 213, and v. 22, pp. 316-24; Peter A. Hains to Francis A. Gibbons, March 10, 1871, and Peter A. Hains to W. B. Shubrick, March 21, 1871, Fifth Dist. Engineer Letter Press, Nov. 1870-May 1871; F. Ross Holland, *The Old Point Loma Lighthouse* (San Diego: Cabrillo Historical Association, 1978), pp. 12-13; and Holland, *America's Lighthouses: An Illustrated History*, pp. 123 and 141.

29. Lighthouse Board, *Light List, 1873*, pp. 64-67; Lighthouse Board, *Annual Report, 1876*, p. 33; Bureau of Lighthouses, Form 60, Description of Light Station, Love Point, Sept. 26, 1927.

30. Lighthouse Board, *Annual Report, 1873*, p. 44; *1874*, p. 45, and *1875*, p. 44.

CHAPTER 4

1. Lighthouse Board, *Annual Report, 1871*, pp. 30-31; *1872*, p. 42; *1873*, pp. 45-46; Site File, Craighill Channel.

2. Lighthouse Board, *Annual Report, 1873*, pp. 45-46, and *1874*, pp. 45-46. The reason for not building the lighthouse on the cylinder right away was because the Lighthouse Board had run out of the appropriation and had to wait until the next year for Congress to provide more funds.

3. Lighthouse Board, Form 60, Description of Lighthouse Tower, Buildings, and Premises, Craighill Channel Front Light Station, July 13, 1909; Lighthouse Board, *Annual Report, 1875*, p. 44.

4. Lighthouse Board, *Annual Report, 1873*, pp. 44-45; *1874*, p. 45; and *1875*, p. 44.

5. Lighthouse Board, Form 60, Description of Lighthouse Tower, Buildings, and Premises, Craighill Channel Rear Light Station, Aug. 14, 1909; Lighthouse Board, *Annual Report, 1873*, p. 45.

6. Site File, Craighill Channel, Record Group 26, National Archives.

7. H. D. King, "Recommendation as to Aids to Navigation", Sept. 26, 1923, Craighill Channel Range Rear Light; Memorandum, King, Baltimore, Aug. 20, 1928 w/attachments; King to Commissioner of Lighthouses, Baltimore, Sept. 17, 1928; N. C. Manyon, "Recommendation as to Aids to Navigation," Aug. 11, 1938, Craighill Channel Range Rear Light; Manyon to Commissioner of Lighthouses, Norfolk, Aug. 18, 1938, all in File 1293, CBL, 1911-1939; Site File, Craighill Channel. Lighthouse Board, *Annual Report, 1889*, p. 91.

8. Lighthouse Board, *Annual Report, 1881*, p. 39, and *1882*, pp. 34-35; Lighthouse Service, Form 60, Sharp's Island Light Station, Md., Sept. 26, 1927.

9. Lighthouse Board, *Annual Report, 1882*, p. 35, and *1883*, pp. 50-51; Lighthouse Board, Form 60, Description of the Lighthouse Tower, Buildings, and Premises, Bloody Point Bar, April 24, 1909.

10. 47th Cong. 1st. Sess. *Report No. 870*, p. 61, bound in "Congressional Reports on Lighthouse Subjects, 1875-1885," in U. S. Coast Guard Library, Headquarters Office; Lighthouse Board, *Annual Report, 1881*, p. 40; *1883*, p. 51; and *1884*, p. 49. The Board in its first requests for a new lighthouse at Sandy Point had said the cost would be $40,000, but later lowered the cost, apparently hoping to induce Congress to make the appropriation. See Lighthouse Board, *Annual Report, 1874*, pp. 44-45 and subsequent reports.

11. Lighthouse Service, Form 60, Sandy Point Light Station, Md., Sept. 26, 1927.

12. Lighthouse Board, *Annual Report, 1872*, p. 40; *1873*, p. 43; *1874*, p. 44; *1875*, p. 43; and *1876*, p. 32; Site File, Solomons Lump.

13. Lighthouse Board, *Annual Report, 1893*, p. 93; *1894*, p. 95; and *1895*, p. 100.

14. Lighthouse Board, *Annual Report, 1895*, p. 100, and *1896*, p. 86-87. Lawrence H. Bradner, *The Plum Beach Light: The Birth, Life, and Death of a Lighthouse* (n. p., n. d.), p. 169 lists Solomons Lump as one of the caisson lighthouses constructed by the pneumatic method. The reports of construction give no indication that the caisson and cylinder were positioned by the pneumatic method. In view of the shallowness of the site (seven feet), it is unlikely the site would require that approach.

15. Lighthouse Board, *Annual Report, 1896*, pp. 86-87; Lighthouse Board, Form 60, Solomons Lump Light Station, Md., Sept. 17, 1909.

16. Petition to Fifth District Lighthouse Inspector, Baltimore, March 4, 1919, and H. D. King, "Recommendation as to Aids to Navigation," April 9, 1919, File 2072, CBL, 1911-1939. In 1950 the Coast Guard downgraded the Solomons Lump light and replaced the fourth-order lens with a 200mm lens. At the same time it automated the light. See de Gast, *The Lighthouses of the Chesapeake*, p. 139, and U. S. Coast Guard, *Light List, Atlantic and Gulf Coasts, 1951*, p. 351.

17. Lighthouse Board, *Annual Report, 1897*, p. 98; *1898*, pp. 106-107; and *1899*, p. 102; Assignee, The Variety Iron Works Co. to Lighthouse Board, Cleveland, June 2, 1903, and W. A. Jones to Comptroller of the Treasury, Baltimore, Feb. 14, 1902, File 477, CLB, 1901-1910.

18. Lighthouse Board, *Annual Report, 1900*, p. 97, *1901*, p. 107, and *1902*, pp. 125-126.

19. Lighthouse Board, *Annual Report, 1902*, pp. 125-126, and "Description of Hooper Island Lighthouse, Md.," [c.1902], File 477, CLB, 1901-1910.

20. Lighthouse Board, *Annual Report, 1891*, p. 89; *1894*, pp. 95-96; *1900*, p. 96; and *1901*, p. 107.

21. Lighthouse Board, *Annual Report, 1901*, p. 107; *1902*, pp. 124-125; *1903*, p. 54; *1904*, pp. 78-79; and *1905*, pp. 80-81; Humphrey Toomey to E. D. Hearne, New York, Oct. 2, 1917, File 1431E, CBL, 1911-1939.

22. Lighthouse Board, *Annual Report, 1890*, p. 99; *1891*, p. 94; *1894*, p. 96; *1895*, p. 101; and *1896*, p. 87. George Dewey, Chairman of the Location Committee, to Lighthouse Board, Washington, Sept. 27, 1894, Site File, Baltimore.

23. Lighthouse Board, *Annual Report, 1897*, p. 98; *1898*, p. 107; *1899*, p. 103; *1900*, p. 97; and *1901*, p. 108-109. *57th Cong., 1st Sess., H. R. 12085*, March 3, 1902, copy, and Engineer Secretary to Secretary of the Treasury, Washington, Dec. 31, 1902, both in File 3920, CLB, 1901-1910.

24. R. L Hoxie to W. A. Jones, Washington, April 24, 1900; W. A. Jones to the Lighthouse Board, Baltimore, Sept, 3, 1902, March 19, April 23, July 2, and Sept. 26, 1903; Peter C. Hains to the Lighthouse Board, Washington, Sept. 22, 1902; George C. Remey to the Lighthouse Board, Washington, April 1, 1903; and George B. Cortelyou to the Lighthouse Board, Washington, Aug. 17 and Nov. 3, 1903 (there are two letters on the latter date), all in File 3920, CLB, 1901-1910. Lighthouse Board, *Annual Report, 1902*, p. 126; *1903*, p. 55; and *1904*, p. 79.

25. Lighthouse Board, *Annual Report, 1904*, p. 79, and *1905*, p. 81. H. B. Bowerman to the Lighthouse Board, Washington, Oct. 25, 1904, and clipping, *Baltimore American*, Oct. 31, 1904, in File 3920, CLB, 1901-1910.

26. R. L Hoxie to the Lighthouse Board, Sept. 22, 1905; Lawrence O. Murray to Lighthouse Board, Washington, May 3 and 9, 1906; W. E. Craighill to the Lighthouse Board, Baltimore, Sept. 10 and 22, 1908; Engineer Secretary to Engineer, 5th District, [Washington}, Sept 12, 1908, all in File 3920, CLB, 1901-1910; and Acting Commissioner to Merritt & Chapman Derrick & Wrecking Co., [Washington], Sept 14, 1911, File 1573E, CBL, 1911-1939. Lighthouse Board, *Annual Report, 1906*, p. 67; *1907*, pp. 76-77; *1908*, p. 19.

27. Lighthouse Board, Form 60, Description of Lighthouse Tower, Buildings and Premises, Baltimore Lighthouse, October 1, 1908.

28. King, "Recommendation as to Aids to Navigation," March 1, 1923; Commissioner of Lighthouses to Secretary of Commerce, [Washington], April 19, 1923; H. D. King to Commissioner of Lighthouses, Baltimore, April 9, 1923; Clifford Hastings to Commissioner of Lighthouses, [Washington], April 17, 1923, all in File 1573E, CBL, 1911-1939. Press Release, May 20, 1964, Public Information Division, U. S. Coast Guard, with picture of Baltimore lighthouse in files of Historian's Office, U. S. C. G. Headquarters.

29. F. Ross Holland, Jr., *A History of the Cape Hatteras Light Station*, Division of History, National Park Service, Dept. of the Interior, Sept. 30, 1968, pp. 112-116. The solution for such ocean sites as Cape Hatteras did not come until the mid-twentieth century, when the Coast Guard erected a number of "Texas Tower" structures off the east coast of the United States. These proved to be quite expensive and the Coast Guard erected only a few of them.

CHAPTER 5

1. Lighthouse Board, *Annual Report, 1872*, p. 41; *1873*, p. 44; *1874*, p. 44; *1875*, p. 43; and *1876*, p. 32; de Gast, *The Lighthouses of the Chesapeake*, p. 79.

2. Lighthouse Board, *Annual Report, 1877*, p. 30. Lighthouse Board, Form 60, Thomas Point Shoal Light Station, Md., July 10, 1909.

3. Lighthouse Board, *Annual Report, 1872*, p. 42; *1873*, pp. 46-47; *1874*, pp. 46-47; *1875*, p. 44; *1876*, p. 33; and *1877*, p. 30. Lighthouse Board, Form 60, Mathias Point Shoal Light Station, June 1, 1909, and Site File, Port Tobacco.

4. Lighthouse Board, *Annual Report, 1885*, p. 50; *1887*, 49; *1888*, p. 84; *1889*, p. 90; and *1890*, pp. 96-97. Lighthouse Board, Form 60, Cobb Point Bar Light Station, Dec. 10, 1889.

5. Lighthouse Board, *Annual Report, 1887*, p. 49; *1888*, p. 85; *1889*, p. 90; *1890*, p. 97; *1891*, p. 89; *1892*, pp. 92-93; *1893*, pp. 92-93. Lighthouse Board, Form 60, Maryland Point Light Station, June 21, 1909.

6. Lighthouse Board, *Annual Report*, p. 29; *1878*, p. 35; *1879*, p. 36; and *1880*, p. 35.

7. *33rd Cong., 1st Sess., Doc. No 2* (Serial # 694), p. 246; *34th Cong., 1st and 2nd Sess., Sen. Exec. Docs* (Serial # 814), p. 282; *35th Cong., 1st Sess., Sen. Exec. Doc. No. 1* (Serial # 918) p. 245; *35th Cong., 2nd Sess., Sen. Exec. Doc. No. 2* (Serial No. 979), p. 289.

8. "47th Cong., 1st Sess., Report No. 1212," p. 81, bound in volume labelled "Congressional Reports on Lighthouse Subjects, 1875-1885," Historian's Office, U. S. Coast Guard Headquarters. Lighthouse Board, *Annual Report, 1883*, pp. 49-50. Lighthouse Board, Form 60, Drum Point Light Station, Aug. 1, 1909.

9. Lighthouse Board, Form 60, Great Shoals Light

Station, Md., Sept. 15, 1909. Lighthouse Board, *Annual Report, 1883*, p. 49; *1884*, p. 48; and *1885*, pp. 48-49. "47th Cong., 1st Sess., Report No. 1213," bound in "Congression Reports on Lighthouse Subjects, 1875-1885" in Historian's Office, U. S. Coast Guard Headquarters.

10. Lighthouse Board, *Annual Report, 1888*, p. 83.

11. *Annual Report, 1889*, pp. 90-91; and *1890*, pp. 96-97. Lighthouse Board, Form 60, Holland Island Bar Light Station, Md. Dec. 16, 1889, and Form 60, Holland Island Bar Light Station, Md., Sept. 17, 1909.

12. *Annual Report, 1896*, p. 86; *1905*, p. 80; *1906*, p. 67.

13. *Annual Report, 1907*, p. 76; *1910*, p. 20.

14. *Annual Report, 1910*, p. 20.

15. Lighthouse Board, *Annual Report, 1879*, p. 36; *1880*, p. 35; *1894*, p. 95; *1895*, p. 100; *1897*, p. 97; and *1921*,

p. 50. de Gast, *The Lighthouses of the Chesapeake*, pp. 156-170.

16. The principal objective of the Living Classroom Foundation, a non-profit organization, is to operate "for the benefit of the community at large, providing hands-on education and job-training, with a special emphasis on at-risk youth and groups from diverse backgrounds. Utilizing maritime settings and a 1:5 staff-to-student ratio, the Foundation provides experience-based educational programs emphasizing the applied learning of math, science, language arts, history, economics, and ecology. Key objectives of all Living Classrooms programs are career development, cooperative learning, community service, elevating self-esteem, and fostering multicultural exchange."

The Foundation reports that "in 1995 Living Classrooms served 30,000 students in experiential programs on [their] vessels and on the shore."

Vessels play a key role in the execution of the programs. For example, "the skipjack *Sigsbee*, built by [the] staff and students in 1994, has provided [a] living classroom for the Oyster Restoration Project. Students are making a lasting contribution to the environment while practicing real-world math and science." In addition, "high school students in [the] new Cetology and Estuarine Studies program [have] had the unique opportunity to sail a 19th century tall ship while working with 20th century scientific technology."

CHAPTER 6

1. Report of Lewis Brantz and James Gibson, Baltimore, May 22, 1822, Barney to Pleasonton, Baltimore, April 25, 1823 w/attachment, May 29 and Aug. 16, 1923, LSCB, 1819-1824; Fifth Auditor's Office, Lighthouse Letters, v. 18, pp. 74-75, 103, 117, 433.

2. Fifth Auditor's Office, Lighthouse Letters, v. 11, pp. 328, 364; George P. Kane to Pleasonton, Baltimore, July 29, 1851 and July 29, 1852, and Kane, advertisement for jetty at North Point, ms, LSCB, 1825-1852.

3. Lighthouse Letters, v. 12, p. 209, v. 13, pp. 323, 459, v. 14, p. 419, v 15, pp. 445, 446, 480, and v. 17, p. 38.

4. Lighthouse Letters, v. 9, pp. 79-80, 101, v. 12, pp. 209, 278, v. 16, p. 298, v. 17, pp. 13, 32, 37-38, 61, v. 18, pp. 27-28, 30-31, 53, 130, 424, v. 21, pp. 3, 117, v. 22, pp. 66, 205-206, 253; and William Frick to Pleasonton, Baltimore, Aug. 26, 1837, LSCB, 1825-1852.

5. Lighthouse Letters, v. 22, pp. 366-367, 415, 511, and v. 29, pp. 311, 361, 372, 503, 505-506; Kane to Pleasonton, Baltimore, June 30, 1851, LSCB, 1825-1852.

6. *38th Cong., 2nd Sess., House Doc. No. 3* (Serial # 1222), p. 166; *39th Cong., 1st Sess., House Exec. Doc No. 3* (Serial # 1254), p. 195; *39th Cong., 2nd Sess., House Exec. Doc No. 4* (Serial # 1287), p. 217; Lighthouse Board, *Annual Report*, 1867, p. 21.

7. Lighthouse Letters, v. 18, pp. 424, 471-472, 510, v. 19, p.75, v. 22, pp. 67, 325-326, 332-333, 349, v. 25, pp. 267-269, 277-278, 456, v. 29, p. 311; Site File, Fog Point.

8. Lighthouse Letters, v. 12 (February 15, 1837-December 30, 1837), pp. 104-105.

9. Lighthouse Letters, v. 18, pp. 77-78, 89-90, 92, 96-97, 152, 433; v. 29, pp. 17, 130; v. 30, 244, 328, 389; Frick to Pleasonton, Baltimore, May 31 and Nov. 30, 1837 and Kane to Pleasonton, Baltimore, April 20, 1850 and July 29, 1851, LSCB, 1825-1852.

10. Lighthouse Letters, v. 11, pp. 252-253; v. 24, pp. 22, 23; v. 30, pp. 244, 268, 305, 328, 435, 379, 389; v. 31 p. 228. Pleasonton in 1847 asked William Gibbs McNeil, because of his "high reputation as an Engineer" and experience "in work of this kind," to visit Sharp's Island, Little Watts Island, and Cove Point and draw up plans to protect these sites from encroachment by the Bay. Pleasonton advanced him $100. McNeil apparently used the revenue cutter to go to the three sites, but went to Old Point Comfort, and then submitted a claim for $300. Pleasonton was indignant and wrote McNeil that five weeks had passed since he agreed to look at the sites and submit a report, and he had used a cutter to visit Old Point Comfort and then submitted a claim for $300 additional. Pleasonton said, "under these circumstance I feel constrained to inform you that I do not wish you to take any further steps in relation to these several lights." See Lighthouse Letters, v. 23, pp. 474-475, and v. 24, pp. 160-161, 176-177.

11. Lighthouse Board, *Annual Report, 1878*, p.35, 1879, p. 37, and 1889, p. 91.

12. Lighthouse Board, *Annual Report, 1890*, p. 98, and 1891, p. 89.

13. *Annual Report, 1892*, pp. 93-95.

14. Lighthouse Board, Form 60, Description of the Lighthouse Tower, Buildings, and Premises, Greenbury Point Shoal, Sept. 10, 1909.

15. *Annual Report, 1893*, p. 93.

16. Barney to Pleasonton, Baltimore, Dec. 27, 1825, and Feb. 13, l826 w/attachment, LSCB, 1825-52, R. G. 26; Letter of Lighthouse Board dated June 7, 1888, in 50th Cong., 1st Sess., *House Exec. Doc. No. 354* (Serial # 2561), p. 1; Lighthouse Board, *Annual Report, 1888*, p. 83, 1892, pp. 93-94, and 1893, p. 93.

17. Cedar Point, Site File, R. G. 26; Lighthouse Board, *Annual Report, 1894*, p. 96, 1895, p. 101, 1896, p. 87, and 1897, p. 98. A report of 1909 adds detail to the descrip-

tion of the lighthouse and its associated structures. The dwelling, resting on a foundation that went six feet into the ground, was brown in color, and the tower was painted white. It had six rooms. A brick cistern holding 4,800 gallons of run-off water was located under the back porch of the dwelling. Wire strainers in the gutters and down spouts helped protect the quality of the water. The lantern, seven feet in diameter, was eight-sided. The lens had ten panels and its red light was achieved by the use of ruby tubes. A clockwork machine rotated the lens. The system's weight-cord ran across the floor of the lantern about three feet and then down a drop tube 16 feet in length. This drop permitted the clockwork system to run for four hours before the weight needed to be rewound. The fog bell weighed 1,962 pounds and a No. 3 Gamewell machine struck it every 30 seconds during thick weather. The tower that held it was located about 12 feet southeast of the light-house. By 1909 the light station, in addition to its original structures, had a chicken house and a stable. Access to the station was by a public road and across a beach.

18. John M. Hawley to Lighthouse Board, Baltimore, June 8, 1903, and Naval Secretary to J. M. Hawley, Washington, May 12, 1903 and June 12, 1903, File 686, CLB, 1900-1910.

19. District Engineer to Lighthouse Board, Baltimore, June 7, 1907; Naval Secretary to Engineer, Fifth District, Washington, July 11, 1907; Engineer Secretary to Secretary of Commerce and Labor, Washington, Feb. 12, 1908; and W. E. Craighill to Lighthouse Board, Baltimore, Jan. 4, 1909, all in File 686, CLB, 1901-1910.

20. Joseph J. Hock to H. D. King, Baltimore, July 16, 1920, File 1702E, Correspondence, Bureau of Lighthouses, 1911-1939.

21. Loch W. Humphreys to Lighthouse Commissioner, Cedar Point Light Station, Sept. 23, 1912; H. B. Bowerman to Commissioner, Cedar Pt., Md., Oct. 23, 1912; "Recommendation for Repairing Aids to Navigation," Nov. 5, 1912; and Ruland to Commissioner, Baltimore, Nov. 30, 1912, all in File 1702A, CBL, l911-1939.

22. Ruland to Commissioner, Baltimore, Oct. 21, 1913; [H. B.] Bowerman to Commissioner, Washington, Nov. 14, 1913 and Jan. 26, 1915; "Recommendation for Repairing Aids to Navigation," Jan. 19, 1914; George W. Willis, Sr. to Lighthouse Inspector, Cedar Pt., Jan. 13, 1915, all in File 1702A, CBL, 1911-1939.

23. [R. L.] Hankinson to Lighthouse Inspector, [Baltimore], Oct. 24, 1916; H. D. King to the Arundel Corporation, Baltimore, July 17, 1920; Acting Commissioner of Lighthouses to [Fifth District] Superintendent of Lighthouses, [Washington], July 29, 1920; Carbon copy of letter to Secretary of Commerce dated May 23, 1914; Edward T. Quigley, "IN RE protection of Cedar Point Light Station from damage by reason of dredging operations in its vicinity," June 6, 1914, all in File 1702E, CBL, 1911-1939.

24. W. S. Stinchcomb to Superintendent of Lighthouses [Fifth Dist.], Cedar Point Light Station, July 13, 1920; King to Arundel Sand and Gravel Co., Baltimore, July 15, 17, 1920; Hock to King, Baltimore, July 16, 1920, all in File 1702E, CBL, 1911-1939.

25. King to Arundel Corporation, Baltimore, Sept. 9, 1920; Hock to King, Baltimore, July 16 and Oct. 19, 1920; [H. D.] King, Memorandum [to files], Oct. 20, 1920; King to Commissioner of Lighthouses, Baltimore, Oct. 20, 1920, all in File 1702E, CBL, 1911-1939.

26. Hock to King, Baltimore, May 26, 1924, and F. C. Hingsburg to Commissioner of Lighthouses, Baltimore, May 29, 1924, in File 1702E, CBL, 1911-1939.

27. J. S. Conway to Secretary of Commerce, [Washington], June 2, 1924; Acting Secretary of Commerce to

Attorney General, [Washington], June 9, 1924; Acting Secretary of Commerce to Secretary of War, [Washington], June 2, 1924; A. W. W. Woodcock to King, Baltimore, July 1, l924; H. B. Bowerman to Superintendent of Lighthouse [Fifth District], [Washington], July 12, 1924; Acting Secretary of War to Secretary of Commerce, Washington, July 12, 1924; Assistant Attorney General to Secretary of Commerce, Washington, July 17, 1924, all in File 1702E, CBL, 1911-1939.

28. Dwight W. Davis to Secretary of Commerce, Washington, Aug. 27 (with endorsements) and Sept. 29, 1924; Acting Secretary of Commerce to Secretary of War, [Washington], Sept 15, 1925, all in File 1702E, CBL, 1911-1939.

29. Gary E. Powell to Superintendent of Lighthouses, Cedar Point, Md., Nov. 14 and 22, and Dec. 12, 1925; Memorandum, Johnson to Superintendent [Fifth District], Nov. 19, 1925; King to Commissioner of Lighthouses, Baltimore, Dec. 7, 1925; and King, "Recommendation as to Aids to Navigation," Jan. 29, 1926, all in File 1702E, CBL, 1911-1939.

30. Hock to King, Baltimore, December 9, 1925, File 1702E, CBL, 1911-1939.

31. King to the Arundel Corporation, Baltimore, Dec. 10, 1925; G. R. Putnam to the Arundel Corporation, Washington, Dec. 15, 1925; King to U. S. Engineer, Baltimore, Dec. 17, 1925; G. R. Putnam to Superintendent [Fifth District], [Washington], Dec. 19, 1925; King to Commissioner of Lighthouses, Baltimore, Dec. 22, 1925; J. A. O'Connor to Superintendent of Lighthouses, 5th District, Washington, Jan. 5, 1926, all in File 1702E, CBL, 1911-1939.

32. Hock to Putnam, Baltimore, December 23, 1925, File 1702E, CBL, 1911-1939.

33. King to Commissioner of Lighthouses, Baltimore, Dec. 26, 1925; Putnam to Secretary of Commerce, [Washington] Dec. 30, 1925, all in File 1702, CBL, 1911-1939.

34. J. Walter Drake to Attorney General, [Washington], Jan. 6 and Feb. 24, 1926; Ira Lloyd Lett to Secretary of Commerce, Washington, Jan. 12, 1926; Acting Solicitor, "IN RE protection of Cedar Point Light Station, Maryland, from damage by reason of dredging operations in its vicinity," Feb. 20, 1926, all in File 1702E, CBL, 1911-1939.

35. Gary E. Powell to King, Cedar Point, Md., February 25, 1926, File 1702E, CBL, 1911-1939.

36. Powell to King, Cedar Point, Md, Feb. 2, 1926; King to Merchants & Miners Transportation Co., etc., Baltimore, Feb. 12, 1926; Thomas P. Pratt to U. S. Lighthouse Inspector, Jacksonville, Fla., Feb. 26, 1926; Wm. (?) J. Bond to King, Norfolk, Feb. 20, 1926; A. H. Seth to King, Baltimore, Feb. 17, 1926 w/attachment; A. L. Stephens to King, Baltimore, Feb. 17, 1926; King to Commissioner of Lighthouses, Baltimore, March 2, 1926, all in File 1702E, CBL, 1911-1939. During this period, King wrote to Joseph Hock asking if the Arundel Corporation would permit the government to put "defensive works" on the north spit to protect it from further erosion so that the light station would retain its last connection to the mainland. Hock responded he would first have to see a plan of what the Bureau of Lighthouses proposed to do. See King to Arundel Corporation, Baltimore, Feb. 11, 1926 and Hock to Superintendent of Lighthouses, Baltimore, Feb. 23, 1926, both in File 1702E.

37. T. S. Johnson to Superintendent of Lighthouses, Fifth District, Baltimore, March 5, 1926, and King to Commissioner of Lighthouses, Baltimore, March 5, 1926, both in File 1702E, CBL, 1911-1939.

38. Powell to Superintendent of Lighthouses, Cedar Point, March 6 and 7, 1926; King to Commissioner of Lighthouses, Baltimore, March 8 and 10, 1926; Putnam

to Secretary of Commerce, Washington, March 9, 1926; Acting Secretary of Commerce to Attorney General, [Washington], March 20, 1926; Ira Lloyd Lett to Secretary of Commerce, Washington, April 1, 1926, all in File 1702E, CBL, 1911-1939.

39. Powell to Superintendent of Lighthouses, Cedar Point, June 22 and Nov. 16, 1926, and Jan. 15, 1927; Hanks to Commissioner of Lighthouses, Baltimore, June 26 and Sept. 27, 1926, Feb. 7 and April 12, 1927; Commissioner of Lighthouses to Superintendent of Lighthouses, [Washington], Sept. 24, 1926, all in File 1702E, CBL, 1911-1939.

40. King to Commissioner of Lighthouses, Baltimore, April 27, June 4 and 8, 1927; Powell to Superintendent of Lighthouses, Cedar Point, May 15, June 1 and 22, 1927; Putnam, memorandum, Cedar Point Lighthouse, June 3, 1927; L. M. Hopkins, "Recommendation as to Aids to Navigation," Cedar Point Gas and Bell Buoy, June 13, 1927, all in File 1702E, CBL, 1911-1939.

41. Powell to Superintendent of Lighthouses, Cedar Point, Md., Oct. 4 and 12, Dec. 12 and 13, 1927; King to Commissioner of Lighthouses, Baltimore, Oct. 14 and 15, 1927, all in File 1702E, CBL, 1911-1939.

42. Commissioner of Lighthouses to Superintendent of Lighthouses, Baltimore, January 16, 1928; L. F. Miles to King, Pearson, Md., January 9, 1928; Putnam to Miles, [Washington], January 20, 1928, all in File 1702E, CBL, 1911-1919.

43. Commissioner of Lighthouses, Washington, Jan. 16, 1928; Miles to King, Pearson, Md., Jan. 9, 1928; Putnam to Miles, [Washington], Jan. 20, 1928; King to Commissioner of Lighthouses, Baltimore, Feb. 15, 1928; Stephen W. Gambrill to Putnam, Washington, Feb. 23, 1928, with endorsements and attachments; Putnam to Gambrill, [Washington], March 2, 1928; L. M. Hopkins to Commissioner of Lighthouses, Baltimore, June 27, 1928; King to Brehon Somervell, [Washington], May 17, 1929, all in File 1702E, CBL, 1911-1939; Cedar Point, Site File. Keeper Gary Powell decided to retire effective Feb. 29, 1928. He was having problems finding a house and

requested that he be permitted to stay at the station after he retired. King recommended that he continue to live there until he found a place or the property was sold. The Bureau approved this action. See King to Commissioner of Lighthouses, Baltimore, Feb. 27, 1928, File 1702E.

44. W. B. Shubrick to S. P. Chase, Treasury Department, May 19 and Sept. 16, 1863, and Henry W. Hoffman to George Harrington, Baltimore, June 2, 1863, all in Treasury Dept., "Lighthouse Letters, 1862-1864," Series P; Site File, Lazaretto; Lighthouse Letters, v. 29, p. 17. *38th Cong., 1st Sess., House Exec. Doc. No. 3* (Serial # 1186), p. 156.

45. *38th Cong., 2nd Sess, House Doc. No. 3* (Serial # 1222), p. 168; Lighthouse Board, *Annual Report, 1870,* p. 39, *1871,* p. 35, *1872,* pp. 46-47, *1873,* p. 51, *1874,* p. 51, and *1875,* p. 47.

46. Lighthouse Board, *Annual Report, 1877,* p. 32, *1878,* pp. 37-38, *1879,* pp. 39-40, *1882,* p. 37, *1883,* p. 55, *1884,* p. 52, *1885,* pp. 52-53.

47. Lighthouse Board, *Annual Report,* pp. 96-97, *1890,* pp. 105-106, *1891,* pp. 95-96, *1892,* pp. 99-100, *1896,* p. 93, *1897,* p. 105, *1898,* pp. 114-115, and *1899,* pp. 111-112.

48. Lighthouse Board, *Annual Report, 1902,* p. 134, *1903,* p.60, and *1910,* p. 38.

49. William H. David to Lighthouse Inspector, Lazaretto Point, Md., Sept. 20, 1911 and May 4, 1913; Ruland to Commissioner of Lighthouses, Baltimore, April 14 and July 3, 1914, and Noble N. Potts to Putnam, Washington, Sept. 14, 1916, File 1403E; and [Commissioner] to Secretary of Commerce, Washington, July 17, 1914, File 651E, all in CBL, 1911-1939. There is nothing like the threat of danger to get the attention of a Washington office bureaucrat. Four months before the second fire in May 1913, the District Inspector had proposed laying water pipes for fire protection purposes. It required getting the permission of Western Maryland Railway to lay pipe across the company's property. Western Maryland responded that it would give permission, if the Lighthouse Service would allow the company

to run a track over a small parcel (8.7 feet) of the depot property. The processing of the permit to lay the track languished somewhere in the bureaucracy until after the second fire, when the District Inspector proposed once again to lay pipe for a water line. When the proposal reached the Washington Office, it was approved in a few days, and within a week after that the Commissioner of Lighthouses sent the completed permit to the District Inspector for transmittal to the railroad company. See Ruland to Commissioner of Lighthouses, Baltimore, Jan. 15, 1913; Ruland, "Recommendation for Repairing Aids to Navigation," May 16, 1913; Putnam, note dated May 26, 1913, all in File 1403E, CBL, 1911-1939.

50. F. P. Dillon to Commissioner of Lighthouses, Baltimore, Nov. 15, 1918; King to Commissioner of Lighthouses, Baltimore, Dec. 16, 1918; Acting Commissioner of Lighthouses to [Secretary of Commerce], Jan. 7, 1919, in File 1403E, CBL, 1911-1939.

51. Memorandum, G[eorge] R. P[utnam], Jan 26, 1921; L. M. Hopkins to Commissioner of Lighthouses, Baltimore, Sept 22, 1934 and Jan. 23, 1935, in File 1403E, CBL, 1911-1939.

52. Memorandum, Radio Laboratory, L. M. Harding, June 21, 1938; Memorandum, C. A. Park to King, Lazaretto Depot Project, June 22, 1938; C. A. Park to Superintendent of Lighthouses, Norfolk, June 22 and 30, 1938; N. C. Manyon to Commissioner of Lighthouses, Norfolk, June 25, 1938; Superintendent of Lighthouses, 11th Dist. to Commissioner of Lighthouses, Detroit, Aug. 3, 1938, all in File 1403E, CBL, 1911-1939.

53. King to W. A. Rhode, [Washington], Oct. 25, 1938, w/attachment, File 1403E, CBL, 1911-1939.

54. N. C. Manyon to Commissioner, Norfolk, Aug. 11, 1938; Memorandum, R. Yates, "Lazaretto Depot Radio Lab.," Aug. 26, 1938; Memorandum, L. M. Harding, "Radio Laboratory; Moving to Baltimore," Nov. 14, 1938; W. P. Harman to Superintendent of Lighthouses, [11th District], [Washington], Dec. 2 and 10, 1938; C. A. Park to Superintendent [11th District], [Washington], Dec. 12, 1938, all in File 1404E, CBL, 1911-1939.

CHAPTER 7

1. Wm. T. Lancaster to George M. Bibb, Baltimore, Oct. 26, 1844, and Charles I. Lancaster to John C. Rives, Milton Hill, Md., Dec. 22, 1844, both in Lighthouse Letters, 1844, Series P, Treasury Dept.; Edward Lucas to Thomas Ewing, Baltimore, Feb. 3, 1849, and Wm. B. Matthews and John Matthews to W. M. Meredith, Port Tobacco, May 15, 1849, Lucas to [unnamed], Baltimore, March 19, 1849, all in Lighthouse Letters, 1849, Series P, Treasury Department; Barney to Pleasonton, Baltimore, Dec. 15, 1821, Lighthouse Superintendent's Correspondence, Baltimore, 1819-1824; Barney to Pleasonton, Baltimore, Nov. 11, 1828, LSCB, 1825-1852; Fifth Auditor's Office, Lighthouse Letters, v. 5, p. 518, v. 7, p. 386, and v. 16, p. 301, all in R. G. 26, National Archives.

2. Wm. T. Leonard to Bibb, Baltimore, Oct. 26, 1844, Daniel H. Wiggins to Secretary of the Treasury, Annapolis, Dec. 28, 1844, both in Lighthouse Letters, Series P, Treasury Department, 1844; Levi Cathell to Meredith, Baltimore, June 29, 1849, Series P, 1849.

3. Lighthouse Letters, v. 7, p. 229 and 259, and v. 10, pp. 423-424; *32nd Cong., 1st Sess., Sen. Exec Doc. No. 28, p. 178.*

4. Barney to Pleasonton, Baltimore, Aug. 26 and 31, 1822, Feb. 10, March 17, May 1, Nov. 17, and Dec. 22, 1823, LSCB, 1819-1824. At some time during this period a Mr. Dunbar also served as ostensible keeper.

5. Lighthouse Letters, v. 10, pp. 306, 308, v. 13 (Jan. 1, 1838-Oct. 17, 1838), p. 460, v. 20 (July 19, 1844-June 6, 1845), pp. 137, 463, v. 22 (April 27, 1846-Dec. 14, 1846), pp. 42, 509, v. 27 (Dec. 22, 1848-May 12, 1849), p. 193, v. 29 (Jan. 25, 1850- Feb. 18, 1851), pp. 289, 365, and v. 30 (Feb. 18, 1851-Feb. 28, 1852), pp. 201, 364.

6. See the various ledgers of personnel listings in Record Group 26; "Lighthouse Appointments, 1843-1880, No. 2," Piney Point.

7. Memorandum, King to Commissioner, Baltimore, Dec. 4, 1917, File 1225, Correspondence of the Bureau of Lighthouses, 1911-1939.

8. Robert H. Sterling to Chairman, Lighthouse Board, Solomons Lump Light Station, Sept. 13, 1902, and John M. Hawley to the Lighthouse Board, Baltimore, Sept 19, 1902, File 1603, Correspondence, Lighthouse Board, 1901-1910; Superintendent of Lighthouses to Commissioner of Lighthouses, Baltimore, Sept. 18, 1920 and Memorandum, Superintendent of Lighthouses, Subject: Drowning accident, Lower Cedar Point, Baltimore, Sept. 25, 1920 and notation dated Oct. 8, 1920, File 2233E, Cor-

respondence, Bureau of Lighthouses, 1911-1939.

9. Lighthouse Letters, v. 11 (June 10, 1835-Feb. 15, 1837), p. 190.

10. Lighthouse Board, Inspecton Book, 5th Dist., 1870.

11. Lighthouse Letters, v. 7, p. 145; Barney to Pleasonton, Baltimore, March 3, 1827, April 9 and June 25, 1828, LCSB 1825-1852; John P. Pickett to Secretary of the Treasury, Havre de Grace, March 30, 1849, Augustine de Caindry (?) to Gen. Taylor, Savannah, Ga., Feb. 2, 1849, and J. J. Sandford to W. Meredith, Port de Posite [sic], Md., April 3, 1849, Lighthouse Letters, Series P. Treasury Department, 1849.

12. Winslow Lewis to Supt., Bodkin Island, Boston, Sept. 15, 1821, L. H. Supt.'s Correspondence, 1819-1824.

13. Lighthouse Letters, v. 26 (Aug. 1, 1848-Dec. 22, 1848), pp. 222, 295.

14. Barney to Pleasonton, Baltimore, April 9 and June 18, 1827, LSCB, 1825-1852; Lighthouse Letters, v. 7, p. 300.

15. Lighthouse Letters, v. 13, p. 498; v. 20, pp. 267, 425, 466-467, v. 21 (June 9, 1854-April 27, 1846), p. 190; George R. Putnam, *Sentinel of the Coasts: The Log of a Lighthouse Engineer* (New York: W. W. Norton & Co., c. 1937), p. 175..

16. Barney to Pleasonton, Baltimore, December 2, 1828, and Barney to Pleasonton, September 18, 1828, both in LSCB, 1825-1852.

17. Lighthouse Letters, v. 13, p. 498; v. 20, pp. 267, 425, 466-467, v. 21, p. 190.

18. Lighthouse Letters, v. 17 (July 21-July 12, 1842), p. 23, v. 27, pp. 213-214, 266, 301.

19. Lighthouse Letters, v. 26 (August 1, 1848-December 22, 1848), v.27, p. 333; Elijah Murphy, et al. to Thomas Corwin, January 29, 1851, Treasury Dept., Lighthouse Letters, 1851-1852, Series P.

20. Lighthouse Letters, v. 10, p. 454.

21. Lighthouse Letters, v. 7, p.443, (Oct. 17, 1838-Aug. 22, 1839), p.466-467, 490-491, and v. 21, p. 190; R. Lyons to S. Pleasonton, Baltimore, June 26 and Sept. 22, 1835.

22. Lighthouse Letters, v. 8, pp. 70, 438, v. 10, pp. 216-217, v. 11, pp. 478-479; R. Lyons to S. Pleasonton, Baltimore, Jan. 10, 1837, w/attachment, and William Frick to S. Pleasonton, Baltimore, July 10, 1840, LSCB, 1825-1852; George C. Havenner to Commissoner of Lighthouses, [Washington], April 7, 1915, File 2307E. Correspondence,

Bureau of Lighthouses, 1911-1939.

23. Bureau of Lighthouses, *Annual Report, 1919,* p. 3, and 1920, p. 8.

24. Lighthouse Letters, v. 8 (April 14, 1829-July 12, 1831), p. 360, v. 10, p. 434. v. 26, p. 201, and v. 28 (May 14, 1849-Jan. 25, 1850), pp. 163-164, 263.

25. *35th Cong., 3rd Sess., Sen. Exec. Doc. No. 3* (Serial # 874), p. 600; Lighthouse Board, *Annual Report, 1877,* p. 29, 1879, p. 36, 1881, p. 39, and 1893, p. 93. In the mid-1830s the was some indication the keepers were not pleased with their dwellings and working conditions in the towers. See R. Lyons to [S. Pleasonton], Baltimore, April 14, 1836, Lighthouse Superintendent's Correspondence, 1825-1852.

26. *Lighthouse Service Bulletin,* v. 2, no. 2 (Feb. 1, 1918), p. 9, no. 3 (March 1, 1918), pp. 13-14, and no. 6 (June 1, 1918), p. 25.

27. *Lighthouse Service Bulletin,* v. 11, no. 27 (March 1, 1920), p. 118.

28. J. J. Daley to Superintendent of Lighthouses, Drum Point Station, Aug. 24, 1933, and J. W. Wilson to Superintendent of Lighthouses, Point No Point, Aug. 24, 1933, File 1431E, Correspondence of the Bureau of Lighthouses, 1911-1939.

29. Lighthouse Board, *Annual Report,* 1894, p. 95; H. D. King to Commissioner of Lighthouses, Baltimore, Dec. 2 and 20, 1919, File 2380, and H. C. Sterling to Superintendent of Lighthouses, Solomons Lump, May 11, 1920, File 2072, Correspondence, Bureau of Lighthouses, 1911-1939.

30. *Lighthouse Service Bulletin,* Jan. 1913 (no. 13), p. 51, June 1913 (no. 18), p. 71, and September 1913 (no. 21), p. 83; Thomas Jacobson to Lighthouse Inspector, Point Lookout, July 27, 1913, File 1321-E, Correspondence of the Bureau of Lighthouses, 1911-1939.

31. *Lighthouse Service Bulletin,* v. 2, no. 9 (Sept. 1, 1918), p. 40, no. 21 (Sept. 1, 1919), p. 91, and no. 67 (July 2, 1923), p. 286; H. D. King to Commissioner of Lighthouses, Baltimore, Aug. 20, 1919, w/attachment, File 1321E, and C. W. Salter to Superintendent of Lighthouses, Turkey Point Light, May 14, 1923, File 2238E, Correspondence, Bureau of Lighthouses, 1911-1939.

32. Memorandum, C. A. Park to Commissioner, Feb. 3, 1936, File 1566A, Correspondence, Bureau of Lighthouses, 1911-1939.

33. Putnam, *Lighthouses and Lightships,* p. 189.

1. Lighthouse Board, *Annual Report, 1867*, p. 21; *1878*, p. 35; *1879*, p. 37; *1894*, p. 98; *34th Cong., 3rd Sess., Sen. Exec. Doc. No. 3* (Serial # 874), p. 600; *58th Cong., 3rd Sess., House Doc. No. 164* (Serial # 4830), pp. 1-2. Clarence Shriver to J. Charles Linthicum, Baltimore, Sept. 19, 1913; Frank O. Smith to Commissioner of Lighthouses, Washington, Sept 20, 1913; Charles G. Homer to Smith, Baltimore, Dec. 24, 1913; Ruland to Commissioner of Lighthouses, Baltimore, June 23, 1914; Commissioner of Lighthouses to Linthicum,[Washington], Sept. 30, 1914; H. D. King to Commissioner of Lighthouses, Baltimore, Dec. 6, 1917, and June 17, 1918; Secretary of War to Secretary of Commerce, Washington, Dec. 13, 1917; Asst. Secretary of Commerce to Secretary of War, [Washington], Dec. 27, 1917; Secretary of Commerce to Secretary of War, Washington, Feb. 8, 1918, all in File 576, Correspondence of the Bureau of Lighthouses, 1911-1939; "Descriptive List of Lighthouses, 5th Dist.," v. II, 1858, p. 58; Lighthouse Board, "Inspection Book, 5th Dist.," 1867, Rpt. # 26; Lighthouse Board, Form 60, "Pooles Island Light Station," July 14, 1909; Site File, Pooles Island, all in Record Group 26. The Bureau of Lighthouses made changes in lighting the way past Pooles Island. To better mark Pooles Island Bay, the Bureau in 1927 placed a light there on a small caisson. The Pooles Island range light in time became the Pooles Island south range light, because a north range light and an east range light were added.

2. Lighthouse Board, *Annual Report, 1881*, p. 40. Site File, Battery Island; Putnam to Commissioner of Fisheries, [Washington], Oct. 24, 1911; [H. D.] King to Commissioner, Baltimore, June 1, 1915; Actg. Commissioner to Commissioner of Fisheries, [Washington], June 5, 1915; H. M. Smith to Commissioner of Lighthouses, Washington, June 30, 1915; [Commission of Lighthouses] to Secretary of Commerce, [Washington], May 10, 1917; King to Commissioner, Baltimore, April 14, 1921; Commissioner of Fisheries to Commissioner of Lighthouses, Washington, May 12, 1921; Commissioner of Lighthouses to Commissioner of Fisheries, [Washington], July 29, 1921; H. D. King, "Recommendation as to Aids to Navigation," Aug. 9, 1921; L. W. L., Handwritten note dated July 31, 1922; Henry O'Malley to Secretary of Commerce, [Washington] June 8, 1922; W. S. Erwin to Surveyor General of Real Estate, [Washington], July 26, 1923; O. E. Weller to Herbert Hoover, [Washington], Aug. 30, 1923; S. B. Davis to H. Arthur Stump, [Washington], Sept. 17, 1923; Stump to Davis, Oct. 2, 1923, handwritten note; J. Walter Drake to Commissioner of Lighthouses, Washington, Aug. 14, 1924; Actg. Secretary of Commerce to Sifford Pearre, [Washington], Oct. 4, 1924 and Oct. 21, 1926; Drake to Pearre, [Washington], Oct. 8, 1925; King to Commissioner of Lighthouses, Baltimore, July 23, 1927; E. F. Morgan to Richard E. Preece, [Washington], June 27, 1929; Morgan to Clay P. Whiteford, [Washington], March 31, 1930, all in File 1667E, Correspondence of the Bureau of Lighthouses, 1911-1939; N.C. Manyon to Commissioner, Norfolk, Nov. 23, 1938; "Survey of Public Property," Fishing Battery Lighthouse, Dec. 6, 1938, all in File 1667, Correspondence of the Bureau of Lighthouses, 1911-1939.

3. Lighthouse Board, *Annual Report, 1869*, p. 46; *1870*, p. 55; *1883*, pp. 51-52; and *1884*, p. 50.

4. Lighthouse Board, *Annual Report, 1885*, p. 50; *1886*, p. 84; *1889*, p. 92; and *1892*, p. 97.

5. Acting Commissioner to Lighthouse Inspector, 5th Dist., [Washington], April 28, 1914; Hankinson to Commissioner, Baltimore, April 30, 1914; Ruland to Commissioner, Baltimore, May 28, 1914, all in File 651A, Correspondence of the Bureau of Lighthouses, 1911-1939; Ruland, "Recommendation as to Aids to Navigation," April 14, 1914, File 1403A, Correspondence of the Bureau of Lighthouses, 1911-1939; [Commissioner] to Secretary of Commerce, Washington, July 17, 1914, w/attachment, File 651E, Correspondence of the Bureau of Lighthouses, 1911-1939; C. H. Vuson to Superintendent [Fifth Dist.], Baltimore, Nov. 17, 1920, File 651, Correspondence of the Bureau of Lighthouses; Ruland to Commissioner, Baltimore, July 3, 1914, File 1403E, Correspondence of the Bureau of Lighthouses, 1911-1939.

6. Newspaper clipping, Baltimore *Evening Sun*, Sept. 30, 1914, and Note, Sept. 30, of J. S. C[onway], both in File 651E, Correspondence of the Bureau of Lighthouses, 1911-1939.

7. Fifth Auditor's Office, Lighthouse Letters, v. 13, p. 459; v. 21, 23; "Descriptive List of Lighthouses, 5th Dist.," v. II, 1858, p. 82; Lighthouse Board, Inspection Book, 5th Dist., 1867, Rpt. # 29; Lighthouse Board, Inspection Book, 5th Dist., 1870, unnumbered; Lighthouse Board, Form 60, Havre de Grace Light Station, July 15, 1909; King to Commissioner, Baltimore, Dec. 22, 1919, File 1666, Correspondence of the Bureau of Lighthouses, 1911-1939.

8. King, "Recommendation as to Aids to Navigation," Havre de Grace, Oct. 21 and Dec. 2, 1918; E. F. Sweet to Commissioner, Washington, Jan. 2, 1919; Millard E. Tydings to King, Havre de Grace, Dec. 17, 1919; Superintendent of Lighthouses to Commissioner, Baltimore, Dec. 18, 1919; J. S. Conway to [H. D. King], Washington, Dec. 23, 1919; Commissioner to Secretary of Commerce, Washington, Jan 23, 1920; King to Commissioner, Baltimore, April 26, May 15, 21, 1920; L. M. Hopkins, "Recommendation as to Aids to Navigation," Havre de Grace Light Station, Nov. 2, 1927.

9. Hopkins, "Recommendation as to Aids to Navigation," July 6, 1933, File 2238E, Correspondence of the Bureau of Lighthouses, 1911-1939; *34th Cong., 3rd Sess., Sen. Exec. Doc. No. 3* (Serial # 874), p. 600; Lighthouse Board, *Annual Report, 1867*, p.21; *1888*, p. 84; *1889*, p. 92; de Gast, *The Lighthouses of the Chesapeake*, p. 119.

10. Fifth Auditor's Office, Lighthouse Letters, v. 12, pp. 31, 115; v. 13, pp. 334, 384, 463, 523-524.

11. Fifth Auditor's Office, Lighthouse Letters, v. 14, pp. 466-467 (two letters), 490-491.

12. Fifth Auditor's Office, Lighthouse Letters, v. 16, pp. 301, 400, 402, 439, 446, 501; v. 19, pp. 137-138, 158-159, 352; v. 20, pp. 87, 137; v. 22, p. 42.

13. Fifth Auditor's Office, Lighthouse Letters, v. 25, pp. 241- 421; v. 26, pp. 222, 295; v. 27, p. 323; v. 28, pp. 24, 410-411, 511, 669; v. 29, pp. 289, 365; Petition to Secretary of the Treasury, Robert J. Walker, undated, in "Lighthouse Letters, 1849, Series P, Treasury Dept.," p. 59.

14. *34th Cong., 1st Sess., House Exec. Doc. No. 10* (Serial # 846), p. 357; *38th Cong., 2nd Sess., House Doc. No. 3* (Serial # 1222), p. 166; Lighthouse Board, *Annual Report, 1880*, p. 36; *1884*, p. 50. At the request of the Navy, the Bureau of Lighthouses in 1921 entered into an agreement whereby the Navy could build a wharf and two large storage sheds for use with a nearby torpedo range. In 1927, the Bureau gave the Navy permission to erect a two-car metal garage in the northeast corner of the station. And in 1940 the Navy was given permission to erect range marker towers at Piney Point. See Site File, Piney Point.

15. Fifth Auditor's Office, Lighthouse Letters, v. 13, p. 460; v. 22, p. 509; v. 29, p. 24; Kane to Pleasonton, Baltimore, June 27, 1849, w/attachment, and July 24, 1849, w/attachment, LSCB, 1825-1852.

16. Lighthouse Board, *Annual Report, 1872*, p.40; *1873*, pp. 43-44; *1883*, pp. 49, 55; *1888*, pp. 82-83; *1889*, p. 90; *1894*, p. 94; *1895*, p. 100; Lighthouse Board, *Light List, 1873*, p. 65.

17. King, "Recommendation as to Aids to Navigation," Pt. Lookout Lighthouse, May 7, 1927 w/attachment, File 1321A, and H. B. Bowerman to Edward H. Booth, [Washington], Aug. 13, 1928, File 1321E, Correspondence of the Bureau of Lighthouses, 1911-1939. See also King to Commissioner of Lighthouses, Baltimore, July 8, 1927, File 1321A, for a slight change in access to the tower on the second floor.

18. Hopkins to Commissioner, Baltimore, Sept. 15, 1930; F. P. Dillon to R. E. L. Yellott, [Washington], Sept. 25, 1930; Putnam, Memorandum, Washington, June 22, 1933; King, Memorandum, Washington, June 23, 1933; Harry H. Hoke, Jr. to Putnam, St. Mary's County, Md., June 24, 1933; Stephen W. Gambrill to Putnam, Washington, June 27, 1933; William P. Cole, Jr. to Putnam, Washington, June 27, 1933; Telegram, Tydings to Putnam, June 28, 1933; G. R. P[utnam], Memorandum, June 28, 1933; Putnam to Gambrill, [Washington], June 29, 1933; Commissioner of Lighthouses to Tydings, Washington, June 29, 1933, all in File 1321E, Correspondence of the Bureau of Lighthouses, 1911-1939.

19. "An Act Authorizing the Erection of Certain Lighthouses," approved June 30, 1834, Early Lighthouse Correspondence, Misc., 1830-1839; *35th Cong., 2nd Sess., Sen. Exec. Doc. No.2* (Serial # 979), p. 284; Lighthouse Board, *Annual Report, 1880*, p. 35; *1887*, p. 48; *1898*, p. 107; *1901*, p. 107; *1902*, p. 126.

20. Lighthouse Board, *Annual Report, 1883*, p. 50.

21. For an example See Lighthouse Board, *Annual Report, 1892*, p.94.

Index

Page numbers in italics refer to illustrations or maps

Designed by Gerard A. Valerio
Bookmark Studio, Annapolis, Maryland

Edited by Lillian Wray

Composed in Cheltenham by Sherri Armstrong
Typeline, Annapolis

Printed on Warren's Lustro Offset Enamel
by Whitmore Print & Imaging
Annapolis